WORDSWORTH CLASSICS
OF WORLD

General Editor

ON UTILITARIANISM
GOVERNMENT

Jeremy Bentham

On Utilitarianism and Government

❖

With an Introduction by
Ross Harrison

WORDSWORTH CLASSICS
OF WORLD LITERATURE

This edition published 2000 by Wordsworth Editions Limited
Cumberland House, Crib Street, Ware, Hertfordshire SG12 9ET

ISBN 1 84022 111 9

Text © Wordsworth Editions Limited 2001
Introduction © Ross Harrison 2001

Wordsworth® is a registered trademark of
Wordsworth Editions Limited

Typeset by Antony Gray
Printed and bound in Great Britain by
Mackays of Chatham, Chatham, Kent

CONTENTS

PRINCIPLES OF THE CIVIL CODE
(*from The Theory of Legislation*)
Part I – Objects of the Civil Law

ANARCHICAL FALLACIES

LEADING PRINCIPLES OF A CONSTITUTIONAL CODE

INTRODUCTION

Three days after Bentham died in 1832 he was publicly dissected by his doctor. Outside was a thunderstorm. Inside, the doctor, his face as white as the corpse before him, gave a funeral oration before carving the body. Watching were many of the leading radical political thinkers and activists of the day. Then, after the body was dissected, its skeleton was padded out, reclothed in Bentham's clothes, and placed in a box with a glass front. Therefore to this day Jeremy Bentham can be seen, the very man himself, sitting in his box in University College, London. Other great philosophers have been buried; Bentham, in accordance with his own instructions, has been preserved.

He has been preserved as what he called an 'auto-icon'. The term comes from a pamphlet which Bentham wrote shortly before his death. He there discusses the best way of producing statues to commemorate important people. The answer is for people to be statues of themselves, auto-icons. The subtitle of the pamphlet is 'further uses of the dead to the living'. For Bentham use is central; everything is to be valued according to the utility it provides. Utility or happiness. The leading principle is that happiness is to be maximised. In his first main work, the *Fragment on Government*, most of which is reprinted here, he talks of a 'principle of utility'. A famous formulation of this principle, enunciated at the start of this work, is that 'it is the greatest happiness of the greatest number that is the measure of right and wrong'.

Bentham takes this principle and pushes it to its logical conclusions, particularly in his writings on law and government. He was systematic. He was radical. He thought everything anew from this single first principle. Sometimes, as with his own body, the conclusions seem merely eccentric. Sometimes proposals which once seemed mad or eccentric now appear commonplace: prohibition of cock-fighting; register of real property; the liberty of the press; the removal of religious tests for office; universal suffrage. Sometimes, as in his view that hunting ought to be prohibited, what he suggested over a hundred and fifty years ago is only now in the centre of contention.

The dissection which preceded Bentham's preservation may also seem to be merely eccentric. But again it was not an accidental flourish. Bentham is always thinking of usefulness; of how most happiness can be gained from something. Dissection for him is part of the 'use of the dead to the living'. Dead bodies can be used for medical research; and hence, if dissected, are of more use to the living than if they are merely buried. The greatest happiness of the greatest number dictates that one person's body should be used to help in the care of other people's bodies. This again seems to us commonplace, or commonsensical. However, again, it was radical, eccentric or innovative in Bentham's day. Only in the following year did it become legal. Up until that time the only source of bodies for medical dissection was robbery of graves, murder, and executed criminals.

Dissection gives a good example not just of what Bentham hoped to achieve (increasing utility) but also of what he was up against. This was superstition or reverence; values based on instinct and emotion. Criminals who had committed murder were dissected after execution because, in the days when you could be hung for stealing, a punishment nastier than mere hanging was needed for murder. So, as the Act instituting dissection put it, 'some further terror and peculiar mark of infamy' had to be added. Dissection deterred. It was treated with horror. It was sacrilege. It was a desecration fit for murderers.

Against this, as he would have thought, superstitious feeling, Bentham wanted to provide cold, hard, reason. He was a child of the movement often called the Enlightenment. Things were to be clarified, illuminated, lit up; clear modern reason rather than ancient gothic imaginings. Bentham started his thought by reading the leading contemporary Enlightenment thinkers such as Helvetius and Beccaria. He translated Voltaire into English. He corresponded with d'Alembert. He was part of a European movement designed to substitute sanity for superstition.

So for Bentham his principle of utility was the path of plain reason. He wished to harness it to the production of a perfect system of law and government. The aim, and the basic principle of utility, Bentham took from people like Helvetius and Beccaria (and Hume in Britain); however, he developed it with a care and reach which was all his own. First he wanted a perfect system of criminal law. This was to be provided by a penal code, for which the *Introduction to the Principles of Morals and Legislation* (reproduced here nearly complete) was to be the introduction. His aim, as he puts it at the end of the first paragraph of the first chapter, is to 'rear the fabric of felicity by the hands of reason and of law'. Felicity, happiness, is the goal; reason and law are the means to be used.

This chapter of the *Introduction* is called 'Of the Principle of Utility'. Bentham starts with a statement of his leading principle. Here we can see that the spread of terms he uses – happiness, felicity, utility, pleasure – does not matter. For, as he puts it here, it all 'comes to the same thing'. Bentham wants to take abstract terms like 'good' and 'bad' which have been given many different kinds of meaning. He wants to analyse them in terms of something easier to understand and hence illuminate them. This is happiness, in its turn understood in terms of pleasure and pain. In this way the terms are clarified, morals are illuminated, and the clear light of reason substituted for the vagaries of emotion and intuition.

When values are handled in this way Bentham thinks that they can be used in public discussion. For, as he puts it in the earlier work reproduced here, *A Fragment on Government*, 'the footing' on which the principle of utility 'rests every dispute, is that of matter of fact; that is, future fact – the probability of certain future contingencies' [IV, 39]. The problems become matters of science, observation, detection. Instead of uncertain and varying emotions, we can experiment and discover. All we have to do is to estimate the happiness which various sorts of action will provide (the pleasure and lack of pain). We have to guess future probabilities. We may get this wrong, but at least we know what we are doing. Otherwise, as Bentham puts it here, we have mere 'scolding and childish altercation'.

The most complete form of this argument is in section 14 of the Utility chapter in the *Introduction*, where Bentham takes the alternative to utility to be 'mere caprice'. It is people just pushing their own individual principles. This, he says, would be 'despotical' or 'anarchical'. There would be as many different standards as there are people, and public discussion about value would be impossible. This is what happens if mere emotion, or the mere feeling that something is right, is the source of values. In chapter two of the *Introduction*, Bentham calls this 'the principle of *sympathy* and *antipathy*'. Instead of antipathy (such as the antipathy people had to posthumous dissection) we have reason. We have utility.

The fabric of felicity is to be raised by the hands not only of reason but also of law. Bentham's early work is in the form of instructions to a legislator, a lawmaker. The legislator is shown how to construct a perfect penal code Then, after writing the *Introduction*, Bentham worked on how to construct a perfect civil code. Some of this *Civil Code* work is reproduced here. These codes aim at maximising utility, happiness. As can be seen in the *Civil Code* (Chapter II) Bentham outlined 'subordinate ends' which the legislator should promote (ends which, if promoted, would lead to greater happiness). In other words, not every thing has to be decided by first principles. We can tell by experience the general effects of other goals on utility. The subordinate ends Bentham outlines here are subsistence, security, equality and abundance.

To know how utility is produced is to know psychology. Thus Bentham outlines in the *Civil Code* certain 'axioms of mental pathology'. He holds that goods, such as wealth, are positively correlated with utility, so the more wealth we have (according to the first axiom) the happier we are. Hence abundance (more wealth and other goods) becomes a subsidiary end: gaining abundance we gain utility. However, in his next axiom Bentham states what we now call the diminishing marginal utility of other goods. Adding equal increments of wealth does not add equal increments of utility. The sixth bar of chocolate does not give us as much pleasure as the first.

From this Bentham derives equality as another subsidiary end. For a unit of wealth provides more pleasure to a poor person than a rich one. Therefore pleasure will be maximised by equal distribution. This, of course, is providing that in doing so happiness is not upset in other ways. In fact, Bentham ranks security over equality (Chapter III); equality will only increase utility providing it is not done at the expense of security. For Bentham, security is the chief goal of law. As he says in chapter II, liberty is really a branch of security. By securing people in their person and goods, the law defends their expectations and gives them freedom to plan their lives and satisfy themselves. Foremost in a person's utility is security of their person and possessions.

Such security is the object of the criminal law. Security is provided, and happiness increased, by laws against particular kinds of behaviour: rape, assault, theft, and so on. For Bentham a law is the threat of punishment for the undesirable kind of activity. He has a deterrent theory of punishment. Punishment is threatened pain which deters people from undesired activities. However, to calculate the deterrent effect of possible punishments the legislator needs an adequate psychology. We can only use threats successfully if we understand their effects. Hence most of the *Introduction is* taken with outlining such a psychology. We need an account of 'sanctions'; the forces which can be applied to people to motivate them. Chief for Bentham here is the 'political' sanction; that is, the threat of legal punishment. We have to be able to calculate the 'value' of a threatened pain, so we know the amount of its deterrent effect; hence Chapter IV on 'value'. We need to know about motives (Chapter X), sensibility (Chapter VI), and so on.

In these early works Bentham aimed to give instructions to a 'legislator'. It was just assumed that the legislator would aim at the right goal, the general happiness. However, as his life moved on, and in particular once he was disappointed in his hope of persuading the British Government to build the circular prison he had designed (the 'panopticon'), he realised that people needed security not only against each other but also against governments. So the chief work of the end of his life was concerned with what he called 'securities against misrule'; that is, with designing a perfect constitutional code. Only a small flavour of this is given here, in an article Bentham wrote to promote the idea, the *Leading Principles of a Constitutional Code*. However, it will be noticed that the principles are the same as those already discussed, starting with an explicit statement of 'the greatest happiness of the greatest number' as the general aim of the constitution.

Whether prison or constitution, whether poor house or penal code, the central idea of Bentham's proposals is the same. It is what he called the 'duty and interest junction principle'. (See, for example, II, 16 of the *Constitutional Code* article.) The idea is that people, naturally following their interest, will be put into a structure in which they will thereby be led into doing their duty. For this Bentham needs an evaluative principle, specifying the duty, and also a descriptive principle, explaining interests and motives. We have already seen what each of these is. The supreme evaluative principle, specifying the duties, is the principle of utility. The supreme descriptive principle, which sums up Bentham's psychology, is that people tend to act in their own interests.

Hence we design the prison so that the prisoners are forced to behave as they ought because they think the unseen warder in the centre of the spider's web is always watching them. We design the penal code so that self-interested people, desiring to avoid punishment, do what they ought. We design the constitution so that self-interested officials nevertheless work towards the general happiness. This is done by having a representative democracy. With it the self-interested representatives, constrained by the desire to be elected, are forced to work in the interests of the electors. The supreme power, thinks Bentham, best resides in the people as a whole. For with the people as a whole, the greatest happiness of the greatest number is both what they actually will aim at and also what they ought to aim at. Interest coincides with duty

The clarification in which Bentham is interested applies to both of the separate principles which he wishes to put into step in this way. In both cases this clarification is in terms of pleasures and pains. As we have seen, the principle of utility is clarified in this way. So also is the psychology. To say that people act in a self-interested way means that they are motivated to seek pleasure and to avoid pain. In both cases this gives clarification. For, as Bentham puts it in the Preface to the *Fragment*, '*pain* and *pleasure,* at least, are words which a man has no need, we may hope, to go to a Lawyer to know the meaning of.'

Because both principles are connected to pleasure and pain, people sometimes confuse them in understanding Bentham. But he is quite clear that there are two separate things here. For example, at the end of the second chapter of the *Introduction* he says that 'the motive or cause' is 'very apt to be confounded' with the 'ground or reason'. We have here both a descriptive thing (motive or cause) and also an evaluative, or normative, one. Similarly, at the start of the first chapter he says of pleasure and pain, that 'on the one hand the standard of right and wrong, on the other the chain of causes and effects, are fastened to their throne.' Again, we clearly have two different things explained by pleasures and pains.

So Bentham clarifies both motives and values. He also clarifies all the more technical terms used in the law, such as *right, duty, power,* and so on. His main work on this (while he was working on the 'metaphysical maze' described in the Preface to the *Introduction*) was unpublished in his lifetime. But some of it appears in a footnote to the *Fragment,* reprinted here (V, 6n). The central idea is, again, that these terms are clarified by being connected to pleasure and pain. For pain (which we don't need to consult lawyers to know the meaning of) is a simple, directly perceptible thing. We understand it by experience. Bentham wants to clarify the more obscure legal terms by connecting them with such understood, directly perceptible things.

So far this is another project he lifts out of the surrounding Enlightenment air. It is the project of Locke and Hume. However, both Locke and Hume tried to analyse single terms, dissolving 'complex ideas' into their elements, 'simple ideas'. Bentham real- ised that this would not work. A right is not just a complex of perceptibles. So he invented a different technique, first introduced in this footnote. This is the device he calls 'paraphrasis'. The idea is to take the problematical term, such as 'duty', and put it in a sentence, such as 'Everyone is under a duty not to assault Jones'. This sentence can then be replaced with another sentence with the same import, such as 'anyone assaulting Jones is liable to be punished'; and this, in turn, is understood as the threat of pain. But, as he says here, 'the idea belonging to the word *pain* is a simple one'. By connection with pain duty becomes comprehensible.

Bentham also analyses rights. They are analysed in terms of duties. Again this is sentence by sentence. A sentence about a right (for example, 'Jones has a right not to be assaulted') is understood in terms of a sentence about duties (such as the one just given). Rights for Bentham are therefore the benefits which someone acquires by duties being placed on others. By connecting rights with duties, and duties with the threat of pain, Bentham gives a meaning to both of them. For, as he puts it in this footnote, 'without the notion of punishment (that is of *pain* annexed to an act . . .) no notion can we have of either *right* or *duty*.'

Rights are important, and in this way Bentham makes legal rights understood. However, legal rights were not the only kind of rights being used at the time when Bentham was writing. In the same year as he published his first main work, the *Fragment*, the Americans revolted. They argued in justification that it was self-evident that people had inalienable rights. In the year Bentham published his next main book, the *Introduction*, it was the turn of the French. They also had a revolution. They also justified it by citing rights. They produced a *Declaration of Rights*; and such citing and use of natural, pre-political, rights (such as in the 1948 Universal Declaration of Human Rights) is still prominent.

Bentham resisted this. He was in favour of the French revolution, but he did not want natural rights cited in justification. He gives a short criticism of an American declaration (that of Massachusetts) at the end of the *Introduction*. But his main work of criticism, in which he tears the French *Declaration* apart article by article, is in a work which in his lifetime was only published in French. This work (under its usual title, *Anarchical Fallacies*, originally given it by its French editor) is reprinted here, but in the form it appeared in English after Bentham's death, edited from his English manuscripts. For Bentham, all the French were doing when talking of natural rights was talking nonsense. Or worse. It is, as he puts it here in a famous phrase, 'nonsense on stilts'. It is 'mischievous nonsense', 'terrorist language'. Its users 'sow the seeds of anarchy'.

Since Bentham manages to use his new fancy technique of paraphrasis to give sense to legal rights, it might be wondered why he cannot also give sense to natural rights. The answer is that a similar analysis will not go through. Natural rights can indeed be analogously analysed as the benefits secured to someone by others being under natural duties. But then we reach a block. Someone would only be under a duty for Bentham if they were threatened with punishment (pain) for non-performance. But here, with natural duties, there is no one threatening them. So there are no natural duties, and therefore no natural rights.

For Bentham, what the French and others are citing are not real rights but imaginary ones. What they are really giving are not rights but reasons for having rights. However, as he puts it here, 'reasons for wishing that there were such things as rights, are not rights . . . hunger is not bread'. In other words, to take again the example of assault, we may think that it is a good thing if Jones is not assaulted. But (for Bentham) this does not mean that he possesses a natural right, independently and prior to all governments. Rather, it means that it would be better if such security could be provided. For this we need a law-giver, a government, some body able to threaten real pain to anyone assaulting Jones. With the government, we have law, and with law we have duties and rights; otherwise it is just anarchy, it is just hunger and no bread.

The vivid, if somewhat excited, language of Bentham in this analysis therefore also gives his reason for having governments. Like everything else it is founded on utility. There will be more utility with governments; for with governments we get rights, and rights are benefits, benefits secured by duties. Similarly, in the *Fragment* (whose main topic is the justification for government), Bentham explicitly wants to found government on utility (and hence, as we saw, prevent 'childish altercation'). As he says there, such justification also shows the limits to government. We should obey governments because they provide good things. But this does not mean that we have to have unquestioning obedience. Rather, we should obey just 'so long as the probable mischiefs of obedience are less than the probable mischiefs of resistance' [I, 43].

The alternative justification, used by Locke and Blackstone, the lawyer Bentham is criticising in the *Fragment*, is to use contract. That is, to suppose that we have contracted to obey the government. However, for Bentham this is hopeless. For apart from the contract just being (in nearly all cases) a fiction, we also need a reason why we should keep our contracts. This, for Bentham, is utility. As he says, here he follows Hume. However, as in the analyses just given, Bentham can be more precise. Someone is only under a contractual obligation if there is a law of contract (if, in Bentham's terms, people are threatened with punishment for breaking contracts). But if that is so, we need governments to explain contracts, and so cannot use contract to explain government. As he puts it in the *Anarchical Fallacies*, 'contracts come from government, not government from contracts'.

The nature of the texts reprinted here is as follows. Both the *Fragment* and the *Introduction* were published by Bentham himself during his lifetime (in 1776 and 1789 respectively). He produced second editions of both in the 1820s, adding a few footnotes which are reproduced here. The *Civil Code* was produced from manuscript which Bentham wrote in French in the 1780s and first appeared in French in the 1802 *Traités de législation civile et pénale*, edited by Etienne Dumont. The text here is from the nineteenth-century translation of this into English by R. Hildreth. *Anarchical Fallacies* was written in the 1790s. Its English version, edited from Bentham's manuscript, first appeared in Volume II of the 1843 *Collected Works* of Bentham, edited by John Bowring, from where the text here comes. Finally, *Leading Principles of a Constitutional Code* was a contribution to a journal called *The Pamphleteer* in 1822. It was reprinted in Volume II of the 1843 *Collected Works*, from where the text here comes.

SUGGESTIONS FOR FURTHER READING

William Hazlitt, 'Bentham', in *The Spirit of the Age,* 1825 (many editions, including OUP World's Classics): contemporary portrait of Bentham, combining sympathy and criticism.

Thomas Peacock, *Crotchet Castle,* 1831: not about Bentham specifically but is a contemporary criticism of the 'march of the mind'; in Chapter 8 the man attacked thinks that he will be made a 'subject for science', i.e. killed and used for dissection.

J.S. Mill, 'Bentham' (originally an 1838 article, reprinted in Vol. X of the modern *Collected Works* of Mill, Routledge 1969): an illuminating analysis by another great philosopher who knew Bentham and grew up in his shadow; again a mixture of sympathy and criticism.

David Lyons, *In the Interest of the Governed* (2nd ed., OUP, 1991; original ed. 1973): a radical reinterpretation of Bentham, more discussed than accepted, which argues that he does not promote universal happiness.

H.L.A. Hart, *Essays on Bentham* (OUP, 1982): much harder and more probing essays on Bentham's philosophy of law.

Ross Harrison, *Bentham*, Routledge, 1983: a full, general account of

Bentham which concentrates on seeing how the different parts of his thought fit together.

Frederick Rosen, *Jeremy Bentham and Representative Democracy* (OUP, 1983): a clear account of the later, political, thought.

John Dinwiddy, *Bentham* (OUP, 1989): short, clear, general account.

P.J. Kelly, *Utilitarianism and Distributive Justice* (OUP, 1990): a reinterpretation, particularly of the *Civil Code* material, which stresses Bentham's use of subsidiary ends.

A FRAGMENT ON GOVERNMENT

Being an Examination of what is delivered, on the
Subject of Government in General,
in the Introduction to Sir William Blackstone's Commentaries
with a Preface in which is given a critique on the work at large

Rien ne recule plus le progrès des connoissances, qu'un mauvais ouvrage d'un Auteur célèbre: parce qu'avant d'instruire, il faut commencer par détromper.

MONTESQUIEU, *Esprit des Loix*

Preface

1. The age we live in is a busy age; in which knowledge is rapidly advancing towards perfection. In the natural world, in particular, every thing teems with discovery and with improvement. The most distant and recondite regions of the earth traversed and explored – the all-vivifying and subtle element of the air so recently analysed and made known to us, – are striking evidences, were all others wanting, of this pleasing truth. *Motives of the present under-taking.*

2. Correspondent to *discovery* and *improvement* in the natural world, is *reformation* in the moral; if that which seems a common notion be, indeed, a true one, that in the moral world there no longer remains any matter for *discovery*. Perhaps, however, this may not be the case: perhaps among such observations as would be best calculated to serve as grounds for reformation, are some which, being observations of matters of fact hitherto either incompletely noticed, or not at all, would, when produced, appear capable of bearing the name of discoveries: with so little method and precision have the consequences of this fundamental axiom, *it is the greatest happiness of the greatest number that is the measure of right and wrong,* been as yet developed.

3. Be this as it may, if there be room for making, and if there be use in publishing, *discoveries* in the *natural* world, surely there is not much less room for making, nor much less use in proposing, *reformation* in the *moral*. If it be a matter of importance and of use to us to be made acquainted with *distant* countries, surely it is not a matter of much less importance, nor of much less use to us, to be made better and better acquainted with the chief means of living happily *in our own*. If it be of importance and of use to us to know the principles of the element we breathe, surely it is not of much

less importance nor of much less use to comprehend the principles, and endeavour at the improvement of those *laws*, by which alone we breathe it in security. If to this endeavour we should fancy any Author, especially any Author of great name, to *be*, and as far as could in such case be expected, to *avow himself* a determined and persevering enemy, what should we say of him? We should say that the interests of reformation, and through them the welfare of mankind, were inseparably connected with the downfall of his works: of a great part, at least, of the esteem and influence, which these works might under whatever title have acquired.

4. Such an enemy it has been my misfortune (and not mine only) to see, or fancy at least I saw, in the Author of the celebrated COMMENTARIES *on the* LAWS *of* ENGLAND; an Author whose works have had beyond comparison a more extensive circulation, have obtained a greater share of esteem, of applause, and consequently of influence (and that by a title on many grounds so indisputable) than any other writer who on that subject has ever yet appeared.

History of it. 5. It is on this account that I conceived, some time since, the design of pointing out some of what appeared to me the capital blemishes of that work, particularly this grand and fundamental one, the antipathy to reformation; or rather, indeed, of laying open and exposing the universal inaccuracy and confusion which seemed to my apprehension to pervade the whole. For, indeed, such an ungenerous antipathy seemed of itself enough to promise a general vein of obscure and crooked reasoning, from whence no clear and sterling knowledge could be derived; so intimate is the connexion between some gifts of the understanding, and some of the affections of the heart.

6. It is in this view that I took in hand that part of the first volume to which the Author has given the name of INTRODUCTION. It is in this part of the work that is contained whatever comes under the denomination of *general principles*. It is in this part of the work that are contained such preliminary views as it seemed proper to him to give of certain objects real or imaginary, which he found connected with his subject LAW by identity of name: two or three

sorts of Laws of *Nature*, the *revealed* Law, and a certain Law of *Nations*. It is in this part of the work that he has touched upon several topics which relate to all laws or institutions[1] in general, or at least to whole classes of institutions without relating to any one more than to another.

7. To speak more particularly, it is in this part of his work that he has given a definition, such as it is, of that whole branch of law which he had taken for his subject; that branch, which some, considering it as a main stock, would term Law without addition; and which he, to distinguish it from those others its *condivident branches*,[2] terms law *municipal*: an account, such as it is, of the nature and origin of *Natural* Society the mother, and of *Political* Society the daughter, of Law *municipal*, duly begotten in the bed of Metaphor: a division, such as it is, of a law, individually considered, into what he fancies to be its *parts*: an account, such as it is, of the method to be taken for *interpreting* any law that may occur.

8. In regard to the Law of England in particular, it is here that he gives an account of the division of it into its two branches (branches, however, that are no ways distinct in the purport of them, when once established, but only in respect of the source from whence their establishment took its rise), the *Statute* or *Written* law, as it is called, and the *Common* or *Unwritten*: an account of what are called *General Customs*, or institutions in force throughout the whole empire, or at least the whole nation; of what are called *Particular Customs*, institutions of local extent established in particular districts; and of such *adopted* institutions of a general extent, as are parcel of what are called the *Civil* and the *Canon* laws; all three in the character of so many branches of what is called the *Common Law*: in fine, a general account of *Equity*, that capricious and incomprehensible mistress of our fortunes, whose features neither our Author, nor perhaps any one is well able to delineate; of *Equity*, who having in the beginning been a rib of

---

1 I add here the word *institutions*, for the sake of including rules of *Common* Law, as well as portions of *Statute* Law.

2 *Membra condividentia* – Saund., Log. I. L. c. 46.

Law, but since in some dark age plucked from her side, when sleeping, by the hands not so much of God as of enterprising Judges, now lords it over her parent sister:

9. All this, I say, together with an account of the different districts of the empire over which different portions of the Law prevail, or over which the Law has different degrees of force, composes that part of our Author's work which he has styled the INTRODUC-TION. His eloquent 'Discourse on the study of the Law', with which, as being a discourse of the rhetorical kind, rather than of the didactic, I proposed not to intermeddle, prefaces the whole.

10. It would have been in vain to have thought of travelling over the whole of so vast a work. My design, therefore, was to take such a portion of it, as might afford a fair and adequate specimen of the character and complexion of the whole. For this purpose the part here marked out would, I thought, abundantly suffice. This, however narrow in extent, was the most conspicuous, the most characteristic part of our Author's work, and that which was most his own. The rest was little more than compilation. Pursuing my examination thus far, I should pursue it, I thought, as far as was necessary for my purpose: and I had little stomach to pursue a task at once so laborious and so invidious any farther. If *Hercules*, according to the old proverb, is to be known *ex pede*: much more, thought I, is he to be known *ex capite*.

11. In these views it was that I proceeded as far as the middle of the definition of the Law *municipal*. It was there, I found, not without surprise, the digression which makes the subject of the present Essay. This threw me at first into no small perplexity. To give no account of it at all; to pass wholly *sub silentio*, so large, and in itself so material a part of the work I was examining, would seem strange: at the same time I saw no possibility of entering into an examination of a passage so anomalous, without cutting in pieces the thread of the discourse. Under this doubt I determined, at any rate for the present, to pass it by; the rather as I could not perceive any connection that it had with any thing that came before or after. I did so; and continuing my examination of the definition from which it digressed, I travelled on to the end of the Introduction. It then became necessary to come to some definitive resolution

concerning this excentric part of it: and the result was, that being loth to leave the enterprise I had begun in this respect, imperfect, I sat down to give what I intended should be a very slight and general survey of it. The farther, however, I proceeded in examining it, the more confused and unsatisfactory it appeared to me: and the greater difficulty I found in knowing what to make of it, the more words it cost me, I found, to say so. In this way, and by these means it was that the present Essay grew to the bulk in which the Reader sees it. When it was nearly completed, it occurred to me, that as the digression itself which I was examining was perfectly distinct from, and unconnected with the text from which it starts, so was, or so at least might be, the *critique* on that digression, from the *critique* on the text. The former was by much too large to be engrafted into the latter: and since if it accompanied it at all, it could only be in the shape of an Appendix, there seemed no reason why the same publication should include them both. To the former, therefore, as being the least, I determined to give that finish which I was able, and which I thought was necessary: and to publish it in this detached manner, as the first, if not the only part of a work, the principal and remaining part of which may possibly see the light some time or other, under some such title as that of '*A* COMMENT *on the* COMMENTARIES'.

12. In the meantime, that I may stand more fully justified, or excused at least, in an enterprise to most perhaps so extraordinary, and to many doubtless so unacceptable, it may be of use to endeavour to state with some degree of precision, the grounds of that war which, for the interests of true science, and of liberal improvement, I think myself bound to wage against this work. I shall therefore proceed to mark out and distinguish those points of view in which it seems principally reprehensible, not forgetting those in which it seems still entitled to our approbation and applause.

13. There are two characters, one or other of which every man who finds any thing to say on the subject of Law, may be said to take upon him; that of the *Expositor*, and that of the *Censor*. To the province of the *Expositor* it belongs to explain to us what, as he supposes, the Law *is*: to that of the *Censor*, to observe to us what he thinks it *ought to be*. The former, therefore, is principally *The business of the Censor distinguished from that of the Expositor.*

occupied in stating, or in enquiring after *facts*:[1] the latter, in discussing *reasons*. The *Expositor*, keeping within his sphere, has no concern with any other faculties of the mind than the *apprehension*, the *memory*, and the *judgment*: the latter, in virtue of those sentiments of pleasure or displeasure which he finds occasion to annex to the objects under his review, holds some intercourse with the *affections*. That which *is* Law, is, in different countries, widely different: while that which *ought to be*, is in all countries to a great degree the same. The *Expositor*, therefore, is always the citizen of this or that particular country: the *Censor* is, or ought to be the citizen of the world. To the *Expositor* it belongs to show what the *Legislator* and his underworkman the *Judge* have done *already*: to the *Censor* it belongs to suggest what the *Legislator ought* to do *in future*. To the Censor, in short, it belongs to *teach* that *science*, which when by change of hands converted into an *art*, the LEGISLATOR *practises*.

The latter alone our Author's. 14. Let us now return to our Author. Of these two perfectly distinguishable functions, the latter alone is that which it fell necessarily within his province to discharge. His professed object was to explain to us what the Laws of England *were*. '*Ita lex scripta est*', was the only motto which he stood engaged to keep in view. The work of *censure* (for to this word, in default of any other, I find it necessary to give a *neutral* sense), the work of *censure*, as it may be styled, or, in a certain sense, of *criticism*, was to him but a *parergon* – a work of supererogation: a work, indeed, which, if aptly executed, could not but be of great ornament to the principal one, and of great instruction as well as entertainment to the Reader, but from which our Author, as well as those that had gone before him on the same line, might, without being chargeable with any deficiency, have stood excused: a work which, when superadded to the principal, would lay the Author

---

1 In practice, the question *of Law* has commonly been spoken of as opposed to that of *fact*: but this distinction is an accidental one. That a Law commanding or prohibiting such a *sort* of action, has been established, is as much a *fact*, as that an *individual* action of that sort has been committed. The establishment of a Law may be spoken of as a *fact*, at least for the purpose of distinguishing it from any consideration that may be offered as a *reason* for such Law.

under additional obligations, and impose on him new duties: which, notwithstanding, whatever else it might differ in from the principal one, agrees with it in this, that it ought to be executed with impartiality, or not at all.

15. If, on the one hand, a hasty and undiscriminating condemner of what is established, may expose himself to contempt; on the other hand, a bigoted or corrupt defender of the works of power, becomes guilty, in a manner, of the abuses which he supports: the more so if, by oblique glances and sophistical glosses, he studies to guard from reproach, or recommend to favour, what he knows not how, and dares not attempt, to justify. To a man who contents himself with simply stating an institution as he thinks it *is*, no share, it is plain, can justly be attributed (nor would any one think of attributing to him any share) of whatever reproach, any more than of whatever applause the institution may be thought to merit. But if not content with this humbler function, he takes upon him to give *reasons* in behalf of it, reasons whether *made* or found by him, it is far otherwise. Every false and sophistical reason that he contributes to circulate, he himself is chargeable with: nor ought he to be holden guiltless even of such as, in a work where *fact* not *reason* is the question, he delivers as from other writers without censure. By officiously adopting them he makes them his own, though delivered under the names of the respective Authors: not much less than if delivered under his own. For the very idea of a *reason* betokens approbation: so that to deliver a remark under that character, and that without censure, is to adopt it. A man will scarcely, therefore, without some note of disapprobation, be the instrument of introducing, in the guise of a reason, an argument which he does not really wish to see approved. Some method or other he will take to wash his hands of it: some method or other he will take to let men see that what he means to be understood to do, is merely to report the judgment of another, not to pass one of his own. Upon that other then he will lay the blame: at least he will take care to repel it from himself. If he omits to do this, the most favourable cause that can be assigned to the omission is indifference: indifference to the public welfare – that indifference which is itself a crime.

Laws ought to be scrutinised with freedom.

16. It is wonderful how forward some have been to look upon it as a kind of presumption and ingratitude, and rebellion, and cruelty, and I know not what besides, not to allege only, nor to own, but to suffer any one so much as to imagine, that an old-established law could in any respect be a fit object of condemnation. Whether it has been a kind of *personification* that has been the cause of this, as if the Law were a living creature, or whether it has been the mechanical veneration for antiquity, or what other delusion of the fancy, I shall not here enquire. For my part, I know not for what good reason it is that the merit of justifying a law when right should have been thought greater, than that of censuring it when wrong. Under a government of Laws, what is the motto of a good citizen? *To obey punctually; to censure freely.*

17. Thus much is certain; that a system that is never to be censured, will never be improved: that if nothing is ever to be found fault with, nothing will ever be mended: and that a resolution to justify every thing at any rate, and to disapprove of nothing, is a resolution which, pursued in future, must stand as an effectual bar to all the *additional* happiness we can ever hope for; pursued hitherto would have robbed us of that share of happiness which we enjoy already.

18. Nor is a disposition to find 'every thing as it should be', less at variance with itself, than with reason and utility. The common-place arguments in which it vents itself justify not what is established, in effect, any more than they condemn it: since whatever *now* is established, *once* was innovation.

19. Precipitate censure, cast on a political institution, does but recoil on the head of him who casts it. From such an attack it is not the institution itself, if well grounded, that can suffer. What a man says against it either makes impression or makes none. If none, it is just as if nothing had been said about the matter: if it *does* make an impression, it naturally calls up some one or other in defence. For if the institution is in truth a beneficial one to the community in general, it cannot but have given an interest in its preservation to a number of individuals. By their industry, then, the reasons on which it is grounded are brought to light: from the observation of which those who acquiesced in it before upon trust, now embrace

it upon conviction. Censure, therefore, though ill-founded, has no other effect upon an institution than to bring it to that test, by which the value of those, indeed, on which prejudice alone has stamped a currency, is cried down, but by which the credit of those of sterling utility is confirmed.

20. Nor is it by any means from passion and ill-humour, that censure, passed upon legal institutions, is apt to take its birth. When it is from passion and ill-humour that men speak, it is with *men* that they are in ill-humour, not with laws: it is men, not laws, that are the butt of 'arrogance'.[1] Spleen and turbulence may

---

1 *Arrogance*; our Author calls it *the utmost arrogance*,[a] 'to censure what has, at least, a better chance to be right, than the singular notions of any particular man': meaning thereby certain ecclesiastical institutions. Vibrating, as it should seem, between passion and discretion, he has thought it necessary, indeed, to insert in the sentence that, which being inserted, turns it into nothing: After the word 'censure', 'with contempt' he adds, 'and rudeness': as if there needed a professor to inform us, that to treat any thing with contempt and rudeness is arrogance. 'Indecency', he had already called it, 'to set up private judgment in opposition to public': and this without restriction, qualification, or reserve. This was in the first transport of a holy zeal, before discretion had come in to his assistance. This passage the Doctors *Priestley*[b] and *Furneaux*[c], who, in quality of Dissenting Ministers, and champions of dissenting opinions, saw themselves particularly attacked in it, have not suffered to pass unnoticed; any more than has the celebrated Author of the *Remarks on the Acts of the 13th Parliament*,[d] who found it adverse to his enterprise, for the same reason that it is hostile to every other liberal plan of political discussion.

My edition of the Commentaries happens to be the first: since the above paragraph was written I have been directed to a later. In this later edition the passage about 'indecency' is, like the other about 'arrogance', explained away into nothing. What we are now told is, that 'to set up private judgment in [*virulent and factious*] opposition to public *authority*' (he might have added – or to *private* either) is 'indecency'. [See the 5th edit., 8vo, p. 50, as in the 1st.] This we owe, I think, to Dr. Furneaux. The Doctors, Furneaux and Priestley, under whose well-applied correction our Author has smarted so severely, have a good deal to answer for: They have been the means of his adding a good deal of this kind of rhetorical lumber to the plentiful stock there was of it before. One passage, indeed, a passage deep-tinctured with religious gall, they have been the means of clearing away entirely:[e] and in this at least, they have done good service. They have made him sophisticate: they have made him even expunge: but all the Doctors in the world, I doubt, would not bring him to confession. See his answer to Dr Priestley.

---

[a] 4 Comm., p. 50.   [b] See Remarks, c.   [c] See Letters to Mr Justice Blackstone, 1771. Second Edition.   [d] In the Preface.   [e] See Furneaux, Letter VII.

indeed prompt men to quarrel with living individuals: but when they make complaint of the dead letter of the Law, the work of departed lawgivers, against whom no personal antipathy can have subsisted, it is always from the observation, or from the belief at least, of some real grievance. The Law is no man's enemy: the Law is no man's rival. Ask the clamorous and unruly multitude — it is never the Law itself that is in the wrong: it is always some wicked interpreter of the Law that has corrupted and abused it.[1]

21. Thus destitute of foundation are the terrors, or pretended terrors, of those who shudder at the idea of a free censure of established institutions. So little does the peace of society require the aid of those lessons which teach men to accept of any thing as reason, and to yield the same abject and indiscriminating homage to the Laws here, which is paid to the despot elsewhere. The fruits of such tuition are visible enough in the character of that race of men who have always occupied too large a space in the circle of the profession: a passive and enervate race, ready to swallow any thing, and to acquiesce in any thing: with intellects incapable of distinguishing right from wrong, and with affections alike indifferent to either: insensible, short-sighted, obstinate: lethargic, yet liable to be driven into convulsions by false terrors: deaf to the voice of reason and public utility: obsequious only to the whisper of interest, and to the beck of power.

---

1 There is only one way in which censure, cast upon the Laws, has a greater tendency to do harm than good; and that is when it sets itself to contest their validity: I mean, when abandoning the question of expediency, it sets itself to contest the right. But this is an attack to which old-established Laws are not so liable. As this is the last though but too common resource of passion and ill-humour; and what men scarce think of betaking themselves to, unless irritated by personal competitions, it is that to which recent Laws are most exposed. I speak of what are called *written* Laws: for as to *unwritten* institutions, as there is no such thing as any certain symbol by which their authority is attested, their validity, how deeply rooted soever, is what we see challenged without remorse. A radical weakness, interwoven into the very constitution of all *un*written Law.

22. This head of mischief, perhaps, is no more than what may seem included under the former. For why is it an evil to a country that the minds of those who have the Law under their management should be thus enfeebled? It is because it finds them impotent to every enterprise of improvement.

23. Not that a race of lawyers and politicians of this enervate breed is much less dangerous to the duration of that share of felicity which the State possesses at any given period, than it is mortal to its chance of attaining to a greater. If the designs of a Minister are inimical to his country, what is the man of all others for him to make an instrument of or a dupe? Of all men, surely none so fit as that sort of man who is ever on his knees before the footstool of Authority, and who, when those *above* him, or *before* him, have pronounced, thinks it a crime to have an opinion of his own.

24. Those who duly consider upon what slight and trivial circumstances, even in the happiest times, the adoption or rejection of a Law so often turns; circumstances with which the utility of it has no imaginable connection – those who consider the desolate and abject state of the human intellect, during the periods in which so great a part of the still subsisting mass of institutions had their birth – those who consider the backwardness there is in most men, unless when spurred by personal interests or resentments, to run a-tilt against the Colossus of authority – those, I say, who give these considerations their due weight, will not be quite so zealous, perhaps, as our Author has been to terrify men from setting up what is now 'private judgment', against what once was 'public':[1] nor to thunder down the harsh epithet of 'arrogance' on those, who, with whatever success, are occupied in bringing rude establishments to the test of polished reason. They will rather do what they can to cherish a disposition at once so useful and so rare:[2] which is so little

1 See note 1, p. 11.
2 One may well say *rare*. It is a matter of fact about which there can be no dispute. The truth of it may be seen in the multitude of *Expositors* which the Jurisprudence of every nation furnished, ere it afforded a single *Censor*. When Beccaria came, he was received by the intelligent as an Angel from heaven would be by the faithful. He may be styled the father of *Censorial Jurisprudence*.

connected with the causes that make popular discontentments dangerous, and which finds so little aliment in those propensities that govern the multitude of men. They will not be for giving such a turn to their discourses as to bespeak the whole of a man's favour for the defenders of what is established: nor all his resentment for the assailants. They will acknowledge that if there be some institutions which it is 'arrogance' to attack, there may be others which it is effrontery to defend. TOURREIL[1] has defended torture: torture established by the 'public judgment' of so many enlightened nations. BECCARIA ('indecent' and 'arrogant' Beccaria!) has condemned it. Of these two whose lot among men would one choose rather – the Apologist's or the Censor's?

Our Author why attacked in the character of an Expositor. 25. Of a piece with the discernment which enables a man to perceive, and with the courage which enables him to avow, the defects of a system of institutions, is that accuracy of conception which enables him to give a clear account of it. No wonder then, in a treatise partly of the *expository* class, and partly of the *censorial*, that if the latter department is filled with imbecility, symptoms of kindred weakness should characterise the former.

26. The former department, however, of our Author's work, is what, on its own account merely, I should scarce have found myself disposed to intermeddle with. The business of simple *exposition* is a harvest in which there seemed no likelihood of there being any want of labourers: and into which therefore I had little ambition to thrust my sickle.

27. At any rate, had I sat down to make a report of it in this character alone, it would have been with feelings very different from those of which I now am conscious, and in a tone very different from that which I perceive myself to have assumed. In determining what conduct to observe respecting it, I should have

---

Montesquieu's was a work of the mixed kind. Before Montesquieu all was unmixed barbarism. Grotius and Puffendorf were to Censorial Jurisprudence what the Schoolmen were to Natural Philosophy.

1 A French Jurist of the last age, whose works had like celebrity, and in many respects much the same sort of merits as our Author's. He was known to most advantage by a translation of Demosthenes. He is now forgotten.

considered whether the taint of error seemed to confine itself to parts, or to diffuse itself through the whole. In the latter case, the least invidious, and considering the bulk of the work, the most beneficial course would have been to have taken no notice of it at all, but to have sat down and tried to give a better. If not the whole in general, but scattered positions only had appeared exceptionable, I should have sat down to rectify those positions with the same apathy with which they were advanced. To fall in an adverse way upon a work simply *expository*, if that were all there were of it, would have been alike ungenerous and unnecessary. In the involuntary errors of the *understanding* there can be little to excite, or at least to justify, resentment. That which alone, in a manner, calls for rigid censure, is the sinister bias of the *affections*. If then I may still continue to mention as separate, parts which in the work itself are so intimately, and, indeed, undistinguishably blended, it is the *censorial* part alone that has drawn from me that sort of animadversion I have been led to bestow indiscriminately on the whole. To lay open, and if possible supply, the imperfections of the *other*, is an operation that might indeed of itself do service; but that which I thought would do still more service, was the weakening the authority of *this*.

28. Under the sanction of a great name every string of words however unmeaning, every opinion however erroneous, will have a certain currency. Reputation adds weight to sentiments from whence no part of it arose, and which had they stood alone might have drawn nothing, perhaps, but contempt. Popular fame enters not into nice distinctions. Merit in one department of letters affords a natural, and in a manner irrecusable presumption of merit in another, especially if the two departments be such between which there is apparently a close alliance.

29. Wonderful, in particular, is that influence which is gained over young minds, by the man who on account of whatever class of merit is esteemed in the character of a *preceptor*. Those who have derived, or fancy themselves to have derived knowledge from what he knows, or appears to know, will naturally be for judging as he judges: for reasoning as he reasons; for approving as he approves; for condemning as he condemns. On these accounts it is, that when the general complexion of a work is unsound, it

may be of use to point an attack against the whole of it without distinction, although such parts of it as are noxious as well as unsound be only scattered here and there.

30. On these considerations then it may be of use to show, that the work before us, in spite of the merits which recommend it so powerfully to the imagination and to the ear, has no better title on one account than on another, to that influence which, were it to pass unnoticed, it might continue to exercise over the judgment.

31. The Introduction is the part to which, for reasons that have been already stated, it was always my intention to confine myself. It is but a part even of this Introduction that is the subject of the present Essay. What determined me to begin with this small part of it is, the facility I found in separating it from every thing that precedes or follows it. This is what will be more particularly spoken to in another place.[1]

32. It is not that this part is among those which seemed most open to animadversion. It is not that stronger traces are exhibited in this part than in another of that spirit in our Author which seems so hostile to Reformation, and to that Liberty which is Reformation's harbinger.

Reprehensible passages from the work at large. 33. It is not here that he tramples on the right of private judgment, that basis of every thing that an Englishman holds dear.[2] It is not here, in particular, that he insults our understandings with nugatory reasons; stands forth the professed champion of religious intolerance; or openly sets his face against civil reformation.

34. It is not here, for example, he would persuade us, that a trader who occupies a booth at a fair is a *fool* for his pains; and on that account no fit object of the Law's protection.[3]

---

1 See the ensuing Introduction.
2 See note 1, p. 5.
3 'Burglary,'[a] says our Author, 'cannot be committed in a tent or a booth erected in a market fair; though the owner may lodge therein: *for* the Law

---

[a] 4 Comm., Ch. XVI, p. 226.

35. It is not here that he gives the presence of *one* man at the *making* of a Law, as a *reason* why *ten thousand* others that are to *obey* it, need know nothing of the matter.[1]

36. It is not here, that after telling us, in express terms, there must be an 'actual breaking' to make burglary, he tells us, in the same breath, and in terms equally express, where burglary may be *without* actual breaking; and this *because* 'the Law will not suffer itself to be trifled with'.[2]

---

regards thus highly nothing but permanent edifices; a house, or church; the wall, or gate of a town; and it is the *folly* of the owner to lodge in so fragile a tenement.' To save himself from this charge of folly, it is not altogether clear which of two things the trader ought to do: quit his business and not go to the fair at all: or leave his goods without any body to take care of them.

1 Speaking of an Act of Parliament,[a] 'There needs,' he says, 'no formal promulgation to give it the force of a Law, as was necessary by the Civil Law with regard to the Emperor's Edicts: *because* every man in England is, *in judgment of Law*, party to the making of an Act of Parliament, being present thereat by *his representatives*.' This, for aught I know, may be good *judgment of Law*, because any thing may be called judgment of Law, that comes from a Lawyer, who has got a name: it seems, however, not much like any thing that can be called *judgment of common sense*. This notable piece of *astutia* was originally, I believe, judgment of Lord Coke: it from thence became judgment of our Author: and may have been judgment of more Lawyers than I know of before and since. What grieves me is, to find many men of the best affections to a cause which needs no sophistry, bewildered and bewildering others with the like jargon.

2 His words are,[b] '*There must be an actual breaking*, not a mere legal *clausum fregit* (by leaping over invisible ideal boundaries, which may constitute a civil trespass) but a *substantial* and *forcible irruption*.' In the next sentence but two he goes on, and says, – 'But to come down a chimney *is* held a burglarious entry; for that is as much closed as the nature of things will permit. So also to knock at a door, and upon opening it to rush in with a felonious intent; or under pretence of taking lodgings, to fall upon the landlord and rob him; or to procure a constable to gain admittance, in order to search for traitors, and then to bind the constable and rob the house; *all these entries have been adjudged burglarious, though there was no actual breaking*: *for* the Law will not suffer itself to be trifled with by such evasions.' . . Can it be more egregiously trifled with than by such *reasons*?

I must own I have been ready to grow out of conceit with these useful little particles, *for, because, since*, and others of that fraternity, from seeing the drudgery they are continually put to in these Commentaries. The appearance of any of them is a sort of warning to me to prepare for some tautology, or some

---

[a] 1 Comm., Ch. II, p. 178.   [b] 4 Comm., Ch. XVI, p. 226.

37. It is not here, that after relating the Laws by which peaceable Christians are made punishable for worshipping God according to their consciences, he pronounces with equal peremptoriness and complacency, that every thing, yes, 'every thing is as it should be.'[1]

38. It is not here, that he commands us to believe, and that on pain of forfeiting all pretensions to either 'sense or probity', that the system of our jurisprudence is, in the whole and every part of it, the very quintessence of perfection.[2]

---

absurdity: for the same thing dished up over again in the shape of a reason for itself: or for a reason which, if a distinct one, is of the same stamp as those we have just seen. Other instances of the like hard treatment given to these poor particles will come under observation in the body of this Essay. As to reasons of the first-mentioned class, of them one might pick out enough to fill a volume.

1 'In what I have now said,' says he,[a] 'I would not be understood to derogate from the rights of the national Church, or to favour a loose latitude of propagating any crude undigested sentiments in religious matters. Of *propagating*, I say; for the bare entertaining them, without an endeavour to diffuse them, seems *hardly* cognizable by any human authority. I only mean to illustrate the excellence of our present establishment, by looking back to former times. *Every thing is now as it should be*; unless, perhaps, that heresy ought to be more strictly defined, and no prosecution permitted, even in the Ecclesiastical Courts, till the tenets in question are by proper authority previously declared to be heretical. Under these restrictions it seems *necessary* for the support of the national religion,' (the national religion being such, we are to understand, as would not be able to support itself were any one at liberty to make objections to it) 'that the officers of the Church should have power to censure heretics, but not to exterminate or destroy them.'

Upon looking into a later edition (the fifth) I find this passage has undergone a modification. After '*Every thing is now as it should be*,' is added, '*with respect to the spiritual cognizance, and spiritual punishment of heresy.*' After '*the officers of the Church should have power to censure heretics*,' is added, '*but not to harass them with temporal penalties, much less to exterminate or destroy them.*'

How far the mischievousness of the original text has been cured by this amendment, may be seen from Dr. Furneaux, Lett. II, p. 30, 2nd edit.

2 1 Comm. 140. I would not be altogether positive, how far it was he meant this persuasion should extend itself in point of time: whether to those institutions only that happened to be in force at the individual instant of his writing: or whether to such opposite institutions also as, within any given distance of time from that instant, either *had* been in force, or were *about* to be. His words are as follow: 'All these rights and liberties it is our birthright to enjoy entire;

---

a 4 Comm., Ch. IV, p. 49.

39. It is not here that he assures us in point of fact, that there never *has* been an alteration made in the Law that men have not afterwards found reason to regret.[1]

---

unless where the Laws of our country have laid them under necessary restraints. Restraints in themselves so gentle and moderate, as will appear upon further enquiry, that no man of *sense* or *probity* would wish to see them slackened. For *all* of us have it in our choice to do *every thing* that a *good* man would desire to do; and are restrained from nothing, but what would be pernicious either to ourselves or our fellow citizens.'

If the Reader would know what these rights and liberties are, I answer him out of the same page, they are those, 'in opposition to one or other of which *every* species of compulsive tyranny and oppression must act, having no other object upon which it can *possibly* be employed.' The liberty, for example, of worshipping God without being obliged to declare a belief in the XXXIX Articles, is a liberty that no '*good man*', 'no man of sense or probity', 'would wish' for.

1 1 Comm. 70. If no reason can be found for an institution, we are to *suppose* one; and it is upon the strength of this supposed one we are to cry it up as reasonable. It is thus that the Law *is justified of her children*.

The words are — 'Not that the particular reason of every rule in the Law can, at this distance of time, be always precisely assigned; but it is sufficient that there be nothing in the rule *flatly* contradictory to reason, and then the Law will *presume* it to be well founded. And it hath been an ancient observation in the Laws of England,' (he might with as good ground have added — *and in all other Laws*) 'That whenever a standing rule of Law, of which the reason, perhaps, could not be remembered or discerned, hath been [*wantonly*] broke in upon by *statutes* or *new resolutions*, the wisdom of the rule hath in the end appeared from the inconveniences that have followed the innovation.'

When a sentiment is expressed, and whether from caution, or from confusion of ideas, a clause is put in by way of qualifying it that turns it into nothing, in this case if we would form a fair estimate of the tendency and probable effect of the whole passage, the way is, I take it, to consider it as if no such clause were there. Nor let this seem strange. Taking the qualification into the account, the sentiment would make no impression on the mind at all: if it makes any, the qualification is dropped, and the mind is affected in the same manner nearly as it would be were the sentiment to stand unqualified.

This, I think, we may conclude to be the case with the passage above mentioned. The word '*wantonly*' is, in pursuance of our Author's standing policy, put in by way of salvo. *With* it the sentiment is as much as comes to nothing. *Without* it, it would be extravagant. Yet in this extravagant form it is, probably, if in any, that it passes upon the Reader.

The pleasant part of the contrivance as, the mentioning of '*Statutes*' and '*Resolutions*' (Resolutions to wit, that is Decisions, of Courts of Justice) in the same breath; as if whether it were by the one of them or the other that a rule of Law was broke in upon, made no difference. By a *Resolution* indeed, a *new* Resolution, to break in upon a *standing* rule, is a practice that in good truth is big

40. It is not here that he turns the Law into a Castle, for the purpose of opposing every idea of 'fundamental' reparation.[1]

---

with mischief. But this mischief on what does it depend? Upon the rule's being a *reasonable* one? By no means: but upon its being a *standing*, an established one. Reasonable or not reasonable, is what makes comparatively but a trifling difference.

A new resolution made in the teeth of an old established rule is mischievous – on what account? In that it puts men's expectations universally to a fault, and shakes whatever confidence they may have in the stability of any rules of Law, reasonable or not reasonable: that stability on which every thing that is valuable to a man depends. Beneficial be it in ever so high a degree to the part in whose favour it is made, the benefit it is of to *him* can never be so great as to outweigh the mischief it is of to the community at large. Make the best of it, it is general evil for the sake of partial good. It is what Lord Bacon calls setting the whole house on fire, in order to roast one man's eggs.

Here then the *salvo* is not wanted: a 'new resolution can never be acknowledged to be contrary to a standing rule', but it must on that very account be acknowledged to be '*wanton*'. Let such a resolution be made, and 'inconveniences' in abundance will sure enough ensue: and then will appear – what? not by any means 'the wisdom of the rule', but, what is a very different thing, the folly of breaking in upon it.

It were almost superfluous to remark, that nothing of all this applies in general to a statute: though particular Statutes may be conceived that would thwart the course of expectation, and by that means produce mischief in the same way in which it is produced by irregular resolutions. A new statute, it is manifest, cannot, unless it be simply a declaratory one, be made in any case, but it must break in upon some standing rule of Law. With regard to a Statute then to tell us that a 'wanton' one has produced 'inconveniences', what is it but to tell us that a thing that has been mischievous has produced mischief?

Of this temper are the argument of all those doting politicians, who, when out of humour with a particular innovation without being able to tell why, set themselves to declaim against *all* innovation, because it is innovation. It is the nature of owls to hate the light: and it is the nature of those politicians who are wise by rote, to detest every thing that forces them either to find (what, perhaps, is impossible) reasons for a favourite persuasion, or (what is not endurable) to discard it.

1 3 Comm. 268, at the end of Ch. XVII which concludes with three pages against Reformation. Our Author had better, perhaps, on this occasion, have kept clear of allegories: he should have considered whether they might not be retorted on him with severe retaliation. He should have considered, that it is not easier to *him* to turn the Law into a Castle, than it is to the imaginations of impoverished suitors to people it with Harpies. He should have thought of the den of Cacus, to whose enfeebled optics, to whose habits of dark and secret rapine, nothing was so hateful, nothing so dangerous, as the light of day.

41. It is not here that he turns with scorn upon those beneficent Legislators whose care it has been to pluck the mask of Mystery from the face of Jurisprudence.[1]

1 3 Comm. 322. It is from the decisions of Courts of Justice that those rules of Law are framed, on the knowledge of which depend the life, the fortune, the liberty of every man in the nation. Of these decisions the Records are, according to our Author [1 Comm. 71] the most authentic histories. These Records were, till within these five-and-forty years, in Law-Latin: a language which, upon a high computation, about one man in a thousand used to fancy himself to understand. In this Law-Latin it is that our Author is satisfied they should have been continued, because the pyramids of Egypt have stood longer than the temples of Palmyra. He observes to us, that the Latin language could not express itself on the subject without borrowing a multitude of words from our own: which is to help to convince us that of the two the former is the fittest to be employed. He gives us to understand that, taking it altogether, there could be no room to complain of it, seeing it was not more unintelligible than the jargon of the schoolmen, some passages of which he instances; and then he goes on, 'This technical Latin continued in use from the time of its first introduction till the subversion of our ancient constitution under Cromwell; when, among many other innovations on the body of the Law, some for the better and some for the worse, the language of our Records was altered and turned into English. But at the Restoration of King Charles, this *novelty* was no longer countenanced; the practisers finding it very difficult to express themselves so concisely or significantly in any other language but the Latin. And thus it continued without any sensible inconvenience till about the year 1730, when it was again thought proper that the Proceedings at Law should be *done* into English, and it was accordingly so ordered by statute, 4 George II, c. 26.

'This was done (continues our Author) in order that the common people might have knowledge and understanding of what was alleged or done for and against them in the process and pleadings, the judgment and entries in a cause. Which purpose I know not how well it has answered, but am *apt to suspect* that the people are now, after many years' experience, *altogether* as ignorant in matters of law as before.'

In this scornful passage the words *novelty* – *done* into English – *apt* to *suspect* – *altogether* as ignorant – sufficiently speak the affection of the mind that dictated it. It is thus that our Author chuckles over the supposed defeat of the Legislature with a fond exultation which all his discretion could not persuade him to suppress.

The case is this. A large portion of the body of the Law was, by the bigotry or the artifice of Lawyers, locked up in an illegible character, and in a foreign tongue. The statute he mentions obliged them to give up their hieroglyphics, and to restore the native language to its rights.

This was doing much; but it was not doing every thing. Fiction, tautology, technicality, circuity, irregularity, inconsistency remain. But above all the pestilential breath of Fiction poisons the sense of every instrument it comes near.

The consequence is, that the Law, and especially that part of it which comes

42. If here,[1] as every where, he is eager to hold the cup of flattery to high station, he has stopped short, however, in this place, of idolatry.[2]

---

under the topic of Procedure, *still* wants much of being generally intelligible. The fault then of the Legislature is their not having done *enough*. His quarrel with them is for having done any thing at all. In doing what they did, they set up a light, which, obscured by many remaining clouds, is still but too apt to prove an *ignis fatuus*: our Author, instead of calling for those clouds to be removed, deprecates all light, and pleads for total darkness.

Not content with representing the alteration as useless, he would persuade us to look upon it as mischievous. He speaks of 'inconveniences'. What these inconveniences are it is pleasant to observe.

In the first place, many young practisers, spoilt by the indulgence of being permitted to carry on their business in their mother-tongue, know not how to read a Record upon the old plan. 'Many Clerks and Attornies,' says our Author, 'are hardly able to read, much less to understand a Record of so modern a date as the reign of George the First.'

What the mighty evil is here, that is to outweigh the mischief of almost universal ignorance, is not altogether clear: Whether it is, that certain Lawyers, in a case that happens very rarely, may be obliged to get assistance: or that the business in such a case may pass from those who do *not* understand it to those who do.

In the next place, he observes to us, 'it has much enhanced the expense of all legal proceedings: for since the practisers are confined (for the sake of the stamp duties, which are thereby considerably increased) to write only a stated number of words in a sheet; and as the English language, through its multitudes of its particles, is much more verbose than the Latin; it follows, that the number of sheets must be very much augmented by the change.'

I would fain persuade myself, were it possible, that this unhappy sophism could have passed upon the inventor. The sum actually levied on the public on that score is, upon the whole, either a proper sum or it is not. If it *is*, why mention it as an evil? if it is *not*, what more obvious remedy than to set the duties lower?

After all, what seems to be the real evil, notwithstanding our Author's unwillingness to believe it, is, that by means of this alteration, men at large are in a somewhat better way of knowing what their Lawyers are about: and that a disinterested and enterprising Legislator, should happily such an one arise, would now with somewhat less difficulty be able to see before him.

1 V. infra, Ch. iii. par. VII, p. 187.

2 In the Seventh Chapter of the First Book. The King has '*attributes*';[a] he possesses '*ubiquity*';[b] he is '*all-perfect* and *immortal*'.[c]

---

[a] 1 Comm. 242.   [b] 1 Comm. Ch. VII, pp. 234, 238, 242, First Edition.
[c] 1 Comm. Ch. VII, p. 260, First Edition.

43. It is not then, I say, *this* part, it is not even any part of that Introduction, to which alone I have any thoughts of extending my examination, that is the principal seat of that poison, against which it was the purpose of this attempt to give an antidote. The subject handled in this part of the work is such, as admits not of much to be said in the person of the Censor. Employed, as we have seen, in settling matters of a preliminary nature – in drawing outlines, it is not in this part that there was occasion to enter into the details of any particular institution. If I chose the Introduction then in preference to any other part, it was on account of its affording the fairest specimen of the whole, and not on account of its affording the greatest scope for censure.

44. Let us reverse the tablet. While with this freedom I expose *Its* our Author's ill deserts, let me not be backward in acknowledging *merits.* and paying homage to his various merits: a justice due, not to him

---

These childish paradoxes, begotten upon servility by false wit, are not more adverse to manly sentiment, than to accurate apprehension. Far from contributing to place the institutions they are applied to in any clear point of view, they serve but to dazzle and confound, by giving to Reality the air of Fable. It is true, they are not altogether of our Author's invention: it is he, however, that has revived them, and that with improvements and additions.

One might be apt to suppose they were no more than so many transient flashes of ornament: it is quite otherwise. He dwells upon them in sober sadness. The attribute of '*ubiquity*', in particular, he lays hold of, and makes it the basis of a chain of reasoning. He spins it out into consequences: he makes one thing '*follow*' from it, and another thing be so and so 'for the same *reason*': and he uses emphatic terms, as if for fear he should not be thought to be in earnest. 'From the ubiquity,' says our Author [1 Comm., p. 260) 'it *follows*, that the King can never be nonsuit; *for* a nonsuit is the desertion of the suit or action by the non-appearance of the plaintiff in Court.' – 'For the same reason also the King is not said to appear by his Attorney, as other men do; for he always appears in contemplation of Law in his *own proper* person.'

This is the case so soon as you come to this last sentence of the paragraph. For so long as you are at the last but two, 'it is the regal office, and *not* the royal person, that is always present.' All this is so drily and so strictly true, that it serves as the groundwork of a metaphor that is brought in to embellish and enliven it. The King, we see, *is*, that is to say is *not*, present in Court. The King's judges are present too. So far is plain downright truth. These Judges, then, speaking metaphorically, are so many looking-glasses, which have this singular property, that when a man looks at them, instead of seeing his own face in them, he sees the King's. 'His Judges,' says our Author, 'are the mirror by which the King's image is reflected.'

alone, but to that Public, which now for so many years has been dealing out to him (it cannot be supposed altogether without title) so large a measure of its applause.

45. Correct, elegant, unembarrassed, ornamented, the *style* is such, as could scarce fail to recommend a work still more vicious in point of *matter* to the multitude of readers.

46. He it is, in short, who, first of all institutional writers, has taught Jurisprudence to speak the language of the Scholar and the Gentleman: put a polish upon that rugged science: cleansed her from the dust and cobwebs of the office: and if he has not enriched her with that precision that is drawn only from the sterling treasury of the sciences, has decked her out, however, to advantage, from the toilette of classic erudition: enlivened her with metaphors and allusions: and sent her abroad in some measure to instruct, and in still greater measure to entertain, the most miscellaneous and even the most fastidious societies.

47. The merit to which, as much perhaps as to any, the work stands indebted for its reputation, is the enchanting harmony of its numbers: a kind of merit that of itself is sufficient to give a certain degree of celebrity to a work devoid of every other. So much is man governed by the ear.

48. The function of the Expositor may be conceived to divide itself into two branches: that of *history*, and that of simple *demonstration*. The business of history is to represent the Law in the state it *has* been in, in past periods of its existence: the business of simple demonstration in the sense in which I will take leave to use the word, is to represent the Law in the state it *is* in for the time being.[1]

---

1 The word *demonstration* may seem here, at first sight, to be out of place. It will be easily perceived that the sense here put upon it is not the same with that in which it is employed by Logicians and Mathematicians. In our own language, indeed, it is not very familiar in any other sense than theirs: but on the Continent it is currently employed in many other sciences. The French, for example, have their *démonstrateurs de botanique, d'anatomie, de physique expérimentale, &c.* I use it out of necessity; not knowing of any other that will suit the purpose.

49. Again, to the head of demonstration belong the several businesses of *arrangement, narration* and *conjecture*. Matter of narration it may be called, where the Law is supposed to be explicit, clear, and settled: matter of conjecture or interpretation, where it is obscure, silent, or unsteady. It is matter of arrangement to *distribute* the several real or supposed institutions into different masses, for the purpose of a general survey; to determine the *order* in which those masses shall be brought to view; and to find for each of them a *name*.

50. The business of narration and interpretation are conversant chiefly about particular institutions. Into the details of particular institutions it has not been my purpose to descend. On these topics, then, I may say, in the language of procedure, *non sum informatus*. Viewing the work in this light, I have nothing to add to or to except against the public voice.

51. *History* is a branch of instruction which our Author, though not rigidly necessary to his design, called in, not without judgment, to cast light and ornament on the dull work of simple *demonstration*: this part he has executed with an elegance which strikes every one: with what fidelity, having not very particularly examined, I will not take upon me to pronounce.

52. Among the most difficult and the most important of the functions of the *demonstrator* is the business of *arrangement*. In this our Author has been thought, and not, I conceive, without justice, to excel; at least in comparison of any thing in that way that has hitherto appeared. 'Tis to him we owe such an arrangement of the elements of Jurisprudence, as wants little, perhaps, of being the best that a technical nomenclature will admit of. A technical nomenclature, so long as it is admitted to mark out and denominate the principal heads, stands an invincible obstacle to every other than a technical arrangement. For to *denominate* in general terms, what is it but to arrange? and to arrange under heads, what is it but to *denominate* upon a large scale? A technical arrangement, governed then in this manner, by a technical nomenclature, can never be otherwise than *confused* and *unsatisfactory*. The reason will be sufficiently apparent, when we understand what sort of an arrangement that must be which can be properly termed a *natural* one.

Idea of a natural arrangement. 53. That arrangement of the materials of any science may, I take it, be termed a *natural* one, which takes such properties to characterise them by, as men in general are, by the common constitution of man's *nature*, disposed to attend to: such, in other words, as *naturally*, that is readily, engage, and firmly fix the attention of any one to whom they are pointed out. The materials, or elements here in question, are such actions as are the objects of what we call Laws or Institutions.

54. Now then, with respect to actions in general, there is no property in them that is calculated so readily to engage, and so firmly to fix the attention of an observer, as the *tendency* that may have *to*, or *divergency* (if one may so say) *from*, that which may be styled the common *end* of all of them. The end I mean is *Happiness*:[1] and this *tendency* in any act is what we style its *utility*: as this *divergency* is that to which we give the name of *mischievousness*. With respect then to such actions in particular as are among the objects of the Law, to point out to a man the *utility* of them or the mischievousness, is the only way to make him see *clearly* that property of them which every man is in search of; the only way, in short, to give him *satisfaction*.

55. From *utility* then we may denominate a *principle*, that may serve to preside over and govern, as it were, such arrangement as shall be made of the several institutions or combinations of institutions that compose the matter of this science: and it is this principle, that by putting its stamp upon the several names given to those combinations, can alone render *satisfactory* and *clear* any arrangement that can be made of them.

56. Governed in this manner by a principle that is recognised by all men, the same arrangement that would serve for the juris-prudence of any one country, would serve with little variation for that of any other.

---

1 Let this be taken for a truth upon the authority of *Aristotle*: I mean by those, who like the authority of Aristotle better than that of their own experience. Πᾶσα τέχνη, says that philosopher, καὶ ᾶσα μέθοδο ϛόμοίως δὲ ρᾱξίς τε καὶ ροαίρεσις, ἀγαθοῦ τινος ἐφίεσθαι δοκεῖ· διὸ καλῶς ἀ εφήναντο τἀγαθὸν, οὗ ἄντα ἐθίεται Διαθυρὰ δέ τις θαίνεται τῶν (understand τοιούτων) Δ∞ΛΩΝ – Arist. Eth. ad Nic. I, c. 1.

57. Yet more. The mischievousness of a bad Law would be detected, at least the utility of it would be rendered suspicious, by the difficulty of finding a place for it in such an arrangement: while, on the other hand, a *technical* arrangement is a sink that with equal facility will swallow any garbage that is thrown into it.

58. That this advantage may be possessed by a natural arrangement, is not difficult to conceive. Institutions would be characterised by it in the only universal way in which they can be characterised; by the nature of the several *modes* of *conduct* which, by prohibiting, they constitute *offences*.[1]

59. These offences would be collected into classes denominated by the various modes of their *divergency* from the common *end*;[2] that is, as we have said, by their various forms and degrees of *mischievousness*: in a word, by those properties which are *reasons* for their being made *offences*: and whether any such mode of conduct possesses any such property is a question of experience. Now, a bad Law is that which prohibits a mode of conduct that is *not* mischievous.[3] Thus would it be found impracticable to place the mode of conduct prohibited by a bad law under any denomination of offence, without asserting such a matter of fact as is contradicted by experience. Thus cultivated, in short, the soil of Jurisprudence would be found to repel in a manner every evil institution; like that country which refuses, we are told, to harbour any thing venomous in its bosom.

60. The *synopsis* of such an arrangement would at once be a compendium of *expository* and of *censorial* Jurisprudence: nor would it serve more effectually to instruct the *subject*, than it would to justify or reprove the *Legislator*.

61. Such a synopsis, in short, would be at once a map, and that an universal one, of Jurisprudence as it *is*, and a slight but

---

1 Offences, the Reader will remember, may as well be offences of *omission* as of *commission*. I would avoid the embarrassment of making separate mention of such Laws as exert themselves in *commanding*. 'Tis on this account I use the phrase '*mode of conduct*', which includes *omissions* or *forbearances*, as well as *acts*.

2 See note 4, p. 29.

3 See note 1.

comprehensive sketch of what it *ought to be*. For, the *reasons* of the several institutions comprised under it would stand expressed, we see, and that uniformly (as in our Author's synopsis they do in scattered instances) by the names given to the several classes under which those institutions are comprised. And what reasons? Not *technical* reasons, such as none but a Lawyer gives, nor any but a Lawyer would put up with;[1] but reasons, such as were they in themselves what they might and ought to be, and expressed too in the manner they might and ought to be, any man might see the force of as well as he.

62. Nor in this is there any thing that need surprise us. The consequences of any Law, or of any act which is made the object of a Law, the only consequences that men are at all interested in, what are they but *pain* and *pleasure*? By some such words then as *pain* and *pleasure*, they may be expressed: and *pain* and *pleasure* at least, are words which a man has no need, we may hope, to go to a Lawyer to know the meaning of.[2] In the synopsis then of that sort of arrangement which alone deserves the name of a natural one, terms such as these, terms which if they can be said to belong to any science, belong rather to Ethics than to Jurisprudence, even than to universal Jurisprudence, will engross the most commanding stations.

---

1 *Technical* reasons: so called from the Greek τέχνη, which signifies an art, science, or profession.

Utility is that standard to which men in general (except in here and there an instance where they are deterred by prejudices of the religious class, or hurried away by the force of what is called *sentiment* or *feeling*), Utility, as we have said, is the standard to which they refer a Law or institution in judging of its title to approbation or disapprobation. Men of Law, corrupted by interests, or seduced by illusions, which it is not here our business to display, have deviated from it much more frequently, and with much less reserve. Hence it is that such reasons as pass with Lawyers, and with no one else, have got the name of *technical* reasons; reasons peculiar to the *art*, peculiar to the profession.

2 The *reason* of a Law, in short, is no other than the *good* produced by the mode of conduct which it enjoins, or (which comes to the same thing) the *mischief* produced by the mode of conduct which it prohibits. This *mischief* or this *good*, if they be real, cannot but show themselves somewhere or other in the shape of *pain* or *pleasure*.

63. What then is to be done with those names of classes that are purely technical? – With offences, for example, against prerogative, with misprisions, contempts, felonies, præmunires?[1] What relation is it that these mark out between the Laws that concern the sorts of acts they are respectively put to signify, and that *common end* we have been speaking of? Not any. In a natural arrangement what then would become of them? They would either be banished at once to the region of *quiddities* and *substantial forms*; or if, and in deference to attachments too inveterate to be all at once dissolved, they were still to be indulged a place, they would be stationed in the corners and bye-places of the Synopsis; stationed, not as now to *give* light, but to *receive* it. But more of this, perhaps, at some future time.

64. To return to our Author. Embarrassed, as a man must needs be, by this blind and intractable nomenclature, he will be found, I conceive, to have done as much as could reasonably be expected of a writer so circumstanced; and more and better than was ever done before by any one. *Merits of the work resumed.*

65. In one part, particularly, of his Synopsis,[2] several fragments of a sort of method which is, or at least comes near to, what may be termed a natural one,[3] are actually to be found. We there read of '*corporal injuries*'; of '*offences against peace*'; against '*health*'; against '*personal security*';[4] '*liberty*': '*property*': light is let in, though irregularly, at various places.

1 See in the Synoptical Table prefixed to our Author's *Analysis*, the last page comprehending Book IV.

2 It is that which comprises his IVth Book, entitled Public Wrongs.

3 *Fragmenta methodi naturalis.* – LINNÆI *Phil. Bot.* Tit. *Systemata*, par. 77.

4 This title affords a pertinent instance to exemplify the use that a natural arrangement may be of in repelling an incompetent institution. What I mean is the sort of filthiness that is termed *unnatural*. This our Author has ranked in his class of *Offences against* '*personal security*', and, in a subdivision of it, entitled '*Corporal injuries*'. In so doing, then, he has asserted a fact: he has asserted that the offence in question is an offence against personal security; is a corporal injury; is, in short, productive of unhappiness *in that way*. Now this is what, in the case where the act is committed *by consent*, is manifestly not true. *Volenti non fit injuria*. If then the Law against the offence in question had no other title to a place in the system than what was founded on this *fact*, it is plain it would have none. It would be a bad Law altogether. The mischief the offence is of to the

66. In an unequal imitation of this Synopsis that has lately been performed upon what is called the *Civil Law*, *all* is technical. All, in short, is darkness. Scarce a syllable by which a man would be led to suspect, that the affair in hand were an affair that happiness or unhappiness was at all concerned in.[1]

67. To return, once more, to our Author's Commentaries. Not even in a *censorial* view would I be understood to deem them altogether without merit. For the institutions commented on, where they are capable of good reasons, good reasons are every now and then given: in which way, so far as it goes, one-half of the Censor's task is well accomplished. Nor is the dark side of the picture left absolutely untouched. Under the head of 'Trial by Jury', are some very just and interesting remarks on the yet-remaining imperfections of that mode of trial:[2] and under that of 'Assurances by matter of Record', on the lying and extortious jargon of *Recoveries*.[3] So little, however, are these particular remarks of a piece with the general disposition, that shows itself so strongly throughout the work, indeed so plainly adverse to the general maxims that we have seen, that I can scarce bring myself to attribute them to our Author. Not only disorder is announced by them, but remedies, well-imagined remedies, are pointed out.

---

community in this case is in truth of quite another nature, and would come under quite another class. When *against* consent, there indeed it does belong really to this class: but then it would come under another name. It would come under that of *Rape*.

1 I think it is Selden, somewhere in his *Table-talk*, that speaks of a whimsical notion he had hit upon when a school-boy, that with regard to *Caesar* and *Justin*, and those other personages of antiquity that gave him so much trouble, there was not a syllable of truth in any thing they said, nor in fact were there ever really any such persons; but that the whole affair was a contrivance of parents to find employment for their children. Much the same sort of notion is that which these technical arrangements are calculated to give us of Jurisprudence: which in them stands represented rather as a game at *Crambo* for Lawyers to whet their wits at, than as that Science which holds in her hand the happiness of nations.

Let us, however, do no man wrong. Where the success has been worse, the difficulty was greater. That detestable chaos of institutions which the Analyst last-mentioned had to do with is still more embarrassed with a technical nomenclature than our own.

2 3 Comm., Ch. XXIII, p. 387.

3 2 Comm., Ch. XXI, p. 360.

One would think some Angel had been sowing wheat among our Author's tares.[1]

68. With regard to this Essay itself, I have not much to say. The principal and professed purpose of it is, to expose the errors and insufficiencies of our Author. The business of it is therefore rather to *overthrow* than to *set up*; which latter task can seldom be performed to any great advantage where the former is the principal one.

Manner in which the present Essay has been conducted.

69. To guard against the danger of misrepresentation, and to make sure of doing our Author no injustice, his own words are given all along: and, as scarce any sentence is left unnoticed, the whole comment wears the form of what is called a perpetual one. With regard to a discourse that is simply institutional, and in which the writer builds upon a plan of his own, a great part of the satisfaction it can be made to afford depends upon the order and connection that are established between the several parts of it. In a comment upon the work of another, no such connection, or at least no such order, can be established commodiously, if at all. The order of the comment is prescribed by the order, perhaps the disorder, of the text.

70. The chief employment of this Essay, as we have said, has necessarily been *to overthrow*. In the little, therefore, which has been done by it in the way of *setting up*, my view has been not so much to think for the Reader, as to put him upon thinking for himself. This I flatter myself with having done on several interesting topics; and this is all that at present I propose.

---

1 The difference between a generous and determined affection, and an occasional, and as it were forced contribution, to the cause of reformation, may be seen, I think, in these Commentaries, compared with another celebrated work on the subject of our Jurisprudence. Mr Barrington, whose agreeable Miscellany has done so much towards opening men's eyes upon this subject; Mr Barrington, like an active General in the service of the Public, storms the strongholds of chicane, wheresoever they present themselves, and particularly fictions, without reserve. Our Author, like an artful partisan in the service of the profession, sacrifices a few, as if it were to save the rest.

Deplorable, indeed, would have been the student's chance for salutary instruction, did not Mr Barrington's work in so many instances, furnish the antidote to our Author's poisons.

71. Among the few positions of my own which I have found occasion to advance, some I observe which promise to be far from popular. These it is likely may give rise to very warm objections: objections which in themselves I do not wonder at, and which in their motive I cannot but approve. The people are a set of masters whom it is not in a man power in every instance fully to please, and at the same time faithfully to serve. He that is resolved to persevere without deviation in the line of truth and utility, must have learnt to prefer the still whisper of enduring approbation, to the short-lived bustle of tumultuous applause.

72. Other passages too there may be, of which some farther explanation may perhaps not unreasonably be demanded. But to give these explanations, and to obviate those objections, is a task which, if executed at all, must be referred to some other opportunity. Consistency forbad our expatiating so far as to lose sight of our Author: since it was the line of his course that marked the boundaries of ours.

Introduction

1. The subject of this examination is a passage contained in that part of Sir W. BLACKSTONE's COMMENTARIES on the LAWS of ENGLAND, which the Author has styled the introduction. This Introduction of his stands divided into four Sections. The *first* contains his discourse 'On *the* STUDY *of the* LAW'. The *second*, entitled 'Of *the* NATURE *of* LAWS *in general*', contains his speculations concerning the various objects, real or imaginary, that are in use to be mentioned under the common name of LAW. The *third*, entitled '*Of the* LAWS *of* ENGLAND', contains such general observations, relative to these last mentioned Laws, as seemed proper to be premised before he entered into the details of any parts of them in particular. In the *fourth*, entitled, '*Of the* COUNTRIES *subject to the* LAWS *of* ENGLAND', is given a statement of the different territorial extents of different branches of those Laws.

Division of our Author's Introduction.

2. 'Tis in the *second* of these sections, that we shall find the passage proposed for examination. It occupies in the edition I happen to have before me, which is the *first* (and all the editions, I believe, are paged alike) the space of *seven* pages; from the 47th to the 53d, inclusive.

What part of it is here to be examined.

3. After treating of 'LAW *in general*', of the 'LAW *of Nature*', 'LAW *of Revelation*', and 'LAW *of Nations*', branches of that imaginary whole, our Author comes at length to what he calls 'LAW *municipal*': that sort of Law, to which men in their ordinary discourse would give the name of Law without addition; the only sort perhaps of them all (unless it be that of *Revelation*) to which the name can, with strict propriety, be applied: in a word, that sort which we see made in each nation, to express the will of that body in it which governs. On this subject of LAW *Municipal* he sets out,

His definition of Law municipal.

as a man ought, with a *definition* of the phrase itself; an important and fundamental phrase, which stood highly in need of a definition, and never so much as since our Author has defined it.

A digression in the middle of it. Its general contents. 4. This definition is ushered in with no small display of accuracy. First, it is given entire: it is then taken to pieces, clause by clause; and every clause by itself, justified and explained. In the very midst of these explanations, in the very midst of the definition, he makes a sudden stand. And now it bethinks him that it is good time to give a dissertation, or rather a bundle of dissertations, upon various subjects – On the *manner* in which *Governments were* established – On the different *forms* they assume when they *are* established – On the peculiar excellence of that form which is established in *this country* – On the *right*, which he thinks it necessary to tell us, the GOVERNMENT in every country has of making laws – On the *duty* of making LAWS; which, he says, is also incumbent on the Government. In stating these two last heads, I give, as near as possible, his own *words*: thinking it premature to engage in discussions, and not daring to decide without discussion on the *sense*.

This digression the subject of the present examination. 5. The digression we are about to examine, is, as it happens, not at all involved with the body of the work from which it starts. No mutual references or allusions: no supports or illustrations communicated or received. It may be considered as one small work inserted into a large one; the contain*ing* and the contain*ed*, having scarce any other connection than what the operations of the press have given them. It is this disconnection that will enable us the better to bestow on the latter a separate examination, without breaking in upon any thread of reasoning, or any principle of Order.

Our Author's sketch of the contents. 6. A general statement of the topics touched upon in the digression we are about to examine has been given above. It will be found, I trust, a faithful one. It will not be thought, however, much of a piece, perhaps, with the following, which our Author himself has given us. 'This,' (says he,[1] meaning an explanation he had been giving of a part of the definition above spoken of) 'will

---

1   1 Comm., p. 47.

naturally lead us into a short enquiry into the nature of society and civil government;[1] and the natural inherent right that belongs to the sovereignty of a state, wherever that sovereignty be lodged, of making and enforcing Laws.'

7. No very explicit mention here, we may observe, of the *manner* *Inadequate.* in which governments have been established, or of the different *forms* they assume when established: no very explicit intimation that these were among the topics to be discussed. None at all of the *duty* of government to make laws; none at all of the *British constitution*; though, of the four other topics we have mentioned, there is no one on which he has been near so copious as on this last. The *right* of Government to make laws, that delicate and invidious topic, as we shall find it when explained, is that which for the moment, seems to have swallowed up almost the whole of his attention.

8. Be this as it may, the contents of the dissertation before us, *Division* taken as I have stated them, will furnish us with the matter of five *of the* chapters: one, which I shall entitle 'FORMATION *of* GOVERN- *present* MENT' – a second, 'FORMS *of* GOVERNMENT' – a third, 'BRITISH CONSTITUTION' – a fourth, 'RIGHT *of the* SUPREME POWER *to make* LAWS' – a fifth, 'DUTY *of the* SUPREME POWER *to make* LAWS'.

---

1 To make sure of doing our Author no injustice, and to show what it is that he thought would 'naturally lead us into' this 'enquiry', it may be proper to give the paragraph containing the explanation above mentioned. It is as follows: 'But farther: municipal law is a rule of civil conduct, prescribed *by the supreme power its a state*.' 'For legislature, as was before observed, is the greatest act of superiority that can be exercised by one being over another. Wherefore it is requisite, to the very essence of a law, that it be made' (he might have added, *or* at *least supported*) 'by the supreme power. Sovereignty and legislature are indeed convertible terms; one cannot subsist without the other.' 1 Comm., p. 46.

CHAPTER I

Formation of Government

1. The first object which our Author seems to have proposed to himself in the dissertation we are about to examine, is to give us an idea of the *manner* in which Governments were formed. This occupies the first paragraph, together with part of the second: for the *typographical* division does not seem to quadrate very exactly with the *intellectual*. As the examination of this passage will unavoidably turn in great measure upon the words, it will be proper the reader should have it under his eye. *Subject of the passage to be examined in the present chapter.*

2. 'The only true and natural foundations of *society*,' (says our Author)[1] 'are the wants and the fears of individuals. Not that we can believe, with some theoretical writers, that there ever was a time when there was no such thing as *society*; and that, from the impulse of reason, and through a sense of their wants and weaknesses, individuals met together in a large plain, entered into an *original contract*, and chose the tallest man present to be their governor. This notion of an actually existing unconnected *state of nature*, is too wild to be seriously admitted; and besides, it is plainly contradictory to the revealed accounts of the primitive origin of mankind, and their preservation two thousand years afterwards; both which were effected by the means of single families. These formed the first *society*, among themselves; which every day extended its limits, and when it grew too large to subsist with convenience in that pastoral state, wherein the patriarchs appear to have lived, it necessarily subdivided itself by various migrations into more. Afterwards, as agriculture increased, which employs and can maintain a much greater number of hands, migrations *The passage recited.*

1 1 Comm., p. 47.

became less frequent; and various tribes which had formerly separated, re-united again; sometimes by compulsion and conquest, sometimes by accident, and sometimes perhaps by compact. But though *society* had not its formal beginning from any convention of individuals, actuated by their wants and their fears; yet it is the *sense* of their weakness and imperfection that *keeps* mankind together; that demonstrates the necessity of this union; and that therefore is the solid and natural foundation, as well as the cement of *society*: And this is what we mean by the *original contract* of *society*; which, though perhaps in no instance it has ever been formally expressed at the first institution of a state, yet in nature and reason must always be understood and implied, in the very act of associating together: namely, that the whole should protect all its parts, and that every part should pay obedience to the will of the whole; or, in other words, that the community should guard the rights of each individual member, and that (in return for this protection) each individual should submit to the laws of the community; without which submission of all it was impossible that protection could be certainly extended to any.'

'For when *society* is once formed, *government* results of course, as necessary to preserve and to keep that *society* in order. Unless some superior were constituted, whose commands and decisions all the members are bound to obey, they would still remain as in a *state of nature*, without any judge upon earth to define their several rights, and redress their several wrongs.' – This far our Author.

Confusion among the leading terms of it. 3. When leading terms are made to chop and change their several significations; sometimes meaning one thing, sometimes another, at the upshot perhaps nothing; and this in the compass of a paragraph; one may judge what will be the complexion of the whole context. This, we shall see, is the case with the chief of those we have been reading: for instance, with the words 'Society', 'State of nature', 'original contract', not to tire the reader with any more. '*Society*', in one place means the same thing as '*a state of nature*' does: in another place it means the same as '*Government*'. Here, we are required to believe there *never was* such a state as a state of nature: there we are given to understand there *has been*. In like manner with respect to an *original contract* we are given to understand that such a thing never existed; that the notion of it is ridiculous: at the same time that there is no speaking nor stirring without supposing there was one.

4. 1st, Society means a *state of nature*. For if by '*a state of nature*' a man means any thing, it is the state, I take it, men are in or supposed to be in, before they are under *government*: the state men quit when they enter into a state of government; and in which were it not for government they would remain. But by the word '*society*' it is plain at one time that he means that state. First, according to him, comes *society*; then afterwards comes *government*. 'For when society,' says our Author, 'is once formed, government results of course; as necessary to preserve and keep that society in order.' − And again, immediately afterwards, 'A state in which a superior has been constituted, whose commands and decisions all the members are bound to obey,' he puts as an explanation (nor is it an inapt one) of a state of '*government*': and 'unless' men were in a state of that description, they would still 'remain', he says, 'as in a *state of nature*'. By *society*, therefore, he means, once more, the same as by a '*state of nature*': he *opposes* it to *government*. And he speaks of it as a state which, in this sense, has actually existed.

'Society' put synonymous to a state of nature − opposed to 'Government' − and spoken of as having existed.

5. 2dly, This is what he tells us in the beginning of the *second* of the two paragraphs: but all the time the *first* paragraph lasted, *society* meant the same as *government*. In shifting then from one paragraph to another, it has changed its nature. 'Tis 'the foundations of society',[1] that he first began to speak of, and immediately he goes on to explain to us, after his manner of explaining, the foundations of *government*. 'Tis of a 'formal beginning' of 'Society',[2] that he speaks soon after; and by this formal beginning, he tells us immediately, that he means, 'the *original contract* of society',[3] which contract entered into, 'a *state*',[4] he gives us to understand, is thereby 'instituted', and men have undertaken to 'submit to Laws'.[5] So long then as this first paragraph lasts, '*society*', I think, it is plain cannot but have been meaning the same as '*government*'.

'Society' put synonymous to 'government'

1 1 Comm., p. 47.
2 1 Comm., p. 47.
3 1 Comm., p. 47.
4 1 Comm., p. 47.
5 1 Comm., p. 48.

A state of nature spoken of, as never having existed.

6. *3dly*, All this while too, this same '*state of nature*' to which we have seen '*Society*' (a state spoken of as existing) put synonymous, and in which were it not for *government*, men, he informs us, in the next page, would '*remain*',[1] is a state in which they never *were*. So he expressly tells us. This 'notion', says he, 'of an actually existing unconnected state of nature' (that is, as he explains himself afterwards,[2] 'a state in which men have no judge to define their rights, and redress their wrongs), is too wild to be seriously admitted.'[3] When he admits it then himself, as he does in his next page, we are to understand, it seems, that he is bantering us: and that the next paragraph is (what one should not otherwise have taken it for) a piece of pleasantry.

Original contract, its reality denied –

7. *4thly*, The *original contract* is a thing, we are to understand, that never had existence; perhaps not in *any* state: certainly therefore not in *all*. 'Perhaps, in no instance,' says our Author, 'has it ever been formally expressed at the first institution of a state.'[4]

– asserted.

8. *5thly*, Notwithstanding all this, we must suppose, it seems, that it had in *every* state: 'yet in nature and reason,' says our Author, 'it must always be understood and implied.'[5] Growing bolder in the compass of four or five pages, where he is speaking of our own Government, he asserts roundly,[6] that such a Contract was actually made at the first formation of it. 'The legislature would be changed,' he says, 'from that which *was originally* set up by the general consent and fundamental act of the society.'

Attempt to reconcile these contradictions – Society distinguished into natural and political.

9. Let us try whether it be not possible for something to be done towards drawing the import of these terms out of the mist in which our Author has involved them. The word 'society', I think it appears, is used by him, and that without notice, in two senses that are opposite. In the one, SOCIETY, or a STATE OF SOCIETY, is put *synonymous* to a STATE OF NATURE; and stands *opposed* to

1 1 Comm., p. 48.
2 1 Comm., p. 48.
3 1 Comm., p. 47.
4 1 Comm., p. 46.
5 1 Comm., p. 46.
6 1 Comm., p. 52.

GOVERNMENT, or a STATE OF GOVERNMENT: in this sense it may be styled, as it commonly is, *natural* SOCIETY. In the other, it is put *synonymous* to GOVERNMENT, or a STATE OF GOVERNMENT; and stands *opposed* to a STATE OF NATURE. In this sense it may be styled, as it commonly is, *political* SOCIETY. Of the difference between these two states, a tolerably distinct idea, I take it, may be given in a word or two.

10. The idea of a natural society is a *negative* one. The idea of a political society is a *positive* one. 'Tis with the latter, therefore, we should begin. *Idea of a political society.*

When a number of persons (whom we may style *subjects*) are supposed to be in the *habit* of paying *obedience* to a person, or an assemblage of persons, of a known and certain description (whom we may call *governor* or *governors*) such persons altogether (*subjects* and *governors*) are said to be in a state of *political* SOCIETY.[1]

11. The idea of a state of *natural* SOCIETY is, as we have said, a *negative* one. When a number of persons are supposed to be in the habit of *conversing* with each other, at the same time that they are not in any such habit as mentioned above, they are said to be in a state of *natural* SOCIETY. *Idea of a natural society.*

12. If we reflect a little, we shall perceive, that, between these two states, there is not that explicit separation which these names, and these definitions might teach one, at first sight, to expect. It is with them as with light and darkness: however distinct the ideas may be, that are, at first mention, suggested by those *names*, the *things* themselves have no determinate bound to separate them. The circumstance that has been spoken of as constituting the difference between these two states, is the presence or absence of an *habit of obedience*. This habit, accordingly, has been spoken of simply as *present* (that is as being *perfectly* present) or, in other words, we have spoken as if there were a *perfect* habit of obedience, in the *one* case: it has been spoken of simply as *absent* (that is, as being *perfectly* absent) or, in other words, we have spoken as if there were *no* habit of obedience at all, in the *other*. But neither of these manners of speaking, perhaps, is strictly just. *Difficulty of drawing the line between the two states.*

---

1 V. infra., par. 12, note 1.

Few, in fact, if any, are the instances of this habit being perfectly *absent*; certainly none at all, of its being perfectly *present*. Governments accordingly, in proportion as the habit of obedience is more perfect, recede from, in proportion as it is less perfect, approach to, a state of nature: and instances may present themselves in which it shall be difficult to say whether a habit, perfect, in the degree in which, to constitute a government, it is deemed necessary it *should* be perfect, *does* subsist or *not*.[1]

---

1   1. A *habit* is but an assemblage of *acts*: under which name I would also include, for the present, *voluntary forbearances*.

2. A *habit of obedience* then is an assemblage of *acts of obedience*.

3. An *act of obedience* is any act done in pursuance of an *expression of will on* the part of some *superior*.

4. *An act of* POLITICAL *obedience* (which is what is here meant) is any act done in pursuance of an expression of will on the part of a person governing.

5. An *expression of will* is either *parole* or *tacit*.

6. A *parole expression of will* is that which is conveyed by the *signs* called *words*.

7. A *tacit expression of will* is that which is conveyed by any other *signs* whatsoever: among which none are so efficacious as *acts* of *punishment* annexed in time past, to the non-performance of acts of the same sort with those that are the objects of the will that is in question.

8. A *parole* expression of the will of a superior is a *command*.

9. When a *tacit* expression of the will of a superior is supposed to have been uttered, it may be styled a *fictitious command*.

10. Were we at liberty to coin words after the manner of the Roman lawyers, we might say a *quasi*-command.

11. The STATUTE LAW is composed of *commands*. The COMMON LAW, of *quasi*-commands.

12. An act which is the object of a command actual or fictitious; such an act, considered before it is performed, is styled a *duty*, or a *point of duty*.

13. These definitions premised, we are now in a condition to give such an idea, of what is meant by the *perfection* or *imperfection* of a *habit of obedience* in a society as may prove tolerably precise.

14. A *period* in the duration of the society; the number of *persons* it is composed of during that period; and the number of *points of duty* incumbent on each person being given; the habit of obedience will be more or less *perfect*, in the ratio of the number of acts of *obedience* to those of *disobedience*.

15. The habit of obedience in this country appears to have been more perfect in the time of the Saxons than in that of the Britons: unquestionably it is more so now than in the time of the Saxons. It is not yet so perfect, as well contrived and well digested laws in time, it is to be hoped, may render it. But absolutely perfect, till man ceases to be man, it never *can* be.

A very ingenious and instructive view of the progress of nations, from the

13. On these considerations, the supposition of a *perfect state of nature*, or, as it may be termed, a state of *society perfectly natural*, may, perhaps, be justly pronounced, what our Author for the moment seemed to think it, an extravagant supposition: but then that of a *government* in this sense *perfect*; or, as it may be termed, a state of society *perfectly political*, a state of *perfect political union*, a state of *perfect submission* in the *subject* of *perfect authority* in the *governor*, is no less so.[1]

A perfect state of nature not more chimerical than a perfect state of government.

---

least perfect states of political union to that highly perfect state of it in which we live, may be found in LORD KAIMS'S *Historical Law Tracts*.

16. For the convenience and accuracy of discourse it may be of use, in this place, to settle the signification of a few other expressions relative to the same subject. Persons who, with respect to each other, are in a state of *political society*, may be said also to be in a state of *political union* or *connection*.

17. Such of them as are *subjects* may, accordingly, be said to be in a state of *submission*, or of *subjection*, with respect to *governors*: such as are *governors* in a state of *authority* with respect to *subjects*.

18. When the subordination is considered as resulting originally from the *will*, or (it may be more proper to say) the *pleasure* of the party governed, we rather use the word '*submission*': when from that of the party governing, the word '*subjection*'. On this account it is, that the term can scarcely be used without apology, unless with a note of disapprobation: especially in this country, where the habit of considering the *consent* of the persons governed as being in some sense or other involved in the notion of all *lawful*, that is, all *commendable* government, has gained so firm a ground. It is on this account, then, that the term '*subjection*,' excluding as it does, or, at least, not including such consent, is used commonly in what is called a BAD sense: that is, in such a sense as, together with the idea of the object in question, conveys the *accessary* idea of disapprobation. This accessary idea, however, annexed as it is to the *abstract* term '*subjection*', does not extend itself to the *concrete* term 'subjects' – a kind of inconsistency of which there are many instances in language.

1 It is true that every person must, for some time, at least, after his birth, necessarily be in a state of subjection with respect to his parents, or those who stand in the place of parents to him; and that a perfect one, or at least as near to being a perfect one, as any that we see. But for all this, the sort of society that is constituted by a state of subjection thus circumstanced, does not come up to the idea that, I believe, is generally entertained by those who speak of a *political* society. To constitute what is meant in general by that phrase, a greater *number* of members is required, or, at least, a *duration* capable of a longer continuance. Indeed, for this purpose nothing less, I take it, than an *indefinite* duration is required. A society, to come within the notion of what is originally meant by a *political* one, must be such as, in its nature, is not incapable of continuing for ever in virtue of the principles which gave it birth. This, it is plain, is not the case with such a family society, of which a parent, or a pair of parents are at the head.

'State of 14. A remark there is, which, for the more thoroughly clearing
nature' a up of our notions on this subject, it may be proper here to make.
relative To some ears, the phrases, 'state of nature', 'state of political
expression. society', may carry the appearance of being *absolute* in their
signification: as if the condition of a man, or a company of men,
in one of these states, or in the other, were a matter that depended
altogether upon themselves. But this is not the case. To the
expression 'state of nature', no more than to the expression 'state
of political society', can any precise meaning be annexed, without
reference to a party different from that one who is spoken of as
being in the state in question. This will readily be perceived. The
difference between the two states lies, as we have observed, in the
habit of obedience. With respect then to a habit of obedience, it can
neither be understood as subsisting in any person, nor as not
subsisting in any person, but with reference to some other person.
For one party to *obey*, there must be another party that is obeyed.
But this party who is obeyed, may at different times be different.
Hence may one and the same party be conceived to obey and *not*
to obey at the same time, so as it be with respect to different
persons, or as we may say, to different *objects of obedience*. Hence it
is, then, that one and the same party may be said to *be* in a state of
nature, and *not* to be in a state of nature, and that at one and the
same time, according as it is this or *that* party that is taken for the
other object of comparison. The case is, that in common speech,
when no particular object of comparison is specified, all persons in

---

In such a society, the only principle of union which is certain and uniform in its
operation, is the natural weakness of those of its members that are in a state of
subjection; that is, the children; a principle which has but a short and limited
continuance. I question whether it be the case even with a family society,
subsisting in virtue of *collateral* consanguinity; and that for the like reason. Not
but that even in this case a habit of obedience, as perfect as any we see examples
of, may subsist for a time; to wit, in virtue of the same *moral* principles which
may protract a habit of *filial* obedience beyond the continuance of the *physical*
ones which gave birth to it: I mean affection, gratitude, awe, the force of habit,
and the like. But it is not long, even in this case, before the bond of connection
must either become imperceptible, or lose its influence by being too extended.
  These considerations therefore, it will be proper to bear in mind in applying
the definition of political society above given [in par. 10] and in order to
reconcile it with what is said further on [in par. 17].

general are intended: so that when a number of persons are said simply to be in a state of nature, what is understood is, that they are so as well with reference to one another, as to all the world.

15. In the same manner we may understand, how the same man, who is *governor* with respect to one man or set of men, may be *subject* with respect to another: how among governors some may be in a *perfect* state of *nature*, with respect to each other: as the KINGS of FRANCE and SPAIN: others, again, in a state of *perfect subjection*, as the HOSPODARS of WALACHIA and MOLDAVIA with respect to the grand signior: others, again, in a state of manifest but *imperfect subjection*, as the GERMAN States with respect to the EMPEROR: others, again, in such a state in which it may be difficult to determine whether they are in a state of *imperfect subjection* or in a *perfect* state of *nature*: as the KING of NAPLES with respect to the POPE.[1]

Different degrees of subjection among governors.

16. In the same manner, also, it may be conceived, without entering into details, how any single person, born, as all persons are, into a state of perfect subjection to his parents,[2] that is into a state of perfect political society with respect to his parents, may from thence pass into a perfect state of nature; and from thence successively into any number of different states of political society more or less perfect, by passing into different societies.

The same person alternately in a state of political and natural society with respect to different societies.

17. In the same manner, also, it may be conceived how, in any political society, the same man may, with respect to the same individuals, be, at different periods, and on different occasions, alternately, in the state of governor and subject: today concurring, perhaps active, in the business of issuing a *general* command for the observance of the whole society, amongst the rest of another man in quality of *Judge*: tomorrow, punished, perhaps, by a *particular* command of that same Judge for not obeying the general command which he himself (I mean the person acting in character of governor) had issued. I need scarce remind the reader how

In the same political society the same persons alternately governors and subjects, with respect to the same persons.

1 The Kingdom of Naples is feudatory to the Papal See: and in token of fealty, the King, at his accession, presents the Holy Father with a white horse. The Royal vassal sometimes treats his Lord but cavalierly: but always sends him his white horse.

2 V. supra, par. 13, note.

happily this alternate state of *authority* and *submission* is exemplified among ourselves.

Hints of several topics that must be passed by. 18. Here might be a place to state the different shares which different persons may have in the issuing of the same command: to explain the nature of *corporate action*: to enumerate and distinguish half a dozen or more different modes in which *subordination* between the same parties may subsist: to distinguish and explain the different senses of the words, '*consent*', '*representation*', and others of connected import: *consent* and *representation*, those interesting but perplexing words, sources of so much debate: and sources or pretexts of so much animosity. But the limits of the present design will by no means admit of such protracted and intricate discussions.

The same society alternately in a state of nature and a state of government. 19. In the same manner, also, it may be conceived, how the same set of men considered *among themselves*, may at one time be in a state of nature, at another time in a state of government. For the habit of obedience, in whatever degree of perfection it be necessary it should subsist in order to constitute a government, may be conceived, it is plain, to suffer interruptions. At different junctures it may take place and cease.

Instance the Aborigines of America. 20. Instances of this state of things appear not to be unfrequent. The sort of society that has been observed to subsist among the AMERICAN INDIANS may afford us one. According to the accounts we have of those people, in most of their tribes, if not in all, the habit we are speaking of appears to be taken up only in time of war. It ceases again in time of peace. The necessity of acting in concert against a common enemy, subjects a whole tribe to the orders of a common Chief. On the return of peace each warrior resumes his pristine independence.

Characteristic of political union. 21. One difficulty there is that still sticks by us. It has been started indeed, but not solved. This is to find a note of distinction, a characteristic mark, whereby to distinguish a society in which there *is* a habit of obedience, and that at the degree of perfection which is necessary to constitute a state of government, from a society in which there is *not*: a mark, I mean, which shall have a visible determinate commencement; insomuch that the instant of its first appearance shall be distinguishable from the last at which it had not as yet appeared. 'Tis only by the help of such a mark that we can be in a condition to determine, at any given time, whether any given society is in a state of government, or in a state of nature. I can find no such mark, I must confess, anywhere, unless it be this; the establishment of names of office: the appearance of a certain man, or set of men, with a certain name, serving to mark them out as objects of obedience: such as King, Sachem, Cacique, Senator, Burgomaster, and the like. This, I think, may serve tolerably well to distinguish a set of men in a state of political union among *themselves* from the *same* set of men not yet in such a state.

22. But suppose an incontestable political society, and that a large one, formed; and from that a smaller body to break off: by this breach the smaller body ceases to be in a state of political union with respect to the larger: and has thereby placed itself, with respect to that larger body, in a state of nature -- What means shall we find of ascertaining the precise juncture at which this change took place? What shall be taken for the *characteristic mark* in this case? The appointment, it may be said, of new governors with new names. But no such appointments, suppose, takes place. The subordinate governors, from whom alone the people at large were in use to receive their commands under the old government, are the same from whom they receive them under the new one. The habit of obedience which these subordinate governors were in with respect to that single person, we will say, who was the supreme governor of the whole, is broken off insensibly and by degrees. The old names by which these subordinate governors were characterised, while they were subordinate, are continued now they are supreme. In this case it seems rather difficult to answer.

Among persons already in a state of political union at what instant a new society can be said to be formed, by defection from a former.

23. If an example be required, we may take that of the DUTCH provinces with respect to SPAIN. These provinces were once branches of the Spanish monarchy. They have now, for a long time, been universally spoken of as independent states: independent as well of that of Spain as of every other. They are now in a state of nature with respect to Spain. They were once in a state of political union with respect to Spain: namely, in a state of subjection to a single *governor*, a King, who was King of Spain. At what precise juncture did the dissolution of this political union take place? At what precise time did these provinces cease to be

1st, in case of defection by whole bodies, instance the Dutch provinces.

subject to the King of Spain? This, I doubt, will be rather difficult to agree upon.[1]

2dly, in case of defection by individuals – instances, Rome – Venice:

24. Suppose the defection to have begun, not by entire provinces, as in the instance just mentioned, but by a handful of fugitives, this augmented by the accession of other fugitives, and so, by degrees, to a body of men too strong to be reduced, the difficulty will be increased still farther. At what precise juncture was it that ancient ROME, or that modern VENICE, became an independent state?

A revolt, at what juncture it can be said to have taken place.

25. In general then, at what precise juncture is it, that persons subject to a government, become, by disobedience, with respect to that government, in a state of nature? When is it, in short, that a *revolt* shall be deemed to have taken place; and when, again, is it, that that revolt shall be deemed to such a degree successful, as to have settled into *independence*?

Dis-obediences what do not amount to a revolt:

26. As it is the obedience of individuals that constitutes a state of submission, so is it their disobedience that must constitute a state of revolt. Is it then every act of disobedience that will do as much? The affirmative, certainly, is what can never be maintained: for then would there be no such thing as government to be found anywhere. Here then a distinction or two obviously presents itself. Disobedience may be distinguished into *conscious* or *unconscious*: and that, with respect as well to the *law* as to the *fact*.[2] Disobedience

---

1 Upon recollection, I have some doubt whether this example would be found historically exact. If not, that of the defection of the Nabobs of Hindostan may answer the purpose. My first choice fell upon the former; supposing it to be rather better known.

2   1. Disobedience may be said to be *unconscious with respect to the fact*, when the party is ignorant either of his having done the act itself, which is forbidden by the law, or else of his having done it in those *circumstances*, in which alone it is forbidden.
   2. Disobedience may be said to be *unconscious*, with respect to the *law*; when although he may know of his having done the *act* that is in reality forbidden, and that, under the *circumstances* in which it is forbidden, he knows not of its being forbidden in these *circumstances*.
   3. So long as the business of spreading abroad the knowledge of the law continues to lie in the neglect in which it has lain hitherto, instances of disobedience *unconscious with respect to the law*, can never be otherwise than abundant.

that is unconscious with respect to either, will readily, I suppose, be acknowledged not to be a revolt. Disobedience again that is conscious with respect to *both*, may be distinguished into *secret* and *open*; or, in other words, into *fraudulent* and *forcible*.[1] Disobedience that is only fraudulent, will likewise, I suppose, be readily acknowledged not to amount to a revolt.

27. The difficulty that will remain will concern such disobedience only as is both *conscious* (and that as well with respect to *law* as *fact*) and *forcible*. This disobedience, it should seem, is to be determined neither by *numbers* altogether (that is of the persons supposed to be disobedient) nor by *acts*, nor by *intentions*: all three may be fit to be taken into consideration. But having brought the difficulty to this point, at this point I must be content to leave it. To proceed any farther in the endeavour to solve it, would be to enter into a discussion of particular local jurisprudence. It would be entering upon the definition of Treason, as distinguished from Murder, Robbery, Riot, and other such crimes, as, in comparison with Treason, are spoken of as being of a more private nature. Suppose the definition of Treason settled, and the commission of an act of Treason is, as far as regards the person committing it, the characteristic mark we are in search of.

Disobediences what do amount to a revolt.

28. These remarks it were easy to extend to a much greater length. Indeed, it is what would be necessary, in order to give them a proper fulness, and method, and precision. But that could not be done without exceeding the limits of the present design. As they are, they may serve as hints to such as shall be disposed to give the subject a more exact and regular examination.

Unfinished state of the above hints.

29. From what has been said, however, we may judge what truth there is in our Author's observation, that 'when society' (understand *natural* society) 'is once formed, government' (that is political society) (whatever quantity or degree of Obedience is necessary to constitute political society) 'results *of course*; as

Our Author's proposition, 'That government results of course', not true.

---

1 If examples be thought necessary, Theft may serve for an example of *fraudulent* disobedience; Robbery of *forcible*. In Theft, the *person* of the disobedient party, and the *act* of disobedience, are both endeavoured to be kept secret. In Robbery, the *act* of disobedience, at least, if not the *person* of him who disobeys, is manifest and avowed.

necessary to preserve and to keep that society in order.' By the words, '*of course*', is meant, I suppose, *constantly* and *immediately*: at least constantly. According to this, political society, in any sense of it, ought long ago to have been established all the world over. Whether this be the case, let any one judge from the instances of the Hottentots, of the Patagonians, and of so many other barbarous tribes, of which we hear from travellers and navigators.

Ambiguity of the sentence. 30. It may be, after all, we have misunderstood his meaning. We have been supposing him to have been meaning to assert a *matter of fact*, and to have written, or at least begun, this sentence in the character of an *historical observer*: whereas, all he meant by it, perhaps, was to speak in the character of a *Censor*, and on a case supposed, to express a *sentiment of approbation*. In short, what he meant, perhaps, to persuade us of, was not that 'government' *does actually* 'result' from natural 'society'; but that it were better that it *should*, to wit, as being necessary to 'preserve and keep' men 'in that state of order', in which it is of advantage to them that they should be. Which of the above-mentioned characters he meant to speak in, is a problem I must leave to be determined. The distinction, perhaps, is what never so much as occurred to him; and indeed the shifting insensibly, and without warning, from one of those characters to the other, is a failing that seems inveterate in our Author; and of which we shall probably have more instances than one to notice.

Darkness of the whole paragraph further shown. 31. To consider the whole paragraph (with its appendage) to-gether, something, it may be seen, our Author struggles to overthrow, and something to establish. But *how* it is he would overthrow, or *what* it is he would establish, are questions I must confess myself unable to resolve. 'The preservation of mankind,' he observes, 'was effected by single families.' This is what upon the authority of the Holy Scriptures, he assumes; and from this it is that he would have us conclude the notion of an original contract (the same notion which he afterwards adopts) to be ridiculous. The force of this conclusion, I must own, I do not see. Mankind was preserved by single families – Be it so. What is there in this to hinder 'individuals' of those families or of families descended from those families, from meeting together 'afterwards, in a large plain', or any where else, 'entering into an *original* contract', or any other contract, 'and choosing the tallest man', or any other man, 'present', or absent, to be their Governor? The 'flat contradiction' our Author finds between this supposed transaction and the 'preservation of mankind by single families', is what I must own myself unable to discover. As to the 'actually existing unconnected state of nature' he speaks of, 'the notion of which', he says, 'is too wild to be seriously admitted', whether this be the case with it, is what, as he has given us no notion of it at all, I cannot judge of.

32. Something positive, however, in one place, we seem to have. These 'single families', by which the preservation of mankind was effected; these single families, he gives us to understand, 'formed the first society'. This is something to proceed upon. A society then of the one kind or the other; a natural society, or else a political society, was formed. I would here then put a case, and then propose a question. In this society we will say no *contract* had as yet been entered into; no *habit of obedience* as yet formed. Was this then a *natural* society merely, or was it a *political* one? For my part, according to my notion of the two kinds of society as above explained, I can have no difficulty. It was a merely *natural* one. But, according to our Author's notion, which was it? If it *was* already a *political* one, what notion would he give us of such an one as shall have been a *natural* one; and by what change should such precedent natural one have turned into *this* political one? If this was *not* a political one, then what sort of a society are we to understand any one to be which *is* political? By what mark are we to distinguish it from a natural one? To this, it is plain, our Author has not given any answer. At the same time, that to give an answer to it, was, if any thing, the professed purpose of the long paragraph before us. *Farther proofs of the darkness of the whole paragraph.*

33. It is time this passage of our Author were dismissed – As among the expressions of it are some of the most striking of those which the vocabulary of the subject furnishes, and these ranged in the most harmonious order, on a distant glance nothing can look fairer: a prettier piece of tinsel-work one shall seldom see exhibited from the show-glass of political erudition. Step close to it, and the delusion vanishes. It is then seen to consist partly of self-evident observations, and partly of contradictions; partly of what every one knows already, and partly of what no one can understand at all. *A general idea of its character.*

Difficulty attending this examination. 34. Throughout the whole of it, what distresses me is, not the meeting with any positions, such as, thinking them false, I find a difficulty in proving so: but the not meeting with any positions, true, or false (unless it be here and there a self-evident one) that I can find a meaning for. If I can find nothing positive to accede to, no more can I to contradict. Of this latter kind of work, indeed, there is the less to do for any one else, our Author himself having executed it, as we have seen, so amply.

The whole of it is, I must confess, to me a riddle: more acute, by far, than I am, must be the Oedipus that can solve it. Happily, it is not necessary, on account of any thing that follows, that it should be solved. Nothing is concluded from it. For aught I can find, it has in itself no use, and none is made of it. There it is, and as well might it be any where else, or no where.

Use that may be made of it. 35. Were it then possible, there would be no use in its being solved: but being, as I take it, *really* unsolvable, it were of use it should *be seen* to be so. Peace may by this means be restored to the breast of many a desponding student, who, now prepossessed with the hopes of a rich harvest of instruction, makes a crime to himself of his inability to reap what, in truth, his Author has not sown.

Original Contract, a fiction. 36. As to the Original Contract, by turns embraced and ridiculed by our Author, a few pages, perhaps, may not be ill bestowed in endeavouring to come to a precise notion about its reality and use. The stress laid on it formerly, and still, perhaps, by some, is such as renders it an object not undeserving of attention. I was in hopes, however, till I observed the notice taken of it by our author, that this chimera had been effectually demolished by Mr. HUME.[1] I think we hear not so much of it now as formerly. The indestructible prerogatives of mankind have no need to be supported upon the sandy foundation of a fiction.

37. With respect to this, and other fictions, there was once a time, perhaps, when they had their use. With instruments of this temper,

---

1   1. In the third Volume of his TREATISE *on* HUMAN NATURE.

    Our Author, one would think, had never so much as opened that celebrated book: of which the criminality in the eyes of some, and the merits in the eyes of others, have since been almost effaced by the splendour of more recent productions of the same pen. The magnanimity of our Author scorned, perhaps, or his circumspection feared, to derive instruction from an enemy: or, what is still more probable, he knew not that the subject had been so much as touched upon by that penetrating and acute metaphysician, whose works lie so much out of the beaten track of Academic reading. But here, as it happens, there is no matter for such fears. Those men, who are most alarmed at the dangers of a free enquiry; those who are most intimately convinced that the surest way to truth is by hearing nothing but on one side, will, I dare answer almost, find nothing of that which they deem poison in this third volume. I would not wish to send the Reader to any other than this, which, if I recollect aright, stands clear of the objections that have of late been urged, with so much vehemence, against the work in general.[a] As to the two first, the Author himself, I am inclined to think, is not ill disposed, at present, to join with those who are of opinion, that they might, without any great loss to the science of Human Nature, be dispensed with. The like might be said, perhaps, of a considerable part, even, of this. But, after all retrenchments, there will still remain enough to have laid mankind under indelible obligations. That the foundations of all *virtue* are laid in *utility*, is there demonstrated, after a few exceptions made, with the strongest force of evidence: but I see not, any more than Helvetius saw, what need there was for the exceptions.

2. For my own part, I well remember, no sooner had I read that part of the work which touches on this subject, than I felt as if scales had fallen from my eyes. I then, for the first time, learnt to call the cause of the people the cause of Virtue.

Perhaps a short sketch of the wanderings of a raw but well-intentioned mind, in its researches after moral truth, may, on this occasion, be not unuseful: for the history of one mind is the history of many. The writings of the honest, but prejudiced, Earl of Clarendon, to whose integrity nothing was wanting, and to whose wisdom little, but the fortune of living something later; and the contagion of a monkish atmosphere; these, and other concurrent causes, had listed my infant affections on the side of despotism. The Genius of the place I dwelt in, the authority of the State, the voice of the Church in her solemn offices; all these taught me to call Charles a Martyr, and his opponents rebels. I saw innovation, where indeed innovation, but a glorious innovation, was, in their efforts to withstand him. I saw falsehood, where indeed falsehood was, in their disavowals of innovation. I saw selfishness, and an obedience to the call of passion, in the efforts of the oppressed to rescue themselves from oppression. I saw strong countenance lent in the sacred writings to monarchic government: and none to any other. I saw *passive obedience* deep stamped with the seal of the Christian Virtues of humility and self-denial.

Conversing with Lawyers, I found them full of the virtues of their Original Contract, as a recipe of sovereign efficacy for reconciling the accidental necessity of resistance with the general duty of submission. This drug of theirs they administered to me to calm my scruples. But my unpractised stomach revolted against their opiate. I bid them open to me

---

[a] By DR BEATTIE, in his *Essay on the Immutability of Truth.*

Fictions in *general mis-chievous in the present state of things.* I will not deny but that some political work may have been done, and that useful work, which, under the then circumstances of things, could hardly have been done with any other. But the season of *Fiction* is now over: insomuch, that what formerly might have been tolerated and countenanced under that name, would, if now attempted to be set on foot, be censured and stigmatised under the harsher appellations of *incroachment* or *imposture*. To attempt to introduce any *new* one, would be *now* a crime: for which reason there is much danger, without any use, in vaunting and propagating such as have been introduced already. In point of political discernment, the universal spread of learning has raised mankind in a manner to a level with each other, in comparison of what they have been in any former time: nor is any man now so far elevated above his fellows, as that he should be indulged in the dangerous licence of cheating them for their good.

This *had a moment-ary use.* 38. As to the fiction now before us, in the character of an *argumentum ad hominem* coming when it did, and managed as it was, it succeeded to admiration.

That compacts, by whomsoever entered into, *ought* to be kept; that men are *bound* by compacts, are propositions which men, without knowing or enquiring why, were disposed universally to accede to. The observance of promises they had been accustomed to see pretty constantly enforced. They had been accustomed to see

---

that page of history in which the solemnisation of this important contract was recorded. They shrunk from this challenge; nor could they, when thus pressed, do otherwise than our Author has done, confess the whole to be a fiction. This, methought, looked ill. It seemed to me the acknowledgment of a bad cause, the bringing a fiction to support it. 'To prove fiction, indeed,' said I, 'there is need of fiction; but it is the characteristic of truth to need no proof but truth. Have you then really any such privilege as that of coining facts? You are spending argument to no purpose. Indulge yourselves in the licence of supposing that to be true which is not, and as well may you suppose that proposition itself to be true, which you wish to prove, as that other whereby you hope to prove it.' Thus continued I unsatisfying, and unsatisfied, till I learnt to see that *utility* was the test and measure of all virtue; of loyalty as much as any; and that the obligation to minister to general happiness, was an obligation paramount to and inclusive of every other. Having thus got the instruction I stood in need of, I sat down to make my profit of it. I bid adieu to the original contract: and I left it to those to amuse themselves with this rattle, who could think they needed it.

Kings, as well as others, behave themselves as if bound by them. This proposition, then, 'that men are bound by *compacts*'; and this other, 'that, if one party performs not his part, the other is released from his', being propositions which no man disputed, were propositions which no man had any call to prove. In theory they were assumed for axioms: and in practice they were observed as rules.[1] If, on any occasion, it was thought proper to make a show of proving them, it was rather for form's sake than for any thing else: and that, rather in the way of memento or instruction to acquiescing auditors, than in the way of proof against opponents. On such an occasion the common place retinue of phrases was at hand; *Justice*, *Right Reason* required it, the *Law of Nature* commanded it, and so forth; all which are but so many ways of intimating that a man is firmly persuaded of the truth of this or that moral proposition, though he either thinks he *need not*, or finds he *can't*, tell *why*. Men were too obviously and too generally interested in the observance of these rules to entertain doubts concerning the force of any arguments they saw employed in their support. – It is an old observation how Interest smooths the road to Faith.

39. A compact, then, it was said, was made by the King and people: the terms of it were to this effect. The people, on their part, promised to the King a *general obedience*. The King, on his part, promised to *govern* the people in such a *particular* manner always, as should be *subservient* to their happiness. I insist not on the words: I undertake only for the sense; as far as an imaginary engagement, so loosely and so variously worded by those who have imagined it, is capable of any decided signification. Assuming then, as a general rule, that promises, when made, ought to be observed; and, as a point of fact, that a promise to this effect in particular had been made by the party in question, men were more ready to deem themselves qualified to judge when it was such a promise was *broken*, than to decide directly and avowedly on the delicate question, when it was that a King acted so far in *opposition* to the happiness of his people, that it were better no longer to obey him.

Terms of the supposed contract stated.

---

1 A *compact* or *contract* (for the two words on this occasion, at least, are used in the same sense) may, I *think*, be defined, a pair of promises, by two persons reciprocally given, the one promise in consideration of the other.

Stated thus generally, it could not dispense men from entering into the question of utility, as was intended. 40. It is manifest, on a very little consideration, that nothing was gained by this manoeuvre after all: no difficulty removed by it. It was still necessary, and that as much as ever, that the question men studied to avoid should be determined, in order to determine the question they thought to substitute in its room. It was still necessary to determine, whether the King in question had, or had not acted so far in *opposition* to the happiness of his people, that it were better no longer to obey him; in order to determine, whether the promise he was supposed to have made, had, or had not been broken. For what was the supposed purport of this promise? It was no other than what has just been mentioned.

Nor, if stated more particularly, could it answer what was designed by it. 41. Let it be said, that part at least of this promise was to govern in *subservience to Law*: that hereby a more precise rule was laid down for his conduct, by means of this supposal of a promise, than that other loose and general rule to govern in subservience to the *happiness of his people*: and that, by this means, it is the letter of the *Law* that forms the tenor of the rule.

Now true it is, that the governing in opposition to Law, is *one* way of governing in opposition to the happiness of the people: the natural effect of such a contempt of the Law being, if not actually to destroy, at least to threaten with destruction, all those rights and privileges that are founded on it: rights and privileges on the enjoyment of which that happiness depends. But still it is not this that can be safely taken for the entire purport of the promise here in question: and that for several reasons. *First*, Because the most mischievous, and under certain constitutions the most feasible, method of governing in opposition to the happiness of the people, is, by setting the Law itself in opposition to their happiness. *Secondly*, Because it is a case very conceivable, that a King may, to a great degree, impair the happiness of his people without violating the letter of any single Law. *Thirdly*, Because extraordinary occasions may now and then occur, in which the happiness of the people may be better promoted by acting, for the moment, in *opposition* to the Law, than in *subservience* to it. *Fourthly*, Because it is not any single violation of the Law, as such, that can properly be taken for a breach of his part of the contract, so as to be understood to have released the people from the obligation of performing theirs. For, to quit the fiction, and resume the language of plain truth, it is scarce ever any single violation of the Law that, by being *submitted to,* can produce so much mischief as shall surpass the probable mischief of *resisting* it. If every single instance whatever of such a violation were to be deemed an entire dissolution of the contract, a man who reflects at all would scarce find anywhere, I believe, under the sun, that Government which he could allow to subsist for twenty years together. It is plain, therefore, that to pass any sound decision upon the question which the inventors of this fiction substituted instead of the true one, the latter was still necessary to be decided. All they gained by their contrivance was, the convenience of deciding it obliquely, as it were, and by a side wind — that is, in a crude and hasty way, without any direct and steady examination.

42. But, after all, for what *reason* is it, that men *ought* to keep their promises? The moment any intelligible reason is given, it is this: that it is for the *advantage* of society they should keep them; and if they do not, that, as far as *punishment* will go, they should be *made* to keep them. It is for the advantage of the whole number that the promises of each individual should be kept: and, rather than they should not be kept, that such individuals as fail to keep them should be punished. If it be asked, how this appears? the answer is at hand: Such is the benefit to gain, and mischief to avoid, by keeping them, as much more than compensates the mischief of so much punishment as is requisite to oblige men to it. Whether the dependence of *benefit* and *mischief* (that is, of *pleasure* and *pain*) upon men's conduct in this behalf, be as here stated, is a question of *fact,* to be decided, in the same manner that all other questions of fact are to be decided, by testimony, observation, and experience.[1]

Nor is it an original independent principle.

---

1 The importance which the observance of promises is of to the happiness of society, is placed in a very striking and satisfactory point of view, in a little apologue of MONTESQUIEU, entitled *The History of the Troglodytes.*[a] The Troglodytes are a people who pay no regard to promises. By the natural consequences of this disposition, they fall from one scene of misery into another; and are at last exterminated. The same Philosopher, in his *Spirit of Laws,* copying and refining upon the current jargon, feigns a LAW for this and other purposes, after defining a Law to be a *relation.* How much more instructive on this head is the fable of the Troglodytes than the pseudo-metaphysical sophistry of the *Esprit des Loix!*

---

a See the Collection of his Works.

Nor can it serve to prove anything, but what may be better proved without it.

43. This then, and no other, being the *reason* why men should be made to keep their promises, viz., that it is for the advantage of society that they should, is a reason that may as well be given at once, why *Kings*, on the one hand, in governing, should in general keep within established Laws, and (to speak universally) abstain from all such measures as tend to the unhappiness of their subjects: and, on the other hand, why *subjects* should obey Kings as long as they so conduct themselves, and no longer; why they should obey in short *so long as the probable mischiefs of obedience are less than the probable mischiefs of resistance*: why, in a word, taking the whole body together, it is their *duty* to obey, just so long as it is their *interest*, and no longer. This being the case, what need of saying of the one, that *he* PROMISED so to *govern*; of the other, that they PROMISED so to *obey*, when the fact is otherwise?

The Coronation-oath does not come up to the notion of it.

44. True it is, that, in this country, according to ancient forms, some sort of vague promise of *good government* is made by Kings at the ceremony of their coronation: and let the acclamations, perhaps given, perhaps not given, by chance persons out of the surrounding multitude, be construed into a promise of *obedience* on the part of the *whole* multitude: that whole multitude itself, a small drop collected together by chance out of the ocean of the state: and let the two promises thus made be deemed to have formed a perfect *compact* – not that either of them is declared to be the *consideration* of the other.[1]

The obligation of a promise will not stand against that of utility: while that of utility will against that of a promise.

45. Make the most of this concession, one experiment there is, by which every reflecting man may satisfy himself, I think, beyond a doubt, that it is the consideration of *utility*, and no other, that, secretly but unavoidably, has governed his judgment upon all these matters. The experiment is easy and decisive. It is but to reverse, in supposition, in the first place the import of the *particular* promise thus feigned; in the next place, the effect in point of *utility* of the observance of promises *in general*. – Suppose the King to promise that he would govern his subjects *not* according to Law; *not* in the view to promote their happiness: would this be binding upon *him*? Suppose the people to promise they would obey him

1 V. supra, par. 38, note, p. 55.

at all events, let him govern as he will; let him govern to their destruction. Would this be binding upon *them*? Suppose the constant and universal effect of an observance of promises were to produce *mischief*, would it *then* be men's *duty* to observe them? Would it *then* be *right* to make Laws, and apply punishment to *oblige* men to observe them?

46. 'No;' (it may perhaps be replied) 'but for this reason; among promises, some there are that, as every one allows, are void: now these you have been supposing, are unquestionably of the number. A promise that is in itself *void*, cannot, it is true, create any obligation. But allow the promise to be *valid*, and it is the promise itself that creates the obligation, and nothing else.' The fallacy of this argument it is easy to perceive. For what is it then that the promise depends on for its *validity*? what is it that being *present* makes it *valid*? what is it that being *wanting* makes it *void*? To acknowledge that any *one* promise may be void, is to acknowledge that if any *other* is *binding*, it is not merely because it is a promise. That circumstance then, whatever it be, on which the validity of a promise depends, that circumstance, I say, and not the promise itself must, it is plain, be the cause of the obligation on which a promise is apt in general to carry with it.

A fallacy obviated.

47. But farther. Allow, for argument's sake, what we have disproved: allow that the obligation of a promise is independent of every other: allow that a promise is binding *propriâ vi* – Binding then on whom? On him certainly who makes it. Admit this: For what reason is the same individual promise to be binding on those who *never* made it? The King, *fifty years ago*, promised my *Great-Grandfather* to govern him according to Law: my Great-Grandfather, *fifty years ago*, promised the King to obey him according to Law. The King, *just now*, promised my *neighbour* to govern him according to Law: my neighbour, *just now*, promised the King to obey him according to Law. – Be it so – What are these promises, all or any of them, to *me*? To make answer to this question, some other principle, it is manifest, must be resorted to, than that of the *intrinsic* obligation of promises upon those who make them.

The obligation of a promise, were it even independent, would not be extensive enough for the purpose.

But the principle of UTILITY *is all-sufficient.* 48. Now this *other* principle that still recurs upon us, what other can it be than the *principle of* utility? The principle which furnishes us with that *reason*, which alone depends not upon any higher reason, but which is itself the sole and all sufficient reason for every point of practice whatsoever.

[*Chapter II – Forms of Government, is omitted.*]

[*Chapter III – British Constitution, is omitted.*]

CHAPTER IV

Right of the Supreme Power to Make Laws

[Paragraphs 1–38 are omitted]

39. I cannot look upon this as a mere dispute of words. I cannot help persuading myself, that the disputes between contending parties – between the defenders of a law and the opposers of it, would stand a much better chance of being adjusted than at present, were they but explicitly and constantly referred at once to the principle of UTILITY. The footing on which this principle rests every dispute is that of matter of fact; that is, future fact – the probability of certain future contingencies. Were the debate then conducted under the auspices of this principle, one of two things would happen: either men would come to an agreement concerning that probability, or they would see at length, after due discussion of the real grounds of the dispute, that no agreement was to be hoped for. They would at any rate see clearly and explicitly, the point on which the disagreement turned. The discontented party would then take their resolution to resist or to submit, upon just grounds, according as it should appear to them worth their while – according to what should appear to them, the importance of the matter in dispute – according to what should appear to them the probability or improbability of *success* – *according*, in short, *as the mischiefs of submission should appear to bear a less, or a greater ratio to the mischiefs of resistance*. But the door to reconcilement would be much more open, when they saw that it might be not a mere affair of passion, but a difference of judgment, and that, for any thing they could know to the contrary, a sincere one, that was the ground of quarrel.

This is not a mere affair of words.

40. All else is but womanish scolding and childish altercation, which is sure to irritate, and which never can persuade. – '*I say,*

The above notion perpetuates wrangling.

the legislature can*not* do this — *I* say, that it *can*. *I* say, that to do this, *exceeds* the bounds of its *authority* — *I* say, it does *not*.' — It is evident, that a pair of disputants setting out in this manner, may go on irritating and perplexing one another for everlasting, without the smallest chance of ever coming to an agreement. It is no more than announcing, and that in an obscure and at the same time, a peremptory and captious manner, their opposite persuasions, or rather affections, on a question of which neither of them sets himself to discuss the grounds. The question of utility, all this while, most probably, is never so much as at all brought upon the carpet: if it be, the language in which it is discussed is sure to be warped and clouded to make it match with the obscure and entangled pattern we have seen.

The principle of UTILITY *puts an end to it.*

41. On the other hand, had the debate been originally and avowedly instituted on the footing of utility, the parties might at length have come to an agreement; or at least to a visible and explicit issue. — 'I say, that the mischiefs of the measure in question are to *such* an amount. — *I* say, *not* so, but to a *less*. — *I* say, the benefits of it are only to *such* an amount. — *I* say, *not* so, but to a *greater*.' — This, we see, is a ground of controversy very different from the former. The question is now manifestly a question of conjecture concerning so many future contingent matters of fact: to solve it, both parties then are naturally directed to support their respective persuasions by the only evidence the nature of the case admits of — the evidence of such *past* matters of fact as appear to be analogous to those contingent *future* ones. Now these *past* facts are almost always numerous: so numerous, that till brought into view for the purpose of the debate, a great proportion of them are what may very fairly have escaped the observation of one of the parties: and it is owing, perhaps, to this and nothing else, that that party is of the persuasion which sets it at variance with the other. Here then, we have a plain and open road, perhaps, to present reconcilement: at the worst to an intelligible and explicit issue — that is, to such a ground of difference as may, when thoroughly trodden and explored, be found to lead on to reconcilement at the last. Men, let them but once clearly understand one another, will not be long ere they agree. It is the perplexity of ambiguous and sophistical discourse

that, while it distracts and eludes the apprehension, stimulates and inflames the passions.

But it is now high time we should return to our Author, from whose text we have been insensibly led astray, by the nicety and intricacy of the question it seemed to offer to our view.

CHAPTER V

Duty of the Supreme Power to Make Laws

Subject of the paragraph examined in the present chapter.

1. We now come to the last topic touched upon in this digression: a certain '*duty*', which, according to our Author's account, the supreme power lies under: the *duty of making laws*.

2. 'Thus far,' says he, 'as to the *right* of the supreme power to make laws; but farther, it is its *duty* likewise. *For since* the respective members are bound to conform themselves to the will of the state, it is expedient that they *receive directions* from the state declaratory of that its will. *But since* it is impossible, in so great a multitude, to give injunctions to every particular man, relative to each particular action, therefore the state establishes general rules for the perpetual information and direction of all persons, in all points, whether of positive or negative duty. And this, in order that every man may know what to look upon as his own, what as another's; what absolute and what relative duties are required at his hands; what is to be esteemed honest, dishonest, or indifferent; what degree every man retains of his natural liberty; what he has given up as the price of the benefits of society; and after what manner each person is to moderate the use and exercise of those rights which the state assigns him, in order to promote and secure the public tranquillity.'

The first sentence examined. The most obvious sense of it nugatory.

3. Still as obscure, still as ambiguous as ever. The '*supreme power*' we may remember, according to the definition so lately given of it by our Author, and so often spoken of, is neither more nor less than the *power to make laws*. Of this power we are now told that it is its '*duty*' to make laws. Hence we learn – what? – that it is its '*duty*' to do what it does; to be, in short, what it is. This then is what the paragraph now before us, with its apparatus of '*fors*', and '*buts*', and '*sinces*', is designed to prove to us. Of this stamp is that

meaning, at least, of the initial sentence, which is apparent upon the face of it.

4. Complete the sense of the phrase, '*to make laws*'; add to it, in this place, what it wants in order to be an adequate expression of the import which the preceding paragraph seemed to annex to it; you have now, for what is mentioned as the object of the '*duty*', another sense indeed, but a sense still more untenable than the foregoing. 'Thus far,' says our Author (recapitulating what he had been saying before) 'as to the *right* of the supreme power to make laws.' – By this '*right*' we saw, in the preceding chapter, was meant, a right to make laws *in all cases whatsoever*. 'But further,' he now adds, 'it is its *duty* likewise.' Its *duty* then to do – what? to do the same thing that it was before asserted to be its *right* to do – to make laws in all cases whatsoever: or (to use another word, and that our Author's own, and that applied to the same purpose) that it is its duty to be '*absolute*'.[1] A sort of duty this which will probably be thought rather a singular one. *The next most obvious extravagant.*

5. Meantime the observation which, if I conjecture right, he really had in view to make, is one which seems very just indeed, and of no mean importance, but which is very obscurely expressed, and not very obviously connected with the purpose of what goes before. The duty he here means is a duty, which respects, I take it, not so much the actual *making* of laws, as the taking of proper measures to *spread abroad* the knowledge of whatever laws happen to *have been* made: a duty which (to adopt some of our Author's own words) is conversant, not so much about *issuing* 'directions' as about providing that such as *are* issued shall be '*received*'. *A third sense proposed.*

6. Meantime to speak of the *duties* of a supreme power – of a *legislature*, meaning a *supreme* legislature; of a set of men acknowledged to be absolute – is what, I must own, I am not very fond of. Not that I would wish the subordinate part of the community to be a whit less watchful over their governors, or more disposed to unlimited submission in point of *conduct*, than if I were to talk with ever so much peremptoriness of the '*duties*' of these latter, and of *Objection to the use of the word 'duty' on this occasion.*

1 1 Comm., p. 49.

the *rights* which the former have against them:[1] what I am afraid of is, running into solecism and confusion in *discourse*.

1 With this note let no man trouble himself who is not used, or does not intend to use himself to what are called *metaphysical* speculations: in whose estimation the benefit of understanding clearly what he is speaking of, is not worth the labour.

1. That may be said to be my *duty* to do (understand political duty) which you (or some other person or persons) have a *right* to have me made to do. I then have a DUTY *towards* you: you have a RIGHT as *against* me.

2. What you have a right to have me made to do (understand a political right) is that which I am liable, according to law, upon a requisition made on your behalf, to be *punished* for not doing.

3: I say *punished*: for without the notion of punishment (that is of *pain* annexed to an act, and accruing on a certain *account*, and from a certain *source*) no notion can we have of either *right* or *duty*.

4. Now the idea belonging to the word *pain* is a simple one. To *define* or rather (to speak more generally) to *expound* a word, is to resolve, or to make a progress towards resolving, the idea belonging to it into simple ones.

5. For expounding the words *duty*, *right*, *power*, *title*, and those other terms of the same stamp that abound so much in ethics and jurisprudence, either I am much deceived, or the only method by which any instruction can be conveyed, is that which is here exemplified. An exposition framed after this method I would term *paraphrasis*.

6. A word may be said to be expounded by *paraphrasis*, when not that *word* alone is translated into other *words*, but some whole *sentence* of which it forms a part is translated into another *sentence*; the words of which latter are expressive of such ideas as are *simple*, or are more immediately resolvable into simple ones than those of the former. Such are those expressive of *substances* and *simple modes*, in respect of such *abstract* terms as are expressive of what LOCKE has called *mixed modes*. This, in short, is the only method in which any abstract terms can, at the long run, be expounded to any instructive purpose: that is in terms calculated to raise *images* either of *substances* perceived, or of *emotions*; *sources*, one or other of which every idea must be drawn from, to be a clear one.

7. The common method of defining – the method *per genus et differentiam*, as logicians call it, will, in many cases, not at all answer the purpose. Among abstract terms we soon come to such as have no *superior genus*. A definition, *per genus et differentiam*, when applied to these, it is manifest, can make no advance: it must either stop short, or turn back, as it were, upon itself; in a *circulate* or a *repetend*.

8. 'Fortitude is a virtue': Very well: but what is a virtue? 'A virtue is a disposition': Good again: but what is a *disposition*? 'A *disposition* is a. . .'; and there we stop. The fact is, a *disposition* has no *superior genus*: a *disposition* is not a. . ., any thing: this is not the way to give us any notion of what is meant by it. 'A *power*', again 'is a *right*': and what is a *right*? It is *power*. – *An estate* is an *interest*, says our Author somewhere; where he begins defining an estate: as well might he have said an *interest* was an *estate*. As well, in short, were it to define in this manner, a conjunction or a preposition. As well were it to say

7. I understand, I think, pretty well, what is meant by the word *The* *duty* (political duty) when applied to myself; and I could not *proper* persuade myself, I think, to apply it in the same sense in a regular *sense of* didactic discourse to those whom I am speaking of as my supreme *it.* governors. That is my *duty* to do, which I am liable to be *punished*, according to law, if I do not do: this is the original, ordinary, and proper sense of the word *duty*.[1] Have these supreme governors

---

of the preposition *through*, or the conjunction *because*; a *through* is a . . ., or a *because* is a . . ., and so go on defining them.

9. Of this stamp, by the bye, are some of his most-fundamental definitions: of consequence they must leave the reader where they found him. But of this, perhaps, more fully and methodically on some future occasion. In the meantime I have thrown out these loose hints for the consideration of the curious.

1   1. One may conceive three sorts of duties: *political*, *moral*, and *religious*; correspondent to the three sorts of *sanctions* by which they are enforced: or the same point of conduct may be a man's duty on these three several accounts. After speaking of the one of these to put the change upon the reader, and without warning begin speaking of another, or not to let it be seen from the first which of them one is speaking of, cannot but be productive of confusion.

2. Political duty is created by punishment: or at least by the will of persons who have punishment in their hands; persons stated and *certain* – political superiors.

3. Religious duty is also created by punishment: by punishment expected at the hands of a person *certain* – the Supreme Being.

4. Moral duty is created by a kind of motive, which from the uncertainty of the *persons* to apply it, and of the *species* and *degree* in which it will be applied, has hardly yet got the name of punishment: by various mortifications resulting from the ill-will of persons *uncertain* and variable – the community in general: that is, such individuals of that community as he, whose duty is in question, shall happen to be connected with.

5. When in any of these three senses a man asserts a point of conduct to be a duty, what he asserts is the existence, actual or probable, of an *external* event: viz, of a punishment issuing from one or other of these sources in consequence of a contravention of the duty: an event *extrinsic* to, and distinct from, as well the conduct of the party spoken of, as the sentiment of him who speaks. If he persists in asserting it to be a duty, but without meaning it should be understood that it is on any one of these three accounts that he looks upon it as such; all he then asserts is his own internal *sentiment*: all he means then is, that he feels himself *pleased* or *displeased* at the thoughts of the point of conduct in question, but without being able to tell *why*. In this case he should e'en say so: and not seek to give an undue influence to his own single suffrage, by delivering it in terms that purport to declare the voice either of God, or of the law, or of the people.

any such duty? No: for if they are at all liable to punishment according to law, whether it be for *not* doing any thing, or for *doing*, then are they not, what they are supposed to be, supreme governors:[1] those are the supreme governors, by whose appointment the former are liable to be punished.

---

6. Now which of all these senses of the word our Author had in mind in which of them all he meant to assert that it was the duty of supreme governors to make laws, I know not. *Political* duty is what they cannot be subject to:[a] and to say that a duty even of the moral or *religious* kind to this effect is incumbent on them, seems rather a precipitate assertion.

In truth what he meant was neither more nor less, I suppose, than that he should be glad to see them do what he is speaking of; to wit, 'make laws': that is, as he explains himself, spread abroad the knowledge of them. Would he so? So indeed should I; and if asked why, what answer our Author would give I know not; but I, for my part, have no difficulty. I answer – because I am persuaded that it is for the benefit of the community that they (its governors) should do so. This would be enough to warrant me in my own opinion for saying that they *ought* to do it. For all this, I should not at any rate say that it was their *duty* in a *political* sense. No more should I venture to say it was in a *moral* or *religious* sense, till I were satisfied whether they themselves *thought* the measures useful and feasible, and whether they were generally *supposed* to think so.

Were I satisfied that they *themselves* thought so, God then, I might say, knows they do. God, we are to suppose, will punish them if they neglect pursuing it. It is then their *religious* duty. Were I satisfied that the *people* supposed they thought so: the people, I might say, in case of such neglect – the people, by various manifestations of its ill-will, will also punish them. It is then their *moral* duty.

In any of these senses it must be observed, there can be no more propriety in averring it to be the duty of the supreme power to pursue the measure in question, than in averring it to be their duty to pursue any other supposeable measure equally beneficial to the community. To usher in the proposal of a measure in this peremptory and assuming guise, may be pardonable in a loose rhetorical harangue, but can never be justifiable in an exact didactic composition. Modes of *private moral* conduct there are indeed many, the tendency whereof is so well known and so generally acknowledged, that the observance of them may well be styled a duty. But to apply the same term to the particular details of *legislative* conduct, especially newly proposed ones, is going, I think, too far, and tends only to confusion.

[a] See the note following.

1 I mean for what they do, or omit to do, when *acting in a body*: in that body in which, when acting, they are supreme. Because for any thing any of them do separately, or acting in bodies that are subordinate, they may any of them be punished without any disparagement to their supremacy. Not only any *may* be, but many *are*: it is what we see examples of every day.

8. The word duty, then, if applied to persons spoken of as *That in* supreme governors, is evidently applied to them in a sense which *which it is* is figurative and improper: nor therefore are the same conclusions *here used* to be drawn from any propositions in which it is used in this sense, *figura-* as might be drawn from them if it were used in the other sense, *tive.* which is its proper one.

9. This explanation, then, being premised; understanding my- *The* self to be using the word *duty* in its improper sense, the *proposition* proposition that it is the duty of the legislature to spread abroad, *acceded to* as much as possible, the knowledge of their will among the *in this last* people, is a proposition I am disposed most unreservedly to *sense.* accede to. If this be our Author's meaning, I join myself to him heart and voice.

10. What particular institutions our Author wished to see estab- *Obscured* lished in this view – what *particular* duties he would have found for *again by* the legislature under this *general* head of duty, is not very apparent: *the next* though it is what should have appeared more precisely than it *sentence* does, ere his meaning could be apprehended to any purpose. *– the* What increases still the difficulty of apprehending it, is a practice *Censor's* which we have already had more than once occasion to detect *part* him in[1] – a kind of versatility, than which nothing can be more *confounded* vexatious to a reader who makes a point of entering into the *with that of* sentiments of his Author. He sets out with the word *duty* in his *the* mouth; and, in the character of a *Censor*, with all due gravity *Histo-* begins talking to us of what *ought* to be. 'Tis in the midst of this *rian.* lecture that our *Proteus* slips aside; puts on the *historian*; gives an insensible turn to the discourse; and, without any warning of the change, finishes with telling us what *is*. Between these two points, indeed, the *is*, and the *ought to be*, so opposite as they frequently are in the eyes of other men, that spirit of obsequious *quietism* that seems constitutional in our Author, will scarce ever let him recognise a difference. 'Tis in the second sentence of the paragraph that he observes that 'it is *expedient* that they' (the people) 'receive directions from the state' (meaning the govern-ing body) 'declaratory of that its will.' 'Tis in the very next

1 V. supra, ch. II par. 11, ch. III par. 7, ch. IV par. 10.

sentence that we learn from him, that what it is thus '*expedient*' that the state *should* do, it *does* do. 'But since it is impossible in so great a multitude, to give particular injunctions to every particular man relative to each particular action, therefore,' says he 'the state establishes' (does *actually* establish) 'general rules' (*the* state generally, *any* state, that is to say, that one can mention, all states, in short, whatever *do* establish) 'general rules for the perpetual information and direction of *all* persons in *all* points, whether of positive or of negative duty.' Thus far our Author; so that, for aught appears, whatever he could *wish* to see done in this view *is* done. Neither this state of our own, nor any other, does he wish to see do any thing more in the matter than he sees done already; nay, nor than what is sure to be done at all events: so that happily the duty he is here so forward to lay on his superiors will not sit on them very heavy. Thus far is he from having any determinate instructive meaning in that part of the paragraph in which, to appearance, and by accident, he comes nearest to it.

Fixed and particularised.
Promulgation
recommended.

11. Not that the passage however is absolutely so remote from meaning, but that the inventive complaisance of a commentator of the admiring breed might find it pregnant with a good deal of useful matter. The design of disseminating the knowledge of the laws is glanced at by it at least, with a show of approbation. Were our Author's writings then as sacred as they are mysterious; and ·were they in the number of those which stamp the seal of authority on whatever doctrines can be fastened on them; what we have read might serve as a text, from which the obligation of adopting as many measures as a man should deem subservient to that design, might, without any unexampled violence, be deduced. In this oracular passage I might find inculcated, if not *totidem syllabis*, at least *totidem literis*, as many points of legislative duty as should seem subservient to the purposes of *digestion* and *promulgation*. Thus fortified, I might press upon the legislature, and that on the score of '*duty*', to carry into execution, and that without delay, many a busy project as yet either unthought of or unheeded. I might call them with a tone of authority to their work: I might bid them go make provision forthwith for the bringing to light such scattered materials as can be found of the judicial decisions of time past − sole and neglected materials of

common law; for the registering and publishing of all future ones as they arise; for transforming, by a digest, the body of the common law thus completed, into statute-law; for breaking down the whole together into *codes* or parcels, as many as there are classes of persons distinguishably concerned in it; for introducing to the notice and possession of every person his respective code: works which public necessity cries aloud for, at which professional interest shudders, and at which legislative indolence stands aghast.

12. All these leading points, I say, of legislative economy, with as many points of detail subservient to each as a meditation not unassiduous has suggested, I might enforce, were it necessary, by our Author's oracular authority. For nothing less than what has been mentioned, I trust, is necessary, in order that every man may be made to know, in the degree in which he *might* and *ought* to be made to know, what (in our Author's words) 'to look upon as his own, what as another's; what absolute and what relative duties are required at his hands; what is to be esteemed honest, dishonest, or indifferent; what degree every man retains of his natural liberty; what he has given up as the price of the benefits of society; and after what manner each person is to moderate the use and exercise of those rights which the state assigns him, in order to promote and secure the public tranquillity.' In taking my leave of our Author, I finish gladly with this pleasing peroration: a scrutinising judgment, perhaps, would not be altogether satisfied with it; but the ear is soothed by it, and the heart is warmed. *The recommend-ation enforced by our Author's concluding sentence.*

13. I now put an end to the tedious and intricate war of words that has subsisted, in a more particular manner during the course of these two last chapters: a logomachy, wearisome enough, perhaps, and insipid to the reader, but beyond description laborious and irksome to the writer. What remedy? Had there been sense, I should have attached myself to the sense: finding nothing but words, to the words I was to attach myself, or to nothing. Had the doctrine been but *false*, the task of exposing it would have been comparatively an easy one: but it was what is worse, *unmeaning*; and thence it came to require all these pains which I have been here bestowing on it: to what profit let the reader judge. *Necessity and use of these verbal criticisms.*

'Well then,' (cries an objector) 'the task you have set yourself is at an end; and the subject of it after all, according to your own representation, teaches nothing; according to your own showing it is not worth attending to. Why then bestow on it so much attention?'

In this view – To do something to instruct, but more to undeceive, the timid and admiring student: to excite him to place more confidence in his own strength, and less in the infallibility of great names: to help him to emancipate his judgment from the shackles of authority; to let him see that the not understanding a discourse may as well be the writer's fault as the reader's: to teach him to distinguish between showy language and sound sense: to warn him not to pay himself with words: to show him that what may tickle the ear, or dazzle the imagination, will not always inform the judgment: to show him what it is our Author can do, and has done: and what it is he has not done, and cannot do: to dispose him rather to fast on ignorance than feed himself with error: to let him see that with regard to an expositor of the law, out Author is not *he that should come*, but that we may be still *looking for another*. – 'Who then,' says my objector, 'shall be that other? Yourself?' – No verily. My mission is at an end, when I have *prepared the way before him*.

AN INTRODUCTION TO THE
PRINCIPLES OF MORALS AND LEGISLATION

Preface

1. The following sheets were, as the title-page expresses,[1] printed so long ago as the year 1780. The design, in pursuance of which they were written, was not so extensive as that announced by the present title. They had at that time no other destination than that of serving as an introduction to a plan of a penal code *in terminis*, designed to follow them, in the same volume.

2. The body of the work had received its completion according to the then present extent of the author's views, when, in the investigation of some flaws be had discovered, he found himself unexpectedly entangled in an unsuspected corner of the metaphysical maze. A suspension, at first not apprehended to be more than a temporary one, necessarily ensued: suspension brought on coolness, and coolness, aided by other concurrent causes, ripened into disgust.

3. Imperfections pervading the whole mass had already been pointed out by the sincerity of severe and discerning friends; and conscience had certified the justness of their censure. The inordinate length of some of the chapters, the apparent inutility of others, and the dry and metaphysical turn of the whole, suggested an apprehension, that, if published in its present form, the work would contend under great disadvantages for any chance, it might on other accounts possess, of being read, and consequently of being of use.

4. But, though in this manner the idea of completing the present work slid insensibly aside, that was not by any means the case with

---

1 The title-page of the 1789 edition reads, after the title – 'printed in the year 1780, and now first published.' W. H.

the considerations which had led him to engage in it. Every opening, which promised to afford the lights he stood in need of, was still pursued: as occasion arose, the several departments connected with that in which he had at first engaged, were successively explored; insomuch that, in one branch or other of the pursuit, his researches have nearly embraced the whole field of legislation.

5. Several causes have conspired at present to bring to light, under this new title, a work which under its original one had been imperceptibly, but as it had seemed irrevocably, doomed to oblivion. In the course of eight years, materials for various works, corresponding to the different branches of the subject of legislation, had been produced, and some nearly reduced to shape: and, in every one of those works, the principles exhibited in the present publication had been found so necessary, that, either to transcribe them piecemeal, or to exhibit them somewhere where they could be referred to in the lump, was found unavoidable. The former course would have occasioned repetitions too bulky to be employed without necessity in the execution of a plan unavoidably so voluminous: the latter was therefore indisputably the preferable one.

6. To publish the materials in the form in which they were already printed, or to work them up into a new one, was therefore the only alternative: the latter had all along been his wish, and, had time and the requisite degree of alacrity been at command, it would as certainly have been realised. Cogent considerations, however, concur, with the irksomeness of the task, in placing the accomplishment of it at present at an unfathomable distance.

7. Another consideration is, that the suppression of the present work, had it been ever so decidedly wished, is no longer altogether in his power. In the course of so long an interval, various incidents have introduced copies into various hands, from some of which they have been transferred, by deaths and other accidents, into others that are unknown to him. Detached, but considerable extracts, have even been published, without any dishonourable views (for the name of the author was very honestly subjoined to them), but without his privity, and in publications undertaken without his knowledge.

8. It may perhaps be necessary to add, to complete his excuse for offering to the public a work pervaded by blemishes, which have not escaped even the author's partial eye, that the censure, so justly bestowed upon the form, did not extend itself to the matter.

9. In sending it thus abroad into the world with all its imperfections upon its head, he thinks it may be of assistance to the few readers he can expect, to receive a short intimation of the chief particulars, in respect of which it fails of corresponding with his maturer views. It will thence be observed how in some respects it fails of quadrating with the design announced by its original title, as in others it does with that announced by the one it bears at present.

10. An introduction to a work which takes for its subject the totality of any science, ought to contain all such matters, and such matters only, as belong in common to every particular branch of that science, or at least to more branches of it than one. Compared with its present title, the present work fails in both ways of being conformable to that rule.

11. As an introduction to the principles of *morals*, in addition to the analysis it contains of the extensive ideas signified by the terms *pleasure*, *pain*, *motive*, and *disposition*, it ought to have given a similar analysis of the not less extensive, though much less determinate, ideas annexed to the terms *emotion*, *passion*, *appetite*, *virtue*, *vice*, and some others, including the names of the particular *virtues* and *vices*. But as the true, and, if he conceives right, the only true ground-work for the development of the latter set of terms, has been laid by the explanation of the former, the completion of such a dictionary, so to style it, would, in comparison of the commencement, be little more than a mechanical operation.

12. Again, as an introduction to the principles of *legislation in general*, it ought rather to have included matters belonging exclusively to the *civil* branch, than matters more particularly applicable to the *penal*: the latter being but a means of compassing the ends proposed by the former. In preference therefore, or at least in priority, to the several chapters which will be found relative to *punishment*, it ought to have exhibited a set of propositions which have since presented themselves to him as

affording a standard for the operations performed by government, in the creation and distribution of proprietary and other civil rights. He means certain axioms of what may be termed *mental pathology*, expressive of the connection betwixt the feelings of the parties concerned, and the several classes of incidents, which either call for, or are produced by, operations of the nature above mentioned.[1]

13. The consideration of the division of offences, and every thing else that belongs to offences, ought, besides, to have preceded the consideration of punishment: for the idea of *punishment* presupposes the idea of *offence*: punishment, as such, not being inflicted but in consideration of offence.

14. Lastly, the analytical discussions relative to the classification of offences would, according to his present views, be transferred to a separate treatise, in which the system of legislation is considered solely in respect of its form: in other words, in respect of its *method* and *terminology*.

15. In these respects the performance fails of coming up to the author's own ideas of what should have been exhibited in a work, bearing the title he has now given it, viz., that of an *Introduction to the Principles of Morals and Legislation*. He knows however of no other that would be less unsuitable: nor in particular would so adequate an intimation of its actual contents have been given, by a title corresponding to the more limited design, with which it was written: viz., that of serving as an *introduction to a penal code*.

16. Yet more. Dry and tedious as a great part of the discussions it contains must unavoidably be found by the bulk of readers, he knows not how to regret the having written them, nor even the having made them public. Under every head, the practical uses,

---

1 For example – *It is worse to lose than simply not to gain.* – *A loss falls the lighter by being divided.* – *The suffering of a person hurt in gratification of enmity, is greater than the gratification produced by the same cause.* – These, and a few others which he will have occasion to exhibit at the head of another publication, have the same claim to the appellation of axioms, as those given by mathematicians under that name; since, referring to universal experience as their immediate basis, they are incapable of demonstration, and require only to be developed and illustrated, in order to be recognised as incontestable.

to which the discussions contained under that head appeared applicable, are indicated: nor is there, he believes, a single proposition that he has not found occasion to build upon in the penning of some article or other of those provisions of detail, of which a body of law, authoritative or unauthoritative, must be composed. He will venture to specify particularly, in this view, the several chapters shortly characterised by the words *Sensibility*, *Actions*, *Intentionality*, *Consciousness*, *Motives*, *Dispositions*, *Consequences*. Even in the enormous chapter on the division of offences, which, notwithstanding the forced compression the plan has undergone in several of its parts, in manner there mentioned, occupies no fewer than one hundred and four closely printed quarto pages, the ten concluding ones are employed in a statement of the practical advantages that may be reaped from the plan of classification which it exhibits. Those in whose sight the Defence of Usury has been fortunate enough to find favour, may reckon as one instance of those advantages the discovery of the principles developed in that little treatise. In the preface to an anonymous tract published so long ago as in 1776,[1] he had hinted at the utility of a natural classification of offences, in the character of a test for distinguishing genuine from spurious ones. The case of usury is one among a number of instances of the truth of that observation. A note at the end of Sect. 35, Chap. XVI of the present publication, may serve to show how the opinions, developed in that tract, owed their origin to the difficulty experienced in the attempt to find a place in his system for that imaginary offence. To some readers, as a means of helping them to support the fatigue of wading through an analysis of such enormous length, he would almost recommend the beginning with those concluding pages.

17. One good at least may result from the present publication; viz., that the more he has trespassed on the patience of the reader on this occasion, the less need he will have so to do on future ones: so that this may do to those, the office which is done, by books of pure mathematics, to books of mixed mathematics and natural philosophy. The narrower the circle of readers is, within

[1] *A Fragment on Government.*

which the present work may be condemned to confine itself, the less limited may be the number of those to whom the fruits of his succeeding labours may be found accessible. He may therefore in this respect find himself in the condition of those philosophers of antiquity, who are represented as having held two bodies of doctrine, a popular and an occult one: but, with this difference, that in his instance the occult and the popular will, he hopes, be found as consistent as in those they were contradictory; and that in his production whatever there is of occultness has been the pure result of sad necessity, and in no respect of choice.

18. Having, in the course of this advertisement, had such frequent occasion to allude to different arrangements, as having been suggested by more extensive and maturer views, it may perhaps contribute to the satisfaction of the reader, to receive a short intimation of their nature: the rather, as, without such explanation, references, made here and there to unpublished works, might be productive of perplexity and mistake. The following then are the titles of the works by the publication of which his present designs would be completed. They are exhibited in the order which seemed to him best fitted for apprehension, and in which they would stand disposed, were the whole assemblage ready to come out at once: but the order, in which they will eventually appear, may probably enough be influenced in some degree by collateral and temporary considerations.

19. Part the 1st. Principles of legislation in matters of *civil*, more distinctively termed *private distributive*, or for shortness, *distributive*, *law*.

20. Part the 2nd. Principles of legislation in matters of *penal law*.

21. Part the 3rd. Principles of legislation in matters of *procedure*: uniting in one view the *criminal* and *civil* branches, between which no line can be drawn, but a very indistinct one, and that continually liable to variation.

22. Part the 4th. Principles of legislation in matters of *reward*.

23. Part the 5th. Principles of legislation in matters of *public distributive*, more concisely as well as familiarly termed *constitutional*, law.

24. Part the 6th. Principles of legislation in matters of *political tactics*: or of the art of maintaining *order* in the proceedings of political assemblies, so as to direct them to the end of their institution: viz., by a system of rules, which are to the constitutional branch, in some respects, what the law of procedure is to the civil and the penal.

25. Part the 7th. Principles of legislation in matters betwixt nation and nation, or, to use a new though not inexpressive appellation, in matters of *international* law.

26. Part the 8th. Principles of legislation in matters of *finance*.

27. Part the 9th. Principles of legislation in matters of *political economy*.

28. Part the 10th. Plan of a body of law, complete in all its branches, considered in respect of its *form*; in other words, in respect of its method and terminology; including a view of the origination and connexion of the ideas expressed by the short list of terms, the exposition of which contains all that can be said with propriety to belong to the head of *universal jurisprudence*.[1]

29. The use of the principles laid down under the above several heads is to prepare the way for the body of law itself exhibited *in terminis*; and which to be complete, with reference to any political state, must consequently be calculated for the meridian, and adapted to the circumstances, of some one such state in particular.

30. Had he an unlimited power of drawing upon *time*, and every other condition necessary, it would be his wish to postpone the publication of each part to the completion of the whole. In particular, the use of the ten parts, which exhibit what appear to him the dictates of utility in every line, being no other than to furnish reasons for the several corresponding provisions contained in the body of law itself, the exact truth of the former can never be precisely ascertained, till the provisions, to which they are destined to apply, are themselves ascertained, and that *in terminis*. But as the

---

1 Such as obligation, tight, power, possession, title, exemption, immunity, franchise, privilege, nullity, validity, and the like.

infirmity of human nature renders all plans precarious in the execution, in proportion as they are extensive in the design, and as he has already made considerable advances in several branches of the theory, without having made correspondent advances in the practical applications, he deems it more than probable, that the eventual order of publication will not correspond exactly with that which, had it been equally practicable, would have appeared most eligible. Of this irregularity the unavoidable result will be, a multitude of imperfections, which, if the execution of the body of law *in terminis* had kept pace with the development of the principles, so that each part had been adjusted and corrected by the other, might have been avoided. His conduct however will be the less swayed by this inconvenience, from his suspecting it to be of the number of those in which the personal vanity of the author is much more concerned, than the instruction of the public: since whatever amendments may be suggested in the detail of the principles, by the literal fixation of the provisions to which they are relative, may easily be made in a corrected edition of the former, succeeding upon the publication of the latter.

31. In the course of the ensuing pages, references will be found, as already intimated, some to the plan of a penal code to which this work was meant as an introduction, some to other branches of the above-mentioned general plan, under titles somewhat different from those, by which they have been mentioned here. The giving this warning is all which it is in the author's power to do, to save the reader from the perplexity of looking out for what has not as yet any existence. The recollection of the change of plan will in like manner account for several similar incongruities not worth particularising.

32. Allusion was made, at the outset of this advertisement, to some unspecified difficulties, as the causes of the original suspension, and unfinished complexion, of the present work. Ashamed of his defeat, and unable to dissemble it, he knows not how to refuse himself the benefit of such an apology as a slight sketch of the nature of those difficulties may afford.

33. The discovery of them was produced by the attempt to solve the questions that will be found at the conclusion of the volume:

Wherein consisted the identity and *completeness* of a law? What the distinction, and where the separation, between a *penal* and a *civil* law? What the distinction, and where the separation, between the *penal* and *other branches* of the law?

34. To give a complete and correct answer to these questions, it is but too evident that the relations and dependencies of every part of the legislative system, with respect to every other, must have been comprehended and ascertained. But it is only upon a view of these parts themselves, that such an operation could have been performed. To the accuracy of such a survey one necessary condition would therefore be, the complete existence of the fabric to be surveyed. Of the performance of this condition no example is as yet to be met with anywhere. *Common* law, as it styles itself in England, *judiciary* law, as it might more aptly be styled everywhere, that fictitious composition which has no known person for its author, no known assemblage of words for its substance, forms everywhere the main body of the legal fabric: like that fancied ether, which, in default of sensible matter, fills up the measure of the universe. Shreds and scraps of real law, stuck on upon that imaginary ground, compose the furniture of every national code. What follows? – that he who, for the purpose just mentioned or for any other, wants an example of a complete body of law to refer to, must begin with making one.

35. There is, or rather there ought to be, a *logic* of the *will*, as well as of the *understanding*: the operations of the former faculty, are neither less susceptible, nor less worthy, than those of the latter, of being delineated by rules. Of these two branches of that recondite art, Aristotle saw only the latter: succeeding logicians, treading the steps of their great founder, have concurred in seeing with no other eyes. Yet so far as a difference can be assigned between branches so intimately connected, whatever difference there is, in point of importance, is in favour of the logic of the will. Since it is only by their capacity of directing the operations of this faculty, that the operations of the understanding are of any consequence.

36. Of this logic of the will, the science of *law*, considered in respect of its *form*, is the most considerable branch, – the most important application. It is, to the art of legislation, what the

science of anatomy is to the art of medicine: with this difference, that the subject of it is what the artist has to work *with*, instead of being what he has to operate *upon*. Nor is the body politic less in danger from a want of acquaintance with the one science, than the body natural from ignorance in the other. One example, amongst a thousand that might be adduced in proof of this assertion, may be seen in the note which terminates this volume.

37. Such then were the difficulties: such the preliminaries: – an unexampled work to achieve, and then a new science to create: a new branch to add to one of the most abstruse of sciences.

38. Yet more: a body of proposed law, how complete soever, would be comparatively useless and uninstructive, unless explained and justified, and that in every tittle, by a continued accompaniment, a perpetual commentary of *reasons*:[1] which reasons, that the comparative value of such as point in opposite directions may be estimated, and the conjunct force, of such as point in the same direction, may be felt, must be marshalled, and put under subordination to such extensive and leading ones as are termed *principles*. There must be therefore, not one system only, but two parallel and connected systems, running on together, the one of legislative provisions, the other of political reasons, each affording to the other correction and support.

39. Are enterprises like these achievable? He knows not. This only he knows, that they have been undertaken, proceeded in, and that some progress has been made in all of them. He will venture to add, if at all achievable, never at least by one, to whom the fatigue of attending to discussions, as arid as those which occupy the ensuing pages, would either appear useless, or feel intolerable. He will repeat it boldly (for it has been said before him), truths that form the basis of political and moral science are not to be discovered but by investigations as severe as mathematical ones, and beyond all comparison more intricate and extensive. The familiarity of the terms is a presumption, but it is a most fallacious one, of the facility of the matter. Truths in general have

---

1 To the aggregate of them a common denomination has since been allotted – *the rationale*. [1823]

been called stubborn things: the truths just mentioned are so in their own way. They are not to be forced into detached and general propositions, unincumbered with explanations and exceptions. They will not compress themselves into epigrams. They recoil from the tongue and the pen of the declaimer. They flourish not in the same soil with sentiment. They grow among thorns; and are not to be plucked, like daisies, by infants as they run. Labour, the inevitable lot of humanity, is in no track more inevitable than here. In vain would an Alexander bespeak a peculiar road for royal vanity, or a Ptolemy, a smoother one, for royal indolence. There is no *King's Road*, no *Stadtholder's Gate*, to legislative, any more than to mathematic science.

CHAPTER I

Of the Principle of Utility

1. Nature has placed mankind under the governance of two sovereign masters, *pain* and *pleasure*. It is for them alone to point out what we ought to do, as well as to determine what we shall do. On the one hand the standard of right and wrong, on the other the chain of causes and effects, are fastened to their throne. They govern us in all we do, in all we say, in all we think: every effort we can make to throw off our subjection, will serve but to demonstrate and confirm it. In words a man may pretend to abjure their empire: but in reality he will remain subject to it all the while. The *principle of utility*[1] recognizes this subjection, and assumes it for the foundation of that system, the object of which is to rear the fabric of felicity by the hands of reason and of law. Systems which attempt to question it, deal in sounds instead of senses, in caprice instead of reason, in darkness instead of light. *Mankind governed by pain and pleasure.*

---

1 Note by the Author, July 1822.

To this denomination has of late been added, or substituted, the *greatest happiness* or *greatest felicity* principle: this for shortness, instead of saying at length *that principle* which states the greatest happiness of all those whose interest is in question, as being the right and proper, and only right and proper and universally desirable, end of human action: of human action in every situation, and in particular in that of a functionary or set of functionaries exercising the powers of Government. The word *utility* does not so clearly point to the ideas of *pleasure* and *pain* as the words *happiness* and *felicity* do: nor does it lead us to the consideration of the *number*, of the interests affected; to the *number*, as being the circumstance, which contributes, in the largest proportion, to the formation of the standard here in question; the *standard of right and wrong*, by which alone the propriety of human conduct, in every situation, can with propriety be tried. This want of a sufficiently manifest connexion between the ideas of *happiness* and *pleasure* on the one hand, and the idea of *utility* on the other, I have every now and then found operating, and with but too much efficiency, as a bar to the acceptance, that might otherwise have been given, to this principle.

But enough of metaphor and declamation: it is not by such means that moral science is to be improved.

Principle of utility, what.

2. The principle of utility is the foundation of the present work: it will be proper therefore at the outset to give an explicit and determinate account of what is meant by it. By the principle[1] of utility is meant that principle which approves or disapproves of every action whatsoever, according to the tendency which it appears to have to augment or diminish the happiness of the party whose interest is in question: or, what is the same thing in other words, to promote or to oppose that happiness. I say of every action whatsoever; and therefore not only of every action of a private individual, but of every measure of government.

Utility what.

3. By utility is meant that property in any object, whereby it tends to produce benefit, advantage, pleasure, good, or happiness, (all this in the present case comes to the same thing) or (what comes again to the same thing) to prevent the happening of mischief, pain, evil, or unhappiness to the party whose interest is considered: if that party be the community in general, then the happiness of the community: if a particular individual, then the happiness of that individual.

Interest of the community, what.

4. The interest of the community is one of the most general expressions that can occur in the phraseology of morals: no wonder that the meaning of it is often lost. When it has a meaning, it is this. The community is a fictitious *body*, composed of the individual persons who are considered as constituting as it were its *members*. The interest of the community then is, what? – the sum of the interests of the several members who compose it.

A principle, what.

1 The word principle is derived from the Latin *principium*: which seems to be compounded of the two words *primus*, first, or chief, and *cipium*, a termination which seems to be derived from *capio*, to take, as in *mancipium*, *municipium*; to which are analogous, *auceps*, *forceps*, and others. It is a term of very vague and very extensive signification: it is applied to any thing which is conceived to serve as a foundation or beginning to any series of operations: in some cases, of physical operations; but of mental operations in the present case.

The principle here in question may be taken for an act of the mind; a sentiment; a sentiment of approbation; a sentiment which, when applied to an action, approves of its utility, as that quality of it by which the measure of approbation or disapprobation bestowed upon it ought to be governed.

5. It is in vain to talk of the interest of the community, without understanding what is the interest of the individual.[1] A thing is said to promote the interest, or to be *for* the interest, of an individual, when it tends to add to the sum total of his pleasures: or, what comes to the same thing, to diminish the sum total of his pains.

6. An action then may be said to be conformable to the principle of utility, or, for shortness sake, to utility, (meaning with respect to the community at large) when the tendency it has to augment the happiness of the community is greater than any it has to diminish it. *An action conformable to the principle of utility, what.*

7. A measure of government (which is but a particular kind of action, performed by a particular person or persons) may be said to be conformable to or dictated by the principle of utility, when in like manner the tendency which it has to augment the happiness of the community is greater than any which it has to diminish it. *A measure of government conformable to the principle of utility, what.*

8. When an action, or in particular a measure of government, is supposed by a man to be conformable to the principle of utility, it may be convenient, for the purposes of discourse, to imagine a kind of law or dictate, called a law or dictate of utility; and to speak of the action in question, as being conformable to such law or dictate. *Laws or dictates of utility, what.*

9. A man may be said to be a partisan of the principle of utility, when the approbation or disapprobation he annexes to any action, or to any measure, is determined by and proportioned to the tendency which he conceives it to have to augment or to diminish the happiness of the community: or in other words, to its conformity or unconformity to the laws or dictates of utility. *A partisan of the principle of utility, who.*

10. Of an action that is conformable to the principle of utility one may always say either that it is one that ought to be done, or at least that it is not one that ought not to be done. One may say also, that it is right it should be done; at least that it is not wrong it should be done: that it is a right action; at least that it is not a wrong action. When thus interpreted, the words *ought*, and *right* *Ought, ought not, right and wrong, etc. how to be understood.*

1 Interest is one of those words, which not having any superior *genus*, cannot in the ordinary way be defined.

and *wrong*, and others of that stamp, have a meaning: when otherwise, they have none.

To prove the rectitude of this principle is at once unnecessary and impossible.

11. Has the rectitude of this principle been ever formally contested? It should seem that it had, by those who have not known what they have been meaning. Is it susceptible of any direct proof? It should seem not: for that which is used to prove everything else, cannot itself be proved: a chain of proofs must have their commencement somewhere. To give such proof is as impossible as it is needless.

It has seldom, however, as yet been consistently pursued.

12. Not that there is or ever has been that human creature breathing, however stupid or perverse, who has not on many, perhaps on most occasions of his life, deferred to it. By the natural constitution of the human frame, on most occasions of their lives men in general embrace this principle, without thinking of it: if not for the ordering of their own actions, yet for the trying of their own actions, as well as of those of other men. There have been, at the same time, not many, perhaps, even of the most intelligent, who have been disposed to embrace it purely and without reserve There are even few who have not taken some occasion or other to quarrel with it, either on account of their not understanding always how to apply it, or on account of some prejudice or other which they were afraid to examine into, or could not bear to part with. For such is the stuff that man is made of: in principle and in practice, in a right track and in a wrong one, the rarest of all human qualities is consistency.

It can never be consistently combated.

13. When a man attempts to combat the principle of utility, it is with reasons drawn, without his being aware of it, from that very principle itself.[1] His arguments, if they prove anything, prove not

---

1 'The principle of utility, (I have heard it said) is a dangerous principle: it is dangerous on certain occasions to consult it.' This is as much as to say, what? that it is not consonant to utility, to consult utility: in short, that it is *not* consulting it, to consult it.

Addition by the Author, July 1822.

Not long after the publication of the *Fragment on Government*, anno 1776, in which, in the character of an all-comprehensive and all-commanding principle, the principle of *utility* was brought to view, one person by whom observation to the above effect was made was *Alexander Wedderburn*, at that time Attorney or

that the principle is *wrong*, but that, according to the applications he supposes to be made of it, it is *misapplied*. Is it possible for a man to move the earth? Yes; but he must first find out another earth to stand upon.

14. To disprove the propriety of it by arguments is impossible; but, from the causes that have been mentioned, or from some confused or partial view of it, a man may happen to be disposed not to relish it. Where this is the case, if he thinks the settling of his opinions on such a subject worth the trouble, let him take the following steps and at length, perhaps, he may come to reconcile himself to it.

Course to be taken for surmounting prejudices that may have been entertained against it.

Solicitor General, afterwards successively Chief Justice of the Common Pleas, and Chancellor of England, under the successive titles of Lord Loughborough and Earl of Rosslyn. It was made – not indeed in my hearing, but in the hearing of a person by whom it was almost immediately communicated to me. So far from being self-contradictory, it was a shrewd and perfectly true one. By that distinguished functionary, the state of the Government was thoroughly understood: by the obscure individual, at that time not so much as supposed to be so: his disquisitions had not been as yet applied, with anything like a comprehensive view, to the field of Constitutional Law, nor therefore to those features of the English Government, by which the greatest happiness of the ruling *one* with or without that of a favoured few, are now so plainly seen to be the only ends to which the course of it has at any time been directed. The *principle of utility* was an appellative, at that time employed – employed by me, as it had been by others, to designate that which in a more perspicuous and instructive manner, may, as above, be designated by the name of the *greatest happiness principle*. 'This principle (said Wedderburn) is a dangerous one.' Saying so, he said that which, to a certain extent, is strictly true: a principle, which lays down, as the only *right* and justifiable end of Government, the greatest happiness of the greatest number – how can it be denied to be a dangerous one? Dangerous it unquestionably is, to every government which has for its *actual* end or object, the greatest happiness of a certain *one*, with or without the addition of some comparatively small number of others, whom it is a matter of pleasure or accommodation to him to admit, each of them, to a share in the concern, on the footing of so many junior partners. *Dangerous* it therefore really was, to the interest – the sinister interest – of all those functionaries, himself included, whose interest it was, to maximize delay, vexation, and expense, in judicial and other modes of procedure, for the sake of the profit, extractible out of the expense. In a Government which had for its end in view the greatest happiness of the greatest number, Alexander Wedderburn might have been Attorney General and then Chancellor: but he would not have been Attorney General with £15,000 a year, nor Chancellor, with a peerage with a veto upon all justice, with £25,000 a year, and with 500 sinecures at his disposal, under the name of Ecclesiastical Benefices, besides *et caeteras*.

1. Let him settle with himself, whether he would wish to discard this principle altogether; if so, let him consider what it is that all his reasonings (in matters of politics especially) can amount to?

2. If he would, let him settle with himself, whether he would judge and act without any principle, or whether there is any other he would judge and act by?

3. If there be, let him examine and satisfy himself whether the principle he thinks he has found is really any separate intelligible principle; or whether it be not a mere principle in words, a kind of phrase, which at bottom expresses neither more nor less than the mere averment of his own unfounded sentiments; that is, what in another person he might be apt to call caprice?

4. If he is inclined to think that his own approbation or disapprobation, annexed to the idea of an act, without any regard to its consequences, is a sufficient foundation for him to judge and act upon, let him ask himself whether his sentiment is to be a standard of right and wrong, with respect to every other man, or whether every man's sentiment has the same privilege of being a standard to itself?

5. In the first case, let him ask himself whether his principle is not despotical, and hostile to all the rest of human race?

6. In the second case, whether it is not anarchical, and whether at this rate there are not as many different standards of right and wrong as there are men? and whether even to the sane man, the same thing, which is right to-day, may not (without the least change in its nature) be wrong to-morrow? and whether the same thing is not right and wrong in the same place at the same time? and in either case, whether all argument is not at an end? and whether, when two men have said, 'I like this,' and 'I don't like it,' they can (upon such a principle) have anything more to say?

7. If he should have said to himself, No: for that the sentiment which he proposes as a standard must be grounded on reflection, let him say on what particulars the reflection is to turn? If on particulars having relation to the utility of the act, then let him say whether this is not deserting his own

principle, and borrowing assistance from that very one in opposition to which he sets it up: or if not on those particulars, on what other particulars?

8. If he should be for compounding the matter, and adopting his own principle in part, and the principle of utility in part, let him say how far he will adopt it?

9. When he has settled with himself where he will stop, then let him ask himself how he justifies to himself the adopting it so far? and why he will not adopt it any farther?

10. Admitting any other principle than the principle of utility to be a right principle, a principle that it is right for a man to pursue; admitting (what is not true) that the word *right* can have a meaning without reference to utility, let him say whether there is any such thing as a *motive* that a man can have to pursue the dictates of it: if there is, let him say what that motive is, and how it is to be distinguished from those which enforce the dictates of utility: if not, then lastly let him say what it is this other principle can be good for?

CHAPTER II

Of Principles Adverse to that of Utility

All other principles than that of utility must be wrong. 1. If the principle of utility be a right principle to be governed by, and that in all cases, it follows from what has been just observed, that whatever principle differs from it in any case must necessarily be a wrong one. To prove any other principle, therefore, to be a wrong one, there needs no more than just to show it to be what it is, a principle of which the dictates are in some point or other different from those of the principle of utility: to state it is to confute it.

Ways in which a principle may be wrong. 2. A principle may be different from that of utility in two ways: 1. By being constantly opposed to it: this is the case with a principle which may be termed the principle of *asceticism*.[1] 2. By being sometimes opposed to it, and sometimes not, as it may happen: this is the case with another, which may be termed the principle of *sympathy* and *antipathy*.

Asceticism, origin of the word. Principles of the monks. 1 Ascetic is a term that has been sometimes applied to Monks. It comes from a Greek word which signifies *exercise*. The practices by which Monks sought to distinguish themselves from other men were called their Exercises. These exercises consisted in so many contrivances they had for tormenting themselves. By this they thought to ingratiate themselves with the Deity. For the Deity, said they, is a Being of infinite benevolence: now a Being of the most ordinary benevolence is pleased to see others make themselves as happy as they can: therefore to make ourselves as unhappy as we can is the way to please the Deity. If any body asked them, what motive they could find for doing all this? Oh! said they, you are not to imagine that we are punishing ourselves for nothing: we know very well what we are about. You are to know, that for every grain of pain it costs us now, we are to have a hundred grains of pleasure by and by. The case is, that God loves to see us torment ourselves at present: indeed he has as good as told us so. But this is done only to try us, in order just to see how we should behave: which it is plain he could not know, without making the experiment. Now then, from the satisfaction it gives him to see us make ourselves as unhappy as we can make ourselves in this present life, we have a sure proof of the satisfaction it will give him to see us as happy as he can make us in a life to come.

3. By the principle of asceticism I mean that principle, which, like the principle of utility, approves or disapproves of any action, according to the tendency which it appears to have to augment or diminish the happiness of the party whose interest is in question; but in an inverse manner: approving of actions in as far as they tend to diminish his happiness; disapproving of them in as far as they tend to augment it.

Principle of asceticism, what.

4. It is evident that any one who reprobates any the least particle of pleasure, as such, from whatever source derived, is *pro tanto* a partisan of the principle of asceticism. It is only upon that principle, and not from the principle of utility, that the most abominable pleasure which the vilest of malefactors ever reaped from his crime would be reprobated, if it stood alone. The case is, that it never does stand alone; but is necessarily followed by such a quantity of pain (or, what comes to the same thing, such a chance for a certain quantity of pain) that the pleasure in comparison of it, is as nothing: and this is the true and sole, but perfectly sufficient, reason for making it a ground for punishment.

A partisan of the principle of asceticism, who.

5. There are two classes of men of very different complexions, by whom the principle of asceticism appears to have been embraced; the one a set of moralists, the other a set of religionists. Different accordingly have been the motives which appear to have recommended it to the notice of these different parties. Hope, that is the prospect of pleasure, seems to have animated the former: hope, the aliment of philosophic pride: the hope of honour and reputation at the hands of men. Fear, that is the prospect of pain, the latter: fear the offspring of superstitious fancy: the fear of future punishment at the hands of a splenetic and revengeful Deity. I say in this case fear: for of the invisible future, fear is more powerful than hope. These circumstances characterize the two different parties among the partisans of the principle of asceticism; the parties and their motives different, the principle the same.

This principle has had in some a philosophical, in others a religious origin.

6. The religious party, however, appear to have carried it farther than the philosophical: they have acted more consistently and less wisely. The philosophical party have scarcely gone farther than to reprobate pleasure: the religious party have frequently gone so far

It has been carried farther by the religious party than by the philosophical.

as to make it a matter of merit and of duty to court pain. The philosophical party have hardly gone farther than the making pain a matter of indifference. It is no evil, they have said: they have not said, it is a good. They have not so much as reprobated all pleasure in the lump. They have discarded only what they have called the gross; that is, such as are organical, or of which the origin is easily traced up to such as are organical: they have even cherished and magnified the refined. Yet this, however, not under the name of pleasure: to cleanse itself from the sordes of its impure original, it was necessary it should change its name: the honourable, the glorious, the reputable, the becoming, the *honestum*, the *decorum*, it was to be called: in short, anything but pleasure.

The philo-sophical branch of it has had most influence among persons of education, the religious among the vulgar. 7. From these two sources have flowed the doctrines from which the sentiments of the bulk of mankind have all along received a tincture of this principle; some from the philosophical, some from the religious, some from both. Men of education more frequently from the philosophical, as more suited to the elevation of their sentiments: the vulgar more frequently from the superstitious, as more suited to the narrowness of their intellect, undilated by knowledge: and to the abjectness of their condition, continually open to the attacks of fear. The tinctures, however, derived from the two sources, would naturally intermingle, insomuch that a man would not always know by which of them he was most influenced: and they would often serve to corroborate and enliven one another. It was this conformity that made a kind of alliance between parties of a complexion otherwise so dissimilar: and disposed them to unite upon various occasions against the common enemy, the partisan of the principle of utility, whom they joined in branding with the odious name of Epicurean.

The principle of asceticism has never been steadily applied by either party to the Business of Government. 8. The principle of asceticism, however, with whatever warmth it may have been embraced by its partisans as a rule of private conduct, seems not to have been carried to any considerable length, when applied to the business of government. In a few instances it has been carried a little way by the philosophical party: witness the Spartan regimen. Though then, perhaps, it may be considered as having been a measure of security: and an application, though a precipitate and perverse application, of the principle of utility. Scarcely in any instances, to any considerable length, by the religious: for the various monastic orders, and the societies of the Quakers, Dumplers, Moravians, and other religionists, have been free societies, whose regimen no man has been astricted to without the intervention of his own consent. Whatever merit a man may have thought there would be in making himself miserable, no such notion seems ever to have occurred to any of them, that it may be a merit, much less a duty, to make others miserable: although it should seem, that if a certain quantity of misery were a thing so desirable, it would not matter much whether it were brought by each man upon himself, or by one man upon another. It is true, that from the same source from whence, among the religionists, the attachment to the principle of asceticism took its rise, flowed other doctrines and practices, from which misery in abundance was produced in one man by the instrumentality of another: witness the holy wars, and the persecutions for religion. But the passion for producing misery in these cases proceeded upon some special ground: the exercise of it was confined to persons of particular descriptions: they were tormented, not as men, but as heretics and infidels. To have inflicted the same miseries on their fellow-believers and fellow-sectaries, would have been as blameable in the eyes even of these religionists, as in those of a partisan of the principle of utility. For a man to give himself a certain number of stripes was indeed meritorious: but to give the same number of stripes to another man, not consenting, would have been a sin. We read of saints, who for the good of their souls, and the mortification of their bodies, have voluntarily yielded themselves a prey to vermin: but though many persons of this class have wielded the reins of empire, we read of none who have set themselves to work, and made laws on purpose, with a view of stocking the body politic with the breed of highwaymen, housebreakers, or incendiaries. If at any time they have suffered the nation to be preyed upon by swarms of idle pensioners, or useless placemen, it has rather been from negligence and imbecility, than from any settled plan for oppressing and plundering of the people. If at any time they have sapped the sources of national wealth, by cramping commerce, and driving the inhabitants into emigration, it has been with other views, and in pursuit of other ends. If they have declaimed against the pursuit of pleasure, and the use of wealth, they have commonly stopped at declamation: they have not, like Lycurgus, made express ordinances for the purpose of banishing the precious metals. If they have established idleness by a law, it has been not because idleness, the mother of vice and misery, is itself a virtue, but because idleness (say they) is the road to holiness. If under the notion of fasting, they have joined in the plan of confining their subjects to a diet, thought by some to be of the most nourishing and prolific nature, it has been not for the sake of making them tributaries to the nations by whom that diet was to be supplied, but for the sake of manifesting their own power, and exercising the obedience of the people. If they have established, or suffered to be established, punishments for the breach of celibacy, they have done no more than comply with the petitions of those deluded rigorists, who, dupes to the ambitious and deep-laid policy of their rulers, first laid themselves under that idle obligation by a vow.

The principle of asceticism, in its origin, was but that of utility misapplied. 9. The principle of asceticism seems originally to have been the reverie of certain hasty speculators, who having perceived, or fancied, that certain pleasures, when reaped in certain circumstances, have, at the long run, been attended with pains more than equivalent to them, took occasion to quarrel with every thing that offered itself under the name of pleasure. Having then got thus far, and having forgot the point which they set out from, they pushed on, and went so much further as to think it meritorious to fall in love with pain. Even this, we see, is at bottom but the principle of utility misapplied.

It can never be consistently pursued. 10. The principle of utility is capable of being consistently pursued; and it is but tautology to say, that the more consistently it is pursued, the better it must ever be for humankind. The principle of asceticism never was, nor ever can be, consistently pursued by any living creature. Let but one tenth part of the inhabitants of this earth pursue it consistently, and in a day's time they will have turned it into a hell.

11. Among principles adverse[1] to that of utility, that which at this day seems to have most influence in matters of government, is what may be called the principle of sympathy and antipathy. By the principle of sympathy and antipathy, I mean that principle which approves or disapproves of certain actions, not on account of their tending to augment the happiness, nor yet on account of

The principle of sympathy and antipathy, what.

---

1 The following Note was first printed in January 1789.

It ought rather to have been styled, more extensively, the principle of *caprice*. Where it applies to the choice of actions to be marked out for injunction or prohibition, for reward or punishment, (to stand, in a word, as subjects for *obligations* to be imposed,) it may indeed with propriety be termed, as in the text, the principle of *sympathy* and *antipathy*. But this appellative does not so well apply to it, when occupied in the choice of the *events* which are to serve as sources of *title* with respect to *rights*: where the actions prohibited and allowed, the obligations and rights, being already fixed, the only question is, under what circumstances a man is to be invested with the one or subjected to the other? from what incidents occasion is to be taken to invest a man, or to refuse to invest him, with the one, or to subject him to the other? In the latter case it may more appositely be characterized by the name of the *phantastic principle*. Sympathy and antipathy are affections of the *sensible* faculty. But the choice of *titles* with respect to *rights*, especially with respect to proprietary rights, upon grounds unconnected with utility, has been in many instances the work, not of the affections but of the imagination.

When, in justification of an article of English Common Law, calling uncles to succeed in certain cases in preference to fathers, Lord Coke produced a sort of ponderosity he had discovered in rights, disqualifying them from ascending in a straight line, it was not that he *loved* uncles particularly, or *hated* fathers, but because the analogy, such as it was, was what his imagination presented him with, instead of a reason, and because, to a judgment unobservant of the standard of utility, or unacquainted with the art of consulting it, where affection is out of the way, imagination is the only guide.

When I know not what ingenious grammarian invented the proposition *Delegatus non potest delegare*, to serve as a rule of law, it was not surely that he had any antipathy to delegates of the second order, or that it was any pleasure to him to think of the ruin which, for want of a manager at home, may befal the affairs of a traveller, whom an unforeseen accident has deprived of the object of his choice: it was, that the incongruity, of giving the same law to objects so contrasted as *active* and *passive* are, was not to be surmounted, and that *-atus* chimes, as well as it contrasts, with *-are*.

When that inexorable maxim, (of which the dominion is no more to be defined, than the date of its birth, or the name of its father, is to be found,) was imported from England for the government of Bengal, and the whole fabric of judicature was crushed by the thunders of *ex post facto* justice, it was not surely that the prospect of a blameless magistracy perishing in prison afforded any enjoyment to the unoffended authors of their misery; but that the music of the maxim, absorbing the whole imagination, had drowned the cries of humanity

their tending to diminish the happiness of the party whose interest is in question, but merely because a man finds himself disposed to approve or disapprove of them: holding up that approbation or disapprobation as a sufficient reason for itself, and disclaiming the necessity of looking out for any extrinsic ground. Thus far in the

---

along with the dictates of common sense.[a] *Fiat Justitia, ruat caelum*, says another maxim, as full of extravagance as it is of harmony: Go heaven to wreck – so justice be but done: – and what is the ruin of kingdoms, in comparison of the wreck of heaven?

So again, when the Prussian chancellor, inspired with the wisdom of I know not what Roman sage, proclaimed in good Latin, for the edification of German ears, *Servitus servitutis non datum*, [Cod. Fred. tom. ii. par. 2. liv. 2. tit. x. § 6. p. 308] it was not that he had conceived any aversion to the life-holder who, during the continuance of his term, should wish to gratify a neighbour with a right of way or water, or to the neighbour who should wish to accept of the indulgence; but that, to a jurisprudential ear, *-tus -tutis* sound little less melodious than *-atus -are*. Whether the melody of the maxim was the real reason of the rule, is not left open to dispute: for it is ushered in by the conjunction *quia*, reason's appointed harbinger: *quia servitus servitutis non datur*.

---

[a]   Additional Note by the Author, July 1822.

Add, and that the bad system, of Mahometan and other native law was to be put down at all events, to make way for the inapplicable and still more mischievous system of English Judge-made law, and, by the hand of his accomplice Hastings, was to be put into the pocket of Impey – Importer of this instrument of subversion, £8,000 a-year contrary to law, in addition to the £8,000 a-year lavished upon him, with the customary profusion, by the hand of law. – See the Account of this transaction in *Mill's British India*.

To this Governor a statue is erecting by a vote of East India Directors and Proprietors: on it should be inscribed – *Let it but put money into our pockets, no tyranny too flagitious to be worshipped by us.*

To this statue of the Arch-malefactor should be added, for a companion, that of the long-robed accomplice: the one lodging the bribe in the hand of the other. The hundred millions of plundered and oppressed Hindoos and Mahometans pay for the one; a Westminster Hall subscription might pay for the other.

What they have done for Ireland with her seven millions of souls, the authorised dealers and perverters of justice have done for Hindostan with her hundred millions. In this there is nothing wonderful. The wonder is – that, under such institutions, men, though in ever such small number, should be found, whom the view of the injustices which, by *English Judge-made law*, they are compelled to commit, and the miseries they are thus compelled to produce, deprive of health and rest. Witness the Letter of an English Hindostan Judge, Sept. 1, 1819, which lies before me. I will not make so cruel a requital for his honesty, as to put his name in print: indeed the House of Commons' Documents already published leave little need of it.

general department of morals: and in the particular department of politics, measuring out the quantum (as well as determining the ground) of punishment, by the degree of the disapprobation.

12. It is manifest, that this is rather a principle in name than in reality: it is not a positive principle of itself, so much as a term employed to signify the negation of all principle. What one

This is rather the negation of all principle, than anything positive.

Neither would equal melody have been produced, nor indeed could similar melody have been called for, in either of these instances, by the opposite provision: it is only when they are opposed to general rules, and not when by their conformity they are absorbed in them, that more specific ones can obtain a separate existence. *Delegatus potest delegare*, and *Servitus servitutis datur*, provisions already included under the general adoption of contracts, would have been as unnecessary to the apprehension and the memory, as, in comparison of their energetic negatives, they are insipid to the ear.

Were the inquiry diligently made, it would be found that the goddess of harmony has exercised more influence, however latent, over the dispensations of Themis, than her most diligent historiographers, or even her most passionate panegyrists, seem to have been aware of. Everyone knows, how, by the ministry of Orpheus, it was she who first collected the sons of men beneath the shadow of the sceptre: yet, in the midst of continual experience, men seem yet to learn, with what successful diligence she has laboured to guide it in its course. Everyone knows, that measured numbers were the language of the infancy of law: none seem to have observed, with what imperious sway they have governed her maturer age. In English jurisprudence in particular, the connexion betwixt law and music, however less perceived than in Spartan legislation, is not perhaps real nor less close. The music of the Office, though not of the same kind, is not less musical in its kind, than the music of the Theatre; that which hardens the heart, than that which softens it: – sostenutos as long, cadences as sonorous; and those governed by rules, though not yet promulgated, not less determinate. Search indictments, pleadings, proceedings in chancery, conveyances: whatever trespasses you may find against truth or common sense, you will find none against the laws of harmony. The English Liturgy, just as this quality has been extolled in that sacred office, possesses not a greater measure of it, than is commonly to be found in an English Act of Parliament. Dignity, simplicity, brevity, precision, intelligibility, possibility of being retained or so much as apprehended, every thing yields to Harmony. Volumes might be filled, shelves loaded, with the sacrifices that are made to this insatiate power. Expletives, her ministers in Grecian poetry are not less busy, though in different shape and bulk, in English legislation: in the former, they are monosyllables:[a] in the latter, they are whole lines.[b]

---

[a] Μεν, τοι, γε, νυν, etc.

[b] And be it further enacted by the authority aforesaid, that – Provided always, and it is hereby further enacted and declared that – etc. etc.

expects to find in a principle is something that points out some external consideration, as a means of warranting and guiding the internal sentiments of approbation and disapprobation: this expectation is but ill fulfilled by a proposition, which does neither more nor less than hold up each of those sentiments as a ground and standard for itself.

Sentiments of a partisan of the principle of antipathy. 13. In looking over the catalogue of human actions (says a partisan of this principle) in order to determine which of them are to be marked with the seal of disapprobation, you need but to take counsel of your own feelings: whatever you find in yourself a propensity to condemn, is wrong for that very reason. For the same reason it is also meet for punishment: in what proportion it is adverse to utility, or whether it be adverse to utility at all, is a

---

To return to the *principle of sympathy and antipathy*: a term preferred at first, on account of its impartiality, to the *principle of caprice*. The choice of an appellative, in the above respects too narrow, was owing to my not having, at that time, extended my views over the civil branch of law, any otherwise than as I had found it inseparably involved in the penal. But when we come to the former branch, we shall see the *phantastic* principle making at least as great a figure there, as the principle of *sympathy and antipathy* in the latter.

In the days of Lord Coke, the light of utility can scarcely be said to have as yet shone upon the face of Common Law. If a faint ray of it, under the name of the *argumentum ab inconvenienti*, is to be found in a list of about twenty topics exhibited by that great lawyer as the co-ordinate leaders of that all-perfect system, the admission, so circumstanced, is as sure a proof of neglect, as, to the status of Brutus and Cassius, exclusion was a cause of notice. It stands, neither in the front, nor in the rear, nor in any post of honour; but huddled in towards the middle, without the smallest mark of preference. [Coke, Littleton, 11. a.] Nor is this Latin *inconvenience* by any means the same thing with the English one. It stands distinguished from *mischief*: and because by the vulgar it is taken for something less bad, it is given by the learned as something worse. *The law prefers a mischief to an inconvenience*, says an admired maxim, and the more admired because as nothing is expressed by it, the more is supposed to be understood.

Not that there is any avowed, much less a constant opposition, between the prescriptions of utility and the operations of the common law: such constancy we have seen to be too much even for ascetic fervor. [Supra, par. x.] From time to time instinct would unavoidably betray them into the paths of reason: instinct which, however it may be cramped, can never be killed by education. The cobwebs spun out of the materials brought together by 'the competition of opposite analogies,' can never have ceased being warped by the silent attraction of the rational principle: though it should have been, as the needle is by the magnet, without the privity of conscience.

matter that makes no difference. In that same *proportion* also is it meet for punishment: if you hate much, punish much: if you hate little, punish little: punish as you hate. If you hate not at all, punish not at all: the fine feelings of the soul are not to be overborne and tyrannized by the harsh and rugged dictates of political utility.

14. The various systems that have been formed concerning the standard of right and wrong, may all be reduced to the principle of sympathy and antipathy. One account may serve for all of them. They consist all of them in so many contrivances for avoiding the obligation of appealing to any external standard, and for prevailing upon the reader to accept of the author's sentiment or opinion as a reason for itself. The phrases different, but the principle the same.[1]

The systems that have been formed concerning the standard of right and wrong, are all reducible to this principle.

1 It is curious enough to observe the variety of inventions men have hit upon, and the variety of phrases they have brought forward, in order to conceal from the world, and, if possible, from themselves, this very general and therefore very pardonable self-sufficiency.

Various phrases that have served as the characteristic marks of so many pretended systems.

   1. One man says, he has a thing made on purpose to tell him what is right and what is wrong; and that it is called a *moral sense*: and then he goes to work at his ease, and says, such a thing is right, and such a thing is wrong – why? 'because my moral sense tells me it is.'

1. Moral Sense.

   2. Another man comes and alters the phrase: leaving out *moral*, and putting in *common*, in the room of it. He then tells you, that his common sense teaches him what is right and wrong, as surely as the other's moral sense did: meaning by common sense, a sense of some kind or other, which, he says, is possessed by all mankind: the sense of those, whose sense is not the same as the author's, being struck out of the account as not worth taking. This contrivance does better than the other; for a moral sense, being a new thing, a man may feel about him a good while without being able to find it out: but common sense is as old as the creation; and there is no man but would be ashamed to be thought not to have as much of it as his neighbours. It has another great advantage: by appearing to share power, it lessens envy: for when a man gets up upon this ground, in order to anathematize those who differ from him, it is not by a *sic volo sic jubeo*, but by a *velitis jubeatis*.

2. Common Sense.

   3. Another man comes, and says, that as to a moral sense indeed, he cannot find that he has any such thing: that however he has an *understanding*, which will do quite as well. This understanding, he says, is the standard of right and wrong: it tells him so and so. All good and wise men understand as he does: if other men's understandings differ in any point from his, so much the worse for them: it is a sure sign they are either defective or corrupt.

3. Understanding.

   4. Another man says, that there is an eternal and immutable Rule of Right: that the rule of right dictates so and so: and then he begins giving you his sentiments upon any thing that comes uppermost: and these sentiments (you are to take for granted) are so many branches of the eternal rule of right.

4. Rule of Right.

This principle will frequently coincide with that of utility.

15. It is manifest, that the dictates of this principle will frequently coincide with those of utility, though perhaps without intending any such thing. Probably more frequently than not: and hence it is that the business of penal justice is carried on upon that tolerable sort of footing upon which we see it carried on in common at this day. For what more natural or more general ground of hatred to a practice can there be, than the mischievousness of such practice? What all men are exposed to suffer by, all men will be disposed to

---

5. Fitness of Things.

5. Another man, or perhaps the same man (it's no matter) says, that there are certain practices conformable, and others repugnant, to the Fitness of Things; and then he tells you, at his leisure, what practices are conformable and what repugnant: just as he happens to like a practice or dislike it.

6. Law of Nature.

6. A great multitude of people are continually talking of the Law of Nature; and then they go on giving you their sentiments about what is right and what is wrong: and these sentiments, you are to understand, are so many chapters and sections of the Law of Nature.

7. Law of Reason, Right Reason, Natural Justice, Natural Equity, Good Order.

7. Instead of the phrase, Law of Nature, you have sometimes, Law of Reason, Right Reason, Natural Justice, Natural Equity, Good Order. Any of them will do equally well. This latter is most used in politics. The three last are much more tolerable than the others, because they do not very explicitly claim to be anything more than phrases: they insist but feebly upon the being looked upon as so many positive standards of themselves, and seem content to be taken, upon occasion, for phrases expressive of the conformity of the thing in question to the proper standard, whatever that may be. On most occasions, however, it will be better to say *utility*: utility is clearer, as referring more explicitly to pain and pleasure.

8. Truth.

8. We have one philosopher, who says, there is no harm in anything in the world but in telling a lie: and that if, for example, you were to murder your own father, this would only be a particular way of saying, he was not your father. Of course, when this philosopher sees anything that he does not like, he says, it is a particular way of telling a lie. It is saying, that the act ought to be done, or may be done, when, *in truth*, it ought not to be done.

9. Doctrine of Election.

9. The fairest and openest of them all is that sort of man who speaks out, and says, I am of the number of the Elect: now God himself takes care to inform the Elect what is right: and that with so good effect, and let them strive ever so, they cannot help not only knowing it but practising it. If therefore a man wants to know what is right and what is wrong, he has nothing to do but to come to me.

Repugnancy to Nature.

It is upon the principle of antipathy that such and such acts are often reprobated on the score of their being *unnatural*: the practice of exposing children, established among the Greeks and Romans, was an unnatural practice. Unnatural, when it means anything, means unfrequent: and there it means something; although nothing to the present purpose. But here it means no such thing: for the frequency of such acts is perhaps the great complaint. It therefore

hate. It is far yet, however, from being a constant ground: for when a man suffers, it is not always that he knows what it is he suffers by. A man may suffer grievously, for instance, by a new tax, without being able to trace up the cause of his sufferings to the injustice of some neighbour, who has eluded the payment of an old one.

16. The principle of sympathy and antipathy is most apt to err on the side of severity. It is for applying punishment in many cases which deserve none: in many cases which deserve some, it is for

This principle is most apt to err on the side of severity.

---

means nothing; nothing, I mean which there is in the act itself. All it can serve to express is, the disposition of the person who is talking of it: the disposition he is in to be angry at the thoughts of it. Does it merit his anger? Very likely it may: but whether it does or no is a question, which, to be answered rightly, can only be answered upon the principle of utility.

Unnatural, is as good a word as moral sense, or common sense; and would be as good a foundation for a system. Such an act is unnatural; that is, repugnant to nature: for I do not like to practise it: and, consequently, do not practise it. It is therefore repugnant to what ought to be the nature of everybody else.

The mischief common to all these ways of thinking and arguing (which, in truth, as we have seen, are but one and the same method, couched in different forms of words) is their serving as a cloke, and pretence, and aliment, to despotism: if not a despotism in practice, a despotism however in disposition: which is but too apt, when pretence and power offer, to show itself in practice. The consequence is, that with intentions very commonly of the purest kind, a man becomes a torment either to himself or his fellow-creatures. If he be of the melancholy cast, he sits in silent grief, bewailing their blindness and depravity: if of the irascible, he declaims with fury and virulence against all who differ from him; blowing up the coals of fanaticism, and branding with the charge of corruption and insincerity, every man who does not think, or profess to think, as he does.

Mischief they produce.

If such a man happens to possess the advantages of style, his book may do a considerable deal of mischief before the nothingness of it is understood.

These principles, if such they can be called, it is more frequent to see applied to morals than to politics: but their influence extends itself to both. In politics, as well as morals, a man will be at least equally glad of a pretence for deciding any question in the manner that best pleases him, without the trouble of inquiry. If a man is an infallible judge of what is right and wrong in the actions of private individuals, why not in the measures to be observed by public men in the direction of those actions? Accordingly (not to mention other chimeras) I have more than once known the pretended law of nature set up in legislative debates, in opposition to arguments derived from the principle of utility.

'But is it never, then, from any other considerations than those of utility, that we derive our notions of right and wrong?' I do not know: I do not care.

applying more than they deserve. There is no incident imaginable, be it ever so trivial, and so remote from mischief, from which this principle may not extract a ground of punishment. Any difference in taste: any difference in opinion: upon one subject as well as upon another. No disagreement so trifling which perseverance and altercation will not render serious. Each becomes in the

---

Whether utility is actually the sole ground of all the approbation we ever bestow, is a different consideration. Whether a moral sentiment can be originally conceived from any other source than a view of utility, is one question: whether upon examination and reflection it can, in point of fact, be actually persisted in and justified on any other ground, by a person reflecting within himself, is another: whether in point of right it can properly be justified on any other ground, by a person addressing himself to the community, is a third. The two first are questions of speculation: it matters not, comparatively speaking, how they are decided. The last is a question of practice: the decision of it is of as much importance as that of any can be.

'I feel in myself,' (say you) 'a disposition to approve of such or such an action in a moral view: but this is not owing to any notions I have of its being a useful one to the community. I do not pretend to know whether it be an useful one or not: it may be, for aught I know, a mischievous one.' 'But is it then,' (say I) 'a mischievous one? examine; and if you can make yourself sensible that it is so, then, if duty means anything, that is, moral duty, it is your *duty* at least to abstain from it: and more than that, if it is what lies in your power, and can be done without too great a sacrifice, to endeavour to prevent it. It is not your cherishing the notion of it in your bosom, and giving it the name of virtue, that will excuse you.'

'I feel in myself,' (say you again) 'a disposition to detest such or such an action in a moral view; but this is not owing to any notions I have of its being a mischievous one to the community. I do not pretend to know whether it be a mischievous one or not: it may be not a mischievous one: it may be, for aught I know, an useful one.' – 'May it indeed,' (say I) 'an useful one? but let me tell you then, that unless duty, and right and wrong, be just what you please to make them, if it really be not a mischievous one, and any body has a mind to do it, it is no duty of yours, but, on the contrary, it would be very wrong in you, to take upon you to prevent him: detest it within yourself as much as you please; that it may be a very good reason (unless it be also a useful one) for your not doing it yourself: but if you go about, by word or deed, to do anything to hinder him, or make him suffer for it, it is you, and not he, that have done wrong: it is not your setting yourself to blame his conduct, or branding it with the name of vice, that will make him culpable, or you blameless. Therefore, if you can make yourself content that he shall be of one mind, and you of another, about this matter, and so continue, it is well: but if nothing will serve you, but that you and he must needs be of the same mind, I'll tell you what you have to do: it is for you to get the better of your antipathy, not for him to truckle to it.'

other's eyes an enemy, and, if laws permit, a criminal.[1] This is one of the circumstances, by which the human race is distinguished (not much indeed to its advantage) from the brute creation.

17. It is not, however, by any means unexampled for this principle to err on the side of lenity. A near and perceptible mischief moves antipathy. A remote and imperceptible mischief, though not less real, has no effect. Instances in proof of this will occur in numbers in the course of the work.[2] It would be breaking in upon the order of it to give them here.

But errs, in some instances, on the side of lenity.

18. it may be wondered, perhaps, that in all this while no mention has been made of the *theological* principle; meaning that principle which professes to recur for the standard of right and wrong to the will of God. But the case is, this is not in fact a distinct principle.

The theological principle, what — not a separate principle.

1 King James the First of England had conceived a violent antipathy against Asians: two of whom be burnt.[a] This gratification he procured himself without much difficulty: the notions of the times were favourable to it. He wrote a furious book against Vorstius, for being what was called an Arminian: for Vorstius was at a distance. He also wrote a furious book, called 'A Counterblast to Tobacco', against the use of that drug, which Sir Walter Raleigh had then lately introduced. Had the notions of the times co-operated with him, he would have burnt the Anabaptist and the smoke of tobacco in the same fire. However, he had the satisfaction of putting Raleigh to death afterwards, though for another crime.

Disputes concerning the comparative excellence of French and Italian music have occasioned very serious bickerings at Paris. One of the parties would not have been sorry (says Mr D'Alembert[b]) to have brought government into the quarrel. Pretences were sought after and urged. Long before that, a dispute of like nature, and of at least equal warmth, had been kindled at London upon the comparative merits of two composers at London; where riots between the approvers and disapprovers of a new play are, at this day, not unfrequent. The ground of quarrel between the Bigendians and the Little-endians in the fable, was not more frivolous than many an one which has laid empires desolate. In Russia, it is said, there was a time when some thousands of persons lost their lives in a quarrel, in which the government had taken part, about the number of fingers to be used in making the sign of the cross. This was in days of yore: the ministers of Catherine II are better *instructed*[c] than to take any other part in such disputes, than that of preventing the parties concerned from doing one another a mischief.

2 See ch. xvi [Division], par. 42, 44.

___

a Hume's Hist. vol. 6.

b Melanges Essai sur la Liberté de la Musique.

c Instruct, art. 474, 475, 476.

It is never anything more or less than one or other of the three before-mentioned principles presenting itself under another shape. The *will* of God here meant cannot be his revealed will, as contained in the sacred writings: for that is a system which nobody ever thinks of recurring to at this time of day, for the details of political administration: and even before it can be applied to the details of private conduct, it is universally allowed, by the most eminent divines of all persuasions, to stand in need of pretty ample interpretations; else to what use are the works of those divines? And for the guidance of these interpretations, it is also allowed, that some other standard must be assumed. The will then which is meant on this occasion, is that which may be called the *presumptive* will: that is to say, that which is presumed to be his will on account of the conformity of its dictates to those of some other principle. What then may be this other principle? It must be one or other of the three mentioned above: for there cannot, as we have seen, be any more. It is plain, therefore, that setting revelation out of the question, no light can ever be thrown upon the standard of right and wrong, by anything that can be said upon the question, what is God's will. We may be perfectly sure, indeed, that whatever is right is conformable to the will of God: but so far is that from answering the purpose of showing us what is right, that it is necessary to know first whether a thing is right, in order to know from thence whether it be conformable to the will of God.[1]

The principle of theology how reducible to one or another of the three principles. 1 The principle of theology refers everything to God's pleasure. But what is God's pleasure? God does not, he confessedly does not now, either speak or write to us. How then are we to know what is his pleasure? By observing what is our own pleasure, and pronouncing it to be his. Accordingly what is called the pleasure of God, is and must necessarily be (revelation apart) neither more nor less than the good pleasure of the person, whoever he be, who is pronouncing what he believes, or pretends, to be God's pleasure. How know you it to be God's pleasure that such or such an act should be abstained from? Whence come you even to suppose as much? 'Because the engaging in it would, I imagine, be prejudicial upon the whole to the happiness of mankind;' says the partisan of the principle of utility: 'Because the commission of it is attended with a gross and sensual, or at least with a trifling and transient satisfaction;' says the partisan of the principle of asceticism: 'Because I detest the thought of it; and I cannot, neither ought I to be called upon to tell why;' says he who proceeds upon the principle of antipathy. In the words of one or other of these must that person necessarily answer (revelation apart) who professes to take for his standard the will of God.

19. There are two things which are very apt to be confounded, but which it imports us carefully to distinguish: – the motive or cause, which, by operating on the mind of an individual, is productive of any act: and the ground or reason which warrants a legislator, or other by-stander, in regarding that act with an eye of approbation. When the act happens, in the particular instance in question, to be productive of effects which we approve of, much more if we happen to observe that the same motive may frequently be productive, in other instances, of the like effects, we ate apt to transfer our approbation to the motive itself, and to assume, as the just ground for the approbation we bestow on the act, the circumstance of its originating from that motive. It is in this way that the sentiment of antipathy has often been considered as a just ground of action. Antipathy, for instance, in such or such a case, is the cause of an action which is attended with good effects: but this does not make it a right ground of action in that case, any more than in any other. Still farther. Not only the effects are good, but the agent sees beforehand that they will be so. This may make the action indeed a perfectly right action: but it does not make antipathy a right ground of action. For the same sentiment of antipathy, if implicitly deferred to, may be, and very frequently is, productive of the very worst effects. Antipathy, therefore, can never be a right ground of action. No more, therefore, can resentment, which, as will be seen more particularly hereafter, is but a modification of antipathy. The only right ground of action, that can possibly subsist, is, after all, the consideration of utility, which if it is a right principle of action, and of approbation, in any one case, is so in every other. Other principles in abundance, that is, other motives, may be the reasons why such and such an act *has* been done: that is, the reasons or causes of its being done: but it is this alone that can be the reason why it might or ought to have been done. Antipathy or resentment requires always to be regulated, to prevent its doing mischief: to be regulated by what? always by the principle of utility. The principle of utility neither requires nor admits of any other regulator than itself.

Antipathy, let the actions it dictates be ever so right, is never of itself a right ground of action.

CHAPTER III

Of the Four Sanctions or Sources of Pain and Pleasure

Connexion of this chapter with the preceding. 1. It has been shown that the happiness of the individuals, of whom a community is composed, that is their pleasures and their security, is the end and the sole end which the legislator ought to have in view: the sole standard, in conformity to which each individual ought, as far as depends upon the legislator, to be *made* to fashion his behaviour. But whether it be this or anything else that is to be *done*, there is nothing by which a man can ultimately be *made* to do it, but either pain or pleasure. Having taken a general view of these two grand objects (*viz.*, pleasure, and what comes to the same thing, immunity from pain) in the character of *final* causes; it will be necessary to take a view of pleasure and pain itself, in the character of *efficient* causes or means.

Four sanctions or sources of pleasure and pain. 2. There are four distinguishable sources from which pleasure and pain are in use to flow: considered separately, they may be termed the *physical*, the *political*, the *moral*, and the *religious*: and inasmuch as the pleasures and pains belonging to each of them are capable of giving a binding force to any law or rule of conduct, they may all of them be termed *sanctions*.[1]

---

1 Sanctio, in Latin, was used to signify the *act of binding*, and, by a common grammatical transition, *anything which serves to bind a man*: to wit, to the observance of such or such a mode of conduct. According to a Latin grammarian,[a] the import of the word is derived by rather a far-fetched process (such as those commonly are, and in a great measure indeed must be, by which intellectual ideas are derived from sensible ones) from the word *sanguis*, blood: because, among the Romans, with a view to inculcate into the people a persuasion that such or such a mode of conduct would be rendered obligatory upon a man by the force of which I call the religious sanction (that is, that

---

a Servius. See Ainsworth's Dict. ad verbum *Sanctio*.

3. If it be in the present life, and from the ordinary course of nature, not purposely modified by the interposition of the will of any human being, nor by any extraordinary interposition of any superior invisible being, that the pleasure or the pain takes place or is expected, it may be said to issue from or to belong to the *physical sanction*.

1. The physical sanction.

4. If at the hands of a *particular* person or set of persons in the community, who under names correspondent to that of *judge*, are chosen for the particular purpose of dispensing it, according to the will of the sovereign or supreme ruling power in the state, it may be said to issue from the *political sanction*.

2. The political.

5. If at the hands of such *chance* persons in the community, as the party in question may happen in the course of his life to have concerns with, according to each man's spontaneous disposition, and not according to any settled or concerted rule, it may be said to issue from the *moral* or *popular sanction*.[1]

3. The moral or popular.

6. If from the immediate hand of a superior invisible being, either in the present life, or in a future, it may be said to issue from the *religious sanction*.

4. The religious.

7. Pleasures or pains which may be expected to issue from the *physical*, *political*, or *moral* sanctions, must all of them be expected to be experienced, if ever, in the *present* life: those which may be expected to issue from the *religious* sanction, may be expected to be experienced either in the *present* life or in a *future*.

The pleasures and pains which belong to the religious sanction, may regard either the present life or future.

---

he would be made to suffer by the extraordinary interposition of some superior being, if he failed to observe the mode of conduct in question) certain ceremonies were contrived by the priests: in the course of which ceremonies the blood of victims was made use of.

A Sanction then is a source of obligatory powers or *motives*: that is, of *pains* and *pleasures*; which, according as they are connected with such or such modes of conduct, operate, and are indeed the only things which can operate, as *motives*. See Chap. x. [Motives].

1 Better termed *popular*, as more directly indicative of its constituent cause; as likewise of its relation to the more common phrase *public opinion*, in French *opinion publique*, the name there given to that tutelary power, of which of late so much is said, and by which so much is done. The latter appellation is however unhappy and inexpressive; since if *opinion* is material, it is only in virtue of the influence it exercises over action, through the medium of the affections and the will.

Those which regard the present life, from which soever source they flow, differ only in the circumstances of their production.

8. Those which can be experienced in the present life, can of course be no others than such as human nature in the course of the present life is susceptible of: and from each of these sources may flow all the pleasures or pains of which, in the course of the present life, human nature is susceptible. With regard to these then (with which alone we have in this place any concern) those of them which belong to any one of those sanctions, differ not ultimately in kind from those which belong to any one of the other three: the only difference there is among them lies in the circumstances that accompany their production. A suffering which befalls a man in the natural and spontaneous course of things, shall be styled, for instance, a *calamity*; in which case, if it be supposed to befall him through any imprudence of his, it may be styled a punishment issuing from the physical sanction. Now this same suffering, if inflicted by the law, will be what is commonly called a *punishment*; if incurred for want of any friendly assistance, which the misconduct, or supposed misconduct, of the sufferer has occasioned to be withholden, a punishment issuing from the *moral* sanction; if through the immediate interposition of a particular providence, a punishment issuing from the religious sanction.

Example.

9. A man's goods, or his person, are consumed by fire. If this happened to him by what is called an accident, it was a calamity: if by reason of his own imprudence (for instance, from his neglecting to put his candle out) it may be styled a punishment of the physical sanction: if it happened to him by the sentence of the political magistrate, a punishment belonging to the political sanction; that is, what is commonly called a punishment: if for want of any assistance which his *neighbour* withheld from him out of some dislike to his *moral* character, a punishment of the *moral* sanction: if by an immediate act of *God's* displeasure, manifested on account of some *sin* committed by him, or through any distraction of mind, occasioned by the dread of such displeasure, a punishment of the *religious* sanction.[1]

---

1 A suffering conceived to befall a man by the immediate act of God, as above, is often, for shortness' sake, called *a judgment*: instead of saying, a suffering inflicted on him in consequence of a special judgment formed, and resolution thereupon taken, by the Deity.

10. As to such of the pleasures and pains belonging to the religious *Those* sanction, as regard a future life, of what kind these may be we *which regard* cannot know. These lie not open to our observation. During the *a future life* present life they are matter only of expectation: and, whether that *specifically* expectation be derived from natural or revealed religion, the *known.* particular kind of pleasure or pain, if it be different from all those which lie open to our observation, is what we can have no idea of. The best ideas we can obtain of such pains and pleasures are altogether unliquidated in point of quality. In what other respects our ideas of them *may* be liquidated will be considered in another place.[1]

11. Of these four sanctions the physical is altogether, we may *The* observe, the ground-work of the political and the moral: so is it *physical* also of the religious, in as far as the latter bears relation to the *sanction* present life. It is included in each of those other three. This may *each of the* operate in any case, (that is, any of the pains or pleasures belonging *other three.* to it may operate) independently of *them*: none of *them* can operate but by means of this. In a word, the powers of nature may operate of themselves; but neither the magistrate, nor men at large, *can* operate, nor is God in the case in question *supposed* to operate, but through the powers of nature.

12. For these four objects, which in their nature have so much in *Use of* common, it seemed of use to find a common name. It seemed of *this* use, in the first place, for the convenience of giving a name to *chapter.* certain pleasures and pains, for which a name equally characteristic could hardly otherwise have been found: in the second place, for the sake of holding up the efficacy of certain moral forces, the influence of which is apt not to be sufficiently attended to. Does the political sanction exert an influence over the conduct of mankind? The moral, the religious sanctions do so too. In every inch of his career are the operations of the political magistrate liable to be aided or impeded by these two foreign powers: who, one or other of them, or both, are sure to be either his rivals or his allies. Does it happen to him to leave them out of his calculations? He will be sure almost to find himself mistaken in the result. Of all

1 See ch. xiii [Cases unmeet] par. 2. note.

this we shall find abundant proofs in the sequel of this work. It behoves him, therefore, to have them continually before his eyes; and that under such a name as exhibits the relation they bear to his own purposes and designs.

CHAPTER IV

Value of a Lot of Pleasure or Pain, How to be Measured

Use of this chapter.

1. Pleasures then, and the avoidance of pains, are the *ends* which the legislator has in view: it behoves him therefore to understand their *value*. Pleasures and pains are the *instruments* he has to work with: it behoves him therefore to understand their force, which is again, in other words, their value.

Circumstances to be taken into the account in estimating the value of a pleasure or pain considered with reference to a single person, and by itself.

2. To a person considered *by himself* the value of a pleasure or pain considered *by itself* will be greater or less, according to the four following circumstances:[1]

 1 Its *intensity*.
 2 Its *duration*.
 3 Its *certainty* or *uncertainty*.
 4 Its *propinquity* or *remoteness*.

3. These are the circumstances which are to be considered in estimating a pleasure or a pain considered each of them by itself. But when the value of any pleasure or pain is considered for the purpose of estimating the tendency of any *act* by which it is produced, there are two other circumstances to be taken into account; these are,

– considered as connected with other pleasures or pains.

---

1 These circumstances have since been dominated *elements* or *dimensions* of *value* in a pleasure or a pain.

Not long after the publication of the first edition, the following memoriter verses were framed, in the view of lodging more effectually, in the memory, these points, on which the whole fabric of morals and legislation may be seen to rest.

> *Intense, long, certain, speedy, fruitful, pure* –
> Such marks in *pleasures* and in *pains* endure.
> Such pleasures seek if *private* be thy end:
> If it be *public*, wide let them *extend*.
> Such *pains* avoid, whichever be thy view:
> If pains *must* come, let them *extend* to few.

5 Its *fecundity*, or the chance it has of being followed by sensations of the *same* kind: that is, pleasures, if it be a pleasure: pains, if it be a pain.

6 Its *purity*, or the chance it has of *not* being followed by sensations of the *opposite* kind: that is, pains, if it be a pleasure: pleasures, if it be a pain.

These two last, however, are in strictness scarcely to be deemed properties of the pleasure or the pain itself; they are not, therefore, in strictness to be taken into the account of the value of that pleasure or that pain. They are in strictness to be deemed properties only of the act, or other event, by which such pleasure or pain has been produced; and accordingly are only to be taken into the account of the tendency of such act or such event.

considered with reference to a number of persons. 4. To a *number* of persons, with reference to each of whom the value of a pleasure or a pain is considered, it will be greater or less, according to seven circumstances: to wit, the six preceding ones; *viz.*

    1 Its *intensity*.

    2 Its *duration*.

    3 Its *certainty* or *uncertainty*.

    4 Its *propinquity* or *remoteness*.

    5 Its *fecundity*.

    6 Its *purity*.

And one other; to wit:

    7 Its *extent*; that is, the number of persons to whom it *extends*; or (in other words) who are affected by it.

Process for estimating the tendency of any act or event. 5. To take an exact account then of the general tendency of any act, by which the interests of a community are affected, proceed as follows. Begin with any one person of those whose interests seem most immediately to be affected by it: and take an account,

    1 Of the value of each distinguishable *pleasure* which appears to be produced by it in the *first* instance.

    2 Of the value of each *pain* which appears to be produced by it in the *first* instance.

    3 Of the value of each pleasure which appears to be produced by it *after* the first. This constitutes the *fecundity* of the first *pleasure* and the *impurity* of the first *pain*.

4 Of the value of each *pain* which appears to be produced by it after the first. This constitutes the *fecundity* of the first *pain*, and the *impurity* of the first pleasure.

5 Sum up all the values of all the *pleasures* on the one side, and those of all the *pains* on the other. The balance, if it be on the side of pleasure, will give the *good* tendency of the act upon the whole, with respect to the interests of that *individual* person; if on the side of pain, the *bad* tendency of it upon the whole.

6 Take an account of the *number* of persons whose interests appear to be concerned; and repeat the above process with respect to each. *Sum up* the numbers expressive of the degrees of *good* tendency, which the act has, with respect to each individual, in regard to whom the tendency of it is *good* upon the whole: do this again with respect to each individual, in regard to whom the tendency of it is *good* upon the whole: do this again with respect to each individual, in regard to whom the tendency of it is *bad* upon the whole. Take the *balance*; which, if on the side of *pleasure*, will give the general *good tendency* of the act, with respect to the total number or community of individuals concerned; if on the side of pain, the general *evil tendency*, with respect to the same community.

6. It is not to be expected that this process should be strictly pursued previously to every moral judgment, or to every legislative or judicial operation. It may, however, be always kept in view: and as near as the process actually pursued on these occasions approaches to it, so near will such process approach to the character of an exact one. *Use of the foregoing process.*

7. The same process is alike applicable to pleasure and pain, in whatever shape they appear: and by whatever denomination they are distinguished: to pleasure, whether it be called *good* (which is properly the cause or instrument of pleasure) or *profit* (which is distant pleasure, or the cause or instrument of distant pleasure,) or *convenience*, or *advantage*, *benefit*, *emolument*, *happiness*, and so forth: to pain, whether it be called *evil*, (which corresponds to *good*) or *mischief* or *inconvenience*, or *disadvantage*, or *loss*, or *unhappiness*, and so forth. *The same process applicable to good and evil, profit and mischief, and all other modifications of pleasure and pain.*

Conformity of men's practice to this theory.

8. Nor is this a novel and unwarranted, any more than it is a useless theory. In all this there is nothing but what the practice of mankind, wheresoever they have a clear view of their own interest, is perfectly conformable to. An article of property, an estate in land, for instance, is valuable, on what account? On account of the pleasures of all kinds which it enables a man to produce, and what comes to the same thing the pains of all kinds which it enables him to avert. But the value of such an article of property is universally understood to rise or fall according to the length or shortness of the time which a man has in it: the certainty or uncertainty of its coming into possession: and the nearness or remoteness of the time at which, if at all, it is to come into possession. As to the *intensity* of the pleasures which a man may derive from it, this is never thought of, because it depends upon the use which each particular person may come to make of it; which cannot be estimated till the particular pleasures he may come to derive from it, or the particular pains he may come to exclude by means of it, are brought to view. For the same reason, neither does he think of the *fecundity* or *purity* of those pleasures.

Thus much for pleasure and pain, happiness and unhappiness, in *general*. We come now to consider the several particular kinds of pain and pleasure.

CHAPTER V

Pleasures and Pains, Their Kinds

1. Having represented what belongs to all sorts of pleasures and pains alike, we come now to exhibit, each by itself, the several sorts of pains and pleasures. Pains and pleasures may be called by one general word, interesting perceptions. Interesting perceptions are either simple or complex. The simple ones are those which cannot any one of them be resolved into more: complex are those which are resolvable into divers simple ones. A complex interesting perception may accordingly be composed either, 1. Of pleasures alone: 2. Of pains alone: or, 3. Of a pleasure or pleasures, and a pain or pains together. What determines a lot of pleasure, for example, to be regarded as one complex pleasure, rather than as divers simple ones, is the nature of the exciting cause. Whatever pleasures are excited all at once by the action of the same cause, are apt to be looked upon as constituting all together but one pleasure. *Pleasures and pains are either 1. Simple: or, 2. Complex.*

2. The several simple pleasures of which human nature is susceptible, seem to be as follows: 1. The pleasures of sense. 2. The pleasures of wealth. 3. The pleasures of skill. 4. The pleasures of amity. 5. The pleasures of a good name. 6. The pleasures of power. 7. The pleasures of piety. 8. The pleasures of benevolence. 9. The pleasures of malevolence. 10. The pleasures of memory. 11. The pleasures of imagination. 12. The pleasures of expectation. 13. The pleasures dependent on association. 14. The pleasures of relief. *The simple pleasures enumerated.*

3. The several simple pains seem to be as follows: 1. The pains of privation. 2. The pains of the senses. 3. The pains of awkwardness. 4. The pains of enmity. 5. The pains of an ill name. 6. The pains of piety. 7. The pains of benevolence. 8. The pains of malevolence. 9. The pains of the memory. 10. The pains of the *The simple pains enumerated.*

imagination. 11. The pains of expectation. 12. The pains dependent on association.[1]

1 Pleasures of sense enumerated. 4. (1) The pleasures of sense seem to be as follows: 1. The pleasures of the taste or palate; including whatever pleasures are experienced in satisfying the appetites of hunger and thirst. 2. The pleasure of intoxication. 3. The pleasures of the organ of smelling. 4. The pleasures of the touch. 5. The simple pleasures of the ear; independent of association. 6. The simple pleasures of the eye; independent of association. 7. The pleasure of the sexual sense. 8. The pleasure of health: or, the internal pleasurable feeling or flow of spirits (as it is called) which accompanies a state of full health and vigour; especially at times of moderate bodily exertion. 9. The pleasures of novelty: or, the pleasures derived from the gratification of the appetite of curiosity, by the application of new objects to any of the senses.[2]

2 Pleasures of wealth, which are either of acquisition or of possession. 5. (2) By the pleasures of wealth may be meant those pleasures which a man is apt to derive from the consciousness of possessing any article or articles which stand in the list of instruments of enjoyment or security, and more particularly at the time of his first acquiring them; at which time the pleasure may be styled a pleasure of gain or a pleasure of acquisition: at other times a pleasure of possession.

3 Pleasures of skill. (3) The pleasures of skill, as exercised upon particular objects, are those which accompany the application of such particular instruments of enjoyment to their uses, as cannot be so applied without a greater or less share of difficulty or exertion.[3]

Analytical view, why none given. 1 The catalogue here given, is what seemed to be a complete list of the several simple pleasures and pains of which human nature is susceptible: insomuch, that if, upon any occasion whatsoever, a man feels pleasure or pain, it is either referable at once to some one or other of these kinds, or resolvable into such as are. It might perhaps have been a satisfaction to the reader, to have seen an analytical view of the subject, taken upon an exhaustive plan, for the purpose of demonstrating the catalogue to be what it purports to be, a complete one. The catalogue is in fact the result of such an analysis; which, however, I thought it better to discard at present, as being of too metaphysical a cast, and not strictly within the limits of this design. See Chap. xiii [Cases unmeet], par. 2. Note.

2 There are also pleasures of novelty, excited by the appearance of new ideas: these are pleasures of the imagination. See infra 13.

3 For instance, the pleasure of being able to gratify the sense of hearing, by

6. (4) The pleasures of amity, or self-recommendation, are the pleasures that may accompany the persuasion of a man's being in the acquisition or the possession of the good-will of such or such assignable person or persons in particular: or, as the phrase is, of being upon good terms with him or them: and as a fruit of it, of his being in a way to have the benefit of their spontaneous and gratuitous services. *4 Pleasures of amity.*

7. (5) The pleasures of a good name are the pleasures that accompany the persuasion of a man's being in the acquisition or the possession of the good-will of the world about him; that is, of such members of society as he is likely to have concerns with; and as a means of it, either their love or their esteem, or both: and as a fruit of it, of his being in the way to have the benefit of their spontaneous and gratuitous services. These may likewise be called the pleasures of good repute, the pleasures of honour, or the pleasures of the moral sanction.[1] *5 Pleasures of a good name.*

8. (6) The pleasures of power are the pleasures that accompany the persuasion of a man's being in a condition to dispose people, by means of their hopes and fears, to give him the benefit of their services: that is, by the hope of some service, or by the fear of some disservice, that he may be in the way to render them. *6 Pleasures of power.*

9. (7) The pleasures of piety are the pleasures that accompany the belief of a man's being in the acquisition or in possession of the good-will or favour of the Supreme Being: and as a fruit of it, of his being in a way of enjoying pleasures to be received by God's special appointment, either in this life, or in a life to come. These may also be called the pleasures of religion, the pleasures of a religious disposition, or the pleasures of the religious sanction.[2] *7 Pleasures of piety.*

10. (8) The pleasures of benevolence are the pleasures resulting from the view of any pleasures supposed to be possessed by the *8 Pleasures of benevolence or good-will.*

---

singing, or performing upon any musical instrument. The pleasure thus obtained, is a thing superadded to, and perfectly distinguishable from, that which a man enjoys from hearing another person perform in the same manner.

1 See Chap. iii [Sanctions].
2 See Chap. iii [Sanctions].

beings who may be the objects of benevolence; to wit, the sensitive beings we are acquainted with; under which are commonly included, 1. The Supreme Being. 2. Human beings. 3. Other animals. These may also be called the pleasures of goodwill, the pleasures of sympathy, or the pleasures of the benevolent or social affections.

9

Pleasures of malevolence or ill-will.

11. (9) The pleasures of malevolence are the pleasures resulting from the view of any pain supposed to be suffered by the beings who may become the objects of malevolence: to wit, 1. Human beings. 2. Other animals. These may also be styled the pleasures of ill-will, the pleasures of the irascible appetite, the pleasures of antipathy, or the pleasures of the malevolent or dissocial affections.

10

Pleasures of the memory.

12. (10) The pleasures of the memory are the pleasures which after having enjoyed such and such pleasures, or even in some case after having suffered such and such pains, a man will now and then experience, at recollecting them exactly in the order and in the circumstances in which they were actually enjoyed or suffered. These derivative pleasures may of course be distinguished into as many species as there are of original perceptions, from whence they may be copied. They may also be styled pleasures of simple recollection.

11

Pleasures of the imagination.

13. (11) The pleasures of the imagination are the pleasures which may be derived from the contemplation of any such pleasures as may happen to be suggested by the memory, but in a different order, and accompanied by different groups of circumstances. These may accordingly be referred to any one of the three cardinal points of time, present, past, or future. It is evident they may admit of as many distinctions as those of the former class.

12

Pleasures of expectation.

14. (12) The pleasures of expectation are the pleasures that result from the contemplation of any sort of pleasure, referred to time *future*, and accompanied with the sentiment of *belief*. These also may admit of the same distinctions.[1]

---

1 In contradistinction to these, all other pleasures may be termed pleasures of *enjoyment*.

15. (13) The pleasures of association are the pleasures which certain objects or incidents may happen to afford, not of themselves, but merely in virtue of some association they have contracted in the mind with certain objects or incidents which are in themselves pleasurable. Such is the case, for instance, with the pleasure of skill, when afforded by such a set of incidents as compose a game of chess. This derives its pleasurable quality from its association partly with the pleasure of skill, as exercised in the production of incidents pleasurable of themselves: partly from its association with the pleasures of power. Such is the case also with the pleasure of good luck, when afforded by such incidents as compose the game of hazard, or any other game of chance, when played at for nothing. This derives its pleasurable quality from its association with one of the pleasures of wealth; to wit, with the pleasure of acquiring it.

13 Pleasures depending on association.

16. (14) Farther on we shall see pains grounded upon pleasures; in like manner may we now see pleasures grounded upon pains. To the catalogue of pleasures may accordingly be added the pleasures of *relief*: or, the pleasures which a man experiences when, after he has been enduring a pain of any kind for a certain time, it comes to cease, or to abate. These may of course be distinguished into as many species as there are of pains: and may give rise to so many pleasures of memory, of imagination, and of expectation.

14 Pleasures of relief.

17. (1) Pains of privation are the pains that may result from the thought of not possessing in the time present any of the several kinds of pleasures. Pains of privation may accordingly be resolved into as many kinds as there are of pleasures to which they may correspond, and from the absence whereof they may be derived.

1 Pains of privation.

18. There are three sorts of pains which are only so many modifications of the several pains of privation. When the enjoyment of any particular pleasure happens to be particularly desired, but without any expectation approaching to assurance, the pain of privation which thereupon results takes a particular name, and is called the pain of *desire*, or of unsatisfied desire.

These include, 1. Pains of desire.

19. Where the enjoyment happens to have been looked for with a degree of expectation approaching to assurance, and that expectation is made suddenly to cease, it is called a pain of disappointment.

2. Pains of disappointment.

3. *Pains of regret.* 20. A pain of privation takes the name of a pain of regret in two cases: 1. Where it is grounded on the memory of a pleasure, which having been once enjoyed, appears not likely to be enjoyed again: 2. Where it is grounded on the idea of a pleasure, which was never actually enjoyed, nor perhaps so much as expected, but which might have been enjoyed (it is supposed), had such or such a contingency happened, which, in fact, did not happen.

2 *Pains of the senses.* 21. (2) The several pains of the senses seem to be as follows: 1. The pains of hunger and thirst: or the disagreeable sensations produced by the want of suitable substances which need at times to be applied to the alimentary canal. 2. The pains of the taste: or the disagreeable sensations produced by the application of various substances to the palate, and other superior parts of the same canal. 3. The pains of the organ of smell: or the disagreeable sensations produced by the effluvia of various substances when applied to that organ. 4. The pains of the touch: or the disagreeable sensations produced by the application of various substances to the skin. 5. The simple pains of the hearing: or the disagreeable sensations excited in the organ of that sense by various kinds of sounds: independently (as before), of association. 6. The simple pains of the sight: or the disagreeable sensations if any such there be, that may be excited in the organ of that sense by visible images, independent of the principle of association. 7.[1] The pains resulting from excessive heat or cold, unless these be referable to the touch. 8. The pains of disease: or the acute and uneasy sensations resulting from the several diseases and indispositions to which human nature is liable. 9. The pain of exertion, whether bodily or mental: or the uneasy sensation which is apt to accompany any intense effort, whether of mind or body.

3 *Pains of awkward-ness.* 22. (3)[2] The pains of awkwardness are the pains which sometimes result from the unsuccessful endeavour to apply any particular

1 The pleasure of the sexual sense seems to have no positive pain to correspond to it: it has only a pain of privation or pain of the mental class, the pain of unsatisfied desire. If any positive pain of body result from the want of such indulgence, it belongs to the head of pains of disease.

2 The pleasures of novelty have no positive pains corresponding to them. The pain which a man experiences when he is in the condition of not knowing what

instruments of enjoyment or security to their uses, or from the difficulty a man experiences in applying them.[1]

23. (4) The pains of enmity are the pains that may accompany the persuasion of a man's being obnoxious to the ill-will of such or such an assignable person or persons in particular: or, as the phrase is, of being upon ill terms with him or them: and, in consequence, of being obnoxious to certain pains of some sort or other, of which he may be the cause.

4 Pains of enmity.

24. (5) The pains of an ill-name, are the pains that accompany the persuasion of a man's being obnoxious, or in a way to be obnoxious to the ill-will of the world about him. These may likewise be called the pains of ill-repute, the pains of dishonour, or the pains of the moral sanction.[2]

5 Pains of an ill-name.

25. (6)[3] The pains of piety are the pains that accompany the belief of a man's being obnoxious to the displeasure of the Supreme

6 Pains of piety.

---

to do with himself, that pain, which in French is expressed by a single word *ennui*, is a pain of privation: a pain resulting from the absence, not only of all the pleasures of novelty, but of all kinds of pleasure whatsoever.

The pleasures of wealth have also no positive pains corresponding to them: the only pains opposed to them are pains of privation. If any positive pains result from the want of wealth, they are referable to some other class of positive pains; principally to those of the senses. From the want of food, for instance, result the pains of hunger; from the want of clothing, the pains of cold; and so forth.

1 It may be a question, perhaps, whether this be a positive pain of itself, or whether it be nothing more than a pain of privation, resulting from the consciousness of a want of skill. It is, however, but a question of words, nor does it matter which way it be determined.

2 In as far as a man's fellow-creatures are supposed to be determined by any event not to regard him with any degree of esteem or *good* will, or to regard him with a less degree of esteem or *good* will than they would otherwise; not to do him any sorts of *good* offices, or not to do him so many *good* offices as they would otherwise; the pain resulting from such consideration may be reckoned a pain of privation: as far as they are supposed to regard him with such a degree of aversion or disesteem as to be disposed to do him positive *ill* offices, it may be reckoned a positive pain. The pain of privation, and the positive pain, in this case run one into another indistinguishably.

3 There seem to be no positive pains to correspond to the pleasures of power. The pains that a man may feel from the want or the loss of power, in as far as power is distinguished from all other sources of pleasure, seem to be nothing more than pains of privation.

Being: and in consequence to certain pains to be inflicted by his especial appointment, either in this life or in a life to come. These may also be called the pains of religion; the pains of a religious disposition; or the pains of the religious sanction. When the belief is looked upon as well-grounded, these pains are commonly called religious terrors; when looked upon as ill-grounded, superstitious terrors.[1]

7 Pains of benevolence. 26. (7) The pains of benevolence are the pains resulting from the view of any pains supposed to be endured by other beings. These may also be called the pains of good-will, of sympathy, or the pains of the benevolent or social affections.

8 Pains of malevolence. 27. (8) The pains of malevolence are the pains resulting from the view of any pleasures supposed to be enjoyed by any beings who happen to be the objects of a man's displeasure. These may also be styled the pains of ill-will, of antipathy, or the pains of the malevolent or dissocial affections.

9 Pains of the memory. 28. (9) The pains of the memory may be grounded on every one of the above kinds, as well of pains of privation as of positive pains. These correspond exactly to the pleasures of the memory.

10 Pains of the imagination. 29. (10) The pains of the imagination may also be grounded on any one of the above kinds, as well of pains of privation as of positive pains; in other respects they correspond exactly to the pleasures of the imagination.

11 Pains of expectation. 30. (11) The pains of expectation may be grounded on each one of the above kinds, as well of pains of privation as of positive pains. These may be also termed pains of apprehension.[2]

12 Pains of association. 31. (12) The pains of association correspond exactly to the pleasures of association.

---

1 The positive pains of piety, and the pains of privation, opposed to the pleasures of piety, run one into another in the same manner as the positive pains of enmity, or of an ill name, do with respect to the pains of privation, opposed to the pleasures of amity, and those of a good name. If what is apprehended at the hands of God is barely the not receiving pleasure, the pain is of the privative class: if, moreover, actual pain be apprehended, it is of the class of positive pains.
2 In contradistinction to these, all other pains may be termed pains of *sufferance*.

32. Of the above list there are certain pleasures and pains which *Pleasures* suppose the existence of some pleasure or pain of some other *and pains* person, to which the pleasure or pain of the person in question has *self-* regard: such pleasures and pains may be termed *extra-regarding*. *regarding* Others do not suppose any such thing: these may be termed *self-* *or extra-* *regarding*.[1] The only pleasures and pains of the extra-regarding *regarding.* class are those of benevolence and those of malevolence: all the rest are self-regarding.[2]

33. Of all these several sorts of pleasures and pains, there is scarce *In what* any one which is not liable, on more accounts than one, to come *ways the* under the consideration of the law. Is an offence committed? It is *law is* the tendency which it has to destroy, in such or such persons, *with the* some of these pleasures, or to produce some of these pains, that *above* constitutes the mischief of it, and the ground for punishing it. It is *pains and* the prospect of some of these pleasures, or of security from some *pleasures.* of these pains, that constitutes the motive or temptation, it is the attainment of them that constitutes the profit of the offence. Is the offender to be punished? It can be only by the production of one or more of these pains, that the punishment can be inflicted.[3]

1 See Chap. x [Motives].
2 By this means the pleasures and pains of amity may be the more clearly distinguished from those of benevolence: and on the other hand, those of enmity from those of malevolence. The pleasures and pains of amity and enmity are of the self-regarding cast: those of benevolence and malevolence of the extra-regarding.
3 It would be a matter not only of curiosity, but of some use, to exhibit a catalogue of the several complex pleasures and pains, analysing them at the same time into the several simple ones, of which they are respectively composed. But such a disquisition would take up too much room to be admitted here. A short specimen, however, for the purpose of illustration, can hardly be dispensed with.

The pleasures taken in at the eye and ear are generally very complex. The pleasures of a country scene, for instance, consist commonly, amongst others, of the following pleasures:

I. Pleasures of the senses.

1 The simple pleasures of sight, excited by the perception of agreeable colours and figures, green fields, waving foliage, glistening water, and the like.
2 The simple pleasure of the ears, excited by the perceptions of the chirping of birds, the murmuring of waters, the rustling of the wind among the trees.
3 The pleasures of the smell, excited by the perceptions of the fragrance of flowers, of new-mown hay, or other vegetable substances, in the first stages of fermentation.

4 The agreeable inward sensation, produced by a brisk circulation of the blood, and the ventilation of it in the lungs by a pure air, such as that in the country frequently is in comparison of that which is breathed in towns.

II. Pleasures of the imagination produced by association.

1 The idea of the plenty, resulting from the possession of the objects that are in view, and of the happiness arising from it.

2 The idea of the innocence and happiness of the birds, sheep, cattle, dogs, and other gentle or domestic animals.

3 The idea of the constant flow of health, supposed to be enjoyed by all these creatures: a notion which is apt to result from the occasional flow of health enjoyed by the supposed spectator.

4 The idea of gratitude, excited by the contemplation of the all-powerful and beneficent Being, who is looked up to as the author of these blessings. These four last are all of them, in some measure at least, pleasures of sympathy.

The depriving a man of this group of pleasures is one of the evils apt to result from imprisonment: whether produced by illegal violence, or in the way of punishment, by appointment of the laws.

CHAPTER VI

Of Circumstances Influencing Sensibility

1. Pain and pleasure are produced in men's minds by the action of certain causes. But the quantity of pleasure and pain runs not uniformly in proportion to the cause; in other words, to the quantity of force exerted by such cause. The truth of this observation rests not upon any metaphysical nicety in the import given to the terms *cause*, *quantity*, and *force*: it will be equally true in whatsoever manner such force be measured. *Pain and pleasure not uniformly proportioned to their causes.*

2. The disposition which anyone has to feel such or such a quantity of pleasure or pain, upon the application of a cause of given force, is what we term the degree or *quantum* of his sensibility. This may be either *general*, referring to the sum of the causes that act upon him during a given period: or *particular*, referring to the action of any one particular cause, or sort of cause. *Degree or quantum of sensibility, what.*

3. But in the same mind such and such causes of pain or pleasure will produce more pain or pleasure than such or such other causes of pain or pleasure: and this proportion will in different minds be different. The disposition which anyone has to have the proportion in which he is affected by two such causes, different from that in which another man is affected by the same two causes, may be termed the quality or *bias* of his sensibility. One man, for instance, may be most affected by the pleasures of the taste; another by those of the ear. So also, if there be a difference in the nature or proportion of two pains or pleasures which they respectively experience from the same cause; a case not so frequent as the former. From the same injury, for instance, one man may feel the same quantity of grief and resentment together as another man: but one of them shall feel a greater share of grief than of resentment: the other, a greater share of resentment than of grief. *Bias or quality of sensibility, what.*

Exciting causes pleasurable and dolorific.

4. Any incident which serves as a cause, either of pleasure or of pain, may be termed an *exciting* cause: if of pleasure, a pleasurable cause: if of pain, a painful, afflictive, or dolorific cause.[1]

Circumstances influencing sensibility, what.

5. Now the quantity of pleasure, or of pain, which a man is liable to experience upon the application of an exciting cause, since they will not depend altogether upon that cause, will depend in some measure upon some other circumstance or circumstances: these circumstances, whatsoever they be, may be termed *circumstances influencing sensibility*.[2]

Circumstances influencing sensibility enumerated.

6. These circumstances will apply differently to different exciting causes; insomuch that to a certain exciting cause, a certain circumstance shall not apply at all, which shall apply with great force to another exciting cause. But without entering for the present into these distinctions, it may be of use to sum up all the circumstances which can be found to influence the effect of *any* exciting cause. These, as on a former occasion, it may be as well first to sum up together in the concisest manner possible, and afterwards to allot a few words to the separate explanation of each article. They seem to be as follows: 1. Health. 2. Strength. 3. Hardiness. 4. Bodily imperfection. 5. Quantity and quality of knowledge. 6. Strength of intellectual powers. 7. Firmness of mind. 8. Steadiness of mind. 9. Bent of inclination. 10. Moral sensibility. 11. Moral biases. 12. Religious sensibility. 13. Religious biases. 14. Sympathetic sensibility. 15. Sympathetic biases. 16. Antipathetic sensibility. 17. Antipathetic biases. 18. Insanity. 19. Habitual occupations. 20. Pecuniary circumstances. 21. Connexions in the

---

1 The exciting cause, the pleasure or pain produced by it, and the intention produced by such pleasure or pain in the character of a motive, are objects so intimately connected, that, in what follows, I fear I have not, on every occasion, been able to keep them sufficiently distinct. I thought it necessary to give the reader this warning; after which, should there be found any such mistakes, it is to be hoped they will not be productive of much confusion.

2 Thus, in physical bodies, the momentum of a ball put in motion by impulse, will be influenced by the circumstance of gravity: being in some directions increased, in others diminished by it. So in a ship, put in motion by the wind, the momentum and direction will be influenced not only by the attraction of gravity, but by the motion and resistance of the water, and several other circumstances.

way of sympathy. 22. Connexions in the way of antipathy. 23. Radical frame of body. 24. Radical frame of mind. 25. Sex. 26. Age. 27. Rank. 28. Education. 29. Climate. 30. Lineage. 31. Government. 32. Religious profession.[1]

7. (1) Health is the absence of disease, and consequently of all   1 *Health.* those kinds of pain which are among the symptoms of disease. A man may be said to be in a state of health when he is not conscious of any uneasy sensations, the primary seat of which can be perceived to be anywhere in his body.[2] In point of general

1 An analytical view of all these circumstances will be given at the conclusion of the chapter: to which place it was necessary to refer it, as it could not well have been understood, till some of them had been previously explained.

To search out the vast variety of exciting or moderating causes, by which the degree or bias of a man's sensibility may be influenced, to define the boundaries of each, to extricate them from the entanglements in which they are involved, to lay the effect of each article distinctly before the reader's eye, is, perhaps, if not absolutely the most difficult task, at least one of the most difficult tasks, within the compass of moral physiology. Disquisitions on this head can never be completely satisfactory without examples. To provide a sufficient collection of such examples, would be a work of great labour as well as nicety: history and biography would need to be ransacked: a vast course of reading would need to be travelled through on purpose. By such a process the present work would doubtless have been rendered more amusing; but in point of bulk, so enormous, that this single chapter would have been swelled into a considerable volume. Feigned cases, although they may upon occasion serve to render the general matter tolerably intelligible, can never be sufficient to render it palatable. On this therefore, as on so many other occasion, I must confine myself to dry and general instruction: discarding illustration, although sensible that without it instruction cannot manifest half its efficacy. The subject, however, is so difficult, and so new, that I shall think I have not ill succeeded, if without pretending to exhaust it, I shall have been able to mark out the principal points of view, and to put the matter in such a method as may facilitate the researches of happier inquirers.

The great difficulty lies in the nature of the words; which are not, like pain and pleasure, names of homogeneous real entities, but names of various fictitious entities, for which no common genus is to be found: and which therefore, without a vast and roundabout chain of investigation, can never be brought under any exhaustive plan of arrangement, but must be picked up here and there as they happen to occur.

2 It may be thought, that in a certain degree of health, this negative account of the matter hardly comes up to the case. In a certain degree of health, there is often such a kind of feeling diffused over the whole frame, such a comfortable feel, or flow of spirits, as it is called, as may with propriety come under the head of positive pleasure. But without experiencing any such pleasurable feeling, if a man experience no painful one, he may be well enough said to be in health.

sensibility, a man who is under the pressure of any bodily indisposition, or, as the phrase is, is in an ill state of health, is less sensible to the influence of any pleasurable cause, and more so to that of any afflictive one, than if he were *well*.

2 *Strength.*   8. (2) The circumstance of strength, though in point of causality closely connected with that of health, is perfectly distinguishable from it. The same man will indeed generally be stronger in a good state of health than in a bad one. But one man, even in a bad state of health, may be stronger than another even in a good one. Weakness is a common concomitant of disease: but in consequence of his radical frame of body, a man may be weak all his life long, without experiencing any disease. Health, as we have observed, is principally a negative circumstance: strength a positive one. The degree of a man's strength can be measured with tolerable accuracy.[1]

3 *Hardiness.*   9. (3) Hardiness is a circumstance which, though closely connected with that of strength, is distinguishable from it. Hardiness is the absence of irritability. Irritability respects either pain, resulting from the action of mechanical causes; or disease, resulting from the action of causes purely physiological. Irritability, in the former sense, is the disposition to undergo a greater or less degree of pain upon the application of a mechanical cause; such as are most of those applications by which simple afflictive punishments are inflicted, as whipping, beating, and the like. In

---

1   The most accurate measure that can be given of a man's strength, seems to be that which is taken from the weight or number of pounds and ounces he can lift with his hands in a given attitude. This indeed relates immediately only to his arms: but these are the organs of strength which are most employed; of which the strength corresponds with most exactness to the general state of the body with regard to strength; and in which the quantum of strength is easiest measured. Strength may accordingly be distinguished into *general* and *particular*.

Weakness is a negative term, and imports the absence of strength. It is, besides, a relative term, and accordingly imports the absence of such a quantity of strength as makes the share, possessed by the person in question, less than that of some person he is compared to. Weakness, when it is at such a degree as to make it painful for a man to perform the motions necessary to the going through the ordinary functions of life, such as to get up, to walk, to dress one's self and so forth, brings the circumstance of health into question, and puts a man into that sort of condition in which he is said to be in ill health.

the latter sense, it is the disposition to contract disease with greater or less facility, upon the application of any instrument acting on the body by its physiological properties; as in the case of fevers, or of colds, or other inflammatory diseases, produced by the application of damp air: or to experience immediate uneasiness, as in the case of relaxation or chilliness produced by an over or under proportion of the matter of heat.

Hardiness, even in the sense in which it is opposed to the action of mechanical causes, is distinguishable from strength. The external indications of strength are the abundance and firmness of the muscular fibres: those of hardiness, in this sense, are the firmness of the muscular fibres, and the callosity of the skin. Strength is more peculiarly the gift of nature: hardiness, of education. Of two persons who have had, the one the education of a gentleman, the other, that of a common sailor, the first may be the stronger, at the same time that the other is the hardier. *Difference between strength and hardiness.*

10. (4) By bodily imperfection may be understood that condition which a person is in, who either stands distinguished by any remarkable deformity, or wants any of those parts or faculties, which the ordinary run of persons of the same sex and age are furnished with: who, for instance, has a hare-lip, is deaf, or has lost a hand. This circumstance, like that of ill-health, tends in general to diminish more or less the effect of any pleasurable circumstance, and to increase that of any afflictive one. The effect of this circumstance, however, admits of great variety: inasmuch as there are a great variety of ways in which a man may suffer in his personal appearance, and in his bodily organs and faculties: all which differences will be taken notice of in their proper places.[1] *4 Bodily imperfection.*

11. (5) So much for circumstances belonging to the condition of the body: we come now to those which concern the condition of the mind: the use of mentioning these will be seen hereafter. In the first place may be reckoned the quantity and quality of the knowledge the person in question happens to possess: that is, of the ideas which he has actually in store, ready upon occasion to call to mind: meaning such ideas as are in some way or other of an interesting nature: that is, of a nature in some way or other to *5 Quantity and quality of knowledge.*

1 See B. I. Tit. [Irrep. corp. Injuries].

influence his happiness, or that of other men. When these ideas are many, and of importance, a man is said to be a man of knowledge; when few, or not of importance, *ignorant*.

6 *Strength of intellectual powers.* 12. (6) By strength of intellectual powers may be understood the degree of facility which a man experiences in his endeavours to call to mind as well such ideas as have been already aggregated to his stock of knowledge, as any others, which, upon any occasion that may happen, he may conceive a desire to place there. It seems to be on some such occasion as this that the words *parts* and *talents* are commonly employed. To this head may be referred the several qualities of readiness of apprehension, accuracy and tenacity of memory, strength of attention, clearness of discernment, amplitude of comprehension, vividity and rapidity of imagination. Strength of intellectual powers, in general, seems to correspond pretty exactly to general strength of body: as any of these qualities in particular does to particular strength.

7 *Firmness of mind.* 13. (7) Firmness of mind on the one hand, and irritability on the other, regard the proportion between the degrees of efficacy with which a man is acted upon by an exciting cause, of which the value lies chiefly in magnitude, and one of which the value lies chiefly in propinquity.[1] A man may be said to be of a firm mind, when small pleasures or pains, which are present or near, do not affect him, in a greater proportion to their value, than greater pleasures or pains, which are uncertain or remote;[2] of an irritable mind, when the contrary is the case.

8 *Steadiness.* 14. (8) Steadiness regards the time during which a given exciting cause of a given value continues to affect a man in nearly the same manner and degree as at first, no assignable external event or change of circumstances intervening to make an alteration in its force.[3]

1 See Chap. iv [Value].
2 When, for instance, having been determined, by the prospect of some inconvenience, not to disclose a fact, although he should be put to the rack, he perseveres in such resolution after the rack is brought into his presence, and even applied to him.
3 The facility with which children grow tired of their play-things, and throw them away, is an instance of unsteadiness: the perseverance with which a

15. (9) By the bent of a man's inclinations may be understood the propensity he has to expect pleasure or pain from certain objects, rather than from others. A man's inclinations may be said to have such or such a bent, when, amongst the several sorts of objects which afford pleasure in some degree to all men, he is apt to expect more pleasure from one particular sort, than from another particular sort, or more from any given particular sort, than another man would expect from that sort; or when, amongst the several sorts of objects, which to one man afford pleasure, whilst to another they afford none, he is apt to expect, or not to expect, pleasure from an object of such or such a sort: so also with regard to pains. This circumstance, though intimately connected with that of the bias of a man's sensibility, is not undistinguishable from it. The quantity of pleasure or pain, which on any given occasion a man may experience from an application of any sort, may be greatly influenced by the expectations he has been used to entertain of pleasure or pain from that quarter; but it will not be absolutely determined by them: for pleasure or pain may come upon him from a quarter from which he was not accustomed to expect it. *9 Bent of inclinations.*

16. (10) The circumstances of *moral, religious, sympathetic*, and *antipathetic sensibility*, when closely considered, will appear to be included in some sort under that of *bent of inclination*. On account of their particular importance they may, however, be worth mentioning apart. A man's moral sensibility may be said to be strong, when the pains and pleasures of the moral sanction[1] show greater in his eyes, in comparison with other pleasures and pains (and consequently exert a stronger influence) than in the eyes of the persons he is compared with; in other words, when he is acted on with more than ordinary efficacy by the sense of honour: it may be said to be weak, when the contrary is the case. *10 Moral sensibility.*

---

merchant applies himself to his traffic, or an author to his book, may be taken for an instance of the contrary. It is difficult to judge of the quantity of pleasure or pain in these cases, but from the effects which it produces in the character of a motive: and even then it is difficult to pronounce, whether the change of conduct happens by the extinction of the old pleasure or pain, or by the intervention of a new one.

1 See Chap. v [Pleasures and Pains].

11 *Moral biases.* 17. (11) Moral sensibility seems to regard the average effect or influence of the pains and pleasures of the moral sanction, upon all sorts of occasions to which it is applicable, or happens to be applied. It regards the average force or *quantity* of the impulses the mind receives from that source during a given period. Moral *bias* regards the particular acts on which, upon so many particular occasions, the force of that sanction is looked upon as attaching. It regards the *quality* or direction of those impulses. It admits of as many varieties, therefore, as there are dictates which the moral sanction may be conceived to issue forth. A man may be said to have such or such a *moral bias*, or to have a moral bias in favour of such or such an action, when he looks upon it as being of the number of those of which the performance is dictated by the moral sanction.

12 *Religious sensibility.* 18. (12) What has been said with regard to moral sensibility, may be applied, *mutatis mutandis*, to religious.

13 *Religious biases.* 19. (13) What has been said with regard to moral biases, may also be applied, *mutatis mutandis*, to religious biases.

14 *Sympathetic sensibility.* 20. (14) By sympathetic sensibility is to be understood the propensity that a man has to derive pleasure from the happiness, and pain from the unhappiness, of other sensitive beings. It is the stronger, the greater the ratio of the pleasure or pain he feels on their account is to that of the pleasure or pain which (according to what appears to him) they feel for themselves.

15 *Sympathetic biases.* 21. (15) Sympathetic bias regards the description of the parties who are the objects of a man's sympathy: and of the acts or other circumstances of or belonging to those persons, by which the sympathy is excited. These parties may be, 1. Certain individuals. 2. Any subordinate class of individuals. 3. The whole nation. 4. Human kind in general. 5. The whole sensitive creation. According as these objects of sympathy are more numerous, the *affection*, by which the man is biased, may be said to be the more *enlarged*.

16, 17 *Antipathetic sensibility and biases.* 22. (16) (17) Antipathetic sensibility and antipathetic biases are just the reverse of sympathetic sensibility and sympathetic biases. By antipathetic sensibility is to be understood the propensity that a man has to derive pain from the happiness, and pleasure from the unhappiness, of other sensitive beings.

23. (18) The circumstance of insanity of mind corresponds to that of bodily imperfection. It admits, however, of much less variety, inasmuch as the soul is (for aught we can perceive) one indivisible thing, not distinguishable, like the body, into parts. What lesser degrees of imperfection the mind may be susceptible of, seem to be comprisable under the already-mentioned heads of ignorance, weakness of mind, irritability, or unsteadiness; or under such others as are reducible to them. Those which are here in view are those extraordinary species and degrees of mental imperfection, which, wherever they take place, are as conspicuous and as unquestionable as lameness or blindness in the body: operating partly, it should seem, by inducing an extraordinary degree of the imperfections above mentioned, partly by giving an extraordinary and preposterous bent to the inclinations.

18 Insanity.

24. (19) Under the head of a man's habitual occupations, are to be understood, on this occasion, as well those which he pursues for the sake of profit, as those which he pursues for the sake of present pleasure. The consideration of the profit itself belongs to the head of a man's pecuniary circumstances. It is evident, that if by any means a punishment, or any other exciting cause, has the effect of putting it out of his power to continue in the pursuit of any such occupation, it must on that account be so much the more distressing. A man's habitual occupations, though intimately connected in point of causality with the bent of his inclinations, are not to be looked upon as precisely the same circumstance. An amusement, or channel of profit, may be the object of a man's *inclinations*, which has never been the subject of his *habitual occupations*: for it may be, that though he wished to betake himself to it, he never did, it not being in his power: a circumstance which may make a good deal of difference in the effect of any incident by which he happens to be debarred from it.

19 Habitual occupations.

25. (20) Under the head of pecuniary circumstances, I mean to bring to view the proportion which a man's *means* bear to his *wants*: the sum total of his means of every kind, to the sum total of his wants of every kind. A man's means depend upon three circumstances: 1. His property. 2. The profit of his labour. 3. His connexions in the way of support. His wants seem to depend upon four circumstances. 1. His habits of expense. 2. His

20 Pecuniary circumstances.

connexions in the way of burthen. 3. Any present casual demand he may have. 4. The strength of his expectation. By a man's property is to be understood, whatever he has in store independent of his labour. By the profit of his labour is to be understood the growing profit. As to labour, it may be either of the body principally, or of the mind principally, or of both indifferently: nor does it matter in what manner, nor on what subject, it be applied, so it produce a profit. By a man's connexions in the way of support, are to be understood the pecuniary assistances, of whatever kind, which he is in a way of receiving from any persons who, on whatever account, and in whatever proportion, he has reason to expect should contribute *gratis* to his maintenance: such as his parents, patrons, and relations. It seems manifest, that a man can have no other means than these. What he uses, he must have either of his own, or from other people: if from other people, either *gratis* or for a price. As to habits of expense, it is well known, that a man's desires are governed in a great degree by his habits. Many are the cases in which desire (and consequently the pain of privation connected with it)[1] would not even subsist at all, but for previous enjoyment. By a man's connexions in the way of burthen, are to be understood whatever expense he has reason to look upon himself as bound to be at in the support of those who by law, or the customs of the world, are warranted in looking up to him for assistance; such as children, poor relations, superannuated servants, and any other dependents whatsoever. As to present casual demand, it is manifest, that there are occasions on which a given sum will be worth infinitely more to a man than the same sum would at another time: where, for example, in a case of extremity, a man stands in need of extraordinary medical assistance: or wants money to carry on a law-suit, on which his all depends: or has got a livelihood waiting for him in a distant country, and wants money for the charges of conveyance. In such cases, any piece of good or ill fortune, in the pecuniary way, might have a very different effect from what it would have at any other time. With regard to strength of expectation; when one man expects to gain or to keep a thing which another does not, it is plain the circumstance of not having

1 See Chap. v [Pleasures and Pains].

it will affect the former very differently from the latter; who, indeed, commonly, will not be affected by it at all.

26. (21) Under the head of a man's connexions in the way of sympathy, I would bring to view the number and description of the persons in whose welfare he takes such a concern, as that the idea of their happiness should be productive of pleasure, and that of their unhappiness of pain to him: for instance, a man's wife, his children, his parents, his near relations, and intimate friends. This class of person, it is obvious, will for the most part include the two classes by which his pecuniary circumstances are affected: those, to wit, from whose means he may expect support, and those whose wants operate on him as a burthen. But it is obvious, that besides these, it may very well include others, with whom he has no such pecuniary connexion: and even with regard to these, it is evident that the pecuniary dependence, and the union of affections, are circumstances perfectly distinguishable. Accordingly, the connexions here in question, independently of any influence they may have on a man's pecuniary circumstances, have an influence on the effect of any exciting causes whatsoever. The tendency of them is to increase a man's general sensibility; to increase, on the one hand, the pleasure produced by all pleasurable causes; on the other, the pain produced by all afflictive ones. When any pleasurable incident happens to a man, he naturally, in the first moment, thinks of the pleasure it will afford immediately to himself: presently afterwards, however (except in a few cases, which is not worth while here to insist on) he begins to think of the pleasure which his friends will feel upon their coming to know of it: and this secondary pleasure is commonly no mean addition to the primary one. First comes the self-regarding pleasure: then comes the idea of the pleasure of sympathy, which you suppose that pleasure of yours will give birth to in the bosom of your friend: and this idea excites again in yours a new pleasure of sympathy, grounded upon his. The first pleasure issuing from your own bosom, as it were from a radiant point, illuminates the bosom of your friend: reverberated from thence, it is reflected with augmented warmth to the point from whence it first proceeded: and so it is with pains.[1]

21
Connexions
in the way
of
sympathy.

---

1   This is one reason why legislators in general like better to have married people

Nor does this effect depend wholly upon affection. Among near relations, although there should be no kindness, the pleasures and pains of the moral sanction are quickly propagated by a peculiar kind of sympathy: no article, either of honour or disgrace, can well fall upon a man, without extending to a certain distance within the circle of his family. What reflects honour upon the father, reflects honour upon the son: what reflects disgrace, disgrace. The *cause* of this singular and seemingly unreasonable circumstance (that is, its analogy to the rest of the phenomena of the human mind,) belongs not to the present purpose. It is sufficient if the effect be beyond dispute.

22
*Connexions
in the
way of
antipathy.*

27. (22) Of a man's connexions in the way of antipathy, there needs not anything very particular to be observed. Happily there is no primeval and constant source of antipathy in human nature, as there is of sympathy. There are no permanent sets of persons who are naturally and of course the objects of antipathy to a man, as there are who are the objects of the contrary affection. Sources, however, but too many, of antipathy, are apt to spring up upon various occasions during the course of a man's life: and whenever they do, this circumstance may have a very considerable influence on the effects of various exciting causes. As on the one hand, a punishment, for instance, which tends to separate a man from those with whom he is connected in the way of sympathy, so on the other hand, one which tends to force him into the company of those with whom he is connected in the way of antipathy, will, on that account, be so much the more distressing. It is to be observed, that sympathy itself multiplies the sources of antipathy. Sympathy for your friend gives birth to antipathy on *your* part against all those who are objects of antipathy, as well as to sympathy for those who are objects of sympathy to *him*. In the same manner does antipathy multiply the sources of sympathy; though commonly perhaps with rather a less degree of efficacy.

---

to deal with than single; and people that have children than such as are childless. It is manifest that the stronger and more numerous a man's connexions in the way of sympathy are, the stronger is the hold which the law has upon him. A wife and children are so many pledges a man gives to the world for his good behaviour.

Antipathy against your enemy is apt to give birth to sympathy on *your* part towards those who are objects of antipathy, as well as to antipathy against those who are objects of sympathy, to *him*.

28. (23). Thus much for the circumstances by which the effect of any exciting cause may be influenced, when applied upon any given occasion, at any given period. But besides these supervening incidents, there are other circumstances relative to a man, that may have their influence, and which are coeval to his birth. In the first place, it seems to be universally agreed, that in the original frame or texture of every man's body, there is a something which, independently of all subsequently intervening circumstances, renders him liable to be affected by causes producing bodily pleasure or pain, in a manner different from that in which another man would be affected by the same causes. To the catalogue of circumstances influencing a man's sensibility, we may therefore add his original or radical frame, texture, constitution, or temperament of body. *23 Radical frame of body.*

29. (24) In the next place, it seems to be pretty well agreed, that there is something also in the original frame or texture of every man's mind, which, independently of all exterior and subsequently intervening circumstances, and even of his radical frame of body, makes him liable to be differently affected by the same exciting causes, from what another man would be. To the catalogue of circumstances influencing a man's sensibility, we may therefore further add his original or radical frame, texture, constitution or temperament of mind.[1] *24 Radical frame of mind.*

30. It seems pretty certain, all this while, that a man's sensibility to causes producing pleasure or pain, even of mind, may depend in a considerable degree upon his original and acquired frame of body. But we have no reason to think that it can depend altogether upon that frame: since, on the one hand, we see persons whose frame of body is as much alike as can be conceived, *This distinct from the circumstances of frame of body:*

---

1 The characteristic circumstances whereby one man's frame of body or mind, considered at any given period, stands distinguished from that of another, have been comprised by metaphysicians and physiologists under the name *idiosyncrasy*, from ιδιος, peculiar, and συνκρασις, composition.

differing very considerably in respect of their mental frame: and, on the other hand, persons whose frame of mind is as much alike as can be conceived, differing very conspicuously in regard to their bodily frame.[1]

– and from all others. 31. It seems indisputable also, that the different sets of external occurrences that may befall a man in the course of his life, will make great differences in the subsequent texture of his mind at any given period: yet still those differences are not solely to be attributed to such occurrences. Equally far from the truth seems that opinion to be (if any such be maintained) which attributes all to nature, and that which attributes all to education. The two circumstances will therefore still remain distinct, as well from one another, as from all others.

Yet the result of them is not separately discernible. 32. Distinct however as they are, it is manifest, that at no period in the active part of a man's life can they either of them make their appearance by themselves. All they do is to constitute the latent ground-work which the other supervening circumstances have to work upon: and whatever influence those original principles may have, is so changed and modified, and covered over, as it were, by those other circumstances, as never to be separately discernible. The effects of the one influence are indistinguishably blended with those of the other.

Frame of body indicates, but not certainly, that of mind. 33. The emotions of the body are received, and with reason, as probable indications of the temperature of the mind. But they are far enough from conclusive. A man may exhibit, for instance, the

---

1 Those who maintain, that the mind and the body are one substance, may here object, that upon that supposition the distinction between frame of mind and frame of body is but nominal, and that accordingly there is no such thing as a frame of mind distinct from the frame of body. But granting, for argument-sake, the antecedent, we may dispute the consequence. For if the mind be but a part of the body, it is at any rate of a nature very different from the other parts of the body.

A man's frame of body cannot in any part of it undergo any considerable alteration without its being immediately indicated by phenomena discernible by the senses. A man's frame of mind may undergo very considerable alterations, his frame of body remaining the same to all appearance; that is, for anything that is indicated to the contrary by phenomena cognizable to the senses: meaning those of other men.

exterior appearances of grief, without really grieving at all, or at least in anything near the proportion in which he appears to grieve. Oliver Cromwell, whose conduct indicated a heart more than ordinarily callous, was as remarkably profuse in tears.[1] Many men can command the external appearances of sensibility with very little real feeling.[2] The female sex commonly with greater facility than the male: hence the proverbial expression of a woman's tears. To have this kind of command over one's self, was the characteristic excellence of the orator of ancient times, and is still that of the player in our own.

34. The remaining circumstances may, with reference to those already mentioned, be termed *secondary* influencing circumstances. These have an influence, it is true, on the quantum or bias of a man's sensibility, but it is only by means of the other primary ones. The manner in which these two sets of circumstances are concerned, is such that the primary ones do the business, while the secondary ones lie most open to observation. The secondary ones, therefore, are those which are most heard of; on which account it will be necessary to take notice of them: at the same

Secondary influencing circumstances.

---

1 Hume's Hist.

2 The quantity of the sort of pain, which is called grief, is indeed hardly to be measured by any external indications. It is neither to be measured, for instance, by the quantity of the tears, nor by the number of moments spent in crying. indications rather less equivocal may, perhaps, be afforded by the pulse. A man has not the motions of his heart at command as he has those of the muscles of his face. But the particular significancy of these indications is still very uncertain. All they can express is, that the man is affected; they cannot express in what manner, nor from what cause. To an affection resulting from such or such a cause, he may give an artificial colouring, and attribute it to such or such another cause. To an affection directed in reality to such or such a person as its object, he may give an artificial bias, and represent it as if directed to such or such another object. Tears of rage he may attribute to contrition. The concern he feels at the thoughts of a punishment that awaits him, he may impute to a sympathetic concern for the mischief produced by his offence.

A very tolerable judgment, however, may commonly be formed by a discerning mind, upon laying all the external indications exhibited by a man together, and at the same time comparing them with his actions.

A remarkable instance of the power of the will, over the external indications of sensibility, is to be found in Tacitus's story of the Roman soldier, who raised a mutiny in the camp, pretending to have lost a brother by the lawless cruelty of the General. The truth was, he never had had a brother.

time that it is only by means of the primary ones that their influence can be explained; whereas the influence of the primary ones will be apparent enough, without any mention of the secondary ones.

25 Sex. 35. (25) Among such of the primary modifications of the corporeal frame as may appear to influence the quantum and bias of sensibility, the most obvious and conspicuous ate those which constitute the *sex*. In point of quantity, the sensibility of the female sex appears in general to be greater than that of the male. The health of the female is more delicate than that of the male: in point of strength and hardiness of body, in point of quantity and quality of knowledge, in point of strength of intellectual powers, and firmness of mind, she is commonly inferior: moral, religious, sympathetic, and antipathetic sensibility are commonly stronger in her than in the male. The quality of her knowledge, and the bent of her inclinations, are commonly in many respects different. Her moral biases are also, in certain respects, remarkably different: chastity, modesty, and delicacy, for instance, are prized more than courage in a woman: courage, more than any of those qualities, in a man. The religious biases in the two sexes are not apt to be remarkably different; except that the female is rather more inclined than the male to superstition; that is, to observances not dictated by the principle of utility; a difference that may be pretty well accounted for by some of the before-mentioned circumstances. Her sympathetic biases are in many respects different; for her own offspring all their lives long, and for children in general while young, her affection is commonly stronger than that of the male. Her affections are apt to be less enlarged: seldom expanding themselves so much as to take in the welfare of her country in general, much less that of mankind, or the whole sensitive creation: seldom embracing any extensive class or division, even of her own countrymen, unless it be in virtue of her sympathy for some particular individuals that belong to it. In general, her antipathetic, as well as sympathetic biases, are apt to be less conformable to the principle of utility than those of the male; owing chiefly to some deficiency in point of knowledge, discernment, and comprehension. Her habitual occupations of the amusing kind are apt to be in many respects different from those

of the male. With regard to her connexions in the way of sympathy, there can be no difference. In point of pecuniary circumstances, according to the customs of perhaps all countries, she is in general less independent.

36. (26) Age is of course divided into divers periods, of which the number and limits are by no means uniformly ascertained. One might distinguish it, for the present purpose, into, 1. Infancy. 2. Adolescence. 3. Youth. 4. Maturity. 5. Decline. 6. Decrepitude. It were lost time to stop on the present occasion to examine it at each period, and to observe the indications it gives, with respect to the several primary circumstances just reviewed. Infancy and decrepitude are commonly inferior to the other periods, in point of health, strength, hardiness, and so forth. In infancy, on the part of the female, the imperfections of that sex are enhanced. on the part of the male, imperfections take place mostly similar in quality, but greater in quantity, to those attending the states of adolescence, youth, and maturity in the female. In the stage of decrepitude both sexes relapse into many of the imperfections of infancy. The generality of these observations may easily be corrected upon a particular review.

26 Age.

37. (27) Station, or rank in life, is a circumstance, that, among a civilized people, will commonly undergo a multiplicity of variations. *Ceteris paribus*, the quantum of sensibility appears to be greater in the higher ranks of men than in the lower. The primary circumstances in respect of which this secondary circumstance is apt to induce or indicate a difference, seem principally to be as follows: 1. Quantity and Quality of knowledge. 2. Strength of mind. 3. Bent of inclination. 4. Moral sensibility. 5. Moral biases. 6. Religious sensibility. 7. Religious biases. 8. Sympathetic sensibility. 9. Sympathetic biases. 10. Antipathetic sensibility. 11. Antipathetic biases. 12. Habitual occupations. 13. Nature and productiveness of a man's means of livelihood. 14. Connexions importing profit. 15. Habit of expense. 16. Connexions importing burthen. A man of a certain rank will frequently have a number of dependents besides those whose dependency is the result of natural relationship. As to health, strength, and hardiness, if rank has any influence on these circumstances, it is but in a remote way, chiefly by the influence it may have on its habitual occupations.

27 Rank.

28   38. (28) The influence of education is still more extensive. Educa-
Education.   tion stands upon a footing somewhat different from that of the
circumstances of age, sex, and rank. These words, though the
influence of the circumstances they respectively denote exerts itself
principally, if not entirely, through the medium of certain of the
primary circumstances before mentioned, present, however, each
of them a circumstance which has a separate existence of itself. This
is not the case with the word education: which means nothing any
farther than as it serves to call up to view some one or more of those
primary circumstances. Education may be distinguished into physical and mental; the education of the body and that of the mind:
mental, again, into intellectual and moral; the culture of the
understanding, and the culture of the affections. The education a
man receives, is given to him partly by others, partly by himself. By
education then nothing more can be expressed than the condition
a man is in in respect of those primary circumstances, as resulting
partly from the management and contrivance of others, principally
of those who in the early periods of his life have had dominion over
him, partly from his own. To the physical part of his education,
belong the circumstances of health, strength, and hardiness: sometimes, by accident, that of bodily imperfection; as where by
intemperance or negligence an irreparable mischief happens to his
person. To the intellectual part, those of quantity and quality of
knowledge, and in some measure perhaps those of firmness of mind
and steadiness. To the moral part, the bent of his inclinations, the
quantity and quality of his moral, religious, sympathetic, and
antipathetic sensibility: to all three branches indiscriminately, but
under the superior control of external occurrences, his habitual
recreations, his property, his means of livelihood, his connexions in
the way of profit and of burthen, and his habits of expense. With
respect indeed to all these points, the influence of education is
modified, in a manner more or less apparent, by that of exterior
occurrences; and in a manner scarcely at all apparent, and altogether out of the reach of calculation, by the original texture and
constitution as well of his body as of his mind.

29   39. (29) Among the external circumstances by which the influence
Climate.   of education is modified, the principal are those which come
under the head of *climate*. This circumstance places itself in front,

and demands a separate denomination, not merely on account of the magnitude of its influence, but also on account of its being conspicuous to everybody, and of its applying indiscriminately to great numbers at a time. This circumstance depends for its *essence* upon the situation of that part of the earth which is in question, with respect to the course taken by the whole planet in its revolution round the sun: but for its *influence* it depends upon the condition of the bodies which compose the earth's surface at that part, principally upon the quantities of sensible heat at different periods, and upon the density, and purity, and dryness or moisture of the circumambient air. Of the so often mentioned primary circumstances, there are few of which the production is not influenced by this secondary one; partly by its manifest effects upon the body; partly by its less perceptible effects upon the mind. In hot climates men's health is apt to be more precarious than in cold: their strength and hardiness less: their vigour, firmness, and steadiness of mind less: and thence indirectly their quantity of knowledge: the bent of their inclinations different: most remarkably so in respect of their superior propensity to sexual enjoyments, and in respect of the earliness of the period at which that propensity begins to manifest itself: their sensibilities of all kinds more intense: their habitual occupations savouring more of sloth than of activity: their radical frame of body less strong, probably, and less hardy: their radical frame of mind less vigorous, less firm, less steady.

40. (30) Another article in the catalogue of secondary circumstances, is that of *race* or *lineage*: the national race or lineage a man issues from. This circumstance, independently of that of climate, will commonly make some difference in point of radical frame of mind and body. A man of negro race, born in France or England, is a very different being, in many respects, from a man of French or English race. A man of Spanish race, born in Mexico or Peru, is at the hour of his birth a different sort of being, in many respects, from a man of the original Mexican or Peruvian race. This circumstance, as far as it is distinct from climate, rank, and education, and from the two just mentioned, operates chiefly through the medium of moral, religious, sympathetic, and antipathetic biases.

30
Lineage.

31 *Govern-* 41. (31) The last circumstance but one, is that of government: the
ment. government a man lives under at the time in question; or rather
that under which he has been accustomed most to live. This
circumstance operates principally through the medium of education: the magistrate operating in the character of a tutor upon all
the members of the state, by the direction he gives to their hopes
and to their fears. Indeed under a solicitous and attentive
government, the ordinary preceptor, nay even the parent himself,
is but a deputy, as it were, to the magistrate: whose controlling
influence, different in this respect from that of the ordinary
preceptor, dwells with a man to his life's end. The effects of the
peculiar power of the magistrate are seen more particularly in the
influence it exerts over the quantum and bias of men's moral,
religious, sympathetic, and antipathetic sensibilities. Under a
well-constituted, or even under a well-administered though ill-
constituted government, men's moral sensibility is commonly
stronger, and their moral biases more conformable to the dictates
of utility: their religious sensibility frequently weaker, but their
religious biases less unconformable to the dictates of utility: their
sympathetic affections more enlarged, directed to the magistrate
more than to small parties or to individuals, and more to the
whole community than to either: their antipathetic sensibilities
less violent, as being more obsequious to the influence of well-
directed moral biases, and less apt to be excited by that of
ill-directed religious ones: their antipathetic biases more conformable to well-directed moral ones, more apt (in proportion) to
be grounded on enlarged and sympathetic than on narrow and
self-regarding affections, and accordingly, upon the whole, more
conformable to the dictates of utility.

32 *Religious* 42. (32) The last circumstance is that of religious profession: the
profession. religious profession a man is of: the religious fraternity of which
he is a member. This circumstance operates principally through
the medium of religious sensibility and religious biases. It operates, however, as an indication more or less conclusive, with
respect to several other circumstances. With respect to some,
scarcely but through the medium of the two just mentioned: this
is the case with regard to the quantum and bias of a man's moral,
sympathetic, and antipathetic sensibility: perhaps in some cases

with regard to quantity and quality of knowledge, strength of intellectual powers, and bent of inclination. With respect to others, it may operate immediately of itself: this seems to be the case with regard to a man's habitual occupations, pecuniary circumstances, and connexions in the way of sympathy and antipathy. A man who pays very little inward regard to the dictates of the religion which he finds it necessary to profess, may find it difficult to avoid joining in the ceremonies of it, and bearing a part in the pecuniary burthens it imposes.[1] By the force of habit and example he may even be led to entertain a partiality for persons of the same profession, and a proportionable antipathy against those of a rival one. In particular, the antipathy against persons of different persuasions is one of the last points of religion which men part with. Lastly, it is obvious, that the religious profession a man is of cannot but have a considerable influence on his education. But, considering the import of the term education, to say this is perhaps no more than saying in other words what has been said already.

43. These circumstances, all or many of them, will need to be attended to as often as upon any occasion any account is taken of any quantity of pain or pleasure, as resulting from any cause. Has any person sustained an injury? They will need to be considered in estimating the mischief of the offence. Is satisfaction to be made to him? They will need to be attended to in adjusting the *quantum* of that satisfaction. Is the injurer to be punished? They will need to be attended to in estimating the force of the impression that will be made on him by any given punishment. *Use of the preceding observations.*

44. It is to be observed, that though they seem all of them, on some account or other, to merit a place in the catalogue, they are not all of equal use in practice. Different articles among them are *How far the circumstances in question can be taken into account.*

---

1 The ways in which a religion may lessen a man's means, or augment his wants, are various. Sometimes it will prevent him from making a profit of his money: sometimes from setting his hand to labour. Sometimes it will oblige him to buy dearer food instead of cheaper: sometimes to purchase useless labour: sometimes to pay men for not labouring: sometimes to purchase trinkets, on which imagination alone has set a value: sometimes to purchase exemptions from punishment, or titles to felicity in the world to come.

applicable to different causes. Of those that may influence the effect of the same exciting cause, some apply indiscriminately to whole classes of persons together; being applicable to all, without any remarkable difference in degree: these may be directly and pretty fully provided for by the legislator. This is the case, for instance, with the primary circumstances of bodily imperfection, and insanity: with the secondary circumstance of sex: perhaps with that of age: at any rate with those of rank, of climate, of lineage, and of religious profession. Others, however they may apply to whole classes of persons, yet in their application to different individuals are susceptible of perhaps an indefinite variety of degrees. These cannot be fully provided for by the legislator; but, as the existence of them, in every sort of case, is capable of being ascertained, and the degree in which they take place is capable of being measured, provision may be made for them by the judge, or other executive magistrate; to whom the several individuals that happen to be concerned may be made known. This is the case, 1. With the circumstance of health. 2. In some sort with that of strength. 3. Scarcely with that of hardiness: still less with those of quantity and quality of knowledge, strength of intellectual powers, firmness or steadiness of mind; except in as far as a man's condition, in respect of those circumstances, may be indicated by the secondary circumstances of sex, age, or rank: hardly with that of bent of inclination, except in as far as that latent circumstance is indicated by the more manifest one of habitual occupations: hardly with that of a man's moral sensibility or biases, except in as far as they may be indicated by his sex, age, rank, and education: not at all with his religious sensibility and religious biases, except in as far as they may be indicated by the religious profession he belongs to: not at all with the quantity or quality of his sympathetic or antipathetic sensibilities, except in as far as they may be presumed from his sex, age, rank, education, lineage, or religious profession. It is the case, however, with his habitual occupations, with his pecuniary circumstances, and with his connexions in the way of sympathy. Of others, again, either the existence cannot be ascertained, or the degree cannot be measured. These, therefore, cannot be taken into account, either by the legislator or the executive magistrate. Accordingly, they would have no claim to be taken notice of, were it not for those secondary circumstances by which they are indicated, and whose influence could not well be understood without them. What these are has been already mentioned.

45. It has already been observed, that different articles in this list of circumstances apply to different exciting causes: the circumstance of bodily strength, for instance, has scarcely any influence of itself (whatever it may have in a roundabout way, and by accident) on the effect of an incident which should increase or diminish the quantum of a man's property. It remains to be considered, what the exciting causes are with which the legislator has to do. These may, by some accident or other, be any whatsoever: but those which he has principally to do, are those of the painful or afflictive kind. With pleasurable ones he has little to do, except now and then by accident: the reasons of which may be easily enough perceived, at the same time that it would take up too much room to unfold them here. The exciting causes with which he has principally to do, are, on the one hand, the mischievous acts, which it is his business to prevent; on the other hand, the punishments, by the terror of which it is his endeavour to prevent them. Now of these two sets of exciting causes, the latter only is of his production: being produced partly by his own special appointment, partly in conformity to his general appointment, by the special appointment of the judge. For the legislator, therefore, as well as for the judge, it is necessary (if they would know what it is they are doing when they are appointing punishment) to have an eye to all these circumstances. For the legislator, lest, meaning to apply a certain quantity of punishment to all persons who shall put themselves in a given predicament, he should unawares apply to some of those persons much more or much less than he himself intended: for the judge, lest, in applying to a particular person a particular measure of punishment, he should apply much more or much less than was intended, perhaps by himself, and at any rate by the legislator. They ought each of them, therefore, to have before him, on the one hand, a list of the several circumstances by which sensibility may be influenced; on the other hand, a list of the several species and degrees of punishment which they purpose to make use of: and then, by making a comparison between the two, to form a detailed estimate of the influence of each of the

To what exciting causes there is most occasion to apply them.

circumstances in question, upon the effect of each species and degree of punishment.

There are two plans or orders of distribution, either of which might be pursued in the drawing up this estimate. The one is to make the name of the circumstance take the lead, and under it to represent the different influences it exerts over the effects of the several modes of punishment: the other is to make the name of the punishment take the lead, and under it to represent the different influences which are exerted over the effects of it by the several circumstances above mentioned. Now of these two sorts of objects, the punishment is that to which the intention of the legislator is directed in the first instance. This is of his own creation, and will be whatsoever he thinks fit to make it: the influencing circumstance exists independently of him, and is what it is whether he will or no. What he has occasion to do is to establish a certain species and degree of punishment: and it is only with reference to that punishment that he has occasion to make any inquiry concerning any of the circumstances here in question. The latter of the two plans therefore is that which appears by far the most useful and commodious. But neither upon the one nor the other plan can any such estimate be delivered here.[1]

Analytical view of the circumstances influencing sensibility. 46. Of the several circumstances contained in this catalogue, it may be of use to give some sort of analytic view; in order that it may be the more easily discovered if any which ought to have been inserted are omitted; and that, with regard to those which are inserted, it may be seen how they differ and agree.

1 This is far from being a visionary proposal, not reducible to practice. I speak from experience, having actually drawn up such an estimate, though upon the least commodious of the two plans, and before the several circumstances in question had been reduced to the precise number and order in which they are here enumerated. This is a part of the matter destined for another work. See Chap. xiii [Cases unmeet], par. 2. Note. There are some of these circumstances that bestow particular denominations on the persons they relate to: thus, from the circumstance of bodily imperfections, persons are denominated, deaf, dumb, blind, and so forth: from the circumstance of insanity, idiots, and maniacs: from the circumstance of age, infants: for all which classes of persons particular provision is made in the Code. See B.I. tit. [Exemptions]. Persons thus distinguished will form so many articles in the *catalogus personarum privilegiatarum*. See Appendix tit. [Composition].

In the first place, they may be distinguished into *primary* and *secondary*: those may be termed primary, which operate immediately of themselves: those secondary, which operate not but by the medium of the former. To this latter head belong the circumstances of sex, age, station in life, education, climate, lineage, government, and religious profession: the rest are primary. These again are either *connate* or *adventitious*: those which are connate, are radical frame of body and radical frame of mind. Those which are adventitious, are either *personal*, or *exterior*. The personal, again, concern either a man's *dispositions*, or his *actions*. Those which concern his dispositions, concern either his *body* or his *mind*. Those which concern his body are health, strength, hardiness, and bodily imperfection. Those which concern his mind, again, concern either his *understanding* or his *affections*. To the former head belong the circumstances of quantity and quality of knowledge, strength of understanding, and insanity. To the latter belong the circumstances of firmness of mind, steadiness, bent of inclination, moral sensibility, moral biases, religious sensibility, religious biases, sympathetic sensibility, sympathetic biases, antipathetic sensibility, and antipathetic biases. Those which regard his actions, are his habitual occupations. Those which are exterior to him, regard either the *things* or the *persons* which he is concerned with; under the former head come his pecuniary circumstances;[1] under the latter, his connexions in the way of sympathy and antipathy.

---

1 As to man's pecuniary circumstances, the causes on which those circumstances depend, do not come all of them under the same class. The absolute quantum of a man's property does indeed come under the same class with his pecuniary circumstances in general: so does the profit he makes from the occupation which furnishes him with the means of livelihood. But the occupation itself concerns his own person, and comes under the same head as his habitual amusements: as likewise his habits of expense: his connexions in the ways of profit and of burthen, under the same head as his connexions in the way of sympathy: and the circumstances of his present demand for money, and strength of expectation, come under the head of those circumstances relative to his person which regard his affections.

CHAPTER VII

Of Human Actions in General

The demand for punishment depends in part upon the tendency of the act.

1. The business of government is to promote the happiness of the society, by punishing and rewarding. That part of its business which consists in punishing, is more particularly the subject of penal law. In proportion as an act tends to disturb that happiness, in proportion as the tendency of it is pernicious, will be the demand it creates for punishment. What happiness consists of we have already seen: enjoyment of pleasures, security from pains.

Tendency of an act determined by its consequences.

2. The general tendency of an act is more or less pernicious, according to the sum total of its consequences: that is, according to the difference between the sum of such as are good, and the sum of such as are evil.

Material consequences only are to be regarded.

3. It is to be observed, that here, as well as henceforward, wherever consequences are spoken of, such only are meant as are *material*. Of the consequences of any act, the multitude and variety must needs be infinite: but such of them only as are material are worth regarding. Now among the consequences of an act, be they what they may, such only, by one who views them in the capacity of a legislator, can be said to be material,[1] as either consist of pain or pleasure, or have an influence in the production of pain or pleasure.[2]

---

1 Or of *importance*.

2 In certain cases the consequences of an act may be material by serving as evidences indicating the existence of some other material fact, which is even *antecedent* to the act of which they are the consequences: but even here, they are material only because, in virtue of such their evidentiary quality, they have an influence, at a subsequent period of time, in the production of pain and pleasure: for example, by serving as grounds for conviction, and thence for punishment. See tit. [Simple Falsehoods], *verbo* [material].

4. It is also to be observed, that into the account of the consequences of the act, are to be taken not such only as might have ensued, were intention out of the question, but such also as depend upon the connexion there may be between these first-mentioned consequences and the intention. The connexion there is between the intention and certain consequences is, as we shall see hereafter,[1] a means of producing other consequences. In this lies the difference between rational agency and irrational.

These depend in part upon the intention.

5. Now the intention, with regard to the consequences of an act, will depend upon two things: 1. The state of the will or intention, with respect to the act itself: and, 2. The state of the understanding, or perceptive faculties, with regard to the circumstances which it is, or may appear to be, accompanied with. Now with respect to these circumstances, the perceptive faculty is susceptible of three states: consciousness, unconsciousness, and false consciousness. Consciousness, when the party believes precisely those circumstances, and no others, to subsist, which really do subsist: unconsciousness, when he fails of perceiving certain circumstances to subsist, which, however, do subsist: false consciousness, when he believes or imagines certain circumstances to subsist, which in truth do not subsist.

The intention depends as well upon the understanding as the will.

6. In every transaction, therefore, which is examined with a view to punishment, there are four articles to be considered: 1. The *act* itself, which is done. 2. The *circumstances* in which it is done. 3. The *intentionality* that may have accompanied it. 4. The *consciousness*, unconsciousness, or false consciousness, that may have accompanied it.

What regards the act and the circumstances will be the subject of the present chapter: what regards intention and consciousness, that of the two succeeding.

In an action are to be considered 1. The act. 2. The circumstances. 3. The intentionality. 4. The consciousness.

7. There are also two other articles on which the general tendency of an act depends: and on that, as well as on other accounts, the demand which it creates for punishment. These are, 1. The particular *motive* or motives which gave birth to it. 2. The

5. The motives. 6. The disposition.

---

1 See B.I. tit. [Exemptions] and tit. [Extenuations].

general *disposition* which it indicates. These articles will be the subject of two other chapters.

Acts positive and negative. 8. Acts may be distinguished in several ways, for several purposes.

They may be distinguished, in the first place, into *positive* and *negative*. By positive are meant such as consist in motion or exertion: by negative, such as consist in keeping at rest; that is, in forbearing to move or exert one's self in such and such circumstances. Thus, to strike is a positive act: not to strike on a certain occasion, a negative one. Positive acts are styled also acts of commission; negative, acts of omission or forbearance.[1]

Negative acts may be so relatively or absolutely. 9. Such acts, again, as are negative, may either be *absolutely* so, or *relatively*: absolutely, when they import the negation of all positive agency whatsoever, for instance, not to strike at all: relatively, when they import the negation of such or such a particular mode of agency; for instance, not to strike such a person or such a thing, or in such a direction.

Negative acts may be expressed positively; and vice-versa. 10. It is to be observed, that the nature of the act, whether positive or negative, is not to be determined immediately by the form of the discourse made use of to express it. An act which is positive in its nature may be characterized by a negative expression: thus, not to be at rest, is as much as to say to move. So also an act, which is negative in its nature, may be characterized by a

---

1 The distinction between positive and negative acts runs through the whole system of offences, and sometimes makes a material difference with regard to their consequences. To reconcile us the better to the extensive, and, as it may appear on some occasions, the inconsistent signification here given to the word *act*, it may be considered, 1. That in many cases, where no exterior or overt act is exercised, the state which the mind is in at the time when the supposed act is said to happen, is as truly and directly the result of the will, as any exterior act, how plain and conspicuous soever. The not revealing a conspiracy, for instance, may be as perfectly the act of the will, as the joining in it. In the next place, that even though the mind should never have had the incident in question in contemplation (insomuch that the event of its not happening should not have been so much as obliquely intentional) still the state the person's mind was in at the time when, if he *had* so willed, the incident might have happened, is in many cases productive of as material consequences; and not only as likely, but as fit to call for the interposition of other agents, as the opposite one. Thus, when a tax is imposed, your not paying it is an act which at any rate must be punished in a certain manner, whether you happened to think of paying it or not.

positive expression: thus, to forbear or omit to bring food to a person in certain circumstances, is signified by the single and positive term *to starve*.

11. In the second place, acts may be distinguished into *external* and *internal*. By external, are meant corporal acts; acts of the body: by internal, mental acts; acts of the mind. Thus, to strike is an external or exterior[1] act: to intend to strike, an internal or interior one.

Acts external and internal.

12. Acts of *discourse* are a sort of mixture of the two: external acts, which are no ways material, nor attended with any consequences, any farther than as they serve to express the existence of internal ones. To speak to another to strike, to write to him to strike, to make signs to him to strike, are all so many acts of discourse.

Acts of discourse, what.

13. Third, Acts that are external may be distinguished into *transitive* and *intransitive*. Acts may be called transitive, when the motion is communicated from the person of the agent to some foreign body: that is, to such a foreign body on which the effects of it are considered as being *material*; as where a man runs against you, or throws water in your face. Acts may be called intransitive, when the motion is communicated to no other body, on which the effects of it are regarded as material, than some part of the same person in whom it originated: as where a man runs, or washes himself.[2]

External acts may be transitive or intransitive.

14. An act of the transitive kind may be said to be in its *commencement*, or in the *first* stage of its progress, while the motion is confined to the person of the agent, and has not yet been communicated to any foreign body, on which the effects of it can

A transitive act, its commencement, termination, and immediate progress.

---

1 An exterior act is also called by lawyers *overt*.

2 The distinction is well known to the latter grammarians: it is with them indeed that it took its rise: though by them it has been applied rather to the names than to the things themselves. To verbs, signifying transitive acts, as here described, they have given the name of transitive verbs: those significative of intransitive acts they have termed intransitive. These last are still more frequently called *neuter*; that is, *neither* active nor passive. The appellation seems improper: since, instead of their being *neither*, they are both in one.

To the class of acts that are here termed intransitive, belong those which constitute the 3rd class in the system of offences. See Chap. [Division] and B.I. tit. [Self regarding Offences].

be material. It may be said to be in its *termination*, or to be in the last stage of its progress, as soon as the motion or impulse has been communicated to some such foreign body. It may be said to be in the *middle* or intermediate stage or stages of its progress, while the motion, having passed from the person of the agent, has not yet been communicated to any such foreign body. Thus, as soon as a man has lifted up his hand to strike, the act he performs in striking you is in its commencement: as soon as his hand has reached you, it is in its termination. If the act be the motion of a body which is separated from the person of the agent before it reaches the object, it may be said, during that interval, to be in its intermediate progress,[1] or in *gradu mediativo*: as in the case where a man throws a stone or fires a bullet at you.

An intransitive act, its commencement, and termination.

15. An act of the intransitive kind may be said to be in its commencement, when the motion or impulse is as yet confined to the member or organ in which it originated; and has not yet been communicated to any member or organ that is distinguishable from the former. It may be said to be in its termination, as soon as it has been applied to any other part of the same person. Thus, where a man poisons himself while he is lifting up the poison to his mouth, the act is in its commencement: as soon as it has reached his lips, it is in its termination.[2]

Acts transient and continued.

16. In the third place, acts may be distinguished into *transient* and *continued*. Thus, to strike is a transient act: to lean, a continued one. To buy, a transient act: to keep in one's possession, a continued one.

Difference between a continued act and a repetition of acts.

17. In strictness of speech there is a difference between a *continued* act and a *repetition* of acts. It is a repetition of acts, when there are intervals filled up by acts of different natures: a continued act, when there are no such intervals. Thus, to lean, is one continued act: to keep striking, a repetition of acts.

Difference between a repetition of acts and a habit.

18. There is a difference, again, between a *repetition* of acts, and a *habit* or *practice*. The term repetition of acts may be employed, let

---

1 Or *in its migration*, or *in transitu*.

2 These distinctions will be referred to in the next chapter: Chap. viii [Intentionality]: and applied to practice in B. I. tit. [Extenuations].

the acts in question be separated by ever such short intervals, and let the sum total of them occupy ever so short a space of time. The term habit is not employed but when the acts in question are supposed to be separated by long-continued intervals, and the sum total of them to occupy a considerable space of time. It is not (for instance) the drinking ever so many times, nor ever so much at a time, in the course of the same sitting, that will constitute a habit of drunkenness: it is necessary that such sittings themselves be frequently repeated. Every habit is a repetition of acts; or, to speak more strictly, when a man has frequently repeated such and such acts after considerable intervals, he is said to have persevered in or contracted a habit: but every repetition of acts is not a habit.[1]

19. Fourth, acts may be distinguished into *indivisible* and *divisible*. Indivisible acts are merely imaginary: they may be easily conceived, but can never be known to be exemplified. Such as are divisible may be so, with regard either to matter or to motion. An act indivisible with regard to matter, is the motion or rest of one single atom of matter. An act indivisible, with regard to motion, is the motion of any body, from one single atom of space to the next to it. *Acts are indivisible, or divisible; and divisible, as well with regard to matter as to motion.*

Fifth, acts may be distinguished into *simple* and *complex*: simple, such as the act of striking, the act of leaning, or the act of drinking, above instanced: complex, consisting each of a multitude of simple acts, which, though numerous and heterogeneous, derive a sort of unity from the relation they bear to some common design or end; such as the act of giving a dinner, the act of maintaining a child, the act of exhibiting a triumph, the act of bearing arms, the act of holding a court, and so forth.

20. It has been every now and then made a question, what it is in such a case that constitutes *one* act: where one act has ended, and another act has begun: whether what has happened has been one act or many.[2] These questions, it is now evident, may frequently *Caution respecting the ambiguity of language.*

---

1 A habit, it should seem, can hardly in strictness be termed an aggregate of acts: acts being a sort of real archetypal entities, and habits a kind of fictitious entities or imaginary beings, supposed to be constituted by, or to result as it were out of, the former.

2 Distinctions like these come frequently in question in the course of Procedure.

be answered, with equal propriety, in opposite ways: and if there be any occasion on which they can be answered only in one way, the answer will depend upon the nature of the occasion, and the purpose for which the question is proposed. A man is wounded in two fingers at one stroke – Is it one wound or several? A man is beaten at 12 o'clock, and again at 8 minutes after 12 – Is it one beating or several? You beat one man, and instantly in the same breath you beat another – Is this one beating or several? In any of these cases it may be *one*, perhaps, as to some purposes, and *several* as to others. These examples are given, that men may be aware of the ambiguity of language: and neither harass themselves with unsolvable doubts, nor one another with interminable disputes.

Circum-stances are to be considered. 21. So much with regard to acts considered in themselves: we come now to speak of the *circumstances* with which they may have been accompanied. These must necessarily be taken into the account before anything can be determined relative to the consequences. What the consequences of an act may be upon the whole can never otherwise be ascertained: it can never be known whether it is beneficial, or indifferent, or mischievous. In some circumstances even to kill a man may be a beneficial act: in others, to set food before him may be a pernicious one.

Circum-stances, what. 22. Now the circumstances of an act, are, what? Any objects[1] whatsoever. Take any act whatsoever, there is nothing in the nature of things that excludes any imaginable object from being a circumstance to it. Any given object may be a circumstance to any other.[2]

Circum-stances material and immaterial. 23. We have already had occasion to make mention for a moment of the *consequences* of an act: these were distinguished into

1 Or entities. See B. II. tit. [Evidence], § [Facts].

2 The etymology of the word circumstance is perfectly characteristic of its import: *circum stantia*, things standing round: objects standing round a given object. I forget what mathematician it was that defined God to be a circle, of which the centre is everywhere, but the circumference nowhere. In like manner the field of circumstances, belonging to any act, may be defined a circle, of which the circumference is nowhere, but of which the act in question is the centre. Now then, as any act may, for the purpose of discourse, be considered as a centre, any other act or object whatsoever may be considered as of the number of those that are standing round it.

material and immaterial. In like manner may the circumstances of it be distinguished. Now *materiality* is a relative term: applied to the consequences of an act, it bore relation to pain and pleasure: applied to the circumstances, it bears relation to the consequences. A circumstance may be said to be material, when it bears a visible relation in point of causality to the consequences: immaterial, when it bears no such visible relation.

24. The consequences of an act are events.[1] A circumstance may be related to an event in point of causality in any one of four ways: 1. In the way of causation or production. 2. In the way of derivation. 3. In the way of collateral connexion. 4. In the way of conjunct influence. It may be said to be related to the event in the way of causation, when it is of the number of those that contribute to the production of such event: in the way of derivation, when it is of the number of the events to the production of which that in question has been contributory: in the way of collateral connexion, where the circumstance in question, and the event in question, without being either of them instrumental in the production of the other, are related, each of them, to some common object, which has been concerned in the production of them both: in the way of conjunct influence, when, whether related in any other way or not, they have both of them concurred in the production of some common consequence.

The circumstances may be related to an event in point of causality, in four ways, viz.:
1 Production.
2 Derivation.
3 Collateral connexion.
4 Conjunct influence

25. An example may be of use. In the year 1628, Villiers, Duke of Buckingham, favourite and minister of Charles I of England, received a wound and died. The man who gave it him was one Felton, who, exasperated at the mal-administration of which that minister was accused, went down from London to Portsmouth, where Buckingham happened then to be, made his way into his anti-chamber, and finding him busily engaged in conversation with a number of people round him, got close to him, drew a knife and stabbed him. In the effort, the assassin's hat fell off, which was found soon after, and, upon searching him, the bloody knife. In the crown of the hat were found scraps of papers, with sentences expressive of the purpose he was come upon. Here then, suppose the event in question is the wound received by

Example. Assassination of Buckingham:

---

1 See B. II. tit. [Evidence], § [Facts].

Buckingham: Felton's drawing out his knife, his making his way into the chamber, his going down to Portsmouth, his conceiving an indignation at the idea of Buckingham's administration, that administration itself, Charles's appointing such a minister, and so on, higher and higher without end, are so many circumstances, related to the event of Buckingham's receiving the wound, in the way of causation or production: the bloodiness of the knife, a circumstance related to the same event in the way of derivation: the finding of the hat upon the ground, the finding the sentences in the hat, and the writing them, so many circumstances related to it in the way of collateral connexion: and the situation and conversations of the people about Buckingham, were circumstances related to the circumstances of Felton's making his way into the room, going down to Portsmouth, and so forth, in the way of conjunct influence; inasmuch as they contributed in common to the event of Buckingham's receiving the wound, by preventing him from putting himself upon his guard upon the first appearance of the intruder.[1]

It is not every event that has circumstances related to it in all those ways.

26. These several relations do not all of them attach upon an event with equal certainty. In the first place, it is plain, indeed, that every event must have some circumstance or other, and in truth, an indefinite multitude of circumstances, related to it in the way of production: it must of course have a still greater multitude of circumstances related to it in the way of collateral connexion. But it does not appear necessary that every event should have circumstances related to it in the way of derivation: nor therefore that it

---

1 The division may be farther illustrated and confirmed by the more simple and particular case of animal generation. To production corresponds paternity: to derivation, filiation: to collateral connexion, collateral consanguinity: to conjunct influence, marriage and copulation.

If necessary, it might be again illustrated by the material image of a chain, such as that which, according to the ingenious fiction of the ancients, is attached to the throne of Jupiter. A section of this chain should then be exhibited by way of specimen, in the manner of the *diagram* of a pedigree. Such a figure I should accordingly have exhibited, had it not been for the apprehension that an exhibition of this sort, while it made the subject a small matter clearer to one man out of a hundred, might, like the mathematical formularies we see sometimes employed for the like purpose, make it more obscure and formidable for the other ninety-nine.

should have any related to it in the way of conjunct influence. But of the circumstances of all kinds which actually do attach upon an event, it is only a very small number that can be discovered by the utmost exertion of the human faculties: it is a still smaller number that ever actually do attract our notice: when occasion happens, more or fewer of them will be discovered by a man in proportion to the strength, partly of his intellectual powers, partly of his inclination.[1] It appears therefore that the multitude and description of such of the circumstances belonging to an act, as may appear to be material, will be determined by two considerations: 1. By the nature of things themselves. 2. By the strength or weakness of the faculties of those who happen to consider them.

27. Thus much it seemed necessary to premise in general concerning acts, and their circumstances, previously to the consideration of the particular sorts of acts with their particular circumstances, with which we shall have to do in the body of the work. An act of some sort or other is necessarily included in the notion of every offence. Together with this act, under the notion of the same offence, are included certain circumstances: which circumstances enter into the essence of the offence, contribute by their conjunct influence to the production of its consequences, and in conjunction with the act are brought into view by the name by which it stands distinguished. These we shall have occasion to distinguish hereafter by the name

Use of this chapter.

---

1 The more remote a connexion of this sort is, of course the more obscure. It will often happen that a connexion, the idea of which would at first sight appear extravagant and absurd, shall be rendered highly probable, and indeed indisputable, merely by the suggestion of a few intermediate circumstances.

At Rome, 390 years before the Christian era, a goose sets up a cackling: two thousand years afterwards a king of France is murdered. To consider these two events, and nothing more, what can appear more extravagant than the notion that the former of them should have had any influence on the production of the latter? Fill up the gap, bring to mind a few intermediate circumstances, and nothing can appear more probable. It was the cackling of a parcel of geese, at the time the Gauls had surprised the Capitol, that saved the Roman commonwealth: had it not been for the ascendancy that commonwealth acquired afterwards over most of the nations of Europe, amongst others over France, the Christian religion, humanly speaking, could not have established itself in the manner it did in that country. Grant then, that such a man as Henry IV would have existed, no man, however, would have had those motives, by which Ravaillac, misled by a mischievous notion concerning the dictates of that religion, was prompted to assassinate him.

of *criminative* circumstances.[1] Other circumstances again entering into combination with the act and the former set of circumstances, are productive of still farther consequences. These additional consequences, if they are of the beneficial kind, bestow, according to the value they bear in that capacity, upon the circumstances to which they owe their birth the appellation of *exculpative*[2] or *extenuative* circumstances:[3] if of the mischievous kind, they bestow on them the appellation of *aggravative* circumstances.[4] Of all these different sets of circumstances, the criminative are connected with the consequences of the original offence, in the way of production; with the act, and with one another, in the way of conjunct influence: the consequences of the original offence with them, and with the act respectively, in the way of derivation: the consequences of the modified offence, with the criminative, exculpative, and extenuative circumstances respectively, in the way also of derivation: these different sets of circumstances, with the consequences of the modified act or offence, in the way of production: and with one another (in respect of the consequences of the modified act or offence) in the way of conjunct influence. Lastly, whatever circumstances can be seen to be connected with the consequences of the offence, whether directly in the way of derivation, or obliquely in the way of collateral affinity (to wit, in virtue of its being connected, in the way of derivation, with some of the circumstances with which they stand connected in the same manner) bear a *material* relation to the offence in the way of evidence, they may accordingly be styled *evidentiary* circumstances, and may become of use, by being held forth upon occasion as so many proofs, indications, or evidences of its having been committed.[5]

1 See B. I. tit. [Crim. circumstances].
2 See B. I. tit. [Justifications].
3 See B. I. tit. [Extenuations].
4 See B. I. tit. [Aggravations].
5 See B. I. tit. [Accessory Offences] and B. II. tit. [Evidence].
   It is evident that this analysis is equally applicable to incidents of a purely physical nature, as to those in which moral agency is concerned. If therefore it be just and useful here, it might be found not impossible, perhaps, to find some use for it in natural philosophy.

CHAPTER VIII

Of Intentionality

1. So much with regard to the two first of the articles upon which the evil tendency of an action may depend: *viz.*, the act itself, and the general assemblage of the circumstances with which it may have been accompanied. We come now to consider the ways in which the particular circumstance of *intention* may be concerned in it.

Recapitulation.

2. First, then, the intention or will may regard either of two objects: 1. The act itself: or, 2. Its consequences. Of these objects, that which the intention regards may be styled *intentional*. If it regards the act, then the act may be said to be intentional:[1] if the consequences, so then also may the consequences. If it regards both the act and consequences, the whole *action* may be said to be intentional. Whichever of those articles is not the object of the intention, may of course be said to be *unintentional*.

The intention may regard, 1. That act: or, 2. The consequences.

3. The act may very easily be intentional without the consequences; and often is so. Thus, you may intend to touch a man

It may regard the act without any of the consequences.

1 On this occasion the words *voluntary* and *involuntary* are commonly employed. These, however, I purposely abstain from, on account of the extreme ambiguity of their signification. By a voluntary act is meant sometimes, any act, in the performance of which the will has had any concern at all; in this sense it is synonymous to *intentional*: sometimes such acts only, in the production of which the will has been determined by motives not of a painful nature; in this sense it is synonymous to unconstrained, or *uncoerced*: sometimes such acts only, in the production of which the will has been determined by motives, which, whether of the pleasurable or painful kind, occurred to a man himself, without being suggested by anybody else; in this sense it is synonymous to *spontaneous*. The sense of the word involuntary does not correspond completely to that of the word voluntary. Involuntary is used in opposition to intentional; and to unconstrained: but not to spontaneous. It might be of use to confine the signification of the words voluntary and involuntary to one single and very narrow case, which will be mentioned in the next note.

without intending to hurt him: and yet, as the consequences turn out, you may chance to hurt him.

– or the consequences without regarding the act in all its stages. 4. The consequences of an act may also be intentional, without the act's being intentional throughout; that is, without its being intentional in every stage of it: but this is not so frequent a case as the former. You intend to hurt a man, suppose, by running against him, and pushing him down: and you run towards him accordingly: but a second man coming in on a sudden between you and the first man, before you can stop yourself, you run against the second man, and by him push down the first.

– but not without regarding the first stage. 5. But the consequences of an act cannot be intentional, without the act's being itself intentional in at least the first stage. If the act be not intentional in the first stage, it is no act of yours: there is accordingly no intention on your part to produce the consequences: that is to say, the individual consequences. All there can have been on your part is a distant intention to produce other consequences, of the same nature, by some act of yours, at a future time: or else, without any intention, a bare *wish* to see such event take place. The second man, suppose, runs of his own accord against the first, and pushes him down. You had intentions of doing a thing of the same nature: *viz.*, To run against him, and push him down yourself; but you had done nothing in pursuance of those intentions: the individual consequences therefore of the act, which the second man performed in pushing down the first, cannot be said to have been on your part intentional.[1]

---

1 To render the analysis here given of the possible states of the mind in point of intentionality absolutely complete, it must be pushed to such a farther degree of minuteness, as to some eyes will be apt to appear trifling. On this account it seemed advisable to discard what follows, from the text to a place where anyone who thinks proper may pass by it. An act of the body, when of the positive kind, is a motion: now in motion there are always three articles to be considered: 1. The quantity of matter that moves: 2. The direction in which it moves: and, 3. The velocity with which it moves. Correspondent to these three articles, are so many modes of intentionality, with regard to an act, considered as being only in its first stage. To be completely unintentional, it must be unintentional with respect to every one of these three particulars. This is the case with those acts which alone are properly termed *involuntary*: acts, in the performance of which the will has no sort of share: such as the contraction of the heart and arteries.

Upon this principle, acts that are unintentional in their first stage, may be

6. Second. A consequence, when it is intentional, may either be *directly* so, or only *obliquely*. It may be said to be directly or lineally intentional, when the prospect of producing it constituted one of the links in the chain of causes by which the person was determined to do the act. It may be said to be obliquely or collaterally intentional, when, although the consequence was in contemplation, and appeared likely to ensue in case of the act's being performed, yet the prospect of producing such consequence did not constitute a link in the aforesaid chain.

A consequence, when intentional, may be directly so, or obliquely.

7. Third. An incident, which is directly intentional, may either be *ultimately* so, or only *mediately*. It may be said to be ultimately intentional, when it stands last of all exterior events in the aforesaid chain of motives; insomuch that the prospect of the production of such incident, could there be a certainty of its taking place, would be sufficient to determine the will, without the prospect of its producing any other. It may be said to be mediately intentional, and no more, when there is some other incident, the prospect of producing which forms a subsequent link in the same chain: insomuch that the prospect of producing the former would not have operated as a motive, but for the tendency which it seemed to have towards the production of the latter.

When directly, ultimately so, or mediately.

8. Fourth. When an incident is directly intentional, it may either be *exclusively* so, or *inexclusively*. It may be said to be exclusively

When directly intentional, it may be exclusively so, or inexclusively.

---

distinguished into such as are completely unintentional, and such as are incompletely unintentional: and these again may be unintentional, either in point of quantity of matter alone, in point of direction alone, in point of velocity alone, or in any two of these points together.

The example given further on may easily be extended to this part of the analysis, by anyone who thinks it worth the whole.

There seem to be occasions in which even these disquisitions, minute as they may appear, may not be without their use in practice. In the case of homicide, for example, and other corporal injuries, all the distinctions here specified may occur, and in the course of trial may, for some purpose or other, require to be brought to mind, and made the subject of discourse. What may contribute to render the mention of them pardonable, is the use that might possibly be made of them in natural philosophy. In the hands of an expert metaphysician, these, together with the foregoing chapter on human actions, and the section on facts in general, in title Evidence of the Book of Procedure, might, perhaps, be made to contribute something towards an exhaustive analysis of the possible varieties of mechanical inventions.

intentional, when no other but that very individual incident would have answered the purpose, insomuch that no other incident had any share in determining the will to the act in question. It may be said to have been inexclusively[1] intentional, when there was some other incident, the prospect of which was acting upon the will at the same time.

When in-exclusively, it may be con-junctively, dis-junctively or indiscrimin-ately so.

9. Fifth. When an incident is inexclusively intentional, it may be either conjunctively so, disjunctively, or *indiscriminately*. It may be said to be conjunctively intentional with regard to such other incident, when the intention is to produce both: disjunctively, when the intention is to produce either the one or the other indifferently, but not both: indiscriminately, when the intention is indifferently to produce either the one or the other, or both, as it may happen.

When dis-junctively, it may be with or without preference.

10. Sixth. When two incidents are disjunctively intentional, they may be so with or without *preference*. They may be said to be so with preference, when the intention is, that one of them in particular should happen rather than the other: without prefer-ence, when the intention is equally fulfilled, whichever of them happens.[2]

Example.

11. One example will make all this clear. William II, king of England, being out a stag-hunting, received from Sir Walter Tyrrel a wound, of which he died.[3] Let us take this case, and diversify it with a variety of suppositions, correspondent to the distinctions just laid down.

---

1 Or concurrently.

2 There is a difference between the case where an incident is altogether unintentional, and that in which, it being disjunctively intentional with reference to another, the preference is in favour of that other. In the first case, it is not the intention of the party that the incident in question should happen at all: in the latter case, the intention is rather that the other should happen: but if that cannot be, then that this in question should happen rather than that neither should, and that both, at any rate, should not happen.

All these are distinctions to be attended to in the use of the particle *or*: a particle of very ambiguous import, and of great importance in legislation. See Append. tit. [Composition].

3 Hume's Hist.

1   First then, Tyrrel did not so much as entertain a thought of the king's death; or, if he did, looked upon it as an event of which there was no danger. In either of these cases the incident of his killing the king was altogether unintentional.

2   He saw a stag running that way, and he saw the king riding that way at the same time: what he aimed at was to kill the stag: he did not wish to kill the king: at the same time he saw, that if he shot, it was as likely he should kill the king as the stag: yet for all that he shot, and killed the king accordingly. In this case the incident of his killing the king was intentional, but obliquely so.

3   He killed the king on account of the hatred he bore him, and for no other reason than the pleasure of destroying him. In this case the accident of the king's death was not only directly but ultimately intentional.

4   He killed the king, intending fully so to do; not for any hatred he bore him, but for the sake of plundering him when dead. In this case the incident of the king's death was directly intentional, but not ultimately: it was mediately intentional.

5   He intended neither more nor less than to kill the king. He had no other aim nor wish. In this case it was exclusively as well as directly intentional: exclusively, to wit, with regard to every other material incident.

6   Sir Walter shot the king in the right leg, as he was plucking a thorn out of it with his left hand. His intention was, by shooting the arrow into his leg through his hand, to cripple him in both those limbs at the same time. In this case the incident of the king's being shot in the leg was intentional: and that conjunctively with another which did not happen; *viz.*, his being shot in the hand.

7   The intention of Tyrrel was to shoot the king either in the hand or in the leg, but not in both; and rather in the hand than in the leg. In this case the intention of shooting in the hand was disjunctively concurrent, with regard to the other incident, and that with preference.

8   His intention was to shoot the king either in the leg or the hand, whichever might happen: but not in both. In this case the intention was inexclusive, but disjunctively so: yet that, however, without preference.

9   His intention was to shoot the king either in the leg or the hand, or in both, as it might happen. In this case the intention was indiscriminately concurrent, with respect to the two incidents.

Intention- 12. It is to be observed, that an act may be unintentional in any
ality of the stage or stages of it, though intentional in the preceding: and, on
act with the other hand, it may be intentional in any stage or stages of it,
respect to and yet unintentional in the succeeding.[1] But whether it be
its different intentional or no in any preceding stage, is immaterial, with
stages, respect to the consequences, so it be unintentional in the last. The
how far only point, with respect to which it is material, is the proof. The
material. more stages the act is unintentional in, the more apparent it will commonly be, that it was unintentional with respect to the last. If a man, intending to strike you on the cheek, strikes you in the eye, and puts it out, it will probably be difficult for him to prove that it was not his intention to strike you in the eye. It will probably be easier, if his intention was really not to strike you, or even not to strike at all.

Goodness 13. It is frequent to hear men speak of a good intention, of a bad
and intention; of the goodness and badness of a man's intention: a
badness of circumstance on which great stress is generally laid. It is indeed of
intention no small importance, when properly understood: but the import
dismissed. of it is to the last degree ambiguous and obscure. Strictly speaking, nothing can be said to be good or bad, but either in itself; which is the case only with pain or pleasure: or on account of its effects; which is the case only with things that are the causes or preventatives of pain and pleasure. But in a figurative and less proper way of speech, a thing may also be, styled good or bad, in consideration of its cause. Now the effects of an intention to do such or such an act, are the same objects which we have been speaking of under the appellation of its *consequences*: and the causes of intention are called *motives*. A man's intention then on any occasion may be styled good or bad with reference either to the consequences of the act, or with reference to his motives. If it be deemed good or bad in any sense, it must be either because it is deemed to be productive of good or of bad consequences, or

---

1 See Chap. vii [Actions], par. 14.

because it is deemed to originate from a good or from a bad motive. But the goodness or badness of the consequences depend upon the circumstances. Now the circumstances are no objects of the intention. A man intends the act: and by his intention produces the act: but as to the circumstances, he does not intend *them*: he does not, inasmuch as they are circumstances of it, produce them. If by accident there be a few which he has been instrumental in producing, it has been by former intentions, directed to former acts, productive of those circumstances as the consequences: at the time in question he takes them as he finds them. Acts, with their consequences, are objects of the will as well as of the understanding: circumstances, as such, are objects of the understanding only. All he can do with these, as such, is to know or not to know them: in other words, to be conscious of them, or not conscious. To the title of Consciousness belongs what is to be said of the goodness or badness of a man's intention, as resulting from the consequences of the act: and to the head of Motives, what is to be said of his intention, as resulting from the motive.

CHAPTER IX

Of Consciousness

Connexion of this chapter with the foregoing. 1. So far with regard to the ways in which the will or intention may be concerned in the production of any incident: we come now to consider the part which the understanding or perceptive faculty may have borne, with relation to such incident.

Acts advised and unadvised; consciousness, what. 2. A certain act has been done, and that intentionally: that act was attended with certain circumstances: upon these circumstances depended certain of its consequences; and amongst the rest, all those which were of a nature purely physical. Now then, take any one of these circumstances, it is plain, that a man, at the time of doing the act from whence such consequences ensued, may have been either conscious, with respect to this circumstance, or unconscious. In other words, he may either have been aware of the circumstance, or not aware: it may either have been present to his mind, or not present. In the first case, the act may be said to have been an *advised* act, with respect to that circumstance: in the other case, an *unadvised* one

Unadvisedness may regard either existence, or materiality. 3. There are two points, with regard to which an act may have been advised or unadvised: 1. The *existence* of the circumstance itself. 2. The *materiality* of it.[1]

4. It is manifest, that with reference to the time of the act, such circumstance may have been either *present*, *past*, or *future*.

An unadvised act may be heedless, or not heedless. 5. An act which is unadvised, is either *heedless*, or not heedless. It is termed heedless, when the case is thought to be such, that a person of ordinary prudence,[2] if prompted by an ordinary share of

---

1 See Chap. vii [Actions], par. 3.
2 See Chap. vi [Sensibility], par. 12.

benevolence, would have been likely to have bestowed such and so much attention and reflection upon the material circumstances, as would have effectually disposed him to prevent the mischievous incident from taking place: not heedless, when the case is not thought to be such as above mentioned.[1]

6. Again. Whether a man did or did not suppose the existence or materiality of a given circumstance, it may be that he *did* suppose the existence and materiality of some circumstance, which either did not exist, or which, though existing, was not material. In such case the act may be said to be *mis-advised*, with respect to such imagined circumstance: and it may be said, that there has been an erroneous supposition, or a *mis-supposal* in the case.

A mis-advised act, what. — A mis-supposal.

7. Now a circumstance, the existence of which is thus erroneously supposed, may be material either, 1. In the way of prevention: or, 2. In that of compensation. It may be said to be material in the way of prevention, when its effect or tendency, had it existed, would have been to prevent the obnoxious consequences: in the way of compensation, when that effect or tendency would have been to produce other consequences, the beneficialness of which would have outweighed the mischievousness of the others.

The supposed circumstance might have been material in the way either of prevention or compensation.

8. It is manifest that, with reference to the time of the act, such imaginary circumstance may in either case have been supposed either to be *present*, *past*, or *future*.

9. To return to the example exhibited in the preceding chapter.

10 Tyrrel intended to shoot in the direction in which he shot; but be did not know that the king was riding so near that way. In this case the act he performed in shooting, the act of shooting, was unadvised, with respect to the *existence* of the circumstance of the king's being so near riding that way.

11 He knew that the king was riding that way: but at the distance at which the king was, he knew not of the probability there was that the arrow would reach him. In this case the act was unadvised, with respect to the *materiality* of the circumstance.

Example, continued from the last chapter.

1 See B. I. tit. [Extenuations].

12 Somebody had dipped the arrow in poison, without Tyrrel's knowing of it. In this case the act was unadvised, with respect to the existence of a *past* circumstance.

13 At the very instant that Tyrrel drew the bow, the king, being screened from his view by the foliage of some bushes, was riding furiously, in such manner as to meet the arrow in a direct line: which circumstance was also more than Tyrrel knew of. In this case the act was unadvised, with respect to the existence of a *present* circumstance.

14 The king being at a distance from court, could get nobody to dress his wound till the next day; of which circumstance Tyrrel was not aware. In this case the act was unadvised with respect to what was then a *future* circumstance.

15 Tyrrel knew of the king's being riding that way, of his being so near, and so forth; but being deceived by the foliage of the bushes, he thought he saw a bank between the spot from which he shot, and that to which the king was riding. In this case the act was *mis-advised*, proceeding on the *mis-supposal* of a *preventive* circumstance.

16 Tyrrel knew that everything was as above, nor was he deceived by the supposition of any preventive circumstance. But he believed the king to be an usurper: and supposed he was coming up to attack a person whom Tyrrel believed to be the rightful king, and who was riding by Tyrrel's side. In this case the act was also mis-advised, but proceeded on the mis-supposal of a *compensative* circumstance.

In what case consciousness extends the intentionality from the act to the consequences. 10. Let us observe the connexion there is between intentionality and consciousness. When the act itself is intentional, and with respect to the existence of all the circumstances *advised*, as also with respect to the materiality of those circumstances, in relation to a given consequence, and there is no mis-supposal with regard to any preventive circumstance, that consequence must also be intentional: in other words, advisedness, with respect to the circumstances, if clear from the mis-supposal of any preventive circumstance, extends the intentionality from the act to the consequences. Those consequences may be either directly intentional, or only obliquely so: but at any rate they cannot but be intentional.

11. To go on with the example. If Tyrrel intended to shoot in the *Example* direction in which the king was riding up, and knew that the king *continued.* was coming to meet the arrow, and knew the probability there was of his being shot in that same part in which he was shot, or in another as dangerous, and with that same degree of force, and so forth, and was not misled by the erroneous supposition of a circumstance by which the shot would have been prevented from taking place, or any such other preventive circumstance, it is plain he could not but have intended the king's death. Perhaps he did not positively wish it; but for all that, in a certain sense he intended it.

12. What heedlessness is in the case of an unadvised act, rashness *A mis-* is in the case of a mis-advised one. A mis-advised act then may be *advised* either rash or not rash. It may be termed rash, when the case is *be rash or* thought to be such, that a person of ordinary prudence, if *not rash.* prompted by an ordinary share of benevolence, would have employed such and so much attention and reflection to the imagined circumstance, as, by discovering to him the non-existence, improbability, or immateriality of it, would have effectually disposed him to prevent the mischievous incident from taking place.

13. In ordinary discourse, when a man does an act of which the *The* consequences prove mischievous, it is a common thing to speak *intention* of him as having acted with a good intention or with a bad *may be* intention, of his intention's being a good one or a bad one. The *good or bad* epithets good and bad are all this while applied, we see, to the *in itself,* intention: but the application of them is most commonly gov- *independ-* erned by a supposition formed with regard to the nature of the *ently of the* motive. The act, though eventually it prove mischievous, is said *eventual* to be done with a good intention, when it is supposed to issue *conse-* from a motive which is looked upon as a good motive: with a bad *quences.* intention, when it is supposed to be the result of a motive which is looked upon as a bad motive. But the nature of the conse-quences intended, and the nature of the motive which gave birth to the intention, are objects which, though intimately connected, are perfectly distinguishable. The intention might therefore with perfect propriety be styled a good one, whatever were the motive. It might be styled a good one, when not only the consequences of

the act *prove* mischievous, but the motive which gave birth to it *was* what is called a bad one. To warrant the speaking of the intention as being a good one, it is sufficient if the consequences of the act, had they proved what to the agent they seemed likely to be, *would* have been of a beneficial nature. And in the same manner the intention may be bad, when not only the consequences of the act prove beneficial, but the motive which gave birth to it was a good one.

It is better, when the intention is meant to be spoken of as being good or bad, not to say, the motive. 14. Now, when a man has a mind to speak of your *intention* as being good or bad, with reference to the consequences, if he speaks of it at all he must use the word intention, for there is no other. But if a man means to speak of the *motive* from which your intention originated, as being a good or a bad one, he is certainly not obliged to use the word intention: it is at least as well to use the word motive. By the supposition he means the motive; and very likely he may *not* mean the intention. For what is true of the one is very often not true of the other. The motive may be good when the intention is bad: the intention may be good when the motive is bad: whether they are both good or both bad, or the one good and the other bad, makes, as we shall see hereafter, a very essential difference with regard to the consequences.[1] It is therefore much better, when motive is meant, never to say intention.

Example. 15. An example will make this clear. Out of malice a man prosecutes you for a crime of which he believes you to be guilty, but of which in fact you are not guilty. Here the *consequences* of his conduct are mischievous: for they are mischievous to you at any rate, in virtue of the shame and anxiety which you are made to suffer while the prosecution is depending: to which is to be added, in case of your being convicted, the evil of the punishment. To you therefore they are mischievous; nor is there anyone to whom they are beneficial. The man's *motive* was also what is called a bad one: for malice will be allowed by everybody to be a bad motive. However, the *consequences* of his conduct, had they proved such as he believed them likely to be, would have been good: for in them

---

1 See Chap. xii [Consequences].

would have been included the punishment of a criminal, which is a benefit to all who are exposed to suffer by a crime of the like nature. The *intention* therefore, in this case, though not in a common way of speaking the motive, might be styled a *good* one. But of motives more particularly in the next chapter.

16. In the same sense the intention, whether it be positively good or no, so long as it is not bad, may be termed innocent. Accordingly, let the consequences have proved mischievous, and let the motive have been what it will, the intention may be termed innocent in either of two cases: 1. In the case of *un*-advisedness with respect to any of the circumstances on which the mischievousness of the consequences depended: 2. In the case of *mis*-advisedness with respect to any circumstance, which, had it been what it appeared to be, would have served either to prevent or to outweigh the mischief.

Intention, in what cases it may be innocent.

17. A few words for the purpose of applying what has been said to the Roman law. Unintentionality, and innocence of intention, seem both to be included in the case of *infortunium*, where there is neither *dolus* nor *culpa*. Unadvisedness coupled with heedlessness, and mis-advisedness coupled with rashness, correspond to the *culpa sine dolo*. Direct intentionality corresponds to *dolus*. Oblique intentionality seems hardly to have been distinguished from direct; were it to occur, it would probably be deemed also to correspond to *dolus*. The division into *culpa, lata, levis,* and *levissima*, is such as nothing certain can correspond to. What is it that it expresses? A distinction, not in the case itself, but only in the sentiments which any person (a judge, for instance) may find himself disposed to entertain with relation to it: supposing it already distinguished into three subordinate cases by other means.

Intentionality and consciousness, how spoken of in the Roman law.

The word *dolus* seems ill enough contrived: the word *culpa* as indifferently. *Dolus*, upon any other occasion, would be understood to imply deceit, concealment,[1] clandestinity;[2] but here it is extended to open force. *Culpa*, upon any other occasion, would

---

1 See B. I. tit. [Theft] *verbo* [amenable].
2 Dolus, an virtus quis in hoste requirit? – VIRGIL.
   —δόλῳ ἠὲ καὶ ἀμφαδόν. – HOMER.

be understood to extend to blame of every kind. It would therefore include *dolus*.[1]

Use of this and the preceding chapter.

18. The above-mentioned definitions and distinctions are far from being mere matters of speculation. They are capable of the most extensive and constant application, as well to moral discourse as to legislative practice. Upon the degree and bias of a man's intention, upon the absence or presence of consciousness or mis-supposal, depend a great part of the good and bad, more especially of the bad consequences of an act; and on this, as well as other grounds, a great part of the demand for punishment.[2] The presence of intention with regard to such or such a consequence, and of consciousness with regard to such or such a circumstance, of the act, will form so many criminative circumstances,[3] or essential ingredients in the composition of this or that offence: applied to other circumstances, consciousness will form a ground of aggravation, annexable to the like offence.[4] In almost all cases,

---

1 I pretend not here to give any determinate explanation of a set of words, of which the great misfortune is, that the import of them is confused and indeterminate. I speak only by approximation. To attempt to determine the precise import that has been given them by a hundredth part of the authors that have used them, would be an endless task. Would anyone talk intelligibly on this subject in Latin? Let him throw out *dolus* altogether: let him keep *culpa*, for the purpose of expressing not the case itself, but the sentiment that is entertained concerning a case described by other means. For intentionality, let him coin a word boldly, and say *intentionalitas*: for unintentionality, *non-intentionalitas*. For unadvisedness, he has already the word *inscitia*; though the words *imprudentia*, *inobservantia*, were it not for the other senses they are used in, would do better: for unadvisedness coupled with heedlessness, let him say *inscitia culpabilis*; for unadvisedness without heedlessness, *inscitia inculpabilis*: for mis-advisedness coupled with rashness, *error culpabilis*, *error temerarius*, or *error cum temeritate*: for mis-advisedness without rashness, *error inculpabilis*, *error non-temerarius*, or *error sine temeritate*.

It is not unfrequent likewise to meet with the phrase, *malo animo*: a phrase still more indeterminate, if possible, than any of the former. It seems to have reference either to intentionality, or to consciousness, or to the motive, or to the disposition, or to any two or more of these taken together; nobody can tell which: these being objects which seem to have never hitherto been properly distinguished and defined.

2 See Chap. xiii [Cases unmeet].

3 See B. I. tit. [Circumstances influencing].

4 See B. I. tit. [Aggravations].

the absence of intention with regard to certain consequences, and the absence of consciousness, or the presence of mis-supposal, with regard to certain circumstances, will constitute so many grounds of extenuation.[1]

1 See B. I. tit. [Extenuations].

CHAPTER X

Of Motives

§ 1. *Different senses of the word motive*[1]

Motives, why considered.

1. It is an acknowledged truth, that every kind of act whatever, and consequently every kind of offence, is apt to assume a different character, and be attended with different effects, according to the nature of the *motive* which gives birth to it. This makes it requisite to take a view of the several motives by which human conduct is liable to be influenced.

Purely speculative motives have nothing to do here.

2. By a motive, in the most extensive sense in which the word is ever used with reference to a thinking being, is meant anything that can contribute to give birth to, or even to prevent, any kind of action. Now the action of a thinking being is the act either of the body, or only of the mind: and an act of the mind is an act either of the intellectual faculty, or of the will. Acts of the intellectual faculty will sometimes rest in the understanding merely, without exerting any influence in the production of any acts of the will. Motives, which are not of a nature to influence any other acts than those, may be styled purely *speculative* motives, or motives resting in speculation. But as to these acts, neither do they exercise any influence over external acts, or over their consequences, nor consequently over any pain or any pleasure that may be in the number of such consequences. Now it is only

---

1 Note by the author, July, 1822.

For a tabular simultaneous view of the whole list of MOTIVES, in conjunction with the correspondent *pleasures* and *pains*, *interests* and *desires*, see, by the same author, *Table of the Springs of Action*, &c., with Explanatory Notes and Observations. London: 1817, Hunter, St Paul's Church Yard, 8vo. pp. 32.

The word *inducement* has of late presented itself, as being in its signification more comprehensive than the word *motive*, and on some occasions more apposite.

on account of their tendency to produce either pain or pleasure, that any acts can be material. With acts, therefore, that rest purely in the understanding, we have not here any concern: nor therefore with any object, if any such there be, which, in the character of a motive, can have no influence on any other acts than those.

3. The motives with which alone we have any concern, are such as are of a nature to act upon the will. By a motive then, in this sense of the word, is to be understood anything whatsoever, which, by influencing the will of a sensitive being, is supposed to serve as a means of determining him to act, or voluntarily to forbear to act,[1] upon any occasion. Motives of this sort, in contradistinction to the former, may be styled *practical* motives, or motives applying to practice.

Motives to the will.

4. Owing to the poverty and unsettled state of language, the word *motive* is employed indiscriminately to denote two kinds of objects, which, for the better understanding of the subject, it is necessary should be distinguished. On some occasions it is employed to denote any of those really existing incidents from whence the act in question is supposed to take its rise. The sense it bears on these occasions may be styled its literal or *unfigurative* sense. On other occasions it is employed to denote a certain fictitious entity, a passion, an affection of the mind, an ideal being which upon the happening of any such incident is considered as operating upon the mind, and prompting it to take that course, towards which it is impelled by the influence of such incident. Motives of this class are Avarice, Indolence, Benevolence, and so forth; as we shall see more particularly farther on. This latter may be styled the *figurative* sense of the term *motive*.

Figurative and unfigurative senses of the word.

---

1 When the effect or tendency of a motive is to determine a man to forbear to act, it may seem improper to make use of the term *motive*; since motive, properly speaking, means that which disposes an object to *move*. We must however use that improper term, or a term which, though proper enough, is scarce in use, the word *determinative*. By way of justification, or at least apology, for the popular usage in this behalf, it may be observed, that even forbearance to act, or the negation of motion (that is, of bodily motion) supposes an act done, when such forbearance is voluntary. It supposes, to wit, an act of the will, which is as much a positive act, as much a motion, as any other act of the thinking substance.

Motives interior and exterior. 5. As to the real incidents to which the name of motive is also given, these too are of two very different kinds. They may be either, 1. The *internal* perception of any individual lot of pleasure or pain, the expectation of which is looked upon as calculated to determine you to act in such or such a manner; as the pleasure of acquiring such a sum of money, the pain of exerting yourself on such an occasion, and so forth: or, 2. Any *external* event, the happening whereof is regarded as having a tendency to bring about the perception of such pleasure or such pain; for instance, the coming up of a lottery ticket, by which the possession of the money devolves to you; or the breaking out of a fire in the house you are in, which makes it necessary for you to quit it. The former kind of motives may be termed interior, or internal: the latter exterior, or external.

Motive in prospect – motive in esse. 6. Two other senses of the term *motive* need also to be distinguished. Motive refers necessarily to action. It is a pleasure, pain, or other event, that prompts to action. Motive then, in one sense of the word, must be previous to such event. But, for a man to be governed by any motive, he must in every case look beyond that event which is called his action; he must look to the consequences of it: and it is only in this way that the idea of pleasure, of pain, or of any other event, can give birth to it. He must look, therefore, in every case, to some event posterior to the act in contemplation: an event which as yet exists not, but stands only in prospect. Now, as it is in all cases difficult, and in most cases unnecessary, to distinguish between objects so intimately connected, as the posterior possible object which is thus looked forward to, and the present existing object or event which takes place upon a man's looking forward to the other, they are both of them spoken of under the same appellation, *motive*. To distinguish them, the one first mentioned may be termed a motive in *prospect*, the other a motive in *esse*: and under each of these denominations will come as well exterior as internal motives. A fire breaks out in your neighbour's house: you are under apprehension of its extending to your own: you are apprehensive, that if you stay in it, you will be burnt: you accordingly run out of it. This then is the act: the others are all motives to it. The event of the fire's breaking out in your neighbour's house is an external motive, and that in *esse*: the idea or belief of the probability of the fire's extending to your own house, that of your being burnt if you continue, and the pain you feel at the thought of such a catastrophe, are all so many internal events, but still in *esse*: the event of the fire's actually extending to your own house, and that of your being actually burnt by it, external motives in prospect: the pain you would feel at seeing your house a burning, and the pain you would feel while you yourself were burning, internal motives in prospect: which events, according as the matter turns out, may come to be in *esse*: but then, of course, they will cease to act as motives.

7. Of all these motives, which stand nearest to the act, to the production of which they all contribute, is that internal motive in *esse*, which consists in the expectation of the internal motive in prospect: the pain or uneasiness you feel at the thoughts of being burnt.[1] All other motives are more or less remote: the motives in prospect, in proportion as the period at which they are expected to happen is more distant from the period at which the act takes place, and consequently later in point of time: the motives in *esse*, in proportion as they also are more distant from that period, and consequently earlier in point of time.[2]

Motives immediate and remote.

8. It has already been observed, that with motives of which the influence terminates altogether in the understanding, we have nothing here to do. If then, amongst objects that are spoken of as

Motives to the understanding, how they may influence the will.

1 Whether it be the expectation of being burnt, or the pain that accompanies that expectation, that is the immediate internal motive spoken of, may be difficult to determine. It may even be questioned, perhaps, whether they are distinct entities. Both questions, however, seem to be mere questions of words, and the solution of them altogether immaterial. Even the other kinds of motives, though for some purposes they demand a separate consideration, are, however, so intimately allied, that it will often be scarce practicable, and not always material, to avoid confounding them, as they have always hitherto been confounded.

2 Under the term *esse* must be included as well *past* existence, with reference to a given period, as *present*. They are equally real, in comparison with what is as yet but future. Language is materially deficient, in not enabling us to distinguish with precision between *existence* as opposed to *unreality* and *present* existence as opposed to past. The word existence in English, and *esse*, adopted by lawyers from the Latin, have the inconvenience of appearing to confine the existence in question to some single period considered as being present,

motives with reference to the understanding, there be any which concern us here, it is only in as far as such objects may, through the medium of the understanding, exercise an influence over the will. It is in this way, and in this way only, that any objects, in virtue of any tendency they may have to influence the sentiment of belief, may in a practical sense act in the character of motives. Any objects, by tending to induce a belief concerning the existence, actual, or probable, of a practical motive; that is, concerning the probability of a motive in prospect, or the existence of a motive in *esse*; may exercise an influence on the will, and rank with those other motives that have been placed under the name of practical. The pointing out of motives such as these, is what we frequently mean when we talk of giving *reasons*. Your neighbour's house is on fire as before. I observe to you, that at the lower part of your neighbour's house is some wood-work, which joins on to yours; that the flames have caught this wood-work, and so forth; which I do in order to dispose you to believe as I believe, that if you stay in your house much longer you will be burnt. In doing this, then, I suggest motives to your understanding; which motives, by the tendency they have to give birth to or strengthen a pain, which operates upon you in the character of an internal motive in *esse*, join their force, and act as motives upon the will.

§ 2. *No motives either constantly good or constantly bad*

Nothing can act of itself as a motive but the ideas of pleasure or pain. 9. In all this chain of motives, the principal or original link seems to be the last internal motive in prospect: it is to this that all the other motives in prospect owe their materiality: and the immediately acting motive its existence. This motive in prospect, we see, is always some pleasure, or some pain; some pleasure, which the act in question is expected to be a means of continuing or producing: some pain which it is expected to be a means of discontinuing or preventing. A motive is substantially nothing more than pleasure or pain, operating in a certain manner.

No sort of motive is in itself a bad one. 10. Now, pleasure is in *itself* a good: nay, even setting aside immunity from pain, the only good: pain is in itself an evil; and, indeed, without exception, the only evil; or else the words good and evil have no meaning. And this is alike true of every sort of pain, and of every sort of pleasure. It follows, therefore, immediately and incontestibly, that *there is no such thing as any sort of motive that is in itself a bad one.*[1]

11. It is common, however, to speak of actions as proceeding from *good* or *bad* motives: in which case the motives meant are such as are internal. The expression is far from being an accurate one; and as it is apt to occur in the consideration of almost every kind of offence, it will be requisite to settle the precise meaning of it, and observe how far it quadrates with the truth of things.

Inaccuracy of expressions in which good or bad are applied to motives.

12. With respect to goodness and badness, as it is with everything else that is not itself either pain or pleasure, so is it with motives. If they are good or bad, it is only on account of their effects: good, on account of their tendency to produce pleasure, or avert pain: bad, on account of their tendency to produce pain, or avert pleasure. Now the case is, that from one and the same motive, and from every kind of motive, may proceed actions that are good, others that are bad, and others that are indifferent. This we shall proceed to shew with respect to all the different kinds of motives, as determined by the various kinds of pleasures and pains.

Any sort of motive may give birth to any sort of act.

13. Such an analysis, useful as it is, will be found to be a matter of no small difficulty; owing, in great measure, to a certain perversity of structure which prevails more or less throughout all languages. To speak of motives, as of anything else, one must call them by their names. But the misfortune is, that it is rare to meet with a motive of which the name expresses that and nothing more. Commonly along with the very name of the motive, is tacitly involved a proposition imputing to it a certain quality; a quality which, in many cases, will appear to include that very goodness or badness, concerning which we are here inquiring whether, properly speaking, it be or be not imputable to motives. To use the common phrase, in most cases, the name of the

Difficulties which stand in the way of an analysis of this sort.

---

1 Let a man's motive be ill-will; call it even malice, envy, cruelty; it is still a kind of pleasure that is his motive: the pleasure he takes at the thought of the pain which he sees, or expects to see, his adversary undergo. Now even this wretched pleasure, taken by itself, is good: it may be faint; it may be short; it must at any rate be impure: yet while it lasts, and before any bad consequences arrive, it is as good as any other that is not more intense. See Chap. iv [Value].

motive is a word which is employed either only in a *good sense*, or else only in a *bad sense*. Now, when a word is spoken of as being used in a good sense, all that is necessarily meant is this: that in conjunction with the idea of the object it is put to signify, it conveys an idea of *approbation*: that is, of a pleasure or satisfaction, entertained by the person who employs the term at the thoughts of such object. In like manner, when a word is spoken of as being used in a bad sense, all that is necessarily meant is this: that, in conjunction with the idea of the object it is put to signify, it conveys an idea of *disapprobation*: that is, of a displeasure entertained by the person who employs the term at the thoughts of such object. Now, the circumstance on which such approbation is grounded will, as naturally as any other, be the opinion of the *goodness* of the object in question, as above explained: such, at least, it must be, upon the principle of utility: so, on the other hand, the circumstance on which any such disapprobation is grounded, will as naturally as any other, be the opinion of the *badness* of the object: such, at least, it must be, in as far as the principle of utility is taken for the standard.

Now there are certain motives which, unless in a few particular cases, have scarcely any other name to be expressed by but such a word as is used only in a good sense. This is the case, for example, with the motives of piety and honour. The consequence of this is, that if, in speaking of such a motive, a man should have occasion to apply the epithet bad to any actions which he mentions as apt to result from it, he must appear to be guilty of a contradiction in terms. But the names of motives which have scarcely any other name to be expressed by, but such a word as is used only in a bad sense, are many more.[1] This is the case, for example, with the motives of lust and avarice. And accordingly, if in speaking of any such motive, a man should have occasion to apply the epithets good or indifferent to any actions which he mentions as apt to result from it, he must here also appear to be guilty of a similar contradiction.[2]

---

1 For the reason, see Chap. xi [Dispositions], par. 17 note.

2 To this imperfection of language, and nothing more, are to be attributed, in great measure, the violent clamours that have from time to time been raised against those ingenious moralists, who, travelling out of the beaten tract of

This perverse association of ideas cannot, it is evident, but throw great difficulties in the way of the inquiry now before us. Confining himself to the language most in use, a man can scarce avoid running, in appearance, into perpetual contradictions. His propositions will appear, on the one hand, repugnant to truth; and on the other hand, adverse to utility. As paradoxes, they will excite contempt: as mischievous paradoxes, indignation. For the truths he labours to convey, however important, and however salutary, his reader is never the better: and he himself is much the worse. To obviate this inconvenience, completely, he has but this one unpleasant remedy; to lay aside the old phraseology and invent a new one. Happy the man whose language is ductile enough to permit him this resource. To palliate the inconvenience, where that method of obviating it is impracticable, he has nothing left for it but to enter into a long discussion, to state the whole matter at large, to confess, that for the sake of promoting the purposes, he has violated the established laws of language, and to throw himself upon the mercy of his readers.[1]

---

speculation, have found more or less difficulty in disentangling themselves from the shackles of ordinary language: such as Rochefoucault, Mandeville and Helvetius. To the unsoundness of their opinions, and, with still greater injustice, to the corruption of their hearts, was often imputed, what was most commonly owing either to a want of skill, in matters of language on the part of the author, or a want of discernment, possibly now and then in some instances a want of probity, on the part of the commentator.

1 Happily, language is not always so intractable, but that by making use of two words instead of one, a man may avoid the inconvenience of fabricating words that are absolutely new. Thus instead of the word lust, by putting together two words in common use, he may frame the neutral expression, sexual desire: instead of the word avarice, by putting together two other words also in common use, he may frame the neutral expression, pecuniary interest. This, accordingly, is the course which I have taken. In these instances, indeed, even the combination is not novel: the only novelty there is consists in the steady adherence to the one neutral expression, rejecting altogether the terms, of which the import is infected by adventitious and unsuitable ideas.

In the catalogue of motives, corresponding to the several sorts of pains and pleasures, I have inserted such as have occurred to me. I cannot pretend to warrant it complete. To make sure of rendering it so, the only way would be to turn over the dictionary from beginning to end: an operation which, in a view to perfection, would be necessary for more purposes than this. See B.I. tit. [Defamation], and Append. tit. [Composition].

§ 3. *Catalogue of motives corresponding to that of pleasures and pains*

Physical desire corresponding to pleasures of sense in general. 14. From the pleasures of the senses, considered in the gross, results the motive which, in a neutral sense, may be termed physical desire: in a bad sense, it is termed sensuality. Name used in a good sense it has none. Of this, nothing can be determined, till it be considered separately, with reference to the several species of pleasures to which it corresponds.

The motive corresponding to the pleasures of the palate. 15. In particular, then, to the pleasures of the taste or palate corresponds a motive, which in a neutral sense having received no name that can serve to express it in all cases, can only be termed, by circumlocution, the love of the pleasures of the palate. In particular cases it is styled hunger: in others, thirst.[1] The love of good cheer expresses this motive, but seems to go beyond: intimating, that the pleasure is to be partaken of in company, and involving a kind of sympathy. In a bad sense, it is styled in some cases greediness, voraciousness, gluttony: in others, principally when applied to children, lickerishness. It may in some cases also be represented by the word daintiness. Name used in a good sense it has none. 1. A boy, who does not want for victuals, steals a cake out of a pastry-cook's shop, and eats it. In this case his motive will be universally deemed a bad one: and if it be asked what it is, it may be answered, perhaps, lickerishness. 2. A boy buys a cake out of a pastry-cook's shop, and eats it. In this case his motive can scarcely be looked upon as either good or bad, unless his master should be out of humour with him; and then perhaps he may call it lickerishness, as before. In both cases, however, his motive is the same. It is neither more nor less than the motive corresponding to the pleasures of the palate.[2]

Sexual desires corresponding to the pleasures of the sexual sense. 16. To the pleasures of the sexual sense corresponds the motive which, in a neutral sense, may be termed sexual desire. In a bad

1 Hunger and thirst considered in the light of motives, import not so much the desire of a particular kind of pleasure, as the desire of removing a positive kind of pain. They do not extend to the desire of that kind of pleasure which depends on the choice of foods and liquors.

2 It will not be worth while, in every case, to give an instance in which the action may be indifferent: if good as well as bad actions may result from the same motive, it is easy to conceive, that also may be indifferent.

sense, it is spoken of under the name of lasciviousness, and a variety of other names of reprobation. Name used in a good sense it has none.[1]

1. A man ravishes a virgin. In this case the motive is, without scruple, termed by the name of lust, lasciviousness, and so forth; and is universally looked upon as a bad one. 2. The same man, at another time, exercises the rights of marriage with his wife. In this case the motive is accounted, perhaps, a good one, or at least indifferent: and here people would scruple to call it by any of those names. In both cases, however, the motive may be precisely the same. In both cases it may be neither more nor less than sexual desire.

17. To the pleasures of curiosity corresponds the motive known by the same name: and which may be otherwise called the love of novelty, or the love of experiment; and, on particular occasions, sport, and sometimes play. *Curiosity, etc. corresponding to the pleasures of curiosity.*

1. A boy, in order to divert himself, reads an improving book: the motive is accounted, perhaps, a good one: at any rate not a bad one. 2. He sets his top a spinning: the motive is deemed, at any rate, not a bad one. 3. He sets loose a mad ox among a crowd; his motive is now, perhaps, termed an abominable one. Yet in all three cases the motive may be the very same: it may be neither more nor less than curiosity.

18. As to the other pleasures of sense they are of too little consequence to have given any separate denominations to the corresponding motives. *None to the pleasures of sense.*

19. To the pleasures of wealth corresponds the sort of motive which, in a neutral sense, may be termed pecuniary interest: in a bad sense, it is termed, in some cases, avarice, covetousness, *Pecuniary interest to the pleasures of wealth.*

---

1 Love indeed includes sometimes this idea: but then it can never answer the purpose of exhibiting it separately: since there are three motives, at least, that may all of them be included in it, besides this: the love of beauty corresponding to the pleasures of the eye, and the motives corresponding to those of amity and benevolence. We speak of the love of children, of the love of parents, of the love of God. These pious uses protect the appellation, and preserve it from the ignominy poured forth upon its profane associates. Even sensual love would not answer the purpose; since that would include the love of beauty.

rapacity, or lucre: in other cases, niggardliness: in a good sense, but only in particular cases, economy and frugality; and in some cases the word industry may be applied to it: in a sense nearly indifferent, but rather bad than otherwise, it is styled, though only in particular cases, parsimony.

1. For money you gratify a man's hatred, by putting his adversary to death. 2. For money you plough his field for him. – In the first case your motive is termed lucre, and is accounted corrupt and abominable: and in the second, for want of a proper appellation, it is styled industry; and is looked upon as innocent at least, if not meritorious. Yet the motive is in both cases precisely the same: it is neither more nor less than pecuniary interest.

None to the pleasures of skill. 20. The pleasures of skill are neither distinct enough, nor of consequence enough, to have given any name to the corresponding motive.

To the pleasures of amity, the desire of ingratiating oneself. 21. To the pleasures of amity corresponds a motive which, in a neutral sense, may be termed the desire of ingratiating one's self. In a bad sense it is in certain cases styled servility: in a good sense it has no name that is peculiar to it: in the cases in which it has been looked on with a favourable eye, it has seldom been distinguished from the motive of sympathy or benevolence, with which, in such cases, it is commonly associated.

1. To acquire the affections of a woman before marriage, to preserve them afterwards, you do everything, that is consistent with other duties, to make her happy: in this case your motive is looked upon as laudable, though there is no name for it. 2. For the same purpose, you poison a woman with whom she is at enmity: in this case your motive is looked upon as abominable, though still there is no name for it. 3. To acquire or preserve the favour of a man who is richer or more powerful than yourself, you make yourself subservient to his pleasures. Let them even be lawful pleasures, if people choose to attribute your behaviour to this motive, you will not get them to find any other name for it than servility. Yet in all three cases the motive is the same: it is neither more nor less than the desire of ingratiating yourself.

22. To the pleasures of the moral sanction, or, as they may otherwise be called, the pleasures of a good name, corresponds a

motive which, in a neutral sense, has scarcely yet obtained any adequate appellative. It may be styled, the love of reputation. It is nearly related to the motive last preceding: being neither more nor less than the desire of ingratiating one's self with, or, as in this case we should rather say, of recommending one's self to, the world at large. In a good sense, it is termed honour, or the sense of honour: or rather, the word honour is introduced somehow or other upon the occasion of its being brought to view: for in strictness the word honour is put rather to signify that imaginary object, which a man is spoken of as possessing upon the occasion of his obtaining a conspicuous share of the pleasures that are in question. In particular cases, it is styled the love of glory. In a bad sense, it is styled, in some cases, false honour; in others, pride; in others, vanity. In a sense not decidedly bad, but rather bad than otherwise, ambition. In an indifferent sense, in some cases, the love of fame: in others, the sense of shame. And, as the pleasures belonging to the moral sanction run undistinguishably into the pains derived from the same source,[1] it may also be styled, in some cases, the fear of dishonour, the fear of disgrace, the fear of infamy, the fear of ignominy, or the fear of shame.

To the pleasures of a good name, the love of reputation.

1. You have received an affront from a man: according to the custom of the country, in order, on the one hand, to save yourself from the shame of being thought to bear it patiently;[2] on the other

---

1 See Chap. vi [Pleasures and Pains], par. 24 note.

2 A man's bearing an affront patiently, that is, without taking this method of doing what is called wiping it off, is thought to import one or other of two things: either that he does not possess that sensibility to the pleasures and pains of the moral sanction, which, in order to render himself a respectable member of society, a man ought to possess: or, that he does not possess courage enough to stake his life for the chance of gratifying that resentment which a proper sense of the value of those pleasures and those pains it is thought would not fail to inspire. True it is, that there are divers other motives, by any of which the same conduct might equally be produced: the motives corresponding to the religious sanction, and the motives that come under the head of benevolence. Piety towards God, the practice in question being generally looked upon as repugnant to the dictates of the religious sanction: sympathy for your antagonist himself, whose life would be put to hazard at the same time with your own; sympathy for his connexions; the persons who are dependent on him in the way of support, or connected with him in the way of sympathy: sympathy for your own connexions: and even sympathy for the public, in cases where the man is such that the public appears to have a material interest in his life. But in comparison with the love of life, the

hand, to obtain the reputation of courage; you challenge him to fight with mortal weapons. In this case your motive will by some people be accounted laudable, and styled honour: by others it will be accounted blameable, and these, if they call it honour, will prefix an epithet of improbation to it, and call it false honour. 2. In order to obtain a post of rank and dignity, and thereby to increase the respects paid you by the public, you bribe the electors who are to confer it, or the judge before whom the title to it is in dispute. In this case your motive is commonly accounted corrupt and abominable, and is styled, perhaps, by some such name as dishonest or corrupt ambition, as there is no single name for it. 3. In order to obtain the good-will of the public, you bestow a large sum in works of private charity or public utility. In this case people will be apt not to agree about your motive. Your enemies will put a bad colour upon it, and call it ostentation: your friends, to save you from this reproach, will choose to impute your conduct not to this motive but to some other; such as that of charity (the denomination in this case given to private sympathy) or that of public spirit. 4. A king, for the sake of gaining the admiration annexed to the name of conqueror (we will suppose power and resentment out of the question) engages his kingdom

---

influence of the religious sanction is known to be in general but weak: especially among people of those classes who are here in question: a sure proof of which is the prevalence of this very custom. Where it is so strong as to preponderate, it is so rare, that, perhaps, it gives a man a place in the calendar: and, at any rate, exalts him to the rank of martyr. Moreover, the instances in which either private benevolence or public spirit predominate over the love of life, will also naturally be but rare: and, owing to the general propensity to detraction, it will also be much rarer for them to be thought to do so. Now, when three or more motives, any one of them capable of producing a given mode of conduct, apply at once, that which appears to be the most powerful, is that which will of course be deemed to have actually done the *most*: and, as the bulk of mankind, on this as on other occasions, are disposed to decide peremptorily upon superficial estimates, it will generally be looked upon as having done the whole.

The consequence is, that when a man of a certain rank forbears to take this chance of revenging an affront, his conduct will, by most people, be imputed to the love of life: which, when it predominates over the love of reputation, is, by a not unsalutary association of ideas, stigmatized with the reproachful name of cowardice.

in a bloody war. His motive, by the multitude (whose sympathy for millions is easily overborne by the pleasure which their imagination finds in gaping at any novelty they observe in the conduct of a single person) is deemed an admirable one. Men of feeling and reflection, who disapprove of the dominion exercised by this motive on this occasion, without always perceiving that it is the same motive which in other instances meets with their approbation, deem it an abominable one; and because the multitude, who are the manufacturers of language, have not given them a simple name to call it by, they will call it by some such compound name as the love of false glory or false ambition. Yet in all four cases the motive is the same: it is neither more nor less than the love of reputation.

23. To the pleasures of power corresponds the motive which, in a neutral sense, may be termed the love of power. People, who are out of humour with it, sometimes call it the lust of power. In a good sense, it is scarcely provided with a name. In certain cases this motive, as well as the love of reputation, are confounded under the same name, ambition. This is not to be wondered at, considering the intimate connexion there is between the two motives in many cases: since it commonly happens, that the same object which affords the one sort of pleasure, affords the other sort at the same time: for instance, offices, which are at once posts of honour and places of trust: and since at any rate reputation is the road to power. *To the pleasures of power, the love of power.*

1. If, in order to gain a place in administration, you poison the man who occupies it. 2. If, in the same view, you propose a salutary plan for the advancement of the public welfare; your motive is in both cases the same. Yet in the first case it is accounted criminal and abominable: in the second case allowable, and even laudable.

24. To the pleasures as well as to the pains of the religious sanction corresponds a motive which has, strictly speaking, no perfectly neutral name applicable to all cases, unless the word religion be admitted in this character: though the word religion, strictly speaking, seems to mean not so much the motive itself, as a kind of fictitious personage, by whom the motive is supposed to be created, or an assemblage of acts, supposed to be dictated by that personage: nor does it seem to be completely settled into a neutral sense. In the same sense it is also, in some cases, styled *The motive belonging to the religious sanction.*

religious zeal: in other cases, the fear of God. The love of God, though commonly contrasted with the fear of God, does not come strictly under this head. It coincides properly with a motive of a different denomination; *viz.*, a kind of sympathy or good-will, which has the Deity for its object. In a good sense, it is styled devotion, piety, and pious zeal. In a bad sense, it is styled, in some cases, superstition, or superstitious zeal: in other cases, fanaticism, or fanatic zeal: in a sense not decidedly bad, because not appropriated to this motive, enthusiasm, or enthusiastic zeal.

1. In order to obtain the favour of the Supreme Being, a man assassinates his lawful sovereign. In this case the motive is now almost universally looked upon as abominable, and is termed fanaticism: formerly it was by great numbers accounted laudable, and was by them called pious zeal. 2. In the same view, a man lashes himself with thongs. In this case, in yonder house, the motive is accounted laudable, and is called pious zeal: in the next house it is deemed contemptible, and called superstition. 3. In the same view, a man eats a piece of bread (or at least what to external appearance is a piece of bread) with certain ceremonies. In this case, in yonder house, his motive is looked upon as laudable, and is styled piety and devotion: in the next house it is deemed abominable, and styled superstition, as before: perhaps even it is absurdly styled impiety. 4. In the same view, a man holds a cow by the tail while he is dying. On the Thames the motive would in this case be deemed contemptible, and called superstition. On the Ganges it is deemed meritorious, and called piety. 5. In the same view, a man bestows a large sum in works of charity, or public utility. In this case the motive is styled laudable, by those at least to whom the works in question appear to come under this description: and by these at least it would be styled piety. Yet in all these cases the motive is precisely the same: it is neither more nor less than the motive belonging to the religious sanction.[1]

---

1 I am aware, or at least I hope, that people in general, when they see the matter thus stated, will be ready to acknowledge, that the motive in these cases, whatever be the tendency of the acts which it produces, is not a bad one: but this will not render it the less true, that hitherto in popular discourse it has been common for men to speak of acts, which they could not but acknowledge to have originated from this source, as proceeding from a bad motive. The same observation will apply to many of the other cases.

25. To the pleasures of sympathy corresponds the motive which, in a neutral sense, is termed good-will. The word sympathy may also be used on this occasion: though the sense of it seems to be rather more extensive. In a good sense, it is styled benevolence: and in certain cases, philanthropy; and, in a figurative way, brotherly love; in others, humanity; in others, charity; in others, pity and compassion; in others, mercy; in others, gratitude; in others, tenderness; in others, patriotism; in others, public spirit. Love is also employed in this as in so many other senses. In a bad sense, it has no name applicable to it in all cases: in particular cases it is styled partiality. The word zeal, with certain epithets prefixed to it, might also be employed sometimes on this occasion, though the sense of it be more extensive; applying sometimes to ill as well as to good will. It is thus we speak of party zeal, national zeal, and public zeal. The word attachment is also used with the like epithets: we also say family-attachment. The French expression, *esprit de corps*, for which as yet there seems to be scarcely any name in English, might be rendered in some cases, though rather inadequately, by the terms corporation spirit, corporation attachment, or corporation zeal.

Good-will, etc. to the pleasures of sympathy.

1. A man who has set a town on fire is apprehended and committed: out of regard or compassion for him, you help him to break prison. In this case the generality of people will probably scarcely know whether to condemn your motive or to applaud it: those who condemn your conduct, will be disposed rather to impute it to some other motive: if they style it benevolence or compassion, they will be for prefixing an epithet, and calling it false benevolence or false compassion.[1] 2. The man is taken again, and is put upon his trial: to save him you swear falsely in his

---

1 Among the Greeks, perhaps the motive, and the conduct it gave birth to, would, in such a case, have been rather approved than disapproved of. It seems to have been deemed an act of heroism on the part of Hercules, to have delivered his friend Theseus from hell: though divine justice, which held him there, should naturally have been regarded as being at least upon a footing with human justice. But to divine justice, even when acknowledged under that character, the respect paid at that time of day does not seem to have been very profound, or well-settled: at present, the respect paid to it is profound and settled enough, though the name of it is but too often applied to dictates which could have had no other origin than the worst sort of human caprice.

favour. People, who would not call your motive a bad one before, will perhaps call it so now. 3. A man is at law with you about an estate: he has no right to it: the judge knows this, yet, having an esteem or affection for your adversary, adjudges it to him. In this case the motive is by everybody deemed abominable, and is termed injustice and partiality. 4. You detect a statesman in receiving bribes: out of regard to the public interest, you give information of it, and prosecute him. In this case, by all who acknowledge your conduct to have originated from this motive, your motive will be deemed a laudable one, and styled public spirit. But his friends and adherents will not choose to account for your conduct in any such manner: they will rather attribute it to party enmity. 5. You find a man on the point of starving: you relieve him; and save his life. In this case your motive will by everybody be accounted laudable, and it will be termed compassion, pity, charity, benevolence. Yet in all these cases the motive is the same: it is neither more nor less than the motive of goodwill.

Ill-will, etc. to the pleasures of antipathy. 26. To the pleasures of malevolence, or antipathy, corresponds the motive which, in a neutral sense, is termed antipathy or displeasure: and, in particular cases, dislike, aversion, abhorrence, and indignation: in a neutral sense, or perhaps a sense leaning a little to the bad side, ill-will: and, in particular cases, anger, wrath, and enmity. In a bad sense it is styled, in different cases, wrath, spleen, ill-humour, hatred, malice, rancour, rage, fury, cruelty, tyranny, envy, jealousy, revenge, misanthropy, and by other names, which it is hardly worth while to endeavour to collect.[1] Like goodwill, it is used with epithets expressive of the persons who are the objects of the affection. Hence we hear of party enmity, party rage, and so forth. In a good sense there seems to be no single name for it. In compound expressions it may be spoken

---

1 Here, as elsewhere, it may be observed, that the same words which are mentioned as names of motives, are also many of them names of passions, appetites, and affections; fictitious entities, which are framed only by considering pleasures or pains in some particular point of view. Some of them are also names of moral qualities. This branch of nomenclature is remarkably entangled: to unravel it completely would take up a whole volume; not a syllable of which would belong properly to the present design.

of in such a sense, by epithets, such as *just* and *laudable*, prefixed to words that are used in a neutral or nearly neutral sense.

1. You rob a man: he prosecutes you, and gets you punished: out of resentment you set upon him, and hang him with your own hands. In this case your motive will universally be deemed detestable, and will be called malice, cruelty, revenge, and so forth. 2. A man has stolen a little money from you: out of resentment you prosecute him, and get him hanged by course of law. In this case people will probably be a little divided in their opinions about your motive: your friends will deem it a laudable one, and call it a just or laudable resentment; your enemies will perhaps be disposed to deem it blameable, and call it cruelty, malice, revenge, and so forth: to obviate which, your friends will try perhaps to change the motive, and call it public spirit. 3. A man has murdered your father: out of resentment you prosecute him, and get him put to death in course of law. In this case your motive will be universally deemed a laudable one, and styled, as before, a just or laudable resentment: and your friends, in order to bring forward the more amiable principle from which the malevolent one, which was your immediate motive, took its rise, will be for keeping the latter out of sight, speaking of the former only, under some such name as filial piety. Yet in all these cases the motive is the same: it is neither more nor less than the motive of ill-will.

27. To the several sorts of pains, or at least to all such of them as are conceived to subsist in an intense degree, and to death, which, as far as we can perceive, is the termination of all the pleasures, as well as all the pains we are acquainted with, corresponds the motive, which in a neutral sense is styled, in general, self-preservation: the desire of preserving one's self from the pain or evil in question. Now in many instances the desire of pleasure, and the sense of pain, run into one another undistinguishably. Self-preservation, therefore, where the degree of the pain which it corresponds to is but slight will scarcely be distinguishable, by any precise line, from the motives corresponding to the several sorts of pleasures. Thus in the case of the pains of hunger and thirst: physical want will in many cases be scarcely distinguishable from physical desire. In some cases it is styled, still in a neutral sense, self-defence. Between the pleasures and the pains of the

Self-preservation, to the several kinds of pains.

moral and religious sanctions, and consequently of the motives that correspond to them, as likewise between the pleasures of amity, and the pains of enmity, this want of boundaries has already been taken notice of.[1] The case is the same between the pleasures of wealth, and the pains of privation corresponding to those pleasures. There are many cases, therefore, in which it will be difficult to distinguish the motive of self-preservation from pecuniary interest, from the desire of ingratiating one's self, from the love of reputation, and from religious hope: in which cases, those more specific and explicit names will naturally be preferred to this general and inexplicit one. There are also a multitude of compound names, which either are already in use, or might be devised, to distinguish the specific branches of the motive of self-preservation from those several motives of a pleasurable origin: such as the fear of poverty, the fear of losing such or such a man's regard, the fear of shame, and the fear of God. Moreover, to the evil of death corresponds, in a neutral sense, the love of life; in a bad sense, cowardice: which corresponds also to the pains of the senses, at least when considered as subsisting in an acute degree. There seems to be no name for the love of life that has a good sense; unless it be the vague and general name of prudence.

1. To save yourself from being hanged, pilloried, imprisoned, or fined, you poison the only person who can give evidence against you. In this case your motive will universally be styled abominable: but as the term self-preservation has no bad sense, people will not care to make this use of it: they will be apt rather to change the motive, and call it malice. 2. A woman, having been just delivered of an illegitimate child, in order to save herself from shame, destroys the child, or abandons it. In this case, also, people will call the motive a bad one, and, not caring to speak of it under a neutral name, they will be apt to change the motive, and call it by some such name as cruelty. 3. To save the expense of a halfpenny, you suffer a man, whom you could preserve at that expense, to perish with want, before your eyes. In this case your motive will be universally deemed an abominable one; and, to avoid calling it by so indulgent a name as self-preservation, people

---

1 See Chap. v [Pleasures and Pains], par. 24, 25.

will be apt to call it avarice and niggardliness, with which indeed in this case it indistinguishably coincides: for the sake of finding a more reproachful appellation, they will be apt likewise to change the motive, and term it cruelty. 4. To put an end to the pain of hunger, you steal a loaf of bread. In this case your motive will scarcely, perhaps, be deemed a very bad one; and, in order to express more indulgence for it, people will be apt to find a stronger name for it than self-preservation, terming it *necessity*. 5. To save yourself from drowning, you beat off an innocent man who has got hold of the same plank. In this case your motive will in general be deemed neither good nor bad, and it will be termed self-preservation, or necessity, or the love of life. 6. To save your life from a gang of robbers, you kill them in the conflict. In this case the motive may, perhaps, be deemed rather laudable than otherwise, and, besides self-preservation, is styled also self-defence. 7. A soldier is sent out upon a party against a weaker party of the enemy: before he gets up with them, to save his life, he runs away. In this case the motive will universally be deemed a contemptible one, and will be called cowardice. Yet in all these various cases, the motive is still the same. It is neither more nor less than self-preservation.

28. In particular, to the pains of exertion corresponds the motive, which, in a neutral sense, may be termed the love of ease, or by a stronger circumlocution, the desire of avoiding trouble. In a bad sense, it is termed indolence.[1] It seems to have no name that carries with it a good sense. *To the pains of exertion, the love of ease.*

1. To save the trouble of taking care of it, a parent leaves his child to perish. In this case the motive will be deemed an abominable one, and, because indolence will seem too mild a name for it, the motive will, perhaps, be changed, and spoken of under some such term as cruelty. 2. To save yourself from an illegal slavery, you make your escape. In this case the motive will be deemed certainly not a bad one: and, because indolence, or even the love of ease, will be thought too unfavourable a name for

1 It may seem odd at first sight to speak of the love of ease as giving birth to action: but exertion is as natural an effect of the love of ease as inaction is, when a smaller degree of exertion promises to exempt a man from a greater.

it, it will, perhaps, be styled the love of liberty. 3. A mechanic, in order to save his labour, makes an improvement in his machinery. In this case, people will look upon his motive as a good one; and finding no name for it that carries a good sense, they will be disposed to keep the motive out of sight: they will speak rather of his ingenuity, than of the motive which was the means of his manifesting that quality. Yet in all these cases the motive is the same; it is neither more nor less than the love of ease.

Motives can only be bad with reference to the most frequent complexion of their effects. 29. It appears then that there is no such thing as any sort of motive which is a bad one in itself: nor, consequently, any such thing as a sort of motive, which in itself is exclusively a good one. And as to their effects, it appears too that these are sometimes bad, at other times either indifferent or good: and this appears to be the case with every sort of motive. *If any sort of motive then is either good or bad on the score of its effects, this is the case only on individual occasions, and with individual motives*; and this is the case with one sort of motive as well as with another. *If any sort of motive then can, in consideration of its effects, be termed with any propriety a bad one*, it can only be with reference to the balance of all the effects it may have had of both kinds within a given period, that is, of its most usual tendency.

How it is that motives, such as lust, avarice, etc. are constantly bad. 30. What then? (it will be said) – are not lust, cruelty, avarice, bad motives? Is there so much as any one individual occasion, in which motives like these can be otherwise than bad? No, certainly: and yet the proposition, that there is no one *sort* of motive but what will on many occasions be a good one, is nevertheless true. The fact is, that these are names which, if properly applied, are never applied but in the cases where the motives they signify happen to be bad. The names of these motives, considered apart from their effects, are sexual desire, displeasure, and pecuniary interest. To sexual desire, when the effects of it are looked upon as bad, is given the name of lust. Now lust is always a bad motive. Why? Because if the case be such, that the effects of the motive are not bad, it does not go, or at least ought not to go, by the name of lust. The case is, then, that when I say, 'Lust is a bad motive' it is a proposition that merely concerns the import of the word lust; and which would be false if transferred to the other word used for the same motive, sexual desire. Hence we see the emptiness of all those rhapsodies of common-place morality, which consist in the taking of such names as lust, cruelty, and avarice, and branding them with marks of reprobation: applied to the *thing*, they are false; applied to the *name*, they are true indeed, but nugatory. Would you do a real service to mankind, show them the cases in which sexual desire *merits* the name of lust; displeasure, that of cruelty; and pecuniary interest, that of avarice.

31. If it were necessary to apply such denominations as good, bad, and indifferent to motives, they might be classed in the following manner, in consideration of the most frequent complexion of their effects. In the class of good motives might be placed the articles of, 1. Good-will, 2. Love of reputation. 3. Desire of amity. And, 4. Religion. In the class of bad motives, 5. Displeasure. In the class of neutral or indifferent motives, 6. Physical desire. 7. Pecuniary interest. 8. Love of power. 9. Self-preservation; as including the fear of the pains of the senses, the love of ease, and the love of life.

Under the above restrictions, motives may be distinguished into good, bad, and indifferent or neutral.

32. This method of arrangement, however, cannot but be imperfect; and the nomenclature belonging to it is in danger of being fallacious. For by what method of investigation can a man be assured, that with regard to the motives ranked under the name of good, the good effects they have had, from the beginning of the world, have, in each of the four species comprised under this name, been superior to the bad? Still more difficulty would a man find in assuring himself, that with regard to those which are ranked under the name of neutral or indifferent, the effects they have had have exactly balanced each other, the value of the good being neither greater nor less than that of the bad. It is to be considered, that the interests of the person himself can no more be left out of the estimate, than those of the rest of the community. For what would become of the species, if it were not for the motives of hunger and thirst, sexual desire, the fear of pain, and the love of life? Nor in the actual constitution of human nature is the motive of displeasure less necessary, perhaps, than any of the others: although a system, in which the business of life might be carried on without it, might possibly be conceived. It seems, therefore, that they could scarcely, without great danger of mistakes, be distinguished in this manner even with reference to each other.

Inconveniences of this distribution.

It is only in individual instances that motives can be good or bad.

33. The only way, it should seem, in which a motive can with safety and propriety be styled good or bad, is with reference to its effects in each individual instance; and principally from the intention it gives birth to: from which arise, as will be shown hereafter, the most material part of its effects. A motive is good, when the intention it gives birth to is a good one; bad, when the intention is a bad one: and an intention is good or bad, according to the material consequences that are the objects of it. So far is it from the goodness of the intention's being to be known only from the species of the motive. But from one and the same motive, as we have seen, may result intentions of every sort of complexion whatsoever. This circumstance, therefore, can afford no clue for the arrangement of the several sorts of motives.

Motives distin-guished into social, dissocial, and self-regarding.

34. A more commodious method, therefore, it should seem, would be to distribute them according to the influence which they appear to have on the interests of the other members of the community, laying those of the party himself out of the question: to wit, according to the tendency which they appear to have to unite, or disunite, his interests and theirs. On this plan they may be distinguished into *social*, *dissocial*, and *self-regarding*. In the social class may be reckoned, 1. Good-will. 2. Love of reputation. 3. Desire of amity. 4. Religion. In the dissocial may be placed, 5. Displeasure. In the self-regarding class, 6. Physical desire. 7. Pecuniary interest. 8. Love of power. 9. Self-preservation; as including the fear of the pains of the senses, the love of ease, and the love of life.

– social, into purely-social, and semi-social.

35. With respect to the motives that have been termed social, if any farther distinction should be of use, to that of good-will alone may be applied the epithet of *purely-social*; while the love of reputation, the desire of amity, and the motive of religion, may together be comprised under the division of *semi-social*: the social tendency being much more constant and unequivocal in the former than in any of the three latter. Indeed these last, social as they may be termed, are self-regarding at the same time.[1]

---

1 'Religion,' says the pious Addison, somewhere in the Spectator, 'is the highest species of self-love.'

§ 4. *Order of pre-eminence among motives*

36. Of all these sorts of motives, good-will is that of which the dictates,[1] taken in a general view, are surest of coinciding with those of the principle of utility. For the dictates of utility are neither more nor less than the dictates of the most extensive[2] and enlightened (that is *well-advised*[3]) benevolence. The dictates of the other motives may be conformable to those of utility, or repugnant, as it may happen.

The dictates of good-will are the surest of coinciding with those of utility.

37. In this, however, it is taken for granted, that in the case in question the dictates of benevolence are not contradicted by those of a more extensive, that is enlarged, benevolence. Now when the dictates of benevolence, as respecting the interests of a certain set of persons, are repugnant to the dictates of the same motive, as respecting the more important[4] interests of another set of persons, the former dictates, it is evident, are repealed, as it were, by the latter: and a man, were he to be governed by the former, could scarcely, with propriety, be said to be governed by the dictates of benevolence. On this account, were the motives on both sides sure to be alike present to a man's mind, the case of such a repugnancy would hardly be worth distinguishing, since the partial benevolence might be considered as swallowed up in the more extensive: if the former prevailed, and governed the action, it must be considered as not owing its birth to benevolence, but to some other motive: if the latter prevailed, the former might be considered as having no effect. But the case is, that a partial benevolence may govern the action, without entering into any direct competition with the more extensive benevolence, which

Yet do not in all cases.

---

1 When a man is supposed to be prompted by any motive to engage, or not to engage, in such or such an action, it may be of use, for the convenience of discourse, to speak of such motive as giving birth to an imaginary kind of *law* or *dictate*, injoining him to engage, or not to engage, in it.[a]

2 See Chap. iv [Value], and Chap. vi [Sensibility], par. 21.

3 See Chap. ix [Consciousness].

4 Or valuable. See Chap. iv [Value].

---

a See Chap. i.

would forbid it; because the interests of the less numerous assemblage of persons may be present to a man's mind, at a time when those of the more numerous are either not present, or, if present, make no impression. It is in this way that the dictates of this motive may be repugnant to utility, yet still be the dictates of benevolence. What makes those of private benevolence conformable upon the whole to the principle of utility, is, that in general they stand unopposed by those of public: if they are repugnant to them, it is only by accident. What makes them the more conformable, is, that in a civilized society, in most of the cases in which they would of themselves be apt to run counter to those of public benevolence, they find themselves opposed by stronger motives of the self-regarding class, which are played off against them by the laws; and that it is only in cases where they stand unopposed by the other more salutary dictates, that they are left free. An act of injustice or cruelty, committed by a man for the sake of his father or his son, is punished, and with reason, as much as if it were committed for his own.

Next to them come those of the love of reputation. 38. After good-will, the motive of which the dictates seem to have the next best chance for coinciding with those of utility, is that of the love of reputation. There is but one circumstance which prevents the dictates of this motive from coinciding in all cases with those of the former. This is, that men in their likings and dislikings, in the dispositions they manifest to annex to any mode of conduct their approbation or their disapprobation, and in consequence to the person who appears to practise it, their good or their ill will, do not govern themselves exclusively by the principle of utility. Sometimes it is the principle of asceticism they are guided by: sometimes the principle of sympathy and antipathy. There is another circumstance, which diminishes, not their conformity to the principle of utility, but only their efficacy in comparison with the dictates of the motive of benevolence. The dictates of this motive will operate as strongly in secret as in public: whether it appears likely that the conduct which they recommend will be known or not: those of the love of reputation will coincide with those of benevolence only in proportion as a man's conduct seems likely to be known. This circumstance, however, does not make so much difference as at first sight might appear. Acts, in proportion as they are material, are apt to become known:[1] and in point of reputation, the slightest suspicion often serves for proof. Besides, if an act be a disreputable one, it is not any assurance a man can have of the secrecy of the particular act in question, that will of course surmount the objections he may have against engaging in it. Though the act in question should remain secret, it will go towards forming a habit, which may give birth to other acts, that may not meet with the same good fortune. There is no human being, perhaps, who is at years of discretion, on whom considerations of this sort have not some weight: and they have the more weight upon a man, in proportion to the strength of his intellectual powers, and the firmness of his mind.[2] Add to this, the influence which habit itself, when once formed, has in restraining a man from acts towards which, from the view of the disrepute annexed to them, as well as from any other cause, he has contracted an aversion. The influence of habit, in such cases, is a matter of fact, which, though not readily accounted for, is acknowledged and indubitable.[3]

39. After the dictates of the love of reputation come, as it should seem, those of the desire of amity. The former are disposed to coincide with those of utility, inasmuch as they are disposed to coincide with those of benevolence. Now those of the desire of amity are apt also to coincide, in a certain sort, with those of benevolence. But the sort of benevolence with the dictates of which the love of reputation coincides, is the more extensive; that with which those of the desire of amity coincide, the less extensive. Those of the love of amity have still, however, the advantage of those of the self-regarding motives. The former, at one period or other of his life, dispose a man to contribute to the happiness of a considerable number of persons: the latter, from the beginning of life to the end of it, confine themselves to the care of

Next, those of the desire of amity.

---

1 See B. II. tit. [Evidence].
2 See Chap. vi [Sensibility], par. 12, 13.
3 Strictly speaking, habit, being but a fictitious entity, and not really anything distinct from the acts or perceptions by which it is said to be formed, cannot be the cause of anything. The enigma, however, may be satisfactorily solved upon the principle of association, of the nature and force of which a very satisfactory account may be seen in Dr Priestley's edition of Hartley on Man.

that single individual. The dictates of the desire of amity, it is plain, will approach nearer to a coincidence with those of the love of reputation, and thence with those of utility, in proportion, *ceteris paribus*, to the number of the persons whose amity a man has occasion to desire: and hence it is, for example, that an English member of parliament, with all his own weaknesses, and all the follies of the people whose amity he has to cultivate, is probably, in general, a better character than the secretary of a visier at Constantinople, or of a naïb in Indostan.

Difficulty of placing those of religion. 40. The dictates of religion are, under the infinite diversity of religions, so extremely variable, that it is difficult to know what general account to give of them, or in what rank to place the motive they belong to. Upon the mention of religion, people's first thoughts turn naturally to the religion they themselves profess. This is a great source of miscalculation, and has a tendency to place this sort of motive in a higher rank than it deserves. The dictates of religion would coincide, in all cases, with those of utility, were the Being, who is the object of religion, universally supposed to be as benevolent as he is supposed to be wise and powerful; and were the notions entertained of his benevolence, at the same time, as correct as those which are entertained of his wisdom and his power. Unhappily, however, neither of these is the case. He is universally supposed to be all-powerful: for by the Deity, what else does any man mean than the Being, whatever he be, by whom every thing is done? And as to knowledge, by the same rule that he should know one thing he should know another. These notions seem to be as correct, for all material purposes, as they are universal. But among the votaries of religion (of which number the multifarious fraternity of Christians is but a small part) there seem to be but few (I will not say how few) who are real believers in his benevolence. They call him benevolent in words, but they do not mean that he is so in reality. They do not mean, that he is benevolent as man is conceived to be benevolent: they do not mean that he is benevolent in the only sense in which benevolence has a meaning. For if they did, they would recognise that the dictates of religion could be neither more nor less than the dictates of utility: not a tittle different: not a tittle less or more. But the case is, that on a thousand occasions they turn their backs on the principle of utility. They go astray after the strange principles its antagonists: sometimes it is the principle of asceticism: sometimes the principle of sympathy and antipathy.[1] Accordingly, the idea they bear in their minds, on such occasions, is but too often the idea of malevolence; to which idea, stripping it of its own proper name, they bestow the specious appellation of the social motive.[2] The dictates of religion, in short, are no other than the dictates of that principle which has been already mentioned under the name of the theological principle.[3] These, as has been observed, are just as it may happen, according to the biases of the person in question, copies of the dictates of one or other of the three original principles: sometimes, indeed, of the dictates of utility: but frequently of those of asceticism, or those of sympathy and antipathy. In this respect they are only on a par with the dictates of the love of reputation: in another they are below it. The dictates of religion are in all places intermixed more or less with dictates unconformable to those of utility, deduced from texts, well or ill interpreted, of the writings held for sacred by each sect: unconformable, by imposing practices sometimes inconvenient to a man's self, sometimes pernicious to the rest of the community. The sufferings of uncalled martyrs, the calamities of holy wars and religious persecutions, the mischiefs of intolerant laws, (objects which can here only be glanced at, not detailed) are so many additional mischiefs over and above the number of those which were ever brought into the world by the love of reputation. On the other hand, it is manifest, that with respect to the power of operating in secret, the dictates of religion have the same

1 Chap. ii [Principles Adverse], par. 18.

2 Sometimes, in order the better to conceal the cheat (from their own eyes doubtless as well as from others) they set up a phantom of their own, which they call Justice: whose dictates are to modify (which being explained, means. to oppose) the dictates of benevolence. But justice, in the only sense in which it has a meaning, is an imaginary personage, feigned for the convenience of discourse, whose dictates are the dictates of utility, applied to certain particular cases. Justice, then, is nothing more than an imaginary instrument, employed to forward on certain occasions, and by certain means, the purposes of benevolence. The dictates of justice are nothing more than a part of the dictates of benevolence, which, on certain occasions, are applied to certain subjects; to wit, to certain actions.

3 See Chap. ii [Principles Adverse, etc.]

advantage over those of the love of reputation, and the desire of amity, as is possessed by the dictates of benevolence.

Tendency they have to improve. 41. Happily, the dictates of religion seem to approach nearer and nearer to a coincidence with those of utility every day. But why? Because the dictates of the moral sanction do so: and those coincide with or are influenced by these. Men of the worst religions, influenced by the voice and practice of the surrounding world, borrow continually a new and a new leaf out of the book of utility: and with these, in order not to break with their religion, they endeavour, sometimes with violence enough, to patch together and adorn the repositories of their faith.

Afterwards come the self-regarding motives: and, lastly, that of displeasure. 42. As to the self-regarding and dissocial motives, the order that takes place among these, and the preceding one, in point of extra-regarding influence, is too evident to need insisting on. As to the order that takes place among the motives of the self-regarding class, considered in comparison with one another, there seems to be no difference which on this occasion would be worth mentioning. With respect to the dissocial motive, it makes a difference (with regard to its extra-regarding effects) from which of two sources it originates; whether from self-regarding or from social considerations. The displeasure you conceive against a man may be founded either on some act which offends you in the first instance, or on an act which offends you no otherwise than because you look upon it as being prejudicial to some other party on whose behalf you interest yourself: which other party may be of course either a determinate individual, or any assemblage. of individuals, determinate or indeterminate.[1] It is obvious enough, that a motive, though in itself dissocial, may, by issuing from a social origin, possess a social tendency; and that its tendency, in this case, is likely to be the more social, the more enlarged the description is of the persons whose interests you espouse. Displeasure, venting itself against a man, on account of a mischief supposed to be done by him to the public, may be more social in its effects than any goodwill, the exertions of which are confined to an individual.[2]

---

1 See Chap. vi [Sensibility], par. 21.
2 See *supra*, par. 37.

§ 5. *Conflict among motives*

43. When a man has it in contemplation to engage in any action, *Motives* he is frequently acted upon at the same time by the force of divers *impelling* motives: one motive, or set of motives, acting in one direction; *and* *restraining,* another motive, or set of motives, acting as it were in an opposite *what.* direction. The motives on one side disposing him to engage in the action: those on the other, disposing him not to engage in it. Now, any motive, the influence of which tends to dispose him to engage in the action in question, may be termed an *impelling* motive: any motive, the influence of which tends to dispose him not to engage in it, a *restraining* motive. But these appellations may of course be interchanged, according as the act is of the positive kind, or the negative.[1]

44. It has been shown, that there is no sort of motive but may *What are* give birth to any sort of action. It follows, therefore, that there are *the motives* no two motives but may come to be opposed to one another. *most* *frequently* Where the tendency of the act is bad, the most common case is for *at variance.* it to have been dictated by a motive either of the self-regarding, or of the dissocial class. In such case the motive of benevolence has commonly been acting, though ineffectually, in the character of a restraining motive.

45. An example may be of use, to show the variety of contending *Example* motives, by which a man may be acted upon at the same time. *to illustrate* Crillon, a Catholic (at a time when it was generally thought *a struggle* *among* meritorious among Catholics to extirpate Protestants), was or- *contending* dered by his king, Charles IX of France, to fall privately upon *motives.* Coligny, a Protestant, and assassinate him: his answer was, 'Excuse me, Sire; but I'll fight him with all my heart.'[2] Here, then, were all the three forces above mentioned, including that of the political sanction, acting upon him at once. By the political sanction, or at least so much of the force of it as such a mandate, from such a sovereign, issued on such an occasion, might be

1 See Chap. vii [Actions], par. 8.

2 The idea of the case here supposed is taken from an anecdote in real history, but varies from it in several particulars.

supposed to carry with it, he was enjoined to put Coligny to death in the way of assassination: by the religious sanction, that is, by the dictates of religious zeal, he was enjoined to put him to death in any way: by the moral sanction, or in other words, by the dictates of honour, that is, of the love of reputation, he was permitted (which permission, when coupled with the mandates of his sovereign, operated, he conceived, as an injunction) to fight the adversary upon equal terms: by the dictates of enlarged benevolence (supposing the mandate to be unjustifiable) he was enjoined not to attempt his life in any way, but to remain at peace with him: supposing the mandate to be unjustifiable, by the dictates of private benevolence he was enjoined not to meddle with him at any rate. Among this confusion of repugnant dictates, Crillon, it seems, gave the preference, in the first place, to those of honour: in the next place, to those of benevolence. He would have fought, had his offer been accepted; as it was not, he remained at peace.

Here a multitude of questions might arise. Supposing the dictates of the political sanction to follow the mandate of the sovereign, of what kind were the motives which they afforded him for compliance? The answer is, of the self-regarding kind at any rate: inasmuch as, by the supposition, it was in the power of the sovereign to punish him for non-compliance or reward him for compliance. Did they afford him the motive of religion (I mean independently of the circumstance of heresy above mentioned)? The answer is, Yes, if his notion was, that it was God's pleasure he should comply with them; No, if it was not. Did they afford him the motive of the love of reputation? Yes, if it was his notion that the world would expect and require that he should comply with them: No, if it was not. Did they afford him that of benevolence? Yes, if it was his notion that the community would upon the whole be the better for his complying with them: No, if it was not. But did the dictates of the political sanction, in the case in question, actually follow the mandates of the sovereign: in other words, was such a mandate legal? This we see is a mere question of local jurisprudence, altogether foreign to the present purpose.

46. What is here said about the goodness and badness of motives, is far from being a mere matter of words. There will be occasion

to make use of it hereafter for various important purposes. I shall have need of it for the sake of dissipating various prejudices, which are of disservice to the community, sometimes by cherishing the flame of civil dissensions,[1] at other times, by obstructing the course of justice. It will be shown, that in the case of many offences,[2] the consideration of the motive is a most material one: for that in the first place it makes a very material difference in the magnitude of the mischief:[3] in the next place, that it is easy to be ascertained; and thence may be made a ground for a difference in the demand for punishment: but that in other cases it is altogether incapable of being ascertained; and that, were it capable of being ever so well ascertained, good or bad, it could make no difference in the demand for punishment: that in all cases, the motive that may happen to govern a prosecutor, is a consideration totally immaterial: whence may be seen the mischievousness of the prejudice that is so apt to be entertained against informers; and the consequence it is of that the judge, in particular, should be proof against the influence of such delusions.

Practical use of the above disquisitions relative to motives.

Lastly, The subject of motives is one with which it is necessary to be acquainted, in order to pass a judgment on any means that may be proposed for combating offences in their source.[4]

But before the theoretical foundation for these practical observations can be completely laid, it is necessary we should say something on the subject of *disposition*: which, accordingly, will furnish matter for the ensuing chapter.

---

1 See B. I. tit. [Rebellion].
2 See B. I. tit. [Simp. corp. injuries]. Ib. tit. [Homicide].
3 See Chap. xi [Dispositions].
4 See Append. tit. [Preventive Institutions].

CHAPTER XI

Of Human Dispositions in General

Disposition what. 1. In the foregoing chapter it has been shown at large, that goodness or badness cannot, with any propriety, be predicated of motives. Is there nothing then about a man that can properly be termed good or bad, when, on such or such an occasion, he suffers himself to be governed by such or such a motive? Yes, certainly: his *disposition*. Now disposition is a kind of fictitious entity, feigned for the convenience of discourse, in order to express what there is supposed to be *permanent* in a man's frame of mind, where, on such or such an occasion, he has been influenced by such or such a motive, to engage in an act, which, as it appeared to him, was of such or such a tendency.

– how far it belongs to the present subject. 2. It is with disposition as with everything else: it will be good or bad according to its effects: according to the effects it has in augmenting or diminishing the happiness of the community. A man's disposition may accordingly be considered in two points of view: according to the influence it has, either, 1. on his own happiness: or, 2. on the happiness of others. Viewed in both these lights together, or in either of them indiscriminately, it may be termed, on the one hand, good; on the other, bad; or, in flagrant cases, depraved.[1] Viewed in the former of these lights, it has

---

1 It might also be termed virtuous, or vicious. The only objection to the use of those terms on the present occasion is, the great quantity of good and bad repute that respectively stand annexed to them. The inconvenience of this is, their being apt to annex an ill-proportioned measure of disrepute to dispositions which are ill-constituted only with respect to the party himself: involving them in such a degree of ignominy as should be appropriated to such dispositions only as are mischievous with regard to others. To exalt weaknesses to a level with crimes, is a way to diminish the abhorrence which ought to be reserved for crimes. To exalt small evils to a level with great ones, is the way to diminish the share of attention which ought to be paid to great ones.

scarcely any peculiar name, which has as yet been appropriated to it. It might be termed, though but inexpressively, frail or infirm, on the one hand: sound or firm, on the other. Viewed in the other light, it might be termed beneficent, or meritorious, on the one hand: pernicious or mischievous, on the other. Now of that branch of a man's disposition, the effects of which regard in the first instance only himself, there needs not much to be said here. To reform it when bad, is the business rather of the moralist than the legislator: nor is it susceptible of those various modifications which make so material a difference in the effects of the other. Again, with respect to that part of it, the effects whereof regard others in the first instance, it is only in as far as it is of a mischievous nature that the penal branch of law has any immediate concern with it: in as far as it may be of a beneficent nature, it belongs to a hitherto but little cultivated, and as yet unnamed branch of law, which might be styled the remuneratory.

3. A man then is said to be of a mischievous disposition, when, by the influence of no matter what motives, he is *presumed* to be more apt to engage, or form intentions of engaging, in acts which are *apparently* of a pernicious tendency, than in such as are apparently of a beneficial tendency: of a meritorious or beneficent disposition in the opposite case.

A mischievous disposition; a meritorious disposition; what.

4. I say presumed: for, by the supposition, all that appears is one single action, attended with one single train of circumstances: but from that degree of consistency and uniformity which experience has shown to be observable in the different actions of the same person, the probable existence (past or future) of a number of acts of a similar nature, is naturally and justly inferred from the observation of one single one. Under such circumstances, such as the motive proves to be in one instance, such is the disposition to be presumed to be in others.

What a man's disposition is, can only be matter for presumption.

5. I say *apparently* mischievous: that is, apparently with regard to him: such as to him appear to possess that tendency: for from the mere event, independent of what to him it appears beforehand likely to be, nothing can be inferred on either side. If to him it appears likely to be mischievous, in such case, though in the upshot it should prove innocent, or even beneficial, it makes no

It depends upon what the act appears to be to him.

difference; there is not the less reason for presuming his disposition to be a bad one: if to him it appears likely to be beneficial or innocent, in such case, though in the upshot it should prove pernicious, there is not the more reason on that account for presuming his disposition to be a good one. And here we see the importance of the circumstances of intentionality,[1] consciousness,[2] unconsciousness,[2] and mis-supposal.[2]

Which position is grounded on two facts: 1. The correspondence between intentions and consequences: 2. Between the intentions of the same person at different times.

6. The truth of these positions depends upon two others, both of them sufficiently verified by experience: The one is, that in the ordinary course of things the consequences of actions commonly turn out conformable to intentions. A man who sets up a butcher's shop, and deals in beef, when he intends to knock down an ox, commonly does knock down an ox; though by some unlucky accident he may chance to miss his blow and knock down a man: he who sets up a grocer's shop, and deals in sugar, when he intends to sell sugar, commonly does sell sugar: though by some unlucky accident he may chance to sell arsenic in the room of it.

7. The other is, that a man who entertains intentions of doing mischief at one time is apt to entertain the like intentions at another.[3]

The disposition is to be inferred: 1. From the apparent tendency of the act: 2. From the nature of the motive.

8. There are two circumstances upon which the nature of the disposition, as indicated by any act, is liable to depend: 1. The apparent tendency of the act: 2. The nature of the motive which gave birth to it. This dependency is subject to different rules, according to the nature of the motive. In stating them, I suppose all along the apparent tendency of the act to be, as it commonly is, the same as the real.

1 See Chap. viii.

2 See Chap. ix.

3 To suppose a man to be of a good disposition, and at the same time likely, in virtue of that very disposition, to engage in an habitual train of mischievous actions, is a contradiction in terms: nor could such a proposition ever be advanced, but from the giving, to the thing which the word disposition is put for, a reality which does *not* belong to it. If then, for example, a man of religious disposition should, in virtue of that very disposition, be in the habit of doing mischief, for instance, by persecuting his neighbours, the case must be, either that his disposition, though good in certain respects, is not good upon the whole: or that a religious disposition is not in general a good one.

9. (1) Where the tendency of the act is *good*, and the motive is of the *self-regarding* kind. In this case the motive affords no inference on either side. It affords no indication of a good disposition: but neither does it afford any indication of a bad one.

Case 1. Tendency, good – motive, self-regarding.

A baker sells his bread to a hungry man who asks for it. This, we see, is one of those acts of which, in ordinary cases, the tendency is unquestionably good. The baker's motive is the ordinary commercial motive of pecuniary interest. It is plain, that there is nothing in the transaction, thus stated, that can afford the least ground for presuming that the baker is a better or a worse man than any of his neighbours.

10. (2) Where the tendency of the act is *bad*, and the motive, as before, is of the *self-regarding* kind. In this case the disposition indicated is a mischievous one.

Case 2. Tendency, bad – motive, self-regarding.

A man steals bread out of a baker's shop: this is one of those acts of which the tendency will readily be acknowledged to be bad. Why, and in what respects it is so, will be stated farther on.[1] His motive, we will say, is that of pecuniary interest; the desire of getting the value of the bread for nothing. His disposition, accordingly, appears to be a bad one: for everyone will allow a thievish disposition to be a bad one.

11. (3) Where the tendency of the act is *good*, and the motive is the purely social one of *good-will*. In this case the disposition indicated is a beneficent one.

Case 3. Tendency, good – motive, goodwill.

A baker gives a poor man a loaf of bread. His motive is compassion; a name given to the motive of benevolence, in particular cases of its operation. The disposition indicated by the baker, in this case, is such as every man will be ready enough to acknowledge to be a good one.

12. (4) Where the tendency of the act is *bad*, and the motive is the purely social one of good-will. Even in this case the disposition which the motive indicates is dubious: it may be a mischievous or a meritorious one, as it happens; according as the mischievousness of the act is more or less apparent.

Case 4. Tendency, bad – motive, good-will.

---

1 See Chap. xii [Consequences], and Code, B. I. tit. [Theft].

This case not an impossible one. 13. It may be thought, that a case of this sort cannot exist; and that to suppose it, is a contradiction in terms. For the act is one, which, by the supposition, the agent knows to be a mischievous one. How then can it be, that good-will, that is, the desire of doing good, could have been the motive that led him into it? To reconcile this, we must advert to the distinction between enlarged benevolence and confined.[1] The motive that led him into it, was that of confined benevolence. Had he followed the dictates of enlarged benevolence, he would not have done what he did. Now, although he followed the dictates of that branch of benevolence, which in any single instance of its exertion is mischievous, when opposed to the other, yet, as the cases which call for the exertion of the former are, beyond comparison, more numerous than those which call for the exertion of the latter, the disposition indicated by him, in following the impulse of the former, will often be such as in a man, of the common run of men, may be allowed to be a good one upon the whole.

Example I. 14. A man with a numerous family of children, on the point of starving, goes into a baker's shop, steals a loaf, divides it all among the children, reserving none of it for himself. It will be hard to infer that that man's disposition is a mischievous one upon the whole. Alter the case, give him but one child, and that hungry perhaps, but in no imminent danger of starving: and now let the man set fire to a house full of people, for the sake of stealing money out of it to buy the bread with. The disposition here indicated will hardly be looked upon as a good one.

Example II. 15. Another case will appear more difficult to decide than either. Ravaillac assassinated one of the best and wisest of sovereigns, at a time when a good and wise sovereign, a blessing at all times so valuable to a state, was particularly precious: and that to the inhabitants of a populous and extensive empire. He is taken, and doomed to the most excruciating tortures. His son, well persuaded of his being a sincere penitent, and that mankind, in case of his being at large, would have nothing more to fear from him, effectuates his escape. Is this then a sign of a good disposition in

---

1 See Chap. x [Motives].

the son, or of a bad one? Perhaps some will answer, of a bad one; for, besides the interest which the nation has in the sufferings of such a criminal, on the score of the example, the future good behaviour of such a criminal is more than anyone can have sufficient ground to be persuaded of.

16. Well then, let Ravaillac, the son, not facilitate his father's *Example* escape; but content himself with conveying poison to him, that at *III.* the price of an easier death he may escape his torments. The decision will now, perhaps, be more difficult. The *act* is a wrong one, let it be allowed, and such as ought by all means to be punished: but is the *disposition* manifested by it a bad one? Because the young man breaks the laws in this one instance, is it probable, that if let alone, he would break the laws in ordinary instances, for the satisfaction of any inordinate desires of his own? The answer of most men would probably be in the negative.

17. (5) Where the tendency of the act is *good*, and the motive is a *Case 5.* semi-social one, the *love of reputation*: in this case the disposition *Tendency,* indicated is a good one. *good –*
                                                                                        motive,
In a time of scarcity, a baker, for the sake of gaining the esteem of *love of* the neighbourhood, distributes bread *gratis* among the industrious *reputation.* poor. Let this be taken for granted: and let it be allowed to be a matter of uncertainty, whether he had any real feeling for the sufferings of those whom he has relieved, or no. His disposition, for all that, cannot, with any pretence of reason, be termed otherwise than a good and beneficent one. It can only be in consequence of some very idle prejudice, if it receives a different name.[1]

---

1 The bulk of mankind, ever ready to depreciate the character of their neighbours, in order, indirectly, to exalt their own, will take occasion to refer a motive to the class of bad ones as often as they can find one still better, to which the act might have owed its birth. Conscious that his own motives are not of the best class, or persuaded that if they be, they will not be referred to that class by others; afraid of being taken for a dupe, and anxious to show the reach of his penetration; each man takes care, in the first place, to impute the conduct of every other man to the least laudable of the motives that can account for it: in the next place, when he has gone as far that way as he can, and cannot drive down the individual motive to any lower class, he changes his battery, and attacks the very class itself. To the love of reputation he will accordingly give a bad name upon every occasion, calling it ostentation, vanity, or vain-glory.

Partly to the same spirit of detraction, the natural consequence of the

Case 6.
Tendency,
bad –
motive,
honour.

18. (6) Where the tendency of the act is *bad*, and the motive, as before, is a semi-social one, the love of reputation. In this case, the disposition which it indicates is more or less good or bad: in the first place, according as the tendency of the act is more or less mischievous: in the next place according as the dictates of the moral sanction, in the society in question, approach more or less to a coincidence with those of utility. It does not seem probable, that in any nation, which is in a state of tolerable civilization, in short, in any nation in which such rules as these can come to be consulted, the dictates of the moral sanction will so far recede from a coincidence with those of utility (that is, of enlightened benevolence) that the disposition indicated in this case can be otherwise than a good one upon the whole.

Example I.

19. An Indian receives an injury, real or imaginary, from an Indian of another tribe. He revenges it upon the person of his antagonist with the most excruciating torments: the case being, that cruelties inflicted on such an occasion, gain him reputation in his own tribe. The disposition manifested in such a case can never be deemed a good one, among a people ever so few degrees advanced, in point of civilization, above the Indians.

Example II.

20. A nobleman (to come back to Europe) contracts a debt with a poor tradesman. The same nobleman, presently afterwards, contracts a debt, to the same amount, to another nobleman, at play. He is unable to pay both: but he pays the whole debt to the companion of his amusements, and no part of it to the tradesman. The disposition manifested in this case can scarcely be termed otherwise than a bad one. It is certainly, however, not so bad as if he had paid neither. The principle of love of reputation, or (as it

---

sensibility of men to the force of the moral sanction, partly to the influence of the principle of asceticism, may, perhaps, be imputed the great abundance of bad names of motives, in comparison of such as are good or neutral: and, in particular, the total want of neutral names for the motives of sexual desire, physical desire in general, and pecuniary interest. The superior abundance, even of good names, in comparison of neutral ones, would, if examined, be found rather to confirm than disprove the above remark. The language of a people on these points may, perhaps, serve in some measure as a key to their moral sentiments. But such speculative disquisitions are foreign to the purpose of the present work.

is called in the case of this partial application of it) honour, is here opposed to the worthier principle of benevolence, and gets the better of it. But it gets the better also of the self-regarding principle of pecuniary interest. The disposition, therefore, which it indicates, although not so good a one as that in which the principle of benevolence predominates, is better than one in which the principle of self-interest predominates. He would be the better for having more benevolence: but would he be the better for having no honour? This seems to admit of great dispute.[1]

21. (7) Where the tendency of the act is *good*, and the motive is the semi-social one of *religion*. In this case, the disposition indicated by it (considered with respect to the influence of it on the man's conduct towards others) is manifestly a beneficent and meritorious one.

Case 7. Tendency, good – motive, piety.

A baker distributes bread *gratis* among the industrious poor. It is not that he feels for their distresses: nor is it for the sake of gaining reputation among his neighbours. It is for the sake of gaining the favour of the Deity: to whom, he takes for granted, such conduct will be acceptable. The disposition manifested by such conduct is plainly what every man would call a good one.

22. (8) Where the tendency of the act is *bad*, and the motive is that of religion, as before. In this case the disposition is dubious. It is good or bad, and more or less good or bad, in the first place, as the tendency of the act is more or less mischievous; in the next place, according as the religious tenets of the person in question approach more or less to a coincidence with the dictates of utility.

Case 8. Tendency, bad – motive, religion.

23. It should seem from history, that even in nations in a tolerable state of civilization in other respects, the dictates of religion have been found so far to recede from a coincidence with those of utility; in other words, from those of enlightened benevolence; that the disposition indicated in this case may even be a bad one upon the whole. This however is no objection to the inference which it affords of a good disposition in those countries (such as

The disposition may be bad in this case.

1 See the case of Duels discussed in B. I. tit. [Homicide].

perhaps are most of the countries of Europe at present) in which its dictates respecting the conduct of a man towards other men approach very nearly to a coincidence with those of utility. The dictates of religion, in their application to the conduct of a man in what concerns himself alone, seem in most European nations to savour a good deal of the ascetic principle: but the obedience to such mistaken dictates indicates not any such disposition as is likely to break out into acts of pernicious tendency with respect to others. Instances in which the dictates of religion lead a man into acts which are pernicious in this latter view, seem at present to be but rare: unless it be acts of persecution, or impolitic measures on the part of government, where the law itself is either the principal actor or an accomplice in the mischief. Ravaillac, instigated by no other motive than this, gave his country one of the most fatal stabs that a country ever received from a single hand: but happily the Ravaillacs are but rare. They have been more frequent, however, in France than in any other country during the same period: and it is remarkable, that in every instance it is this motive that has produced them. When they do appear, however, nobody, I suppose, but such as themselves, will be for terming a disposition, such as they manifest, a good one. It seems hardly to be denied, but that they are just so much the worse for their notions of religion; and that had they been left to the sole guidance of benevolence, and the love of reputation, without any religion at all, it would have been but so much the better for mankind. One may say nearly the same thing, perhaps, of those persons who, without any particular obligation, have taken an active part in the execution of laws made for the punishment of those who have the misfortune to differ with the magistrate in matters of religion, much more of the legislator himself, who has put it in their power. If Louis XIV had had no religion, France would not have lost 800,000 of its most valuable subjects. The same thing may be said of the authors of the wars called holy ones; whether waged against persons called Infidels, or persons branded with the still more odious name of Heretics. In Denmark, not a great many years ago, a sect is said to have arisen, who, by a strange perversion of reason, took it into their heads, that, by leading to repentance, murder, or any other horrid crime, might be made the road to heaven. It should all along, however, be observed, that instances of this latter kind were always rare: and that in almost all the countries of Europe, instances of the former kind, though once abundantly frequent, have for some time ceased. In certain countries, however, persecution at home, or (what produces a degree of restraint, which is one part of the mischiefs of persecution) I mean the *disposition* to persecute, whensoever occasion happens, is not yet at an end: insomuch that if there is no *actual* persecution, it is only because there are no heretics; and if there are no heretics, it is only because there are no thinkers.[1]

24. (9) Where the tendency of the act is *good*, and the motive (as before) is the dissocial one of ill-will. In this case the motive seems not to afford any indication on either side. It is no indication of a good disposition; but neither is it any indication of a bad one.

Case 9. Tendency, good— motive, malevolence.

You have detected a baker in selling short weight: you prosecute him for the cheat. It is not for the sake of gain that you engaged in the prosecution; for there is nothing to be got by it: it is not from public spirit: it is not for the sake of reputation; for there is no reputation to be got by it: it is not in the view of pleasing the Deity: it is merely on account of a quarrel you have with the man you prosecute. From the transaction, as thus stated, there does not seem to be anything to be said either in favour of your disposition or against it. The tendency of the act is good: but you would not have engaged in it, had it not been from a motive which there seems no particular reason to conclude will ever prompt you to engage in an act of the same kind again. Your motive is of that sort which may, with least impropriety, be termed a bad one: but the act is of that sort, which, were it engaged in ever so often, could never have any evil tendency; nor indeed any other tendency than a good one. By the supposition, the motive it happened to be dictated by was that of ill-will: but the act itself is of such a nature as to have wanted nothing but sufficient discernment on your part in order to have been dictated by the most enlarged benevolence. Now, from a man's having suffered himself to be induced to gratify his resentment by means of an act of which the tendency is good, it by no means follows

Example.

---

1 See B. I. tit. [Offences against Religion].

that he would be ready on another occasion, through the influence of the same sort of motive, to engage in any act of which the tendency is a bad one. The motive that impelled you was a dissocial one: but what social motive could there have been to restrain you? None, but what might have been outweighed by a more enlarged motive of the same kind. Now, because the dissocial motive prevailed when it stood alone, it by no means follows that it would prevail when it had a social one to combat it.

Case 10.
Tendency,
bad —
motive,
malevolence.

25. (10) Where the tendency of the act is *bad*, and the motive is the dissocial one of malevolence. In this case the disposition it indicates is of course a mischievous one.

Example.

The man who stole the bread from the baker, as before, did it with no other view than merely to impoverish and afflict him: accordingly, when he had got the bread, he did not eat, or sell it; but destroyed it. That the disposition, evidenced by such a transaction, is a bad one, is what everybody must perceive immediately.

Problem —
to measure
the
depravity
in a man's
disposition.

26. Thus much with respect to the circumstances from which the mischievousness or meritoriousness of a man's disposition is to be inferred in the gross: we come now to the *measure* of that mischievousness or meritoriousness, as resulting from those circumstances. Now with meritorious acts and dispositions we have no direct concern in the present work. All that penal law is concerned to do, is to measure the depravity of the disposition where the act is mischievous. To this object, therefore, we shall here confine ourselves.

A man's
disposition is
constituted
by the sum
of his
intentions:

27. It is evident, that the nature of a man's disposition must depend upon the nature of the motives he is apt to be influenced by: in other words, upon the degree of his sensibility to the force of such and such motives. For his disposition is, as it were, the sum of his intentions: the disposition he is of during a certain period, the sum or result of his intentions during that period. If, of the acts he has been intending to engage in during the supposed period, those which are apparently of a mischievous tendency, bear a large proportion to those which appear to him to be of the contrary tendency, his disposition will be of the mischievous cast: if but a small proportion, of the innocent or upright.

28. Now intentions, like everything else, are produced by the *— which owe their birth to motives.* things that are their causes: and the causes of intentions are motives. If, on any occasion, a man forms either a good or a bad intention, it must be by the influence of some motive.

29. When the act, which a motive prompts a man to engage in, *A seducing or corrupting motive, what — a tutelary or preservatory motive.* is of a mischievous nature, it may, for distinction's sake, be termed a *seducing* or corrupting motive: in which case also any motive which, in opposition to the former, acts in the character of a restraining motive, may be styled a *tutelary*, preservatory, or preserving motive.

30. Tutelary motives may again be distinguished into *standing* or *Tutelary motives are either standing or occasional.* constant, and *occasional*. By standing tutelary motives, I mean such as act with more or less force in all, or at least in most cases, tending to restrain a man from *any* mischievous acts he may be prompted to engage in; and that with a force which depends upon the general nature of the act, rather than upon any accidental circumstance with which any individual act of that sort may happen to be accompanied. By occasional tutelary motives, I mean such motives as may chance to act in this direction or not, according to the nature of the act, and of the particular occasion on which the engaging in it is brought into contemplation.

31. Now it has been shown, that there is no sort of motive by *Standing tutelary motives are, 1. Good-will.* which a man may not be prompted to engage in acts that are of a mischievous nature; that is, which may not come to act in the capacity of a seducing motive. It has been shown, on the other hand, that there are some motives which are remarkably less likely to operate in this way than others. It has also been shown, that the least likely of all is that of benevolence or good-will: the most common tendency of which, it has been shown, is to act in the character of a tutelary motive. It has also been shown, that even when by accident it acts in one way in the character of a seducing motive, still in another way it acts in the opposite character of a tutelary one. The motive of good-will, in as far as it respects the interests of one set of persons, may prompt a man to engage in acts which are productive of mischief to another and more extensive set: but this is only because his good-will is imperfect and confined: not taking into contemplation the interests of all the

persons whose interests are at stake. The same motive, were the affection it issued from more enlarged, would operate effectually, in the character of a constraining motive, against that very act to which, by the supposition, it gives birth. This same sort of motive may therefore, without any real contradiction or deviation from truth, be ranked in the number of standing tutelary motives, notwithstanding the occasions in which it may act at the same time in the character of a seducing one.

2. *The love of reputation.* 32. The same observation, nearly, may be applied to the semi-social motive of love of reputation. The force of this, like that of the former, is liable to be divided against itself. As in the case of good-will, the interests of some of the persons, who may be the objects of that sentiment, are liable to be at variance with those of others: so in the case of love of reputation, the sentiments of some of the persons, whose good opinion is desired, may be at variance with the sentiments of other persons of that number. Now in the case of an act, which is really of a mischievous nature, it can scarcely happen that there shall be no persons whatever who will look upon it with an eye of disapprobation. It can scarcely ever happen, therefore, that an act really mischievous shall not have some part at least, if not the whole, of the force of this motive to oppose it; nor, therefore, that this motive should not act with some degree of force in the character of a tutelary motive. This, therefore, may be set down as another article in the catalogue of standing tutelary motives.

3. *The desire of amity.* 33. The same observation may be applied to the desire of amity, though not in altogether equal measure. For, notwithstanding the mischievousness of an act, it may happen, without much difficulty, that all the persons for whose amity a man entertains any particular present desire which is accompanied with expectation, may concur in regarding it with an eye rather of approbation than the contrary. This is but too apt to be the case among such fraternities as those of thieves, smugglers, and many other denominations of offenders. This, however, is not constantly, nor indeed most commonly the case: insomuch, that the desire of amity may still be regarded, upon the whole, as a tutelary motive, were it only from the closeness of its connexion with the love of reputation. And it may be ranked among standing tutelary

motives, since, where it does apply, the force with which it acts, depends not upon the occasional circumstances of the act which it opposes, but upon principles as general as those upon which depend the action of the other semi-social motives.

34. The motive of religion is not altogether in the same case with the three former. The force of it is not, like theirs, liable to be divided against itself. I mean in the civilized nations of modern times, among whom the notion of the unity of the Godhead is universal. In times of classical antiquity it was otherwise. If a man got Venus on his side, Pallas was on the other: if Aeolus was for him, Neptune was against him. Aeneas, with all his pity, had but a partial interest at the court of heaven. That matter stands upon a different footing now-a-days. In any given person, the force of religion, whatever it be, is now all of it on one side. It may balance, indeed, on which side it shall declare itself: and it may declare itself, as we have seen already in but too many instances, on the wrong as well as on the right. It has been, at least till lately, perhaps is still, accustomed so much to declare itself on the wrong side, and that in such material instances, that on that account it seemed not proper to place it, in point of social tendency, on a level altogether with the motive of benevolence. Where it does act, however, as it does in by far the greatest number of cases, in opposition to the ordinary seducing motives, it acts, like the motive of benevolence, in an uniform manner, not depending upon the particular circumstances that may attend the commission of the act; but tending to oppose it, merely on account of its mischievousness; and therefore, with equal force, in whatsoever circumstances it may be proposed to be committed. This, therefore, may also be added to the catalogue of standing tutelary motives.

4. The motive of religion.

35. As to the motives which may operate occasionally in the character of tutelary motives, these, it has been already intimated, are of various sorts, and various degrees of strength in various offences: depending not only upon the nature of the offence, but upon the accidental circumstances in which the idea of engaging in it may come in contemplation. Nor is there any sort of motive which may not come to operate in this character; as may be easily conceived. A thief, for instance, may be prevented from engaging in a projected scheme of house-breaking, by sitting too long over

Occasional tutelary motives may be any whatsoever.

his bottle,[1] by a visit from his doxy, by the occasion he may have to go elsewhere, in order to receive his dividend of a former booty;[2] and so on.

Motives that are particularly apt to act in this character are, 1. Love of ease. 2. Self-preservation.

36. There are some motives, however, which seem more apt to act in this character than others; especially as things are now constituted, now that the law has everywhere opposed to the force of the principal seducing motives, artificial tutelary motives of its own creation. Of the motives here meant it will be necessary to take a general view. They seem to be reducible to two heads; *viz.* 1. The love of ease; a motive put into action by the prospect of the trouble of the attempt; that is, the trouble which it may be necessary to bestow, in overcoming the physical difficulties that may accompany it. 2. Self-preservation, as opposed to the dangers to which a man may be exposed in the prosecution of it.

Dangers to which self-preservation is most apt in this case to have respect, are, 1. Dangers purely physical. 2. Dangers depending on detection.

37. These dangers may be either, 1. Of a purely physical nature: or, 2. Dangers resulting from moral agency; in other words, from the conduct of any such persons to whom the act, if known, may be expected to prove obnoxious. But moral agency supposes knowledge with respect to the circumstances that are to have the effect of external motives in giving birth to it. Now the obtaining such knowledge, with respect to the commission of any obnoxious act, on the part of any persons who may be disposed to make the agent suffer for it, is called *detection*; and the agent concerning whom such knowledge is obtained, is said to be detected. The dangers, therefore, which may threaten an offender from this quarter, depend, whatever they may be, on the event of his detection; and may, therefore, be all of them comprised under the article of the *danger of detection*.

Danger depending on detection may result from, 1. Opposition on the spot: 2. Subsequent punishment.

38. The danger depending upon detection may be divided again into two branches: 1. That which may result from any opposition that may be made to the enterprise by persons on the spot; that is, at the very time the enterprise is carrying on: 2. That which respects the legal punishment, or other suffering, that may await at a distance upon the issue of the enterprise.

1 Love of the pleasures of the palate.
2 Pecuniary interest.

39. It may be worth calling to mind on this occasion, that among the tutelary motives, which have been styled constant ones, there are two of which the force depends (though not so entirely as the force of the occasional ones which have been just mentioned, yet in a great measure) upon the circumstance of detection. These, it may be remembered, are, the love of reputation, and the desire of amity. In proportion, therefore, as the chance of being detected appears greater, these motives will apply with the greater force: with the less force, as it appears less. This is not the case with the two other standing tutelary motives, that of benevolence, and that of religion. *The force of the two standing tutelary motives of love of reputation, and desire of amity, depend upon detection.*

40. We are now in a condition to determine, with some degree of precision, what is to be understood by the *strength of a temptation*, and what indication it may give of the degree of mischievousness in a man's disposition in the case of any offence. *Strength of a temptation, what is meant by it.* When a man is prompted to engage in any mischievous act, we will say, for shortness, in an offence, the strength of the temptation depends upon the ratio between the force of the seducing motives on the one hand, and such of the occasional tutelary ones, as the circumstances of the case call forth into action, on the other. The temptation, then, may be said to be strong, when the pleasure or advantage to be got from the crime is such as in the eyes of the offender must appear great in comparison of the trouble and danger that appear to him to accompany the enterprise: slight or weak, when that pleasure or advantage is such as must appear small in comparison of such trouble and such danger. It is plain the strength of the temptation depends not upon the force of the impelling (that is of the seducing) motives altogether: for let the opportunity be more favourable, that is, let the trouble, or any branch of the danger, be made less than before, it will be acknowledged, that the temptation is made so much the stronger: and on the other hand, let the opportunity become less favourable, or, in other words, let the trouble, or any branch of the danger, be made greater than before, the temptation will be so much the weaker.,

Now, after taking account of such tutelary motives as have been styled occasional, the only tutelary motives that can remain are those which have been termed standing ones. But those which have been termed the standing tutelary motives, are the same that we have been styling social. It follows, therefore, that the strength of the temptation, in any case, after deducting the force of the social motives, is as the sum of the forces of the seducing, to the sum of the forces of the occasional tutelary motives.

Indications afforded by this and other circumstances respecting the depravity of an offender's disposition. 41. It remains to be inquired, what indication concerning the mischievousness or depravity of a man's disposition is afforded by the strength of the temptation, in the case where any offence happens to have been committed. It appears, then, that the weaker the temptation is, by which a man has been overcome, the more depraved and mischievous it shows his disposition to have been. For the goodness of his disposition is measured by the degree of his sensibility to the action of the social motives:[1] in other words, by the strength of the influence which those motives have over him: now, the less considerable the force is by which their influence on him has been overcome, the more convincing is the proof that has been given of the weakness of that influence.

Again, The degree of a man's sensibility to the force of the social motives being given, it is plain that the force with which those motives tend to restrain him from engaging in any mischievous enterprise, will be as the apparent mischievousness of such enterprise, that is, as the degree of mischief with which it appears to *him* likely to be attended. In other words, the less mischievous the offence appears to him to be, the less averse he will be, as far as he is guided by social considerations, to engage in it; the more mischievous, the more averse. If then the nature of the offence is such as must appear to him highly mischievous, and yet he engages in it notwithstanding, it shows, that the degree of his sensibility to the force of the social motives is but slight; and consequently that his disposition is proportionately depraved. Moreover, the less the strength of the temptation was, the more pernicious and depraved does it show his disposition to have been. For the less the strength of the temptation was, the less was the force which the influence of those motives had to overcome: the clearer therefore is the proof that has been given of the weakness of that influence.

1 *Supra*, par. 27, 28.

42. From what has been said, it seems, that, for judging of the indication that is afforded concerning the depravity of a man's disposition by the strength of the temptation, compared with the mischievousness of the enterprise, the following rules may be laid down.

Rules for measuring the depravity of disposition indicated by an offence.

Rule 1. *The strength of the temptation being given, the mischievousness of the disposition manifested by the enterprise, is as the apparent mischievousness of the act.*

Thus, it would show a more depraved disposition, to murder a man for a reward of a guinea, or falsely to charge him with a robbery for the same reward, than to obtain the same sum from him by simple theft: the trouble he would have to take, and the risk he would have to run, being supposed to stand on the same footing in the one case as in the other.

Rule 2. *The apparent mischievousness of the act being given, a man's disposition is the more depraved, the slighter the temptation is by which he has been overcome.*

Thus, it shows a more depraved and dangerous disposition, if a man kill another out of mere sport, as the Emperor of Morocco, Muley Mahomet, is said to have done great numbers, than out of revenge, as Sylla and Marius did thousands, or in the view of self-preservation, as Augustus killed many, or even for lucre, as the same Emperor is said to have killed some. And the effects of such a depravity, on that part of the public which is apprized of it, run in the same proportion. From Augustus, some persons only had to fear, under some particular circumstances. From Muley Mahomet, every man had to fear at all times.

Rule 3. *The apparent mischievousness of the act being given, the evidence which it affords of the depravity of a man's disposition is the less conclusive, the stronger the temptation is by which he has been overcome.*

Thus, if a poor man, who is ready to die with hunger, steal a loaf of bread, it is a less explicit sign of depravity, than if a rich man were to commit a theft to the same amount. It will be observed, that in this rule all that is said is, that the evidence of depravity is in this case the less conclusive: it is not said that the depravity is positively the less. For in this case it is possible, for anything that appears to the contrary, that the theft might have been committed, even had the temptation been not so strong. In this case, the alleviating circumstance is only a matter of presumption; in the former, the aggravating circumstance is a matter of certainty.

Rule 4. *Where the motive is of the dissocial kind, the apparent mischievousness of the act, and the strength of the temptation, being given, the depravity is as the degree of deliberation with which it is accompanied.*

For in every man, be his disposition ever so depraved, the social motives are those which, wherever the self-regarding ones stand neuter, regulate and determine the general tenor of his life. If the dissocial motives are put in action, it is only in particular circumstances, and on particular occasions; the gentle but constant force of the social motives being for a while subdued. The general and standing bias of every man's nature is, therefore, towards that side to which the force of the social motives would determine him to adhere. This being the case, the force of the social motives tends continually to put an end to that of the dissocial ones; as, in natural bodies, the force of friction tends to put an end to that which is generated by impulse. Time, then, which wears away the force of the dissocial motives, adds to that of the social. The longer, therefore, a man continues, on a given occasion, under the dominion of the dissocial motives, the more convincing is the proof that has been given of his insensibility to the force of the social ones.

Thus, it shows a worse disposition, where a man lays a deliberate plan for beating his antagonist, and beats him accordingly, than if he were to beat him upon the spot, in consequence of a sudden quarrel: and worse again, if, after having had him a long while together in his power, he beats him at intervals, and at his leisure.[1]

Use of this chapter. 43. The depravity of disposition, indicated by an act, is a material consideration in several respects. Any mark of extraordinary depravity, by adding to the terror already inspired by the crime, and by holding up the offender as a person from whom there may be more mischief to be apprehended in future, adds in that way to the demand for punishment. By indicating a general want of sensibility on the part of the offender, it may add in another way

---

1 See B. I. tit. [Confinement].

also to the demand for punishment. The article of disposition is of the more importance, inasmuch as, in measuring out the quantum of punishment, the principle of sympathy and antipathy is apt to look at nothing else. A man who punishes because he hates, and only because he hates, such a man, when he does not find anything odious in the disposition, is not for punishing at all; and when he does, he is not for carrying the punishment further than his hatred carries him. Hence the aversion we find so frequently expressed against the maxim, that the punishment must rise with the strength of the temptation; a maxim, the contrary of which, as we shall see, would be as cruel to offenders themselves, as it would be subversive of the purposes of punishment.

CHAPTER XII

Of the Consequences of a Mischievous Act

§ 1. *Shapes in which the mischief of an act may show itself*

*Recapitul-
ation*

1. Hitherto we have been speaking of the various articles or objects on which the consequences or tendency of an act may depend: of the bare *act* itself: of the *circumstances* it may have been, or may have been supposed to be, accompanied with: of the *consciousness* a man may have had with respect to any such circumstances: of the *intentions* that may have preceded the act: of the *motives* that may have given birth to those intentions: and of the *disposition* that may have been indicated by the connexion between such intentions and such motives. We now come to speak of *consequences* or tendency: an article which forms the concluding link in all this chain of causes and effects, involving in it the materiality of the whole. Now, such part of this tendency as is of a mischievous nature, is all that we have any direct concern with; to that, therefore, we shall here confine ourselves.

*Mischief of
an act,
the aggregate
of its
mischievous
conse-
quences.*

2. The tendency of an act is mischievous when the consequences of it are mischievous; that is to say, either the certain consequences or the probable. The consequences, how many and whatsoever they may be, of an act, of which the tendency is mischievous, may, such of them as are mischievous, be conceived to constitute one aggregate body, which may be termed the mischief of the act.

*The mischief
of an act,
primary or
secondary.*

3. This mischief may frequently be distinguished, as it were, into two shares or parcels: the one containing what may be called the primary mischief; the other, what may be called the secondary. That share may be termed the *primary*, which is sustained by an assignable individual, or a multitude of assignable individuals. That share may be termed the *secondary*, which, taking its origin

from the former, extends itself either over the whole community, or over some other multitude of unassignable individuals.

4. The primary mischief of an act may again be distinguished into two branches: 1. The *original*: and, 2. The *derivative*. By the original branch, I mean that which alights upon and is confined to any person who is a sufferer in the first instance, and on his own account: the person, for instance, who is beaten, robbed, or murdered. By the derivative branch, I mean any share of mischief which may befall any other assignable persons in consequence of his being a sufferer, and no otherwise. These persons must, of course, be persons who in some way or other are connected with him. Now the ways in which one person may be connected with another, have been already seen: they may be connected in the way of *interest* (meaning self-regarding interest) or merely in the way of *sympathy*. And again, persons connected with a given person, in the way of interest, may be connected with him either by affording *support* to him, or by deriving it from him.[1]

Primary – original, or derivative.

5. The secondary mischief, again, may frequently be seen to consist of two other shares or parcels: the first consisting of *pain*; the other of *danger*. The pain which it produces is a pain of apprehension: a pain grounded on the apprehension of suffering such mischiefs or inconveniences, whatever they may be, as it is the nature of the primary mischief to produce. It may be styled, in one word, the *alarm*. The danger is the *chance*, whatever it may be, which the multitude it concerns may in consequence of the primary mischief stand exposed to, of suffering such mischiefs or inconveniences. For danger is nothing but the chance of pain, or, what comes to the same thing, of loss of pleasure.

The secondary – 1. Alarm; or, 2. Danger.

6. An example may serve to make this clear. A man attacks you on the road, and robs you. You suffer a pain on the occasion of losing so much money:[2] you also suffered a pain at the thoughts of the personal ill-treatment you apprehended he might give you, in case of your not happening to satisfy his demands.[3] These together

Example.

---

1 See Chap. vi [Sensibility].
2 Viz., a *pain of privation*. See Chap. v [Pleasures and Pains], 17.
3 Viz., *a pain of apprehension*, grounded on the prospect of organical pain, or whatever other mischiefs might have ensued from the ill treatment. Ib. 30.

constitute the original branch of the primary mischief, resulting from the act of robbery. A creditor of yours, who expected you to pay him with part of that money, and a son of yours, who expected you to have given him another part, are in consequence disappointed. You are obliged to have recourse to the bounty of your father, to make good part of the deficiency. These mischiefs together make up the derivative branch. The report of this robbery circulates from hand to hand, and spreads itself in the neighbourhood. It finds its way into the newspapers, and is propagated over the whole country. Various people, on this occasion, call to mind the danger which they and their friends, as it appears from this example, stand exposed to in travelling; especially such as may have occasion to travel the same road. On this occasion they naturally feel a certain degree of pain: slighter or heavier, according to the degree of ill-treatment they may understand you to have received; the frequency of the occasion each person may have to travel in that same road, or its neighbourhood; the vicinity of each person to the spot; his personal courage; the quantity of money he may have occasion to carry about with him; and a variety of other circumstances. This constitutes the first part of the secondary mischief, resulting from the act of robbery; viz., the alarm. But people of one description or other, not only are disposed to conceive themselves to incur a chance of being robbed, in consequence of the robbery committed upon you, but (as will be shown presently) they do really incur such a chance. And it is this chance which constitutes the remaining part of the secondary mischief of the act of robbery; viz., the danger.

The danger, whence it arises – a past offence affords no direct motive to a future.

7. Let us see what this chance amounts to; and whence it comes. How is it, for instance, that one robbery can contribute to produce another? In the first place, it is certain that it cannot create any direct motive. A motive must be the prospect of some pleasure, or other advantage, to be enjoyed in future: but the robbery in question is past: nor would it furnish any such prospect were it to come: for it is not one robbery that will furnish pleasure to him who may be about to commit another robbery. The consideration that is to operate upon a man, as a motive or inducement to commit a robbery, must be the idea of the pleasure

he expects to derive from the fruits of that very robbery: but this pleasure exists independently of any other robbery.

8. The means, then, by which one robbery tends, as it should seem, to produce another robbery, are two. 1. By suggesting to a person exposed to the temptation, the idea of committing such another robbery (accompanied, perhaps, with the belief of its facility). In this case the influence it exerts applies itself, in the first place, to the understanding. 2. By weakening the force of the tutelary motives which tend to restrain him from such an action, and thereby adding to the strength of the temptation.[1] In this case the influence applies itself to the will. These forces are, 1. The motive of benevolence, which acts as a branch of the physical sanction.[2] 2. The motive of self-preservation, as against the punishment that may stand provided by the political sanction. 3. The fear of shame; a motive belonging to the moral sanction. 4. The fear of the divine displeasure; a motive belonging to the religious sanction. On the first and last of these forces it has, perhaps, no influence worth insisting on: but it has on the other two.

But it suggests feasibility, and weakens the force of restraining motives;

9. The way in which a past robbery may weaken the force with which the *political* sanction tends to prevent a future robbery, may be thus conceived. The way in which this sanction tends to prevent a robbery, is by denouncing some particular kind of punishment against any who shall be guilty of it: the *real* value of which punishment will of course be diminished by the *real* uncertainty: as also, if there be any difference, the *apparent* value by the *apparent* uncertainty. Now this uncertainty is proportionably increased by every instance in which a man is known to commit the offence, without undergoing the punishment. This, of course, will be the case with every offence for a certain time; in short, until the punishment allotted to it takes place. If punishment takes place at last, this branch of the mischief of the offence is then at last, but not till then, put a stop to.

viz. 1. Those issuing from the political section.

---

1 See Chap. xi [Dispositions], 40.

2 To wit, in virtue of the pain it may give a man to be a witness to, or otherwise conscious of, the sufferings of a fellow-creature: especially when he is himself the cause of them: in a word, the pain of sympathy. See Chap. v [Pleasures and Pains], 26.

2. Those issuing from the moral.

10. The *way* in which a past robbery may weaken the force with which the *moral* sanction tends to prevent a future robbery, may be thus conceived. The way in which the moral sanction tends to prevent a robbery, is by holding forth the indignation of mankind as ready to fall upon him who shall be guilty of it. Now this indignation will be the more formidable, according to the number of those who join in it: it will be the less so, the fewer they are who join in it. But there cannot be a stronger way of showing that a man does not join in whatever indignation may be entertained against a practice, than the engaging in it himself. It shows not only that he himself feels no indignation against it, but that it seems to him there is no sufficient reason for apprehending what indignation may be felt against it by others. Accordingly, where robberies are frequent, and unpunished, robberies are committed without shame. It was thus amongst the Grecians formerly.[1] It is thus among the Arabs still.

It is said to operate by the influence of example.

11. In whichever way then a past offence tends to pave the way for the commission of a future offence, whether by suggesting the idea of committing it, or by adding to the strength of the temptation, in both cases it may be said to operate by the force or *influence of example*.

The alarm and the danger, though connected, are distinguishable.

12. The two branches of the secondary mischief of an act, the alarm and the danger, must not be confounded: though intimately connected, they are perfectly distinct: either may subsist without the other. The neighbourhood may be alarmed with the report of a robbery, when, in fact, no robbery either has been committed or is in a way to be committed: a neighbourhood may be on the point of being disturbed by robberies, without knowing anything of the matter. Accordingly, we shall soon perceive, that some acts produce alarm without danger: others, danger without alarm.

Both may have respect to the same person, or to others.

13. As well the danger as the alarm may again be divided, each of them, into two branches: the first, consisting of so much of the alarm or danger as may be apt to result from the future behaviour

---

1 See Hom. Odyss. xix. 395; ib. iii. 71. Plato de Rep. i. p. 576, edit. Ficin. Thucyd. i – and see B. I. tit. [Offences against external security].

of the same agent: the second, consisting of so much as may be apt to result from the behaviour of other persons: such others, to wit, as may come to engage in acts of the same sort and tendency.[1]

14. The distinction between the primary and the secondary consequences of an act must be carefully attended to. It is so just, that the latter may often be of a directly opposite nature to the former. In some cases, where the primary consequences of the act are attended with a mischief, the secondary consequences may be beneficial, and that to such a degree, as even greatly to outweigh the mischief of the primary. This is the case, for instance, with all acts of punishment, when properly applied. Of these, the primary mischief being never intended to fall but upon such persons as may happen to have committed some act which it is expedient to prevent, the secondary mischief, that is, the alarm and the danger, extends no farther than to such persons as are under temptation to commit it: in which case, in as far as it tends to restrain them from committing such acts, it is of a beneficial nature.

The primary consequences of an act may be mischievous, and the secondary beneficial.

15. Thus much with regard to acts that produce positive pain, and that immediately. This case, by reason of its simplicity, seemed the fittest to take the lead. But acts may produce mischief in various other ways; which, together with those already specified, may all be comprised by the following abridged analysis.

Analysis of the different shapes in which the mischief of an act may show itself.

Mischief may admit of a division in any one of three points of view. 1. According to its own *nature*. 2. According to its *cause*. 3. According to the person, or other party, who is the *object* of it.[2] With regard to its nature, it may be either *simple* or *complex*:[3] when simple, it may either be *positive* or *negative*: positive, consisting of

---

1 To the former of these branches is opposed so much of the force of any punishment, as is said to operate in the way of *reformation*: to the latter, so much as is said to operate in the way of *example*. See Chap. xiii [Cases unmeet], par. 2. note.

2 There may be other points of view, according to which mischief might be divided, besides these: but this does not prevent the division here given from being an exhaustive one. A line may be divided in any one of an infinity of ways, and yet without leaving in any one of those cases any remainder. See Chap. xvi [Division] par. 1 note.

3 Chap. v. [Pleasures and Pains] par. 1.

actual pain: negative, consisting of the loss of pleasure. Whether simple or complex, and whether positive or negative, it may be either *certain* or *contingent*. When it is negative, it consists of the loss of some benefit or advantage: this benefit may be material in both or either of two ways: 1. By affording actual pleasure: or, 2. By averting pain or *danger*, which is the chance of pain: that is, by affording *security*. In as far, then, as the benefit which a mischief tends to avert, is productive of security, the tendency of such mischief is to produce *insecurity*. 2. With regard to its *cause*, mischief may be produced either by one *single* action, or not without the *concurrence* of other actions: if not without the concurrence of other actions, these others may be the actions either of the *same person*, or of *other* persons: in either case, they may be either acts of the *same kind as* that in question, or of *other* kinds. 3. Lastly, with regard to the party who is the *object* of the mischief, or, in other words, who is in a way to be affected by it, such party may be either an *assignable*[1] individual, or assemblage of individuals, or else a multitude of *unassignable* individuals. When the object is an assignable individual, this individual may either be the person *himself* who is the author of the mischief, or some *other* person. When the individuals who are the objects of it, are an unassignable multitude, this multitude may be either the *whole* political community or state, or some *subordinate* division of it. Now when the object of the mischief is the author himself, it may be styled *self-regarding*: when any other party is the object, *extra-regarding*: when such other party is an individual, it may be styled *private*: when a subordinate branch of the community, *semi-public*: when the whole community, *public*. Here, for the present, we must stop. To pursue the subject through its inferior distinctions, will be the business of the chapter which exhibits the division of offences.[2]

– applied to the preceding cases.   The cases which have been already illustrated, are those in which the primary mischief is not necessarily otherwise than a simple one, and that positive: present, and therefore certain: producible by a single action, without any necessity of the

---

1 See Chap. xvi [Division] par. 4. note.
2 Chap. xvi.

concurrence of any other action, either on the part of the same agent, or of others; and having for its object an assignable individual, or, by accident, an assemblage of assignable individuals: extra-regarding therefore, and private. This primary mischief is accompanied by a secondary: the first branch of which is sometimes contingent and sometimes certain, the other never otherwise than contingent: both extra-regarding and semi-public: in other respects, pretty much upon a par with the primary mischief: except that the first branch, *viz.* the alarm, though inferior in magnitude to the primary, is, in point of extent, and therefore, upon the whole, in point of magnitude, much superior.

16. Two instances more will be sufficient to illustrate the most material of the modifications above exhibited.

A man drinks a certain quantity of liquor, and intoxicates himself. The intoxication in this particular instance does him no sort of harm: or, what comes to the same thing, none that is perceptible. But it is probable, and indeed next to certain, that a given number of acts of the same kind would do him a very considerable degree of harm: more or less according to his constitution and other circumstances: for this is no more than what experience manifests every day. It is also certain, that one act of this sort, by one means or other, tends considerably to increase the disposition a man may be in to practise other acts of the same sort: for this also is verified by experience. This, therefore, is one instance where the mischief producible by the act is contingent; in other words, in which the tendency of the act is no otherwise mischievous than in virtue of its producing a *chance* of mischief. This chance depends upon the concurrence of other acts of the same kind; and those such as must be practised by the same person. The object of the mischief is that very person himself who is the author of it, and he only, unless by accident. The mischief is therefore private and self-regarding.

As to its secondary mischief, alarm, it produces none: it produces indeed a certain quantity of danger by the influence of example: but it is not often that this danger will amount to a quantity worth regarding.

– to examples of other cases where the mischief is less conspicuous. Example I. An act of self-intox-ication.

Example II.
Non-
payment
of a tax.

17. Again. A man omits paying his share to a public tax. This we see is an act of the negative kind.[1] Is this then to be placed upon the list of mischievous acts? Yes, certainly. Upon what grounds? Upon the following. To defend the community against its external as well as its internal adversaries, are tasks, not to mention others of a less indispensable nature, which cannot be fulfilled but at a considerable expense. But whence is the money for defraying this expense to come? It can be obtained in no other manner than by contributions to be collected from individuals; in a word, by taxes. The produce then of these taxes is to be looked upon as a kind of *benefit* which it is necessary the governing part of the community should receive for the use of the whole. This produce, before it can be applied to its destination, requires that there should be certain persons commissioned to receive and to apply it. Now if these persons, had they received it, would have applied it to its proper destination, it would have been a benefit: the not putting them in a way to receive it, is then a mischief. But it is possible, that if received, it might not have been applied to its proper destination; or that the services, in consideration of which it was bestowed, might not have been performed. It is possible, that the under-officer, who collected the produce of the tax, might not have paid it over to his principal: it is possible that the principal might not have forwarded it on according to its further destination; to the judge, for instance, who is to protect the community against its clandestine enemies from within, or the soldier, who is to protect it against its open enemies from without: it is possible that the judge, or the soldier, had they received it, would not however have been induced by it to fulfil their respective duties: it is possible, that the judge would not have sat for the punishment of criminals, and the decision of controversies: it is possible that the soldier would not have drawn his sword in the defence of the community. These, together with an infinity of other intermediate acts, which for the sake of brevity I pass over, form a connected chain of duties, the discharge of which is necessary to the preservation of the community. They must every one of them be discharged, ere the benefit to which they are

---

1 See Chap. vii [Actions] 8.

contributory can be produced. If they are all discharged, in that case the benefit subsists, and any act, by tending to intercept that benefit, may produce a mischief. But if any of them are not, the benefit fails: it fails of itself: it would not have subsisted, although the act in question (the act of non-payment) had not been committed. The benefit is therefore contingent; and, accordingly, upon a certain supposition, the act which consists in the averting of it is not a mischievous one. But this supposition, in any tolerably-ordered government, will rarely indeed be verified. In the very worst-ordered government that exists, the greatest part of the duties that are levied are paid over according to their destination: and, with regard to any particular sum, that is attempted to be levied upon any particular person upon any particular occasion, it is therefore manifest, that, unless it be certain that it will not be so disposed of, the act of withholding it is a mischievous one.

The act of payment, when referable to any particular sum, especially if it be a small one, might also have failed of proving beneficial on another ground: and, consequently, the act of non-payment, of proving mischievous. It is possible that the same services, precisely, might have been rendered without the money as with it. If, then, speaking of any small limited sum, such as the greatest which any one person is called upon to pay at a time, a man were to say, that the non-payment of it would be attended with mischievous consequences; this would be far from certain: but what comes to the same thing as if it were, it is perfectly certain when applied to the whole. It is certain, that if all of a sudden the payment of all taxes was to cease, there would no longer be anything effectual done, either for the maintenance of justice, or for the defence of the community against its foreign adversaries: that therefore the weak would presently be oppressed and injured in all manner of ways, by the strong at home, and both together overwhelmed by oppressors from abroad. Upon the whole, therefore, it is manifest, that in this case, though the mischief is remote and contingent, though in its first appearance it consists of nothing more than the interception of a *benefit*, and though the individuals, in whose favour that benefit would have been reduced into the explicit form of pleasure or security, are altogether unassignable, yet the mischievous tendency of the act is not on all these accounts the less indisputable. The mischief, in point of *intensity* and *duration*, is indeed unknown: it is *uncertain*: it is *remote*. But in point of *extent* it is immense; and in point of *fecundity*, pregnant to a degree that baffles calculation.

No alarm, when no assignable person is the object. 18. It may now be time to observe, that it is only in the case where the mischief is extra-regarding, and has an assignable person or persons for its object, that so much of the secondary branch of it as consists in *alarm* can have place. When the individuals it affects are uncertain, and altogether out of sight, no alarm can be produced: as there is nobody whose sufferings you can see, there is nobody whose sufferings you can be alarmed at. No alarm, for instance, is produced by non-payment to a tax. If at any distant and uncertain period of time such offence should chance to be productive of any kind of alarm, it would appear to proceed, as indeed immediately it would proceed, from a very different cause. It might be immediately referable, for example, to the act of a legislator, who should deem it necessary to lay on a new tax, in order to make up for the deficiency occasioned in the produce of the old one. Or it might be referable to the act of an enemy, who, under favour of a deficiency thus created in the fund allotted for defence, might invade the country, and exact from it much heavier contributions than those which had been thus withholden from the sovereign.[1]

As to any alarm which such an offence might raise among the few who might chance to regard the matter with the eyes of statesmen, it is of too slight and uncertain a nature to be worth taking into the account.

---

1 The investigation might, by a process rendered obvious by analogy, be extended to the consequences of an act of a beneficial nature. In both instances a *third* order of consequences may be reckoned to have taken place, when the influence of the act, through the medium of the passive faculty of the patient, has come to affect his active faculty. In this way, 1. *Evil* may flow out of *evil*: – instance; the exertions of industry put a stop to by the extinction of inducement, resulting from a continued chain of acts of robbery or extortion. 2. *Good out of evil*: – instance; habits of depredation put a stop to by a steady course of punishment. 3. *Evil out good*: – instance; habits of industry put a stop to by an excessive course of gratuitous bounty. 4. *Good out of good*: – instance; a constant and increasing course of industry, excited and kept up by the rewards afforded by a regular and increasing market for the fruits of it.

§ 2. *How intentionality, etc. may influence the mischief of an act*

19. We have seen the nature of the secondary mischief, which is apt to be reflected, as it were, from the primary, in the cases where the individuals who are the objects of the mischief are assignable. It is now time to examine into the circumstances upon which the production of such secondary mischief depends. These circumstances are no others than the four articles which have formed the subjects of the four last preceding chapters: viz. 1. The intentionality. 2. The consciousness. 3. The motive. 4. The disposition. It is to be observed all along, that it is only the *danger* that is immediately governed by the *real* state of the mind in respect to those articles: it is by the *apparent* state of it that the *alarm* is governed. It is governed by the real only in as far as the apparent happens, as in most cases it may be expected to do, to quadrate with the real. The different influences of the articles of intentionality and consciousness may be represented in the several cases following. *Secondary mischief influenced by the state of the agent's mind.*

20. Case 1. Where the act is so completely unintentional, as to be altogether *involuntary*. In this case it is attended with no secondary mischief at all. *Case 1. Involuntariness.*

A bricklayer is at work upon a house: a passenger is walking in the street below. A fellow-workman comes and gives the bricklayer a violent push, in consequence of which he falls upon the passenger, and hurts him. It is plain there is nothing in this event that can give other people, who may happen to be in the street, the least reason to apprehend anything in future on the part of the man who fell, whatever there may be with regard to the man who pushed him.

21. Case 2. Where the act, though not unintentional, is *unadvised*, insomuch that the mischievous part of the consequences is unintentional, but the unadvisedness is attended with *heedlessness*. In this case the act is attended with some small degree of secondary mischief, in proportion to the degree of heedlessness. *Case 2. Unintentionality with heedlessness.*

A groom being on horseback, and riding through a frequented street, turns a corner at a full pace, and rides over a passenger, who happens to be going by. It is plain, by this behaviour of the groom, some degree of alarm may be produced, less or greater, according to the degree of heedlessness betrayed by him: according to the quickness of his pace, the fulness of the street, and so forth. He has done mischief, it may be said, by his carelessness, already: who knows but that on other occasions the like cause may produce the like effect?

Case 3.
Mis-
supposal of
a complete
justific-
ation,
without
rashness.

22. Case 3. Where the act is *mis-advised* with respect to a circumstance, which, had it existed, would *fully* have excluded or (what comes to the same thing) outweighed the primary mischief: and there is no rashness in the case. In this case the act is attended with no secondary mischief at all.

It is needless to multiply examples any farther.

Case 4.
Mis-
supposal
of a partial
justific-
ation,
without
rashness.

23. Case 4. Where the act is mis-advised with respect to a circumstance which would have excluded or counterbalanced the primary mischief *in part*, but not entirely: and still there is no rashness. In this case the act is attended with some degree of secondary mischief, in proportion to that part of the primary which remains unexcluded or uncounterbalanced.

Case 5.
Mis-
supposal,
with
rashness.

24. Case 5. Where the act is mis-advised with respect to a circumstance, which, had it existed, would have excluded or counterbalanced the primary mischief entirely, or in part: and there is a degree of *rashness* in the supposal. In this case, the act is also attended with a farther degree of secondary mischief, in proportion to the degree of rashness.

Case 6.
Con-
sequences
completely
free from
mis-
supposal.

25. Case 6. Where the consequences are *completely* intentional, and there is no mis-supposal in the case. In this case the secondary mischief is at the highest.

26. Thus much with regard to intentionality and consciousness. We now come to consider in what manner the secondary mischief is affected by the nature of the *motive*.

The nature
of a motive
takes not
away the
mischief
of the
secondary
con-
sequences.

Where an act is pernicious in its primary consequences, the secondary mischief is not obliterated by the *goodness* of the motive; though the motive be of the best kind. For, notwith-standing the goodness of the motive, an act of which the primary consequences are pernicious, is produced by it in the instance in question, by the supposition. It may, therefore, in other instances:

although this is not so likely to happen from a good motive as from a bad one.[1]

27. An act, which, though pernicious in its primary consequences, is rendered in other respects beneficial upon the whole, by virtue of its secondary consequences, is not changed back again and rendered pernicious upon the whole by the *badness* of the motive: although the motive be of the worst kind.[2]

Nor the beneficialness.

28. But when not only the primary consequences of an act are pernicious, but, in other respects, the secondary likewise, the

But it may aggravate the mischievousness, where they are mischievous.

---

1 An act of homicide, for instance, is not rendered innocent, much less beneficial, merely by its proceeding from a principle of religion, of honour (that is, of love of reputation) or even of benevolence. When Ravaillac assassinated Henry IV it was from a principle of religion. But this did not so much as abate from the mischief of the act. It even rendered the act still more mischievous, for a reason that we shall see presently, than if it had originated from a principle of revenge. When the conspirators against the late king of Portugal attempted to assassinate him, it is said to have been from a principle of honour. But this, whether it abated or no, will certainly not be thought to have outweighed, the mischief of the act. Had a son of Ravaillac's, as in the case before supposed,[a] merely on the score of filial affection, and not in consequence of any participation in his crime, put him to death in order to rescue him from the severer hands of justice, the motive, although it should not be thought to afford any proof of a mischievous disposition, and should, even in case of punishment have made such rescuer an object of pity, would hardly have made the act of rescue a beneficial one.

2 The prosecution of offences, for instance, proceeds most commonly from one or other, or both together, of two motives, the one of which is of the self-regarding, the other of the dissocial kind: viz. pecuniary interest, and ill-will: from pecuniary interest, for instance, whenever the obtaining pecuniary amends for damage suffered is one end of the prosecution. It is common enough indeed to hear men speak of prosecutions undertaken from *public spirit*; which is a branch, as we have seen,[b] of the principle of benevolence. Far be it from me to deny but that such a principle may very frequently be an ingredient in the sum of motives, by which men are engaged in a proceeding of this nature. But whenever such a proceeding is engaged in from the sole influence of public spirit, uncombined with the least tincture of self-interest, or ill-will, it must be acknowledged to be a proceeding of the heroic kind. Now acts of heroism are, in the very essence of them, but rare: for if they were common, they would not be acts of heroism. But prosecutions for crimes are very frequent, and yet, unless in very particular circumstances indeed, they are never otherwise than beneficial.

---

[a] Chap. xi [Disposition] 15.
[b] Chap. x [Motives] 25.

secondary mischief may be *aggravated* by the nature of the motive: so much of that mischief, to wit, as respects the future behaviour of the same person.

29. It is not from the worst kind of motive, however, that the secondary mischief of an act receives its greatest aggravation.

It does the more, the more considerable the tendency of the motive to produce such acts.

30. The aggravation which the secondary mischief of an act, in as far as it respects the future behaviour of the same person, receives from the nature of a motive in an individual case, is as the tendency of the motive to produce, on the part of the same person, acts of the like bad tendency with that of the act in question.

– which is as its strength and constancy.

31. The tendency of a motive to produce acts of the like kind, on the part of any given person, is as the *strength* and *constancy* of its influence on that person, as applied to the production of such effects.

General efficacy of a species of motive, how measured.

32. The tendency of a species of motive to give birth to acts of any kind, among persons in general, is as the *strength*, *constancy*, and *extensiveness*[1] of its influence, as applied to the production of such effects.

A mischievous act is more so, when issuing from a self-regarding than when from a dissocial motive.

33. Now the motives, whereof the influence is at once most powerful, most constant, and most extensive, are the motives of physical desire, the love of wealth, the love of ease, the love of life, and the fear of pain: all of them self-regarding motives. The motive of displeasure, whatever it may be in point of strength and extensiveness, is not near so constant in its influence (the case of mere antipathy excepted) as any of the other three. A pernicious act, therefore, when committed through vengeance, or otherwise through displeasure, is not near so mischievous as the same pernicious act, when committed by force of any one of those other motives.[2]

---

1 Chap. iv [Value].

2 It is for this reason that a threat, or other personal outrage, when committed on a stranger, in pursuance of a scheme of robbery, is productive of more mischief in society, and accordingly is, perhaps, everywhere more severely punished, than an outrage of the same kind offered to an acquaintance, in prosecution of a scheme of vengeance. No man is always in a rage. But, at all times, every man, more or less, loves money. Accordingly, although a man by

34. As to the motive of religion, whatever it may sometimes prove to be in point of strength and constancy, it is not in point of extent so universal, especially in its application to acts of a mischievous nature, as any of the three preceding motives. It may, however, be as universal in a particular state, or in a particular district of a particular state. It is liable indeed to be very irregular in its operations. It is apt, however, to be infrequently as powerful as the motive of vengeance, or indeed any other motive whatsoever. It will sometimes even be more powerful than any other motive. It is, at any rate, much more constant.[1] A pernicious act, therefore, when committed through the motive of religion, is more mischievous than when committed through the motive of ill-will.

– so even when issuing from the motive of religion.

35. Lastly, The secondary mischief, to wit, so much of it as hath respect to the future behaviour of the same person, is aggravated or lessened by the apparent depravity or beneficence of his disposition: and that in the proportion of such apparent depravity or beneficence.

How the secondary mischief is influenced by disposition.

36. The consequences we have hitherto been speaking of, are the *natural* consequences, of which the act, and the other articles we have been considering, are the causes: consequences that result

Connexion of this with the succeeding chapter.

---

his quarrelsomeness should for once have been engaged in a bad action, he may nevertheless remain a long while, or even his whole life-time, without engaging in another bad action of the same kind: for he may very well remain his whole life-time without engaging in so violent a quarrel: nor at any rate will he quarrel with more than one, or a few people at a time. But if a man, by his love of money, has once been engaged in a bad action, such as a scheme of robbery, he may at any time, by the influence of the same motive, be engaged in acts of the same degree of enormity. For take men throughout, if a man loves money to a certain degree to-day, it is probable that he will love it, at least in equal degree, to-morrow. And if a man is disposed to acquire it in that way, he will find inducement to rob, wheresoever and whensoever there are people to be robbed.

1 If a man happen to take it into his head to assassinate with his own hands, or with the sword of justice, those whom he calls heretics, that is, people who think, or perhaps only speak, differently upon a subject which neither party understands, he will be as much inclined to do this at one time as at another. Fanaticism never sleeps: it is never glutted: it is never stopped by philanthropy; for it makes a merit of trampling on philanthropy: it is never stopped by conscience; for it has pressed conscience into its service. Avarice, lust, and vengeance, have piety, benevolence, honour; fanaticism has nothing to oppose it.

from the behaviour of the individual, who is the offending agent, without the interference of political authority. We now come to speak of *punishment*: which, in the sense in which it is here considered, is an *artificial* consequence, annexed by political authority to an offensive act, in one instance; in the view of putting a stop to the production of events similar to the obnoxious part of its natural consequences, in other instances.

CHAPTER XIII

Cases Unmeet for Punishment

§ 1. General view of cases unmeet for punishment

1. The general object which all laws have, or ought to have, in common, is to augment the total happiness of the community; and therefore, in the first place, to exclude, as far as may be, everything that tends to subtract from that happiness: in other words, to exclude mischief. *The end of law is, to augment happiness.*

2. But all punishment is mischief: all punishment in itself is evil. Upon the principle of utility, if it ought at all to be admitted, it ought only to be admitted in as far as it promises to exclude some greater evil.[1] *But punishment is an evil.*

---

1 What follows, relative to the subject of punishment, ought regularly to be preceded by a distinct chapter on the ends of punishment. But having little to say on that particular branch of the subject, which has not been said before, it seemed better, in a work, which will at any rate be but too voluminous, to omit this title, reserving it for another, hereafter to be published, intituled *The Theory of Punishment*.[a] To the same work I must refer the analysis of the several possible modes of punishment, a particular and minute examination of the nature of each, and of its advantages and disadvantages, and various other disquisitions, which did not seem absolutely necessary to be inserted here. A very few words, however, concerning the *ends* of punishment, can scarcely be dispensed with.

The immediate principal end of punishment is to control action. This action is either that of the offender, or of others: that of the offender it controls by its influence, either on his will, in which case it is said to operate in the way of *reformation*; or on his physical power, in which case it is said to operate by *disablement*: that of others it can influence no otherwise than by its influence over their wills; in which case it is said to operate in the way of *example*. A kind of

---

a This is the work which, from the Author's papers, has since been published by Mr Dumont in French, in company with *The Theory of Reward* added to it, for the purpose of mutual illustration. It is in contemplation to publish them both in English, from the Author's manuscripts, with the benefit of any amendments that have been made by Mr Dumont. [*Note to Edition of* 1823.]

Therefore ought not to be admitted:
1. Where groundless.

2. Inefficacious.

3. Unprofitable.

4. Or needless.

3. It is plain, therefore, that in the following cases punishment ought not to be inflicted:

1   Where it is *groundless*: where there is no mischief for it to prevent: the act not being mischievous upon the whole.

2   Where it must be *inefficacious*: where it cannot act so as to prevent the mischief.

3   Where it is *unprofitable*, or too *expensive*: where the mischief it would produce would be greater than what it prevented.

4   Where it is *needless*: where the mischief may be prevented, or cease of itself, without it: that is, at a cheaper rate.

§ 2. *Cases in which punishment is groundless*

These are,

1. Where there has never been any mischief: as in the case of consent.

4. (1) Where there has never been any mischief: where no mischief has been produced to anybody by the act in question. Of this number are those in which the act was such as might, on some occasions, be mischievous or disagreeable, but the person whose interest it concerns gave his *consent* to the performance of it.[1] This consent, provided it be free, and fairly obtained,[1] is the best proof that can be produced, that, to the person who gives it, no mischief, at least no immediate mischief, upon the whole, is done. For no man can be so good a judge as the man himself, what it is gives him pleasure or displeasure.

---

collateral end, which it has a natural tendency to answer, is that of affording a pleasure or satisfaction to the party injured, where there is one, and, in general, to parties whose ill-will, whether on a self-regarding account, or on the account of sympathy or antipathy, has been excited by the offence. This purpose, as far as it can be answered *gratis*, is a beneficial one. But no punishment ought to be allotted merely to this purpose, because (setting aside its effects in the way of control) no such pleasure is ever produced by punishment as can be equivalent to the pain. The punishment, however, which is allotted to the other purpose, ought, as far as it can be done without expense, to be accommodated to this. Satisfaction thus administered to a party injured, in the shape of a dissocial pleasure,[a] may be styled a vindictive satisfaction or compensation: as a compensation, administered in the shape of a self-regarding profit, or stock of pleasure, may be styled a lucrative one. See B. I. tit. vi [Compensation]. Example is the most important end of all, in proportion as the *number* of the persons under temptation to offend is to *one*.

1 See B. I. tit. [Justifications].

---

a See Chap. x [Motives].

5. (2) Where the mischief was *outweighed*: although a mischief was produced by that act, yet the same act was necessary to the production of a benefit which was of greater value[1] than the mischief. This may be the case with anything that is done in the way of precaution against instant calamity, as also with anything that is done in the exercise of the several sorts of powers necessary to be established in every community, to wit, domestic, judicial, military, and supreme.[2]

2. Where the mischief was outweighed: as in precaution against calamity, and the exercise of powers.

6. (3) Where there is a certainty of an adequate compensation: and that in all cases where the offence can be committed. This supposes two things: 1. That the offence is such as admits of an adequate compensation: 2. That such a compensation is sure to be forthcoming. Of these suppositions, the latter will be found to be a merely ideal one: a supposition that cannot, in the universality here given to it, be verified by fact. It cannot, therefore, in practice, be numbered amongst the grounds of absolute impunity. It may, however, be admitted as a ground for an abatement of that punishment, which other considerations, standing by themselves, would seem to dictate.[3]

3. – or will for a certainty be cured by compensation.

§ 3. Cases in which punishment must be inefficacious

These are,

7. (1) Where the penal provision is *not established* until after the act is done. Such are the cases, 1. Of an *ex post facto* law; where the legislator himself appoints not a punishment till after the act is done. 2. Of a sentence beyond the law; where the judge, of his own authority, appoints a punishment which the legislator had not appointed.

1. Where the penal provision comes too late

---

1 See supra, Chap. iv [Value].
2 See Book I. tit. [Justifications].
3 This, for example, seems to have been one ground, at least, of the favour shown by perhaps all systems of laws, to such offenders as stand upon a footing. of responsibility: shown, not directly indeed to the persons themselves; but to such offences as none but responsible persons are likely to have the opportunity of engaging in. In particular, this seems to be the reason why embezzlement, in certain cases, has not commonly been punished upon the footing of theft: nor mercantile frauds upon that of common sharping.[a]

---

a See tit. [Simple merc. Defraudment].

2. Or is not made known: as in a law not sufficiently promulgated.

8. (2) Where the penal provision, though established, is *not conveyed* to the notice of the person on whom it seems intended that it should operate. Such is the case where the law has omitted to employ any of the expedients which are necessary, to make sure that every person whatsoever, who is within the reach of the law, be apprized of all the cases whatsoever, in which (being in the station of life he is in) he can be subjected to the penalties of the law.[1]

3. Where the will cannot be deterred from any act: as in, [a] Infancy.

[b] Insanity.

[c] Intox-ication.

9. (3) Where the penal provision, though it were conveyed to a man's notice, *could produce no effect* on him, with respect to the preventing him from engaging in any act of the *sort* in question. Such is the case, 1. In extreme *infancy*; where a man has not yet attained that state or disposition of mind in which the prospect of evils so distant as those which are held forth by the law, has the effect of influencing his conduct. 2. In *insanity*; where the person, if he has attained to that disposition, has since been deprived of it through the influence of some permanent though unseen cause. 3. In *intoxication*; where he has been deprived of it by the transient influence of a visible cause: such as the use of wine, or opium, or other drugs, that act in this manner on the nervous system: which condition is indeed neither more nor less than a temporary insanity produced by an assignable cause.[2]

1 See B. II. Appendix. tit. iii [Promulgation].

2 Notwithstanding what is here said, the cases of infancy and intoxication (as we shall see hereafter) cannot be looked upon in practice as affording sufficient grounds for absolute impunity. But this exception in point of practice is no objection to the propriety of the rule in point of theory. The ground of the exception is neither more nor less than the difficulty there is of ascertaining the matter of fact: viz. whether at the requisite point of time the party was actually in the state in question; that is, whether a given case comes really under the rule. Suppose the matter of fact capable of being perfectly ascertained, without danger or mistake, the impropriety of punishment would be as indubitable in these cases as in any other.[a]

The reason that is commonly assigned for the establishing an exemption from punishment in favour of infants, insane persons, and persons under intoxication, is either false in fact, or confusedly expressed. The phrase is, that the will of these persons concurs not with the act; that they have no vicious will; or, that they have not the free use of their will. But suppose all this to be true? What is it to the purpose? Nothing: except in as far as it implies the reason given in the text.

a See B. I. tit. iv [Exemptions], and tit. vii [Extenuations].

10. (4) Where the penal provision (although, being conveyed to the party's notice, it might very well prevent his engaging in acts of the sort in question, provided he knew that it related to those acts) could not have this effect, with regard to the *individual* act he is about to engage in: to wit, because he knows not that it is of the number of those to which the penal provision relates. This may happen, 1. In the case of *unintentionality*; where he intends not to engage, and thereby knows not that he is about to engage, in the *act* in which eventually he is about to engage.[1] 2. In the case of *unconsciousness*; where, although he may know that he is about to engage in the *act* itself, yet, from not knowing all the material *circumstances* attending it, he knows not of the *tendency* it has to produce that mischief, in contemplation of which it has been made penal in most instances. 3. In the case of *mis-supposal*; where, although he may know of the tendency the act has to produce that degree of mischief, he supposes it, though mistakenly, to be attended with some circumstance, or set of circumstances, which, if it had been attended with, it would either not have been productive of that mischief, or have been productive of such a greater degree of good, as has determined the legislator in such a case not to make it penal.[2]

4. Or not from the individual act in question, as in,

[a] Unintentionality.

[b] Unconsciousness.

[c] Mis-supposal.

11. (5) Where, though the penal clause might exercise a full and prevailing influence, were it to act alone, yet by the *predominant* influence of some opposite cause upon the will, it must necessarily be ineffectual; because the evil which he sets himself about to undergo, in the case of his *not* engaging in the act, is so great, that the evil denounced by the penal clause, in case of his engaging in it, cannot appear greater. This may happen, 1. In the case of *physical danger*; where the evil is such as appears likely to be brought about by the unassisted powers of *nature*. 2. In the case of a *threatened mischief*; where it is such as appears likely to be brought about through the intentional and conscious agency of man.[3]

5. Or is acted on by an opposite superior force: as by,

[a] Physical danger.

[b] Threatened mischief.

---

1 See Chap. viii [Intentionality].
2 See Chap. ix [Consciousness].
3 The influences of the *moral* and *religious* sanctions, or, in other words, of the motives of *love of reputation* and *religion*, are other causes, the force of which may, upon particular occasions, come to be greater than that of any punishment which

6. – or
the bodily
organs
cannot
follow its
determin-
ation: as
under
physical
compulsion
or restraint.

12. (6) Where (though the penal clause may exert a full and prevailing influence over the *will* of the party) yet his *physical faculties* (owing to the predominant influence of some physical cause) are not in a condition to follow the determination of the will: insomuch that the act is absolutely *involuntary*. Such is the case of physical *compulsion* or *restraint*, by whatever means brought about; where the man's hand, for instance, is pushed against some object which his will disposes him *not* to touch; or tied down from touching some object which his will disposes him to touch.

§ 4. *Cases where punishment is unprofitable*

These are,

1. Where the
punishment
would
produce more
evil than the
offence.

13. (1) Where, on the one hand, the nature of the offence, on the other hand, that of the punishment, are, *in the ordinary state of things*, such, that when compared together, the evil of the latter will turn out to be greater than that of the former.

Evil
producible by
punish-ment
– its four
branches –
viz.
[a] Restraint.
[b] Appre-
hension.
[c] Suffer-
ance.

14. Now the evil of the punishment divides itself into four branches, by which so many different sets of persons are affected. 1. The evil of *coercion* or *restraint*: or the pain which it gives a man not to be able to do the act, whatever it be, which by the apprehension of the punishment he is deterred from doing. This is felt by those by whom the law is *observed*. 2. The evil of *apprehension*: or the pain which a man, who has exposed himself to punishment, feels at the thoughts of undergoing it. This is felt by those by whom the law has been *broken*, and who feel themselves in *danger* of its being executed upon them. 3. The evil of *sufferance*:[1] or the pain which a man feels, in virtue of the punishment itself, from the time when he begins to undergo it. This is felt by those by whom the law is broken, and upon whom

---

the legislator is *able*, or at least which he will *think proper*, to apply. These, therefore, it will be proper for him to have his eye upon. But the force of these influences is variable and different in different times and places: the force of the foregoing influences is constant and the same, at all times and everywhere. These, therefore, it can never be proper to look upon as safe grounds for establishing absolute impunity: owing (as in the above-mentioned cases of infancy and intoxication) to the impracticability of ascertaining the matter of fact.

1 See Chap. v [Pleasures and Pains].

it comes actually to be executed. 4. The pain of sympathy, and the other *derivative* evils resulting to the persons who are in *connection* with the several classes of original sufferers just mentioned.[1] Now of these four lots of evil, the first will be greater or less, according to the nature of the act from which the party is restrained: the second and third according to the nature of the punishment which stands annexed to that offence. [d] *Derivative evils.*

15. On the other hand, as to the evil of the offence, this will also, of course, be greater or less, according to the nature of each offence. The proportion between the one evil and the other will therefore be different in the case of each particular offence. The cases, therefore, where punishment is unprofitable on this ground, can by no other means be discovered, than by an examination of each particular offence; which is what will be the business of the body of the work.

16. (2) Where, although in the *ordinary state* of things, the evil resulting from the punishment is not greater than the benefit which is likely to result from the force with which it operates, during the same space of time, towards the excluding the evil of the offences, yet it may have been rendered so by the influence of some *occasional circumstances*. In the number of these circumstances may be, 1. The multitude of delinquents at a particular juncture; being such as would increase, beyond the ordinary measure, the *quantum* of the second and third lots, and thereby also of a part of the fourth lot, in the evil of the punishment. 2. The extraordinary value of the services of some one delinquent; in the case where the effect of the punishment would be to deprive the community of the benefit of those services. 3. The displeasure of the *people*; that is, of an indefinite number of the members of the *same* community, in cases where (owing to the influences of some occasional incident) they happen to conceive, that the offence or the offender ought not to be punished at all, or at least ought not to be punished in the way in question. 4. The displeasure of *foreign powers*; that is, of the governing body, or a considerable number of the members of some *foreign* community or communities, with which the community in question is connected. 2. – *or in the individual case in question: by reason of*

[a] *The multitude of delinquents.*

[b] *The value of a delinquent's service.*

[c] *The displeasure of the people.*

[d] *The displeasure of foreign powers.*

1 See Chap. xii [Consequences] 4.

§ 5. *Cases where punishment is needless*

These are,

Where the mischief is to be prevented at a cheaper rate; as, by instruction. 17. Where the purpose of putting an end to the practice may be attained as effectually at a cheaper rate: by instruction, for instance, as well as by terror: by informing the understanding, as well as by exercising an immediate influence on the will. This seems to be the case with respect to all those offences which consist in the disseminating pernicious principles in matters of *duty*; of whatever kind the duty be; whether political, or moral, or religious. And this, whether such principles be disseminated *under*, or even *without*, a sincere persuasion of their being beneficial. I say, even *without*: for though in such a case it is not instruction that can prevent the writer from endeavouring to inculcate his principles, yet it may the readers from adopting them: without which, his endeavouring to inculcate them will do no harm. In such a case, the sovereign will commonly have little need to take an active part: if it be the interest of *one* individual to inculcate principles that are pernicious, it will as surely be the interest of *other* individuals to expose them. But if the sovereign must needs take a part in the controversy, the pen is the proper weapon to combat error with, not the sword.

CHAPTER XIV

Of the Proportion Between Punishments and Offences

1. We have seen that the general object of all laws is to prevent mischief; that is to say, when it is worth while; but that, where there are no other means of doing this than punishment, there are four cases in which it is *not* worth while.

2. When it *is* worth while, there are four subordinate designs or objects, which, in the course of his endeavours to compass, as far as may be, that one general object, a legislator, whose views are governed by the principle of utility, comes naturally to propose to himself.

3. (1) His first, most extensive, and most eligible object, is to prevent, in as far as it is possible, and worth while, all sorts of offences whatsoever:[1] in other words, so to manage, that no offence whatsoever may be committed.

4. (2) But if a man must needs commit an offence of some kind or other, the next object is to induce him to commit an offence *less* mischievous, rather than one *more* mischievous, of two offences that will either of them suit his purpose.

5. (3) When a man has resolved upon a particular offence, the next object is to dispose him to do *no more* mischief than is *necessary* to his purpose: in other words, to do as little mischief as is consistent with the benefit he has in view.

6. (4) The last object is, whatever the mischief be, which it is proposed to prevent, to prevent it at as *cheap* a rate as possible.

---

1 By *offences* I mean, at present, acts which appear to him to have a tendency to produce mischief.

Rules of
proportion

7. Subservient to these four objects, or purposes, must be the rules or canons by which the proportion of punishments[1] to offences is to be governed.

Rule 1.
Outweigh
the profits of
the offence.

8. Rule 1. The first object, it has been seen, is to prevent, in as far as it is worth while, all sorts of offences; therefore,

The value of the punishment must not be less in any case than what is sufficient to outweigh that of the profit[2] of the offence.[3]

If it be, the offence (unless some other considerations, independent of the punishment, should intervene and operate efficaciously in the character of tutelary motives[4]) will be sure to be committed notwithstanding:[5] the whole lot of punishment will

---

1 The same rules (it is to be observed) may be applied, with little variation, to rewards as well as punishment: in short, to motives in general, which, according as they are of the pleasurable or painful kind, are of the nature of *reward* or *punishment*: and, according as the act they are applied to produce is of the positive or negative kind, are styled impelling or restraining. See Chap. x [Motives] 47.

2 By the profit of an offence, is to be understood, not merely the pecuniary profit, but the pleasure or advantage, of whatever kind it be, which a man reaps, or expects to reap, from the gratification of the desire which prompted him to engage in the offence.[a]

It is the profit (that is, the expectation of the profit) of the offence that constitutes the *impelling* motive, or, where there are several, the sum of the impelling motives, by which a man is prompted to engage in the offence. It is the punishment, that is, the expectation of the punishment, that constitutes the *restraining* motive, which, either by itself, or in conjunction with others, is to act upon him in a *contrary* direction, so as to induce him to abstain from engaging in the offence. Accidental circumstances apart, the strength of the temptation is as the force of the seducing, that is, of the impelling motive or motives. To say then, as authors of great merit and great name have said, that the punishment ought not to increase with the strength of the temptation, is as much as to say in mechanics, that the moving force or *momentum* of the *power* need not increase in proportion to the momentum of the *burthen*.

3 Beccaria, dei diletti, § 6, id. trad. par. Morellet, § 23.

4 See Chap. xi [Dispositions] 29.

5 It is a well-known adage, though it is to be hoped not a true one, that every man has his price. It is commonly meant of a man's virtue. This saying, though in a very different sense, was strictly verified by some of the Anglo-Saxon laws: by which a fixed price was set, not upon a man's virtue indeed, but upon his life:

---

a See Chap. x [Motives] § 1.

be thrown away: it will be altogether *inefficacious*.[1]

9. The above rule has been often objected to, on account of its seeming harshness: but this can only have happened for want of its being properly understood. The strength of the temptation, *ceteris paribus*, is as the profit of the offence: the quantum of the punishment must rise with the profit of the offence: *ceteris paribus*, it must therefore rise with the strength of the temptation. This there is no disputing. True it is, that the stronger the temptation, the less conclusive is the indication which the act of delinquency affords of the depravity of the offender's disposition.[2] So far then as the absence of any aggravation, arising from extraordinary depravity of disposition, may operate, or at the utmost, so far as the presence of a ground of extenuation, resulting from the innocence or beneficence of the offender's disposition, can operate, the strength of the temptation may operate in abatement of the demand for punishment. But it can never operate so far as to indicate the propriety of making the punishment ineffectual, which it is sure to be when brought below the level of the apparent profit of the offence.

The propriety of taking the strength of the temptation for a ground of abatement, no objection to this rule.

---

that of the sovereign himself among the rest. For 200 shillings you might have killed a peasant: for six times as much, a nobleman: for six-and-thirty times as much you might have killed the king.[a] A king in those days was worth exactly 7,200 shillings. If then the heir to the throne, for example, grew weary of waiting for it, he had a secure and legal way of gratifying his impatience: he had but to kill the king with one hand, and pay himself with the other, and all was right. An earl Godwin, or a duke Streon, could have bought the lives of a whole dynasty. It is plain, that if ever a king in those days died in his bed, he must have had something else, besides this law, to thank for it. This being the production of a remote and barbarous age, the absurdity of it is presently recognized: but, upon examination, it would be found, that the freshest laws of the most civilized nations are continually falling into the same error.[b] This, in short, is the case wheresoever the punishment is fixed while the profit of delinquency is indefinite: or, to speak more precisely, where the punishment is limited to such a mark, that the profit of delinquency may reach beyond it.

1 See Chap. xiii. Cases unmeet], § 1.
2 See Chap. xi. [Dispositions), 42.

---

[a] Wilkins' Leg. Anglo-Sax. p. 71, 72. See Hume, Vol. I, App. I. p. 219.
[b] See in particular the *English Statute laws* throughout, *Bonaparte's* Penal Code, and the recently enacted or not enacted *Spanish* Penal *Code. – Note by the Author, July* 1822.

The partial benevolence which should prevail for the reduction of it below this level, would counteract as well those purposes which such a motive would actually have in view, as those more extensive purposes which benevolence ought to have in view: it would be cruelty not only to the public, but to the very persons in whose behalf it pleads: in its effects, I mean, however opposite in its intention. Cruelty to the public, that is cruelty to the innocent, by suffering them, for want of an adequate protection, to lie exposed to the mischief of the offence: cruelty even to the offender himself; by punishing him to no purpose, and without the chance of compassing that beneficial end, by which alone the introduction of the evil of punishment is to be justified.

Rule 2.
Venture
more
against a
great offence
than a small
one.

10. Rule 2. But whether a given offence shall be prevented in a given degree by a given quantity of punishment, is never anything better than a chance; for the purchasing of which, whatever punishment is employed, is so much expended in advance. However, for the sake of giving it the better chance of outweighing the profit of the offence,

The greater the mischief of the offence, the greater is the expense, which it may be worth while to be at, in the way of punishment.[1]

Rule 3.
Cause the
least of two
offences to
be preferred.

11. Rule 3. The next object is, to induce a man to choose always the least mischievous of two offences; therefore

Where two offences come in competition, the punishment for the greater offence must be sufficient to induce a man to prefer the less.[2]

Rule 4.
Punish for
each particle
of the
mischief.

12. Rule 4. When a man has resolved upon a particular offence, the next object is, to induce him to do no more mischief than what is necessary for his purpose: therefore

The punishment should be adjusted in such manner to each particular offence, that for every part of the mischief there may be a motive to restrain the offender from giving birth to it.[3]

---

1 For example, if it can ever be worth while to be at the expense of so horrible a punishment as that of burning alive, it will be more so in the view of preventing such a crime as that of murder or incendiarism, than in the view of preventing the uttering of a piece of bad money. See B. I. tit. [Defraudment touching the Coin] and [Incendiarism].

2 Espr. des Loix, L. vi. c. 16.

3 If anyone have any doubt of this, let him conceive the offence to be divided into as many separate offences as there are distinguishable parcels of mischief that

13. Rule 5. The last object is, whatever mischief is guarded against, to guard against it at as cheap a rate as possible: therefore

The punishment ought in no case to be more than what is necessary to bring it into conformity with the rules here given.

Rule 5.
Punish in
no degree
without
special
reason.

14. Rule 6. It is further to be observed, that owing to the different manners and degrees in which persons under different circumstances are affected by the same exciting cause, a punishment which is the same in name will not always either really produce, or even so much as appear to others to produce, in two different persons the same degree of pain: therefore

That the quantity actually inflicted on each individual offender may correspond to the quantity intended for similar offenders in general, the several circumstances influencing sensibility ought always to be taken into account.[1]

15. Of the above rules of proportion, the four first, we may perceive, serve to mark out the limits on the side of diminution; the limits *below* which a punishment ought not to be *diminished*: the fifth, the limits on the side of increase; the limits *above* which it ought not to be *increased*. The five first are calculated to serve as guides to the legislator: the sixth is calculated, in some measure, indeed, for the same purpose; but principally for guiding the judge in his endeavours to conform, on both sides, to the intentions of the legislator.

---

result from it. Let it consist, for example, in a man's giving you ten blows, or stealing from you ten shillings. If then, for giving you ten blows, he is punished no more than for giving you five, the giving you five of these ten blows is an offence for which there is no punishment at all: which being understood, as often as a man gives you five blows, he will be sure to give you five more, since he may have the pleasure of giving you these five for nothing. In like manner, if for stealing from you ten shillings, he is punished no more than for stealing five, the stealing of the remaining five of those ten shillings is an offence for which there is no punishment at all. This rule is violated in almost every page of every body of laws I have ever seen.

The profit, it is to be observed, though frequently, is not constantly, proportioned to the mischief: for example, where a thief, along with the things he covets, steals others which are of no use to him. This may happen through wantonness, indolence, precipitation, &c. &c.

1 Sec Chap. vi [Sensibility].

Into the account of the value of a punishment, must be taken its deficiency in point of certainty and proximity.

16. Let us look back a little. The first rule, in order to render it more conveniently applicable to practice, may need perhaps to be a little more particularly unfolded. It is to be observed, then, that for the sake of accuracy, it was necessary, instead of the word *quantity* to make use of the less perspicuous term *value*. For the word *quantity* will not properly include the circumstances either of certainty or proximity: circumstances which, in estimating the value of a lot of pain or pleasure, must always be taken into the account.[1] Now, on the one hand, a lot of punishment is a lot of pain; on the other hand, the profit of an offence is a lot of pleasure, or what is equivalent to it. But the profit of the offence is commonly more *certain* than the punishment, or, what comes to the same thing, *appears* so at least to the offender. It is at any rate commonly more *immediate*. It follows, therefore, that, in order to maintain its superiority over the profit of the offence, the punishment must have its value made up in some other way, in proportion to that whereby it falls short in the two points of *certainty* and *proximity*. Now there is no other way in which it can receive any addition to its *value*, but by receiving an addition in point of *magnitude*. Wherever then the value of the punishment falls short, either in point of *certainty*, or of *proximity*, of that of the profit of the offence, it must receive a proportionable addition in point of *magnitude*.[2]

Also, into the account of the mischief, and profit of the offence, the mischief and profit of other offences of the same habit.

17. Yet farther. To make sure of giving the value of the punishment the superiority over that of the offence, it may be necessary, in some cases, to take into the account the profit not only of the *individual* offence to which the punishment is to be annexed, but also of such *other* offences of the *same sort* as the offender is likely to have already committed without detection. This random mode of calculation, severe as it is, it will be impossible to avoid having recourse to, in certain cases: in such, to wit, in which the profit is pecuniary, the chance of detection very small, and the obnoxious act of such a nature as indicates a habit: for example, in the case of frauds against the coin. If it be *not* recurred to, the practice of committing the offence will be sure to be, upon the balance of the

---

1 See Chap. iv [Value].
2 It is for this reason, for example, that simple compensation is never looked upon as sufficient punishment for theft or robbery.

account, a gainful practice. That being the case, the legislator will be absolutely sure of *not* being able to suppress it, and the whole punishment that is bestowed upon it will be thrown away. In a word (to keep to the same expressions we set out with) that whole quantity of punishment will be *inefficacious*.

18. Rule 7. These things being considered, the three following rules may be laid down by way of supplement and explanation to Rule 1.

Rule 7.
Want of certainty must be made up in magnitude.

To enable the value of the punishment to outweigh that of the profit of the offence, it must be increased, in point of magnitude, in proportion as it fails short in point of certainty.

19. Rule 8. *Punishment must be further increased in point of magnitude, in proportion as it falls short in point of proximity.*

Rule 8.
So also want of proximity.

20. Rule 9. *Where the act is conclusively indicative of a habit, such an increase must be given to the punishment as may enable it to outweigh the profit not only of the individual offence, but of such other like offences as are likely to have been committed with impunity by the same offender.*

Rule 9.
For acts indicative of a habit punish as for the habit.

21. There may be a few other circumstances or considerations which may influence, in some small degree, the demand for punishment: but as the propriety of these is either not so demonstrable, or not so constant, or the application of them not so determinate, as that of the foregoing, it may be doubted whether they be worth putting on a level with the others.

22. Rule 10. *When a punishment, which in point of quality is particularly well calculated to answer its intention, cannot exist in less than a certain quantity, it may sometimes be of use, for the sake of employing it, to stretch a little beyond that quantity which, on other accounts, would be strictly necessary.*

Rule 10.
For the sake of quality, increase in quantity.

23. Rule 11. *In particular, this may sometimes be the case, where the punishment proposed is of such a nature as to be particularly well calculated to answer the purpose of a moral lesson.*[1]

Rule 11.
Particularly for a moral lesson.

---

1 A punishment may be said to be calculated to answer the purpose of a moral lesson, when, by reason of the ignominy it stamps upon the offence, it is calculated to inspire the public with sentiments of aversion towards those pernicious habits and dispositions with which the offence appears to be connected; and thereby to inculcate the opposite beneficial habits and dispositions.

Rule 12.
Attend to
circum-
stances
which may
render
punish-
ment
unprofit-
able.

24. Rule 12. The tendency of the above considerations is to dictate an augmentation in the punishment: the following rule operates in the way of diminution. There are certain cases (it has been seen)[1] in which, by the influence of accidental circumstances, punishment may be rendered unprofitable in the whole: in the same cases it may chance to be rendered unprofitable as to a part only. Accordingly,

In adjusting the quantum of punishment, the circumstances, by which all punishment may be rendered unprofitable, ought to be attended to.

Rule 13.
For
simplicity's
sake, small
dispro-
portions
may be
neglected.

25. Rule 13. It is to be observed, that the more various and minute any set of provisions are, the greater the chance is that any article in them will not be borne in mind: without which, no benefit can ensue from it. Distinctions, which are more complex than what the conceptions of those whose conduct it is designed to influence can take in, will even be worse than useless. The whole system will present a confused appearance: and thus the effect, not only of the proportions established by the articles in question, but of whatever is connected with them, will be destroyed.[2] To draw a precise line of direction in such case seems impossible. However, by way of memento, it may be of some use to subjoin the following rule.

Among provisions designed to perfect the proportion between punishments and offences, if any occur, which, by their own particular good effects, would not make up for the harm they would do by adding to the intricacy of the Code, they should be omitted.[3]

It is this, for example, if anything, that must justify the application of so severe a punishment as the infamy of a public exhibition, hereinafter proposed, for him who lifts up his hand against a woman, or against his father. See B. I. tit. [Simp. corporal injuries].

It is partly on this principle, I suppose, that military legislators have justified to themselves the inflicting death on the soldier who lifts up his hand against his superior officer.

1 See Chap. xiii [Cases unmeet] § 4.

2 See B. II. tit. [Purposes], Append. tit. [Composition].

3 Notwithstanding this rule, my fear is, that in the ensuing model, I may be thought to have carried my endeavours at proportionality too far. Hitherto scarce any attention has been paid to it. Montesquieu seems to have been almost the first who has had the least idea of any such thing. In such a matter, therefore, excess seemed more eligible than defect. The difficulty is to invent: that done, if anything seems superfluous, it is easy to retrench.

26. It may be remembered, that the political sanction, being that *Auxiliary* to which the sort of punishment belongs, which in this chapter is *force of the* all along in view, is but one of four sanctions, which may all of *physical,* them contribute their share towards producing the same effects. It *moral, and* may be expected, therefore, that in adjusting the quantity of *sanction,* political punishment, allowance should be made for the assistance *not here* it may meet with from those other controlling powers. True it is, *– why.* that from each of these several sources a very powerful assistance may sometimes be derived. But the case is, that (setting aside the moral sanction, in the case where the force of it is expressly adopted into and modified by the political)[1] the force of those other powers is never determinate enough to be depended upon. It can never be reduced, like political punishment, into exact lots, nor meted out in number, quantity, and value. The legislator is therefore obliged to provide the full complement of punishment, as if he were sure of not receiving any assistance whatever from any of those quarters. If he does, so much the better: but lest he should not, it is necessary he should, at all events, make that provision which depends upon himself.

27. It may be of use, in this place, to recapitulate the several *Recapit-* circumstances, which, in establishing the proportion betwixt *ulation.* punishments and offences, are to be attended to. These seem to be as follows:

(1) *On the part of the offence*:

1   The profit of the offence;

2   The mischief of the offence;

3   The profit and mischief of other greater or lesser offences, of different sorts, which the offender may have to choose out of;

4   The profit and mischief of other offences, of the same sort, which the same offender may probably have been guilty of already.

(2) *On the part of the punishment*:

5   The magnitude of the punishment: composed of its intensity and duration;

3 See B. I. tit. [Punishments].

6   The deficiency of the punishment in point of certainty;

7   The deficiency of the punishment in point of proximity;

8   The quality of the punishment;

9   The accidental advantage in point of quality of a punishment, not strictly needed in point of quantity;

10   The use of a punishment of a particular quality, in the character of a moral lesson.

(3) *On the part of the offender.*

11   The responsibility of the class of persons in a way to offend;

12   The sensibility of each particular offender;

13   The particular merits or useful qualities of any particular offender, in case of a punishment which might deprive the community of the benefit of them;

14   The multitude of offenders on any particular occasion.

(4) *On the part of the public*, at any particular conjuncture:

15   The inclinations of the people, for or against any quantity or mode of punishment;

16   The inclinations of foreign powers.

(5) *On the part of the law*; that is, of the public for a continuance:

17   The necessity of making small sacrifices, in point of proportionality, for the sake of simplicity.

The nicety here observed vindicated from the charge of inutility. 28. There are some, perhaps, who, at first sight, may look upon the nicety employed in the adjustment of such rules, as so much labour lost: for gross ignorance, they will say, never troubles itself about laws, and passion does not calculate. But the evil of ignorance admits of cure:[1] and as to the proposition that passion does not calculate this, like most of these very general and oracular propositions, is not true. When matters of such importance as pain and pleasure are at stake, and these in the highest degree (the only matters, in short, that can be of importance) who is there that does not calculate? Men calculate, some with less exactness, indeed, some with more: but all men calculate. I would not say, that even a madman does not calculate.[2] Passion calculates, more or less, in

1 See Append. tit. [Promulgation].

2 There are few madmen but what are observed to be afraid of the strait waistcoat.

every man: in different men, according to the warmth or coolness of their dispositions: according to the firmness or irritability of their minds: according to the nature of the motives by which they are acted upon. Happily, of all passions, that is the most given to calculation, from the excesses of which, by reason of its strength, constancy, and universality, society has most to apprehend:[1] I mean that which corresponds to the motive of pecuniary interest: so that these niceties, if such they are to be called, have the best chance of being efficacious, where efficacy is of the most importance.

1 Sec Chap. xii [Consequences] 33.

CHAPTER XV

Of the Properties to be Given to a Lot of Punishment

Properties are to be governed by proportion. 1. It has been shown what the rules are, which ought to be observed in adjusting the proportion between the punishment and the offence. The properties to be given to a lot of punishment, in every instance, will of course be such as it stands in need of, in order to be capable of being applied, in conformity to those rules: the *quality* will be regulated by the *quantity*.

Property 1. Variability. 2. The first of those rules, we may remember, was, that the quantity of punishment must not be less, in any case, than what is sufficient to outweigh the profit of the offence: since, as often as it is less, the whole lot (unless by accident the deficiency should be supplied from some of the other sanctions) is thrown away: it is *inefficacious*. The fifth was, that the punishment ought in no case to be more than what is required by the several other rules: since, if it be, all that is above that quantity is *needless*. The fourth was, that the punishment should be adjusted in such manner to each individual offence, that every part of the mischief of that offence may have a penalty (that is, a tutelary motive) to encounter it: otherwise, with respect to so much of the offence as has not a penalty to correspond to it, it is as if there were no punishment in the case. Now to none of those rules can a lot of punishment be conformable, unless, for every variation in point of quantity, in the mischief of the species of offences to which it is annexed, such lot of punishment admits of a correspondent variation. To prove this, let the profit of the offence admit of a multitude of degrees. Suppose it, then, at any one of these degrees: if the punishment be less than what is suitable to that degree, it will be *inefficacious*; it will be so much thrown away: if it be more, as far as the difference extends, it will be *needless*; it will therefore be thrown away also in that case.

The first property, therefore, that ought to be given to a lot of punishment, is that of being variable in point of quantity, in conformity to every variation which can take place in either the profit or mischief of the offence. This property might, perhaps, be termed, in a single word, *variability*.

3. A second property, intimately connected with the former, may be styled *equability*. It will avail but little, that a mode of punishment (proper in all other respects) has been established by the legislator; and that capable of being screwed up or let down to any degree that can be required; if, after all, whatever degree of it be pitched upon, that same degree shall be liable, according to circumstances, to produce a very heavy degree of pain, or a very slight one, or even none at all. In this case, as in the former, if circumstances happen one way, there will be a great deal of pain produced which will be *needless*: if the other way, there will be no pain at all applied, or none that will be *efficacious*. A punishment, when liable to this irregularity, may be styled an unequable one: when free from it, an equable one. The quantity of pain produced by the punishment will, it is true, depend in a considerable degree upon circumstances distinct from the nature of the punishment itself: upon the condition which the offender is in, with respect to the circumstances by which a man's sensibility is liable to be influenced. But the influence of these very circumstances will in many cases be reciprocally influenced by the nature of the punishment: in other words, the pain which is produced by any mode of punishment, will be the joint effect of the punishment which is applied to him, and the circumstances in which he is exposed to it. Now there are some punishments, of which the effect may be liable to undergo a greater alteration by the influence of such foreign circumstances, than the effect of other punishments is liable to undergo. So far, then, as this is the case, equability or unequability may be regarded as properties belonging to the punishment itself.

Property 2. Equability.

4. An example of a mode of punishment which is apt to be unequable, is that of *banishment*, when the *locus a quo* (or place the party is banished from) is some determinate place appointed by the law, which perhaps the offender cares not whether he ever see or no. This is also the case with *pecuniary*, or *quasi-pecuniary*

Punishments which are apt to be deficient in this respect.

punishment, when it respects some particular species of property, which the offender may have been possessed of, or not, as it may happen. All these punishments may be split down into parcels, and measured out with the utmost nicety: being divisible by time, at least, if by nothing else. They are not, therefore, any of them defective in point of variability: and yet, in many cases, this defect in point of equability may make them as unfit for use as if they were.[1]

Property 3. Commensurability to other punishments. 5. The third rule of proportion was, that where two offences come in competition, the punishment for the greater offence must be sufficient to induce a man to prefer the less. Now, to be sufficient for this purpose, it must be evidently and uniformly greater: greater, not in the eyes of some men only, but of all men who are liable to be in a situation to take their choice between the two offences; that is, in effect, of all mankind. In other words, the two punishments must be perfectly *commensurable*. Hence arises a third property, which may be termed *commensurability*: to wit, with reference to other punishments.[2]

How two lots of punishment may be rendered perfectly commensurable. 6. But punishments of different kinds are in very few instances uniformly greater one than another; especially when the lowest degrees of that which is ordinarily the greater, are compared with the highest degrees of that which is ordinarily the less; in other words, punishments of different kinds are in few instances uniformly commensurable. The only certain and universal means of making two lots of punishment perfectly commensurable, is by making the lesser an ingredient in the composition of the greater.

---

1 By the English law, there are several offences which are punished by a total forfeiture of moveables, not extending to immoveables. This is the case with suicide, and with certain species of theft and homicide. In some cases, this is the principal punishment: in others, even the only one. The consequence is, that if a man's fortune happens to consist in moveables, he is ruined; if in immoveables, he suffers nothing.

2 See *View of the Hard-Labour Bill*, Lond. 1778, p. 100.

For the idea of this property, I muse acknowledge myself indebted to an anonymous letter in the St James's Chronicle, of the 27th of September, 1777; the author of which is totally unknown to me. If anyone should be disposed to think lightly of the instruction, on account of the channel by which it was first communicated, let him tell me where I can find an idea more ingenious or original.

This may be done in either of two ways. 1. By adding to the lesser punishment another quantity of punishment of the same kind. 2. By adding to it another quantity of a different kind. The latter mode is not less certain than the former: for though one cannot always be absolutely sure, that to the same person a given punishment will appear greater than another given punishment; yet one may be always absolutely sure, that any given punishment, so as it does but come into contemplation, will appear greater than none at all.

7. Again: Punishment cannot act any farther than in as far as the idea of it, and of its connection with the offence, is present in the mind. The idea of it, if not present, cannot act at all; and then the punishment itself must be *inefficacious*. Now, to be present, it must be remembered, and to be remembered it must have been learnt. But of all punishments that can be imagined, there are none of which the connection with the offence is either so easily learnt, or so efficaciously remembered, as those of which the idea is already in part associated with some part of the idea of the offence: which is the case when the one and the other have some circumstance that belongs to them in common. When this is the case with a punishment and an offence, the punishment is said to bear an *analogy* to, or to be *characteristic* of, the offence.[1] *Characteristicalness* is, therefore, a fourth property, which on this account ought to be given, whenever it can conveniently be given, to a lot of punishment.

Property 4. Characteristicalness

8. It is obvious, that the effect of this contrivance will be the greater, as the analogy is the closer. The analogy will be the closer, the more *material*[2] that circumstance is, which is in common. Now the most material circumstance that can belong to an offence and a punishment in common, is the hurt or damage which they produce. The closest analogy, therefore, that can subsist between an offence and the punishment annexed to it, is that which subsists between them when the hurt or damage they produce is of the

The mode of punishment the most eminently characteristic, is that of retaliation.

---

1 See Montesq. Esp. des Loix, L. xii, chap. iv. He seems to have the property of characteristicalness in view; but that the idea he had of it was very indistinct, appears from the extravagant advantages he attributes to it.

2 See Chap. vii [Actions] 3.

same nature: in other words, that which is constituted by the circumstance of identity in point of damage.[1] Accordingly, the mode of punishment, which of all others bears the closest analogy to the offence, is that which in the proper and exact sense of the word is termed *retaliation*. Retaliation, therefore, in the few cases in which it is practicable, and not too expensive, will have one great advantage over every other mode of punishment.

Property 5.
Exemplarity.
9. Again: It is the idea only of the punishment (or, in other words, the *apparent* punishment) that really acts upon the mind; the punishment itself (the *real* punishment) acts not any farther than as giving rise to that idea. It is the apparent punishment, therefore, that does all the service, I mean in the way of example, which is the principal object.[2] It is the real punishment that does all the mischief.[3] Now the ordinary and obvious way of increasing the magnitude of the apparent punishment, is by increasing the magnitude of the real. The apparent magnitude, however, may to a certain degree be increased by other less expensive means: whenever, therefore, at the same time that these less expensive means would have answered that purpose, an additional real punishment is employed, this additional real punishment is *needless*. As to these less expensive means, they consist, 1. In the choice of a particular mode of punishment, a punishment of a particular quality, independent of the quantity.[4] 2. In a particular set of *solemnities* distinct from the punishment itself, and accompanying the execution of it.[5]

The most effective way of rendering a punishment exemplary is by means of analogy.
10. A mode of punishment, according as the appearance of it bears a greater proportion to the reality, may be said to be the more *exemplary*. Now as to what concerns the choice of the punishment itself, there is not any means by which a given quantity of punishment can be rendered more exemplary, than by

---

1 Besides this, there are a variety of other ways in which the punishment may bear an analogy to the offence. This will be seen by looking over the table of punishments.

2 See Chap. xiii [Cases unmeet], § 1, 2 note.

3 Ib. § 4 par. 3.

4 See B. I. tit. [Punishments].

5 See B. II. tit. [Execution].

choosing it of such a sort as shall bear an *analogy* to the offence. Hence another reason for rendering the punishment analogous to, or in other words characteristic of, the offence.

11. Punishment, it is still to be remembered, is in itself an expense: it is in itself an evil.[1] Accordingly the fifth rule of proportion is, not to produce more of it than what is demanded by the other rules. But this is the case as often as any particle of pain is produced, which contributes nothing to the effect proposed. Now if any mode of punishment is more apt than another to produce any such superfluous and needless pain, it may be styled *unfrugal*; if less, it may be styled *frugal*. *Frugality*, therefore, is a sixth property to be wished for in a mode of punishment. *Property 6. Frugality.*

12. The perfection of frugality, in a mode of punishment, is where not only no superfluous pain is produced on the part of the person punished, but even that same operation, by which he is subjected to pain, is made to answer the purpose of producing pleasure on the part of some other person. Understand a profit or stock of pleasure of the self-regarding kind: for a pleasure of the dissocial kind is produced almost of course, on the part of all persons in whose breasts the offence has excited the sentiment of ill-will. Now this is the case with pecuniary punishment, as also with such punishments of the *quasi-pecuniary* kind as consist in the subtraction of such a species of possession as is transferable from one party to another. The pleasure, indeed, produced by such an operation, is not in general equal to the pain:[2] it may, however, be so in particular circumstances, as where he, from whom the thing is taken, is very rich, and he, to whom it is given, very poor: and, be it what it will, it is always so much more than can be produced by any other mode of punishment. *Frugality belongs in perfection to pecuniary punishment.*

13. The properties of exemplarity and frugality seem to pursue the same immediate end, though by different courses. Both are occupied in diminishing the ratio of the real suffering to the apparent: but exemplarity tends to increase the apparent; frugality to reduce the real. *Exemplarity and frugality, in what they differ and agree.*

1 Ch. xiii [Cases unmeet], par. 3.
2 Ib. note.

Other properties of inferior importance. 14. Thus much concerning the properties to be given to punishments in general, to whatsoever offences they are to be applied. Those which follow are of less importance, either as referring only to certain offences in particular, or depending upon the influence of transitory and local circumstances.

In the first place, the four distinct ends into which the main and general end of punishment is divisible,[1] may give rise to so many distinct properties, according as any particular mode of punishment appears to be more particularly adapted to the compassing of one or of another of those ends. To that of *example*, as being the principal one, a particular property has already been adapted. There remain the three inferior ones of *reformation*, *disablement*, and *compensation*.

Property 7. Subserviency to reformation. 15. A seventh property, therefore, to be wished for in a mode of punishment, is that of *subserviency to reformation*, or *reforming tendency*. Now any punishment is subservient to reformation in proportion to its *quantity*: since the greater the punishment a man has experienced, the stronger is the tendency it has to create in him an aversion towards the offence which was the cause of it: and that with respect to all offences alike. But there are certain punishments which, with regard to certain offences, have a particular tendency to produce that effect by reason of their *quality*: and where this is the case, the punishments in question, as applied to the offences in question, will *pro tanto* have the advantage over all others. This influence will depend upon the nature of the motive which is the cause of the offence: the punishment most subservient to reformation will be the sort of punishment that is best calculated to invalidate the force of that motive.

– applied to offences originating in ill-will. 16. Thus, in offences originating from the motive of ill-will,[2] that punishment has the strongest reforming tendency, which is best calculated to weaken the force of the irascible affections. And more particularly, in that sort of offence which consists in an obstinate refusal, on the part of the offender, to do something which is lawfully required of him,[3] and in which the obstinacy is

---

1 See Chap. xiii [Cases unmeet], par. 2 note.
2 See Chap. x [Motives].
3 See B. I. tit. [Offences against Justice].

in great measure kept up by his resentment against those who have an interest in forcing him to compliance, the most efficacious punishment seems to be that of confinement to spare diet.

17. Thus, also, in offences which owe their birth to the joint influence of indolence and pecuniary interest, that punishment seems to possess the strongest reforming tendency, which is best calculated to weaken the force of the former of those dispositions. And more particularly, in the cases of theft, embezzlement, and every species of defraudment, the mode of punishment best adapted to this purpose seems, in most cases, to be that of penal labour. *– to offences originating in indolence joined to pecuniary interest.*

18. An eighth property to be given to a lot of punishment in certain cases, is that of *efficacy with respect to disablement*, or, as it might be styled more briefly, *disabling efficacy*. This is a property which may be given in perfection to a lot of punishment; and that with much greater certainty than the property of subserviency to reformation. The inconvenience is, that this property is apt, in general, to run counter to that of frugality: there being, in most cases, no certain way of disabling a man from doing mischief, without, at the same time, disabling him, in a great measure, from doing good, either to himself or others. The mischief therefore of the offence must be so great as to demand a very considerable lot of punishment, for the purpose of example, before it can warrant the application of a punishment equal to that which is necessary for the purpose of disablement. *Property 8. Efficacy with respect to disablement.*

19. The punishment, of which the efficacy in this way is the greatest, is evidently that of death. In this case the efficacy of it is certain. This accordingly is the punishment peculiarly adapted to those cases in which the name of the offender, so long as he lives, may be sufficient to keep a whole nation in a flame. This will now and then be the case with competitors for the sovereignty, and leaders of the factions in civil wars: though, when applied to offences of so questionable a nature, in which the question concerning criminality turns more upon success than anything else; an infliction of this sort may seem more to savour of hostility than punishment. At the same time this punishment, it is evident, is in an eminent degree *unfrugal*; which forms one among the *– is most conspicuous in capital punishment.*

many objections there are against the use of it, in any but very extraordinary cases.[1]

Other punishments in which it is to be found.　20. In ordinary cases the purpose may be sufficiently answered by one or other of the various kinds of confinement and banishment: of which, imprisonment is the most strict and efficacious. For when an offence is so circumstanced that it cannot be committed but in a certain place, as is the case, for the most part, with offences against the person, all the law has to do, in order to disable the offender from committing it, is to prevent his being in that place. In any of the offences which consist in the breach or the abuse of any kind of trust, the purpose may be compassed at a still cheaper rate, merely by forfeiture of the trust; and in general, in any of those offences which can only be committed under favour of some relation in which the offender stands with reference to any person, or sets of persons, merely by forfeiture of that relation: that is, of the right of continuing to reap the advantages belonging to it. This is the case, for instance, with any of those offences which consist in an abuse of the privileges of marriage, or of the liberty of carrying on any lucrative or other occupation.

Property 9. Subserviency to compensation.　21. The *ninth* property is that of *subserviency to compensation*. This property of punishment, if it be *vindictive* compensation that is in view, will, with little variation, be in proportion to the quantity: if *lucrative*, it is the peculiar and characteristic property of pecuniary punishment.

Property 10. Popularity.　22. In the rear of all these properties may be introduced that of *popularity*; a very fleeting and indeterminate kind of property, which may belong to a lot of punishment one moment, and be lost by it the next. By popularity is meant the property of being acceptable, or rather not unacceptable, to the bulk of the people, among whom it is proposed to be established. In strictness of speech, it should rather be called *absence of unpopularity*: for it cannot be expected, in regard to such a matter as punishment, that any species or lot of it should be positively acceptable and grateful to the people: it is sufficient, for the most part, if they have no decided aversion to the thoughts of it. Now the property of

---

1　See B. 1. tit. (Punishments].

characteristicalness, above noticed, seems to go as far towards conciliating the approbation of the people to a mode of punishment, as any: insomuch that popularity may be regarded as a kind of secondary quality, depending upon that of characteristicalness.[1] The use of inserting this property in the catalogue, is chiefly to make it serve by way of memento to the legislator not to introduce, without a cogent necessity, any mode or lot of punishment, towards which he happens to perceive any violent aversion entertained by the body of the people.

23. The effects of unpopularity in a mode of punishment are analogous to those of unfrugality. The unnecessary pain, which denominates punishment unfrugal, is most apt to be that which is produced on the part of the offender. A portion of superfluous pain is in like manner produced when the punishment is unpopular: but in this case it is produced on the part of persons altogether innocent, the people at large. This is already one mischief; and another is, the weakness which it is apt to introduce into the law. When the people are satisfied with the law, they voluntarily lend their assistance in the execution: when they are dissatisfied, they will naturally withhold that assistance; it is well if they do not take a positive part in raising impediments. This contributes greatly to the uncertainty of the punishment; by which, in the first instance, the frequency of the offence receives an increase. In process of time that deficiency, as usual, is apt to draw on an increase in magnitude: an addition of a certain quantity which otherwise would be *needless*.[2]

Mischiefs resulting from the unpopularity of a punishment – discontent among the people, and weakness in the law.

24. This property, it is to be observed, necessarily supposes, on the part of the people, some prejudice or other, which it is the business of the legislator to endeavour to correct. For if the aversion to the punishment in question were grounded on the principle of utility, the punishment would be such as, on other

This property supposes a prejudice which the legislator ought to cure.

1 The property of characteristicalness, therefore, is useful in a mode of punishment in three different ways: 1. It renders a mode of punishment, before infliction, more easy to be borne in mind; 2. It enables it, especially after infliction, to make the stronger impression, when it is there; that is, renders it the more *exemplary*; 3. It tends to render it more acceptable to the people, that is, it renders it the more *popular*.

2 See Chap. xiii [Cases unmeet], § v.

accounts, ought not to be employed: in which case its popularity or unpopularity would never be worth drawing into question. It is properly therefore a property not so much of the punishment as of the people: a disposition to entertain an unreasonable dislike against an object which merits their approbation. It is the sign also of another property, to wit, indolence or weakness, on the part of the legislator: in suffering the people, for the want of some instruction, which ought to be and might be given them, to quarrel with their own interest. Be this as it may, so long as any such dissatisfaction subsists, it behoves the legislator to have an eye to it, as much as if it were ever so well grounded. Every nation is liable to have its prejudices and its caprices, which it is the business of the legislator to look out for, to study, and to cure.[1]

Property 11. Remissibility. 25. The eleventh and last of all the properties that seem to be requisite in a lot of punishment, is that of *remissibility*.[2] The general presumption is, that when punishment is applied, punishment is needful: that it ought to be applied, and therefore cannot want to be *remitted*. But in very particular, and those always very deplorable cases, it may by accident happen otherwise. It may happen that punishment shall have been inflicted, where, according to the intention of the law itself, it ought not to have been inflicted: that is, where the sufferer is innocent of the offence. At the time of the sentence passed he appeared guilty: but since then, accident has brought his innocence to light. This being the case, so much of the destined punishment as he has suffered already, there is no help for. The business is then to free him from as much as is yet to come. But *is* there any yet to come? There is very little chance of there being any, unless it be so much as consists of *chronical* punishment: such as imprisonment, banishment, penal labour, and the like. So much as consists of *acute* punishment, to wit where the penal process itself is over presently, however permanent the punishment may be in its effects, may be considered as *ir*remissible. This is the case, for example, with whipping, branding, mutilation, and capital punishment. The most perfectly irremissible of any is capital punishment. For though other punishments cannot, when

---

1 See Chap. xiii [Cases unmeet] § 4, par. 4.
2 See View of the Hard Labour Bill, p. 109.

they are over, be remitted, they may be compensated for; and although the unfortunate victim cannot be put into the same condition, yet possibly means may be found of putting him into as good a condition, as he would have been in if he had never suffered. This may in general be done very effectually where the punishment has been no other than pecuniary.

There is another case in which the property of remissibility may appear to be of use: this is, where, although the offender has been justly punished, yet on account of some good behaviour of his, displayed at a time subsequent to that of the commencement of the punishment, it may seem expedient to remit a part of it. But this it can scarcely be, if the proportion of the punishment is, in other respects, what it ought to be. The purpose of example is the more important object, in comparison of that of reformation.[1] It is not very likely, that less punishment should be required for the former purpose than for the latter. For it must be rather an extraordinary case, if a punishment, which is sufficient to deter a man who has only thought of it for a few moments, should not be sufficient to deter a man who has been feeling it all the time. Whatever, then, is required for the purpose of example, must abide at all events: it is not any reformation on the part of the offender, that can warrant the remitting of any part of it: if it could, a man would have nothing to do but to reform immediately, and so free himself from the greatest part of that punishment which was deemed necessary. In order, then, to warrant the remitting of any part of a punishment upon this ground, it must first be supposed that the punishment at first appointed was more than was necessary for the purpose of example, and consequently that a part of it was *needless* upon the whole. This indeed, is apt enough to be the case, under the imperfect systems that are as yet on foot: and therefore, during the continuance of those systems, the property of remissibility may, on this second ground likewise, as well as on the former, be deemed a useful one. But this would not be the case in any new-constructed system, in which the rule of proportion above laid down should be observed. In such a system, therefore, the utility of this property would rest solely on the former ground.

---

1 See Chap. xiii [Cases unmeet], 2 note.

To obtain all these properties, punishments must be mixed.

26. Upon taking a survey of the various possible modes of punishment, it will appear evidently, that there is not any one of them that possesses all the above properties in perfection. To do the best that can be done in the way of punishment, it will therefore be necessary, upon most occasions, to compound them, and make them into complex lots, each consisting of a number of different modes of punishment put together; the nature and proportions of the constituent parts of each lot being different, according to the nature of the offence which it is designed to combat.

The foregoing properties recapitulated.

27. It may not be amiss to bring together, and exhibit in one view, the eleven properties above established. They are as follows:

Two of them are concerned in establishing a proper proportion between a single offence and its punishment; viz.

1 Variability.
2 Equability.

One, in establishing a proportion, between more offences than one, and more punishments than one; viz.

3 Commensurability.

A fourth contributes to place the punishment in that situation in which alone it can be efficacious; and at the same time to be bestowing on it the two farther properties of exemplarity and popularity; viz.

4 Characteristicalness.

Two others are concerned in excluding all useless punishment; the one indirectly, by heightening the efficacy of what is useful; the other in a direct way; viz.

5 Exemplarity.
6 Frugality.

Three others contribute severally to the three inferior ends of punishment; viz.

7 Subserviency to reformation.
8 Efficacy in disabling.
9 Subserviency to compensation.

Another property tends to exclude a collateral mischief, which a particular mode of punishment is liable accidentally to produce; viz.

10 Popularity.

The remaining property tends to palliate a mischief, which all punishment, as such, is liable accidentally to produce; viz.

11 Remissibility.

The properties of commensurability, characteristicalness, exemplarity, subserviency to reformation, and efficacy in disabling, are more particularly calculated to augment the *profit* which is to be made by punishment: frugality, subserviency to compensation, popularity, and remissibility, to diminish the *expense*: variability and equability are alike subservient to both those purposes.

28. We now come to take a general survey of the system of *offences*: that is, of such *ads* to. which, on account of the mischievous *consequences* they have a *natural* tendency to produce, and in the view of putting a stop to those consequences, it may be proper to annex a certain *artificial* consequence, consisting of punishment, to be inflicted on the authors of such acts, according to the principles just established.

Connection of this with the ensuing chapter.

[*Chapter XVI is omitted.*]

CHAPTER XVII

Of the Limits of the Penal Branch of Jurisprudence

§ 1. *Limits between private ethics and the art of legislation*

1. So much for the division of offences in general. Now an offence is an act prohibited, or (what comes to the same thing) an act of which the contrary is commanded, by the law: and what is it that the law can be employed in doing, besides prohibiting and commanding? It should seem then, according to this view of the matter, that were we to have settled what may be proper to be done with relation to offences, we should thereby have settled everything that may be proper to be done in the way of law. Yet that branch which concerns the method of dealing with offences, and which is termed sometimes the *criminal*, sometimes the *penal*, branch, is universally understood to be but one out of two branches which compose the whole subject of the art of legislation; that which is termed the *civil* being the other.[1] Between these two branches then, it is evident enough, there cannot but be a very intimate connection; so intimate is it indeed, that the limits between them are by no means easy to mark out. The case is the same in some degree between the whole business of legislation (civil and penal branches taken together) and that of private

---

1 And the *constitutional* branch, what is become of it? Such is the question which many a reader will be apt to put. An answer that might be given is – that the matter of it might without much violence be distributed under the two other heads. But, as far as recollection serves, that branch, notwithstanding its importance, and its capacity of being lodged separately from the other matter, had at that time scarcely presented itself to my view in the character of a distinct one: the thread of my enquiries had not as yet reached it. But in the concluding note of this same chapter, in paragraphs 22 to the end, the omission may be seen in some measure supplied.

ethics. Of these several limits however it will be in a manner necessary to exhibit some idea: lest, on the one hand, we should seem to leave any part of the subject that *does* belong to us untouched, or, on the other hand, to deviate on any side into a track which does not belong to us.

In the course of this enquiry, that part of it I mean which concerns the limits between the civil and the penal branch of law, it will be necessary to settle a number of points, of which the connection with the main question might not at first sight be suspected. To ascertain what sort of a thing a *law* is; what the *parts* are that are to be found in it; what it must contain in order to be *complete*; what the connection is between that part of a body of laws which belongs to the subject of *procedure* and the rest of the law at large: – all these, it will be seen, are so many problems, which must be solved before any satisfactory answer can be given to the main question above mentioned.

Nor is this their only use: for it is evident enough, that the notion of a complete law must first be fixed, before the legislator can in any case know what it is he has to do, or when his work is done.

2. Ethics at large may be defined, the art of directing men's actions to the production of the greatest possible quantity of happiness, on the part of those whose interest is in view. *Ethics in general, what.*

3. What then are the actions which it can be in a man s power to direct? They must be either his own actions, or those of other agents. Ethics, in as far as it is the art of directing a man's own actions, may be styled the *art of self-government*, or *private ethics*. *Private ethics.*

4. What other agents then are there, which, at the same time that they are under the influence of man's direction, are susceptible of happiness? They are of two sorts: 1. Other human beings who are styled persons. 2. Other animals, which, on account of their interests having been neglected by the insensibility of the ancient jurists, stand degraded into the class of *things*.[1] As to other human *The art of government: that is, of legislation and administration.*

---

1 Under the Gentoo and Mahometan religions, the interests of the rest of the animal creation seem to have met with some attention. Why have they not, universally, with as much as those of human creatures, allowance made for the difference in point of sensibility? Because the laws that are have been the work of mutual fear; a sentiment which the less rational animals have not had the same

beings, the art of directing their actions to the above end is what we mean, or at least the only thing which, upon the principle of utility, we *ought* to mean, by the art of government: which, in as far as the measures it displays itself in are of a permanent nature, is generally distinguished by the name of *legislation*: as it is by that of *administration*, when they are of a temporary nature, determined by the occurrences of the day.

Art of education. 5. Now human creatures, considered with respect to the maturity of their faculties, are either in an *adult*, or in a *non-adult* state. The art of government, in as far as it concerns the direction of the actions of persons in a non-adult state, may be termed the art of *education*. In as far as this business is entrusted with those who, in virtue of some private relationship, are in the main the best

---

means as man has of turning to account. Why *ought* they not? No reason can be given. If the being eaten were all, there is very good reason why we should be suffered to eat such of them as we like to eat: we are the better for it. and they are never the worse. They have none of those long-protracted anticipations of future misery which we have. The death they suffer in our hands commonly is, and always may be, a speedier, and by that means a less painful one, than that which would await them in the inevitable course of nature. If the being killed were all, there is very good reason why we should be suffered to kill such as molest us: we should be the worse for their living, and they are never the worse for being dead. But is there any reason why we should be suffered to torment them? Not any that I can see. Are there any why we should *not* be suffered to torment them? Yes, several. See B. I. tit. [Cruelty to animals]. The day has been, I grieve to say in many places it is not yet past, in which the greater part of the species, under the denomination of slaves, have been treated by the law exactly upon the same footing as, in England for example, the inferior races of animals are still. The day *may* come, when the rest of the animal creation may acquire those rights which never could have been withholden from them but by the hand of tyranny. The French have already discovered that the blackness of the skin is no reason why a human being should be abandoned without redress to the caprice of a tormentor.[a] It may come one day to be recognized, that the number of the legs, the villosity of the skin, or the termination of the *os sacrum*, are reasons equally insufficient for abandoning a sensitive being to the same fate. What else is it that should trace the insuperable line? Is it the faculty of reason, or, perhaps, the faculty of discourse? But a full-grown horse or dog is beyond comparison a more rational, as well as a more conversable animal, than an infant of a day, or a week, or even a month, old. But suppose the case were otherwise, what would it avail? The question is not, Can they *reason*? nor, Can they *talk*? but, Can they *suffer*?

---

a See Lewis XIVth's Code Noir.

disposed to take upon them, and the best able to discharge, this office, it may be termed the art of *private education*: in as far as it is exercised by those whose province it is to superintend the conduct of the whole community, it may be termed the art of *public education*.

6. As to ethics in general, a man's happiness will depend, in the first place, upon such parts of his behaviour as none but himself are interested in; in the next place, upon such parts of it as may affect the happiness of those about him. In as far as his happiness depends upon the first-mentioned part of his behaviour, it is said to depend upon his *duty to himself*. Ethics then, in as far as it is the art of directing a man's actions in this respect, may be termed the art of discharging one's duty to one's self: and the quality which a man manifests by the discharge of this branch of duty (if duty it is to be called) is that of *prudence*. In as far as his happiness, and that of any other person or persons whose interests are considered, depends upon such parts of his behaviour as may affect the interests of those about him, it may be said to depend upon his *duty to others*; or, to use a phrase now somewhat antiquated, his *duty to his neighbour*. Ethics then, in as far as it is the art of directing a man's actions in this respect, may be termed the art of discharging one's duty to one's neighbour. Now the happiness of one's neighbour may be consulted in two ways: 1. In a negative way, by forbearing to diminish it. 2. In a positive way, by studying to increase it. A man's duty to his neighbour is accordingly partly negative and partly positive: to discharge the negative branch of it, is *probity*: to discharge the positive branch, *beneficence*.

Ethics exhibits the rules of,
1. Prudence.
2. Probity.
3. Beneficence.

7. It may here be asked, How it is that upon the principle of private ethics, legislation and religion out of the question, a mans happiness depends upon such parts of his conduct as affect, immediately at least, the happiness of no one but himself: this is as much as to ask, What motives (independent of such as legislation and religion may chance to furnish) can one man have to consult the happiness of another? By what motives, or, which comes to the same thing, by what obligations, can he be bound to obey the dictates *of probity* and *beneficence*? In answer to this, it cannot but be admitted, that the only interests which a man at all times and upon all occasions is sure to find *adequate* motives for consulting, are his own. Notwithstanding this, there are no occasions in which a

Probity and beneficence, how they connect with prudence.

man has not some motives for consulting the happiness of other men. In the first place, he has, on all occasions, the purely social motive of sympathy or benevolence: in the next place, he has, on most occasions, the semi-social motives of love of amity and love of reputation. The motive of sympathy will act upon him with more or less effect, according to the *bias* of his sensibility:[1] the two other motives, according to a variety of circumstances, principally according to the strength of his intellectual powers, the firmness and steadiness of his mind, the quantum of his moral sensibility, and the characters of the people he has to deal with.

Every act which is a proper object of ethics is not of legislation. 8. Now private ethics has happiness for its end: and legislation can have no other. Private ethics concerns every member, that is, the happiness and the actions of every member, of any community that can be proposed; and legislation can concern no more. Thus far, then, private ethics and the art of legislation go hand in hand. The end they have, or ought to have, in view, is of the same nature. The persons whose happiness they ought to have in view, as also the persons whose conduct they ought to be occupied in directing, are precisely the same. The very acts they ought to be conversant about, are even in a *great measure* the same. Where then lies the difference? In that the acts which they ought to be conversant about, though in a great measure, are not *perfectly and throughout* the same. There is no case in which a private man ought not to direct his own conduct to the production of his own happiness, and of that of his fellow-creatures: but there are cases in which the legislator ought not (in a direct way at least, and by means of punishment applied immediately to particular *individual* acts) to attempt to direct the conduct of the several other members of the community. Every act which promises to be beneficial upon the whole to the community (himself included) each individual ought to perform of himself: but it is not every such act that the legislator ought to compel him to perform. Every act which promises to be pernicious upon the whole to the community (himself included) each individual ought to abstain from of himself: but it is not every such act that the legislator ought to compel him to abstain from.

1 Chap. vi [Sensibility], 3.

9. Where then is the line to be drawn? – We shall not have far to seek for it. The business is to give an idea of the cases in which ethics ought, and in which legislation ought not (in a direct manner at least) to interfere. If legislation interferes in a direct manner, it must be by punishment.[1] Now the cases in which punishment, meaning the punishment of the political sanction, ought not to be inflicted, have been already stated.[2] If then there be any of these cases in which, although legislation ought not, private ethics does or ought to interfere, these cases will serve to point out the limits between the two arts or branches of science. These cases, it may be remembered, are of four sorts: 1. Where punishment would be groundless. 2. Where it would be inefficacious. 3. Where it would be unprofitable. 4. Where it would be needless. Let us look over all these cases, and see whether in any of them there is room for the interference of private ethics, at the same time that there is none for the direct interference of legislation.

The limits between the provinces of private ethics and legislation, marked out by the cases unmeet for punishment.

10. (1) First then, as to the cases where punishment would be *groundless*. In these cases it is evident, that the restrictive interference of ethics would be groundless too. It is because, upon the whole, there is no evil in the act, that legislation ought not to endeavour to prevent it. No more, for the same reason, ought private ethics.

1. Neither ought to apply where punishment is groundless.

11. (2) As to the cases in which punishment would be *inefficacious*. These, we may observe, may be divided into two sets or classes. The first do not depend at all upon the nature of the act: they turn only upon a defect in the timing of the punishment. The punishment in question is no more than what, for anything that appears, ought to have been applied to the act in question. It ought, however, to have been applied at a different time; viz., not till after it had been properly denounced. These are the cases of an *ex-post-facto* law; of a judicial sentence beyond the law; and of a law not sufficiently promulgated. The acts here in question then

2. How far private ethics can apply in the cases where punishment would be inefficacious.

---

1 I say nothing in this place of reward: because it is only in a few extraordinary cases that it can be applied, and because even where it is applied, it may be doubted perhaps whether the application of it can, properly speaking, be termed an act of legislation. See infra, § 3.

2 Chap. xiii [Cases unmeet].

might, for anything that appears, come properly under the department even of coercive legislation: of course do they under that of private ethics. As to the other set of cases, in which punishment would be inefficacious; neither do these depend upon the nature of the act, that is, of the *sort* of act: they turn only upon some extraneous *circumstances*, with which an act of *any* sort may chance to be accompanied. These, however, are of such a nature as not only to exclude the application of legal punishment, but in general to leave little room for the influence of private ethics. These are the cases where the will could not be deterred from any act, even by the extraordinary force of artificial punishment: as in the cases of extreme infancy, insanity, and perfect intoxication: of course, therefore, it could not by such slender and precarious force as could be applied by private ethics. The case is in this respect the same, under the circumstances of unintentionality with respect to the event of the action, unconsciousness with regard to the circumstances, and mis-supposal with regard to the existence of circumstances which have not existed; as also where the force, even of extraordinary punishment, is rendered inoperative by the superior force of a physical danger or threatened mischief. It is evident, that in these cases, if the thunders of the law prove impotent, the whispers of simple morality can have but little influence.

3. How far, where it would be unprofitable. 12. (3) As to the cases where punishment would be *unprofitable*. These are the cases which constitute the great field for the exclusive interference of private ethics. When a punishment is unprofitable, or in other words too expensive, it is because the evil of the punishment exceeds that of the offence. Now the evil of the punishment, we may remember,[1] is distinguishable into four branches: 1. The evil of coercion, including constraint or restraint, according as the act commanded is of the positive kind or the negative. 2. The evil of apprehension. 3. The evil of sufferance. 4. The derivative evils resulting to persons in *connection* with those by whom the three above-mentioned original evils are sustained. Now with respect to those original evils, the persons who lie exposed to them may be two very different sets of

---

1 See Chap. xiii [Cases unmeet], § iv.

persons. In the first place, persons who may have actually committed, or been prompted to commit, the acts really meant to be prohibited. In the next place, persons who may have performed, or been prompted to perform, such other acts as they fear may be in danger of being involved in the punishment designed only for the former. But of these two sets of acts, it is the former only that are pernicious: it is, therefore, the former only that it can be the business of private ethics to endeavour to prevent. The latter being by the supposition not mischievous, to prevent them is what it can no more be the business of ethics to endeavour at, than of legislation. It remains to show how it may happen, that there should be acts really pernicious, which, although they may very properly come under the censure of private ethics, may yet be no fit objects of the legislator to control.

13. Punishment then, as applied to delinquency, may be unprofitable in both or either of two ways: 1. By the expense it would amount to, even supposing the application of it to be confined altogether to delinquency: 2. By the danger there may be of its involving the innocent in the fate designed only for the guilty. First then, with regard to the cases in which the expense of the punishment as applied to the guilty, would outweigh the profit to be made by it. These cases, it is evident, depend upon a certain proportion between the evil of the punishment and the evil of the offence. Now were the offence of such a nature, that a punishment which, in point of *magnitude*, should but just exceed the profit of it, would be sufficient to prevent it, it might be rather difficult perhaps to find an instance in which such punishment would clearly appear to be unprofitable. But the fact is, there are many cases in which a punishment, in order to have any chance of being efficacious, must, in point of magnitude, be raised a great deal above that level. Thus it is, wherever the danger of detection is, or, what comes to the same thing, is likely to appear to be, so small, as to make the punishment appear in a high degree uncertain. In this case it is necessary, as has been shown,[1] if punishment be at all applied, to raise it in point of magnitude as much as it falls short in point of certainty. It is evident, however,

Which it may be, 1. Although confined to the guilty.

---

1 Chap. xiv [Proportion] 17, Rule 7.

that all this can be but guess-work: and that the effect of such a proportion will be rendered precarious, by a variety of circumstances: by the want of sufficient promulgation on the part of the law:[1] by the particular circumstances of the temptation:[2] and by the circumstances influencing the sensibility of the several individuals who are exposed to it.[3] Let the *seducing* motives be strong, the offence then will at any rate be frequently committed. Now and then indeed, owing to a coincidence of circumstances more or less extraordinary, it will be detected, and by that means punished. But for the purpose of example, which is the principal one, an act of punishment, considered in itself, is of no use: what use it can be of, depends altogether upon the expectation it raises of similar punishment, in future cases of similar delinquency. But this future punishment, it is evident, must always depend upon detection. If then the want of detection is such as must in general (especially to eyes fascinated by the force of the seducing motives) appear too improbable to be reckoned upon, the punishment, though it should be inflicted, may come to be of no use. Here then will be two opposite evils running on at the same time, yet neither of them reducing the quantum of the other: the evil of the disease and the evil of the painful and inefficacious remedy. It seems to be partly owing to some such considerations, that fornication, for example, or the illicit commerce between the sexes, has commonly either gone altogether unpunished, or been punished in a degree inferior to that in which, on other accounts, legislators might have been disposed to punish it.

2. By enveloping the innocent.   14. Secondly, with regard to the cases in which political punishment, as applied to delinquency, may be unprofitable, in virtue of the danger there may be of its involving the innocent in the fate designed only for the guilty. Whence should this danger then arise? From the difficulty there may be of fixing the idea of the guilty action: that is, of subjecting it to such a definition as shall be clear and precise enough to guard effectually against misapplication. This difficulty may arise from either of two sources: the one permanent, to wit, the nature of the *actions*

1 Chap. xiii [Cases unmeet], § 3. Append tit. [Promulgation].
2 Chap. xi [Disposition] 35, etc.
3 Chap. vi [Sensibility].

themselves: the other occasional, I mean the qualities of the *men* who may have to deal with those actions in the way of government. In as far as it arises from the latter of these sources, it may depend partly upon the use which the *legislator* may be *able* to make of language; partly upon the use which, according to the apprehension of the legislator, the *judge* may be *disposed* to make of it. As far as legislation is concerned, it will depend upon the degree of perfection to which the arts of language may have been carried, in the first place, in the nation in general; in the next place, by the *legislator* in particular. It is to a sense of this difficulty, as it should seem, that we may attribute the caution with which most legislators have abstained from subjecting to censure, on the part of the law, such actions as come under the notion of rudeness, for example, or treachery, or ingratitude. The attempt to bring acts of so vague and questionable a nature under the control of law, will argue either a very immature age, in which the difficulties which give birth to that danger are not descried; or a very enlightened age, in which they are overcome.[1]

15. For the sake of obtaining the clearer idea of the limits between the art of legislation and private ethics, it may now be time to call to mind the distinctions above established with regard to ethics in general. The degree in which private ethics stands in need of the assistance of legislation, is different in the three branches of duty above distinguished. Of the rules of moral duty, those which seem to stand least in need of the assistance of legislation are the rules of *prudence*. It can only be through some defect on the part of the understanding, if a man be ever deficient in point of duty to himself. If he does wrong, there is nothing else that it can be owing to but either some *inadvertence*[2] or some *mis-supposal*[2] with regard to the circumstances on which his happiness depends. It is a

Legislation how far necessary for the enforcement of the dictates of prudence.

---

1 In certain countries, in which the voice of the people has a more especial control over the hand of the legislator, nothing can exceed the dread which they are under of seeing any effectual provision made against the offences which come under the head of *defamation*, particularly that branch of it which may be styled the *political*. This dread seems to depend partly upon the apprehension they may think it prudent to entertain of a defect in point of ability or integrity on the part of the legislator, partly upon a similar apprehension of a defect in point of integrity on the part of the judge.

2 See Chap. ix [Consciousness].

standing topic of complaint, that a man knows too little of himself. Be it so: but is it so certain that the legislator must know more?[1] It is plain, that of individuals the legislator can know nothing: concerning those points of conduct which depend upon the particular circumstances of each individual, it is plain, therefore, that he can determine nothing to advantage. It is only with respect to those broad lines of conduct in which all persons, or very large and permanent descriptions of persons, may be in a way to engage, that he can have any pretence for interfering; and even here the propriety of his interference will, in most instances, lie very open to dispute. At any rate, he must never expect to produce a perfect compliance by the mere force of the sanction of which he is himself the author. All he can hope to do, is to increase the efficacy of private ethics, by giving strength and direction to the influence of the moral sanction. With what chance of success, for example, would a legislator go about to extirpate drunkenness and fornication by dint of legal punishment? Not all the tortures which ingenuity could invent would compass it: and, before he had made any progress worth regarding, such a mass of evil would be produced by the punishment, as would exceed, a thousand-fold, the utmost possible mischief of the offence. The great difficulty would be in the procuring evidence; an object which could not be attempted, with any probability of success, without spreading dismay through every family,[2] tearing the bonds of sympathy asunder,[3] and rooting out the influence of all the social motives. All that he can do then, against offences of this nature, with any prospect of advantage, in the way of direct legislation, is to subject them, in cases of notoriety, to a slight censure, so as thereby to cover them with a slight shade of artificial disrepute.

---

1 Chap. xvi [Division] 52.

On occasions like this the legislator should never lose sight of the well-known story of the oculist and the sot. A countryman who had hurt his eyes by drinking, went to a celebrated oculist for advice. He found him at table, with a glass of wine before him. 'You must leave off drinking,' said the oculist. 'How so?' says the countryman. '*You* don't, and yet methinks your own eyes are none of the best.' – 'That's very true, friend,' replied the oculist: 'but you are to know, I love my bottle better than my eyes.'

2 Evil of apprehension: third branch of the evil of a punishment. Chap. xiii § 4.

3 Derivative evils: fourth branch of the evil of a punishment. Ib.

16. It may be observed, that with regard to this branch of duty, legislators have, in general, been disposed to carry their interference full as far as is expedient. The great difficulty here is, to persuade them to confine themselves within bounds. A thousand little passions and prejudices have led them to narrow the liberty of the subject in this line, in cases in which the punishment is either attended with no profit at all, or with none that will make up for the expense.

– Apt to go too far in this respect.

17. The mischief of this sort of interference is more particularly conspicuous in the article of religion. The reasoning, in this case, is of the following stamp. There are certain errors, in matters of belief, to which all mankind are prone: and for these errors in judgment, it is the determination of a Being of infinite benevolence, to punish them with an infinity of torments. But from these errors the legislator himself is necessarily free: for the men, who happen to be at hand for him to consult with, being men perfectly enlightened, unfettered, and unbiassed, have such advantages over all the rest of the world, that when they sit down to enquire out the truth relative to points so plain and so familiar as those in question, they cannot fail to find it. This being the case, when the sovereign sees his people ready to plunge headlong into an abyss of fire, shall he not stretch out a hand to save them? Such, for example, seems to have been the train of reasoning, and such the motives, which led Lewis the XIVth into those coercive measures which he took for the conversion of heretics and the confirmation of true believers. The ground-work, pure sympathy and loving-kindness: the super-structure, all the miseries which the most determined malevolence could have devised.[1]

– Particularly in matters of religion.

---

1 I do not mean but that other motives of a less social nature might have introduced themselves, and probably, in point of fact, did introduce themselves, in the progress of the enterprise. But in point of possibility, the motive above mentioned, when accompanied with such a thread of reasoning, is sufficient, without any other, to account for all the effects above alluded to. If any others interfere, their interference, how natural soever, may be looked upon as an accidental and inessential circumstance, not necessary to the production of the effect. Sympathy, a concern for the danger they appear to be exposed to, gives birth to the wish of freeing them from it; that wish shows itself in the shape of a command: this command produces disobedience: disobedience on the one part produces disappointment on the other: the pain of disappointment produces

But of this more fully in another place.[1]

– How far necessary for the enforcement of the dictates of probity. 18. The rules of *probity* are those, which in point of expediency stand most in need of assistance on the part of the legislator, and in which, in point of fact, his interference has been most extensive. There are few cases in which it *would* be expedient to punish a man for hurting *himself*: but there are few cases, if any, in which it would *not* be expedient to punish a man for injuring his neighbour. With regard to that branch of probity which is opposed to offences against property, private ethics depends in a manner for its very existence upon legislation. Legislation must first determine what things are to be regarded as each man's property, before the general rules of ethics, on this head, can have any particular application. The case is the same with regard to offences against the state. Without legislation there would be no such thing as a *state*: no particular persons invested with powers to be exercised for the benefit of the rest. It is plain, therefore, that in this branch the interference of the legislator cannot anywhere be dispensed with. We must first know what are the dictates of legislation, before we can know what are the dictates of private ethics.[2]

– of the dictates of beneficence. 19. As to the rules of beneficence, these, as far as concerns matters of detail, must necessarily be abandoned in great measure to the jurisdiction of private ethics. In many cases the beneficial quality of the act depends essentially upon the disposition of the agent; that is, upon the motives by which he appears to have been prompted to perform it: upon their belonging to the head of

---

ill-will towards those who are the authors of it. The affections will often make this progress in less time than it would take to describe it. The sentiment of wounded pride, and other modifications of the love of reputation and the love of power, add fuel to the flame. A kind of revenge exasperates the seve,rities of coercive policy.

1 See B. I. tit. [Self-regarding offences.]

2 But suppose the dictates of legislation *are* not what they *ought to be*: what are then, or (what in this case comes to the same thing) what ought to be, the dictates of private ethics? Do they coincide with the dictates of legislation, or do they oppose them, or do they remain neuter? A very interesting question this, but one that belongs not to the present subject. It belongs exclusively to that of private ethics. Principles which may lead to the solution of it may be seen in A Fragment on Government, p. 150, Lond. edit. 1776 – and p. 114, edit. 1823.

sympathy, love of amity, or love of reputation; and not to any head of self-regarding motives, brought into play by the force of political constraint: in a word, upon their being such as denominate his conduct *free* and *voluntary*, according to one of the many senses given to those ambiguous expressions.[1] The limits of the law on this head seem, however, to be capable of being extended a good deal farther than they seem ever to have been extended hitherto. In particular, in cases where the person is in danger, why should it not be made the duty of every man to save another from mischief, when it can be done without prejudicing himself, as well as to abstain from bringing it on him? This accordingly is the idea pursued in the body of the work.[2]

20. To conclude this section, let us recapitulate and bring to a point the difference between private ethics, considered as an art or science, on the one hand, and that branch of jurisprudence which contains the art or science of legislation, on the other. Private ethics teaches how each man may dispose himself to pursue the course most conducive to his own happiness, by means of such motives as offer of themselves: the art of legislation (which may be considered as one branch of the science of jurisprudence) teaches how a multitude of men, composing a community, may be disposed to pursue that course which upon the whole is the most conducive to the happiness of the whole community, by means of motives to be applied by the legislator.

Difference between private ethics and the art of legislation recapitulated.

---

1 If we may believe M. Voltaire,[a] there was a time when the French ladies who thought themselves neglected by their husbands, used to petition *pour être embesoignées*: the technical word which, he says, was appropriated to this purpose. This sort of law-proceedings seems not very well calculated to answer the design: accordingly we hear nothing of them now-a-days. The French ladies of the present age seem to be under no such difficulties.

2 A woman's head-dress catches fire: water is at hand: a man, instead of assisting to quench the fire, looks on, and laughs at it. A drunken man, falling with his face downwards into a puddle, is in danger of suffocation: lifting his head a little on one side would save him: another man sees this and lets him lie. A quantity of gunpowder lies scattered about a room: a man is going into it with a lighted candle: another, knowing this, lets him go in without warning. Who is there that in any of these cases would think punishment misapplied?

---

a Quest. sur l'Encyclop. tom. 7. art. Impuissance.

We come now to exhibit the limits between penal and civil jurisprudence. For this purpose it may be of use to give a distinct though summary view of the principal branches into which jurisprudence, considered in its utmost extent, is wont to be divided.

§ 2. *Jurisprudence, its branches*

Juris-
prudence,
expository
or censorial.

21. Jurisprudence is a fictitious entity: nor can any meaning be found for the word, but by placing it in company with some word that shall be significative of a real entity. To know what is meant by jurisprudence, we must know, for example, what is meant by a book of jurisprudence. A book of jurisprudence can have but one or the other of two objects: 1. To ascertain what the law[1] is: 2. to ascertain what it ought to be. In the former case it may be styled a book of *expository* jurisprudence; in the latter, a book of *censorial* jurisprudence: or, in other words, a book on the *art of legislation*.

Expository
juris-
prudence,
author-
itative or
unauthor-
itative.

22. A book of expository jurisprudence, is either *authoritative* or *unauthoritative*. It is styled authoritative, when it is composed by him who, by representing the state of the law to be so and so, causeth it so to be; that is, of the legislator himself: unauthoritative, when it is the work of any other person at large.

Sources
of the
distinctions
yet
remaining.

23. Now *law*, or *the law*, taken indefinitely, is an abstract and collective term; which, when it means anything, can mean neither more nor less than the sum total of a number of individual laws taken together.[2] It follows, that of whatever other modifica-

---

1 The word *law* itself, which stands so much in need of a definition, must wait for it awhile (see § 3): for there is no doing everything at once. In the mean time every reader will understand it according to the notion he has been accustomed to annex to it.

2 In most of the European languages there are two different words for distinguishing the abstract and the concrete senses of the word *law*: which words are so wide asunder as not even to have any etymological affinity. In Latin, for example, there is *lex* for the concrete sense, *jus* for the abstract: in Italian, *legge* and *diritto*: in French, *loi* and *droit*: in Spanish, *ley* and *derecho*: in German, *gesetz* and *recht*. The English is at present destitute of this advantage.

In the Anglo-Saxon, besides *lage*, and several other words, for the concrete sense, there was the word *right*, answering to the German *recht*, for the abstract; as may be seen in the compound *folc-right*, and in other instances. But the word *right* having long ago lost this sense, the modern English no longer possesses this advantage.

tions the subject of a book of jurisprudence is susceptible, they must all of them be taken from some circumstance or other of which such individual laws, or the assemblages into which they may be sorted, are susceptible. The circumstances that have given rise to the principal branches of jurisprudence we are wont to hear of, seem to be as follows: 1. The *extent* of the laws in question in point of dominion. 2. The *political quality* of the persons whose conduct they undertake to regulate. 3. The *time* of their being in force. 4. The manner in which they are *expressed*. 5. The concern which they have with the article of *punishment*.

24. In the first place, in point of extent, what is delivered concerning the laws in question, may have reference either to the laws of such or such a nation or nations in particular, or to the laws of all nations whatsoever: in the first case, the book may be said to relate to *local*, in the other, to *universal*, *jurisprudence*. *Jurisprudence, local and universal.*

Now of the infinite variety of nations there are upon the earth, there are no two which agree exactly in their laws: certainly not in the whole: perhaps not even in any single article: and let them agree to-day, they would disagree tomorrow. This is evident enough with regard to the *substance* of the laws: and it would be still more extraordinary if they agreed in point of *form*; that is, if they were conceived in precisely the same strings of words. What is more, as the languages of nations are commonly different, as well as their laws, it is seldom that, strictly speaking, they have so much as a single *word* in common. However, among the words that are appropriated to the subject of law, there are some that in all languages are pretty exactly correspondent to one another: which comes to the same thing nearly as if they were the same. Of this stamp, for example, are those which correspond to the words *power*, *right*, *obligation*, *liberty*, and many others.

It follows, that if there are any books which can, properly speaking, be styled books of universal jurisprudence, they must be looked for within very narrow limits. Among such as are expository, there can be none that are authoritative: nor even, as far as the *substance* of the laws is concerned, any that are unauthoritative. To be susceptible of an universal application, all that a book of the expository kind can have to treat of, is the import of words: to be, strictly speaking, universal, it must confine itself to terminology. Accordingly the definitions which there has been occasion here and there to intersperse in the course of the present work, and particularly the definition hereafter given of the word *law*, may be considered as matter belonging to the head of universal jurisprudence. Thus far in strictness of speech: though in point of usage, where a man, in laying down what he apprehends to be the law, extends his view to a few of the nations with which his own is most connected, it is common enough to consider what he writes as relating to universal jurisprudence,

It is in the censorial line that there is the greatest room for disquisitions that apply to the circumstances of all nations alike: and in this line what regards the substance of the laws in question is as susceptible of an universal application, as what regards the words. That the laws of all nations, or even of any two nations, should coincide in all points, would be as ineligible as it is impossible: some leading points, however, there seem to be, in respect of which the laws of all civilized nations might, without inconvenience, be the same. To mark out some of these points will, as far as it goes, be the business of the body of this work.

– internal and international. 25. In the second place, with regard to the *political quality* of the persons whose conduct is the object of the law. These may, on any given occasion, be considered either as members of the same state, or as members of different states: in the first case, the law may be referred to the head of *internal*, in the second case, to that of *international*[1] jurisprudence.

Now as to any transactions which may take place between individuals who are subjects of different states, these are regulated by the internal laws, and decided upon by the internal tribunals, of

---

1. The word *international*, it must be acknowledged, is a new one; though, it is hoped, sufficiently analogous and intelligible. It is calculated to express, in a more significant way, the branch of law which goes commonly under the name of the *law of nations*: an appellation so uncharacteristic, that, were it not for the force of custom, it would seem rather to refer to internal jurisprudence. The chancellor D'Aguesseau has already made, I find, a similar remark: he says that what is commonly called *droit des gens*, ought rather to be termed *droit entre les gens*.[a]

---

[a] Oeuvres, Tom. ii, p. 337, edit. 1773, 12mo.

the one or the other of those states: the case is the same where the sovereign of the one has any immediate transactions with a private member of the other: the sovereign reducing himself, *pro re nata*, to the condition of a private person, as often as he submits his cause to either tribunal; whether by claiming a benefit, or defending himself against a burthen. There remain then the mutual transactions between sovereigns, as such, for the subject of that branch of jurisprudence which may be properly and exclusively termed *international*.[1]

With what degree of propriety rules for the conduct of persons of this description can come under the appellation of *laws*, is a question that must rest till the nature of the thing called a *law* shall have been more particularly unfolded.

It is evident enough, that international jurisprudence may, as well as internal, be censorial as well as expository, unauthoritative as well as authoritative.

26. Internal jurisprudence, again, may either concern all the members of a state indiscriminately, or such of them only as are connected in the way of residence, or otherwise, with a particular district. Jurisprudence is accordingly sometimes distinguished into *national* and *provincial*. But as the epithet *provincial* is hardly applicable to districts so small as many of those which

Internal jurisprudence, national and provincial, local or particular.

---

1 In the times of James I of England and Philip III of Spain, certain merchants at London happened to have a claim upon Philip, which his ambassador Gondemar did not think fit to satisfy. They applied for counsel to Selden, who advised them to sue the Spanish monarch in the court of King's Bench, and prosecute him to an outlawry. They did so: and the sheriffs of London were accordingly commanded, in the usual form, to take the body of the defendant Philip, wherever it was to be found within their bailiwick. As to the sheriffs, Philip, we may believe, was in no great fear of them: but what answered the same purpose, he happened on his part to have demands upon some other merchants, whom, so long as the outlawry remained in force, there was no proceeding against. Gondemar paid the money.[a] This was internal jurisprudence: if the dispute had been betwixt Philip and James himself, it would have been international.

As to the word *international*, from this work, or the first of the works edited in French by Mr Dumont, it has taken root in the language. Witness reviews and newspapers.

---

a Selden's Table-Talk, tit. Law.

have laws of their own are wont to be, such as towns, parishes, and manors; the term *local* (where universal jurisprudence is plainly out of the question) or the term *particular*, though this latter is not very characteristic, might either of them be more commodious.[1]

Juris-prudence, ancient or living. 27. Thirdly, with respect to *time*. In a work of the expository kind, the laws that are in question may either be such as are still in force at the time when the book is writing, or such as have ceased to be in force. In the latter case the subject of it might be termed *ancient*; in the former, *present* or *living* jurisprudence: that is, if the substantive *jurisprudence*, and no other, must at any rate be employed, and that with an epithet in both cases. But the truth is, that a book of the former kind is rather a book of history than a book of jurisprudence; and, if the word *jurisprudence* be expressive of the subject, it is only with some such words as *history* or *antiquities* prefixed. And as the laws which are anywhere in question are supposed, if nothing appears to the contrary, to be those which are in force, no such epithet as that of *present* or *living* commonly appears.

Where a book is so circumstanced, that the laws which form the subject of it, though in force at the time of its being written, are in force no longer, that book is neither a book of living jurisprudence, nor a book on the history of jurisprudence: it is no longer the former, and it never was the latter. It is evident that, owing to the changes which from time to time must take place, in a greater or less degree, in every body of laws, every book of jurisprudence, which is of an expository nature, must in the course of a few years, come to partake more or less of this condition.

The most common and most useful object of a history of jurisprudence, is to exhibit the circumstances that have attended the establishment of laws actually in force. But the exposition of the dead laws which have been superseded, is inseparably interwoven with that of the living ones which have superseded them.

---

1 The term *municipal* seemed to answer the purpose very well, till it was taken by an English author of the first eminence to signify internal law in general, in contradistinction to international law, and the imaginary law of nature. It might still be used in this sense, without scruple, in any other language.

The great use of both these branches of *science*, is to furnish examples for the *art* of legislation.[1]

28. Fourthly, in point of *expression*, the laws in question may subsist either in the form of *statute* or in that of *customary* law.

Juris-prudence, statutory or customary.

As to the difference between these two branches (which respects only the article of form or expression) it cannot properly be made appear till some progress has been made in the definition of a law.

29. Lastly, the most intricate distinction of all, and that which comes most frequently on the carpet, is that which is made between the *civil* branch of jurisprudence and the *penal*, which letter is wont, in certain circumstances, to receive the name of *criminal*.

Juris-prudence, civil or penal (criminal).

What is a penal code of laws? What a civil code? Of what nature are their contents? Is it that there are two sorts of laws, the one penal the other civil, so that the laws in a penal code are all penal laws, while the laws in a civil code are all civil laws? Or is it, that in every law there is some matter which is of a penal nature, and which therefore belongs to the penal code; and at the same time other matter which is of a civil nature, and which therefore belongs to the civil code? Or is it, that some laws belong to one code or the other exclusively, while others are divided between the two? To answer these questions in any manner that shall be tolerably satisfactory, it will be necessary to ascertain what a *law* is; meaning one entire but single law: and what are the parts into

Question concerning the distinction between the civil branch and the penal, stated.

---

1 Of what stamp are the works of Grotius, Puffendorf and Burlamaqui? Are they political or ethical, historical or juridical, expository or censorial? – Sometimes one thing, sometimes another: they seem hardly to have settled the matter with themselves. A defect this to which all books must almost unavoidably be liable, which take for their subject the pretended *law of nature*: an obscure phantom, which, in the imaginations of those who go in chase of it, points sometimes to *manners*, sometimes to *laws*; sometimes to what law *is*, sometimes to what it *ought* to be.[a] Montesquieu sets out upon the censorial plan: but long before the conclusion, as if he had forgot his first design, he throws off the censor, and puts on the antiquarian. The Marquis Beccaria's book, the first of any account that is uniformly censorial, concludes as it sets out, with penal jurisprudence.

---

[a] See Chap. ii [Principles Adverse], 14.

which a law, as such, is capable of being distinguished: or, in other words, to ascertain what the properties are that are to be found in every object which can with propriety receive the appellation of a law. This then will be the business of the third and fourth sections: what concerns the import of the word *criminal*, as applied to law, will be discussed separately in the fifth.[1]

1 Here ends the original work, in the state into which it was brought in November, 1780. What follows is now added in January, 1789.

The third, fourth, and fifth sections intended, as expressed in the text, to have been added to this chapter, will not here, nor now be given; because to give them in a manner tolerably complete and satisfactory, might require a considerable volume. This volume will form a work of itself closing the series of works mentioned in the preface.

What follows here may serve to give a slight intimation of the nature of the task, which such a work will have to achieve: it will at the same time furnish, not anything like a satisfactory answer to the questions mentioned in the text, but a slight and general indication of the course to be taken for giving them such an answer.

What is a Law? What the parts of a law? The subject of these questions, it is to be observed, is the *logical*, the *ideal*, the *intellectual* whole, not the *physical* one: the *law*, and not the *statute*. An enquiry, directed to the latter sort of object, could neither admit of difficulty nor afford instruction. In this sense whatever is given for law by the person or persons recognized as possessing the power of making laws, is *law*. The Metamorphoses of Ovid, if thus given, would be law. So much as was embraced by one and the same act of authentication, so much as received the touch of the sceptre at one stroke, is *one* law: a whole law, and nothing more. A statute of George II made to substitute an *or* instead of an *and* in a former statute is a complete law; a statute containing an entire body of laws, perfect in all its parts, would not be more so. By the word *law* then, as often as it occurs in the succeeding pages is meant that ideal object, of which the part, the whole, or the multiple, or an assemblage of parts, wholes, and multiples mixed together, is exhibited by a statute; not the statute which exhibits them.

Every law, when complete, is either of a *coercive* or an *uncoercive* nature.

A coercive law is a *command*.

An uncoercive, or rather a *dis*coercive, law is the *revocation*, in whole or in part, of a coercive law.

What has been termed a *declaratory* law, so far as it stands distinguished from either a coercive or a discoercive law, is not properly speaking a law. It is not the expression of an act of the will exercised at the time: it is a mere notification of the existence of a law, either of the coercive or the discoercive kind, as already subsisting: of the existence of some document expressive of some act of the will, exercised, not at the time, but at some former period. If it does anything more than give information of this fact, viz. of the prior existence of a law of either the coercive or the discoercive kind, it ceases *pro tanto* to be what is meant by a declaratory law, and assumes either the coercive or the discoercive quality.

Every coercive law creates an *offence*, that is, converts an act of some sort or other into an offence. It is only by so doing that it can *impose obligation*, that it can *produce coercion*.

A law confining itself to the creation of an offence, and a law commanding a punishment to be administered in case of the commission of such an offence, are two distinct laws; not parts (as they seem to have been generally accounted hitherto) of one and the same law. The acts they command are altogether different; the persons they are addressed to are altogether different. Instance, *Let no man steal*; and, *Let the judge cause whoever is convicted of stealing to be hanged*.

They might be styled; the former, *a simply imperative* law; the other a *punitory*: but the punitory, if it commands the punishment to be inflicted, and does not merely permit it, is as truly *imperative* as the other: only it is punitory besides, which the other is not.

A law of the discoercive kind, considered in itself, can have no punitory law belonging to it: to receive the assistance and support of a punitory law, it must first receive that of a simply imperative or coercive law, and it is to this latter that the punitory law will attach itself, and not to the discoercive one. Example; discoercive law. *The sheriff has power to hang all such as the judge, proceeding in due course of law, shall order him to hang*. Example of a coercive law, made in support of the above discoercive one. *Let no man hinder the sheriff from hanging such as the judge, proceeding in due course of law, shall order him to hang*. Example of a punitory law, made in support of the above coercive one. *Let the judge cause to be imprisoned whosoever attempts to hinder the sheriff from hanging one, whom the judge, proceeding in due course of law, has ordered him to hang*.

But though a simply imperative law, and the punitory law attached to it, are so far distinct laws, that the former contains nothing of the latter, and the latter, in its direct tenor, contains nothing of the former; yet by *implication*, and that a necessary one, the punitory does involve and include the import of the simply imperative law to which it is appended. To say to the judge, *Cause to be hanged whoever in due form of law is convicted of stealing*, is, though not a direct, yet as intelligible a way of intimating to men in general that they must not steal, as to say to them directly, *Do not steal*: and one sees, how much more likely to be efficacious.

It should seem then, that, wherever a simply imperative law is to have a punitory one appended to it, the former might be spared altogether: in which case, saving the exception (which naturally should seem not likely to be a frequent one) of a law capable of answering its purpose without such an appendage, there should be no occasion in the whole body of the law for any other than punitory, or in other words than *penal*, laws. And this, perhaps, would be the case, were it not for the necessity of a large quantity of matter of the *expository* kind, of which we come now to speak.

It will happen in the instance of many, probably of most, possibly of all commands endued with the force of a public law, that, in the expression given to such a command, it shall be necessary to have recourse to terms too complex in their signification to exhibit the requisite ideas, without the assistance of a greater or less quantity of matter of an expository nature. Such terms, like the symbols used in algebraical notation, are rather substitutes and indexes to the terms capable of themselves of exhibiting the ideas in question, than the real and immediate representatives of those ideas.

Take for instance the law, *Thou shalt not steal*. Such a command, were it to rest there, could never sufficiently answer the purpose of a law. A word of so vague and unexplicit a meaning can no otherwise perform this office, than by giving a general intimation of a variety of propositions, each requiring, to convey it to the apprehension, a more particular and ample assemblage of terms. Stealing, for example, (according to a definition not accurate enough for use, but sufficiently so for the present purpose), is *the taking of a thing which is another's, by one who has the* TITLE *so to do* and *is conscious of his having none*. Even after this exposition, supposing it a correct one, can the law be regarded as completely expressed? Certainly not. For what is meant by *a man's having* a TITLE *to take a thing*? To be complete, the law must have exhibited, amongst a multitude of other things, two catalogues: the one of events to which it has given the quality of *conferring title* in such a case; the other of the events to which it has given the quality of *taking it away*. What follows? That for a man to have *stolen*, for a man to *have had no title to what he took*, either no one of the articles contained in the first of those lists must have happened in his favour, or if there has, some one of the number of those contained in the second must have happened to his prejudice.

Such then is the nature of a general law, that while the imperative part of it, the *punctum saliens* as it may be termed, of this artificial body, shall not take up above two or three words, its expository appendage, without which that imperative part could not rightly perform its office, may occupy a considerable volume.

But this may equally be the case with a private order given in a family. Take for instance one from a bookseller to his foreman. *Remove, from this shop to my new one, my whole stock, according to this printed catalogue. – Remove, from this shop to my new one, my whole stock*, is the imperative matter of this order; the catalogue referred to contains the expository appendage.

The same mass of expository matter may serve in common for, may appertain in common to, many commands, many masses of imperative matter. Thus, amongst other things, the catalogue of *collative* and *ablative* events, with respect to *titles* above spoken of, will belong in common to all or most of the laws constitutive of the various offences against property. Thus, in mathematical diagrams, one and the same base shall serve for a whole cluster of triangles.

Such expository matter, being of a complexion so different from the imperative it would.be no wonder if the connection of the former with the latter should escape the observation: which, indeed, is perhaps pretty generally the case. And so long as any mass of legislative matter presents itself, which is not itself imperative or the contrary, or of which the connection with matter of one of those two descriptions is not apprehended, so long and so far the truth of the proposition, *That every law is a command or its opposite*, may remain unsuspected, or appear questionable; so long also may the incompleteness of the greater part of those masses of legislative matter, which wear the complexion of complete laws upon the face of them, also the method to be taken for rendering them really complete, remain undiscovered.

A circumstance, that will naturally contribute to increase the difficulty of the discovery, is the great variety of ways in which the imperation of a law may be conveyed – the great variety of forms which the imperative part of a law may indiscriminately assume: some more directly, some less directly expressive of the imperative quality. *Thou shalt not steal. Let no man steal. Whoso stealeth shall be punished so and so. If any man steal, he shall be punished so and so. Stealing is where a man does so and so; the punishment for stealing is so and so. To judges* so and so named, and so and so constituted, *belong the cognizance of such and such offences;* viz. *stealing* – and so on. These are but part of a multitude of forms of words, in any of which the command by which stealing is prohibited might equally be couched: and it is manifest to what a degree, in some of them, the imperative quality is clouded and concealed from ordinary apprehension.

After this explanation, a general proposition or two, that may be laid down, may help to afford some little insight into the structure and contents of a complete body of laws. – So many different sorts of *offences* created, so many different laws of the *coercive* kind: so many *exceptions* taken out of the descriptions of those offences, so many laws of the *discoercive* kind.

To class *offences*, as hath been attempted to be done in the preceding chapter, is therefore to class *laws*: to exhibit a complete catalogue of all the offences created by law, including the whole mass of expository matter necessary for fixing and exhibiting the import of the terms contained in the several laws, by which those offences are respectively created, would be to exhibit a complete collection of the laws in force: in a word a complete body of law; a *pannomion*, if so it might be termed.

From the obscurity in which the limits of a *law*, and the distinction betwixt a law of the civil or simply imperative kind and a punitory law, are naturally involved, results the obscurity of the limits betwixt a civil and a penal *code*, betwixt a civil branch of the law and the penal.

The question, *What parts of the total mass of legislative matter belong to the civil branch, and what to the penal?* supposes that divers political states, or at least that some one such state, are to be found, having as well a civil code as a penal code, each of them complete in its kind, and marked out by certain limits. But no *one* such state has ever yet existed.

To put a question to which a true answer can be given, we must substitute to the foregoing question some such a one as that which follows:

Suppose two masses of legislative matter to be drawn up at this time of day, the one under the name of a civil code, the other of a penal code, each meant to be complete in its kind – in what general way, is it natural to suppose, that the different sorts of matter, as above distinguished, would be distributed between them?

To this question the following answer seems likely to come as near as any other to the truth.

The *civil* code would not consist of a collection of civil laws, each complete in itself, as well as clear of all penal ones:

Neither would the *penal* code (since we have seen that it *could* not) consist of a collection of punitive laws, each not only complete it itself, but clear of all civil ones. But:

The civil code would consist chiefly of mere masses of expository matter. The imperative matter, to which those masses of expository matter respectively appertained, would be found – not in that same code – not in the civil code – nor in a pure state, free from all admixture of punitory laws; but in the penal code –

in a state of combination – involved, in manner as above explained, in so many correspondent punitory laws.

The penal code then would consist principally of punitive laws, involving the imperative matter of the whole number of civil laws: along with which would probably also be found various masses of expository matter, appertaining not to the civil, but to the punitory laws. The body of penal law, enacted by the Empress-Queen Maria Theresa, agrees pretty well with this account.

The mass of legislative matter published in French as well as German, under the auspices of Frederic II of Prussia, by the name of Code Frederic, but never established with force of law,[a] appears, for example, to be almost wholly composed of masses of expository matter, the relation of which to any imperative matter appears to have been but very imperfectly apprehended.

In that enormous mass of confusion and inconsistency, the ancient Roman, or, as it is termed by way of eminence, the *civil* law, the imperative matter, and even all traces of the imperative character, seem at last to have been smothered in the expository. *Esto* had been the language of primaeval simplicity: *esto* had been the language of the twelve tables. By the time of Justinian (so thick was the darkness raised by clouds of commentators) the penal law had been crammed into an odd corner of the civil – the whole catalogue of offences, and even of crimes, lay buried under a heap of *obligations* – *will* was hid in *opinion* – and the original *esto* had transformed itself into *videtur*, in the mouths even of the most despotic sovereigns.

Among the barbarous nations that grew up out of the ruins of the Roman Empire, Law, emerging from under the mountain of expository rubbish, reassumed for a while the language of command: and then she had simplicity at least, if nothing else, to recommend her.

Besides the civil and the penal, every complete body of law must contain a third branch, the *constitutional*.

The constitutional branch is chiefly employed in conferring, on particular classes of persons, *powers*, to be exercised for the good of the whole society, or of considerable parts of it, and prescribing *duties* to the persons invested with those powers.

The powers are principally constituted, in the first instance, by discoercive or permissive laws, operating as exceptions to certain laws of the coercive or imperative kind. Instance: *A tax-gatherer, as such, may, on such and such an occasion, take such and such things, without any other* TITLE.

The duties are created by imperative laws, addressed to the persons on whom the powers are conferred. Instance: *On such and such an occasion, such and such a tax-gatherer shall take such and such things. Such and such a judge shall, in such and such a case, cause persons so and so offending to be hanged.*

The parts which perform the function of indicating who the individuals are, who, in every case, shall be considered as belonging to those classes, have neither a permissive complexion, nor an imperative.

They are so many masses of expository matter, appertaining in common to all laws, into the texture of which, the names of those classes of persons have occasion to be inserted. Instance: imperative matter: – *Let the judge cause whoever,*

---

[a] Mirabeau sur la Monarchie Prussienne, Tom. v. Liv. 8, p. 215.

in due course of law, is convicted of stealing, to be hanged. Nature of the expository matter: – Who is the person meant by the word *judge*? He who has been *invested* with that office in such a manner: and in respect of whom no *event* has happened, of the number of those, to which the effect is given, of reducing him to the condition of one *divested* of that office.

Thus it is, that one and the same law, one and the same command, will have its matter divided, not only between two great codes, or main branches of the whole body of the laws, the civil and the penal; but amongst three such branches, the civil, the penal, and the constitutional.

In countries, where a great part of the law exists in no other shape, than that of which in England it called *common* law but might be more expressively termed *judiciary*, there must be a great multitude of laws, the import of which cannot be sufficiently made out for practice, without referring to this common law, for more or less of the expository matter belonging to them. Thus in England the exposition of the word *title*, that basis of the whole fabric of the laws of property, is nowhere else to be found. And, as uncertainty is of the very essence of every particle of law so denominated (for the instant it is clothed in a certain authoritative form of words it changes its nature, and passes over to the other denomination) hence it is that a great part of the laws in being in such countries remain uncertain and incomplete. What are those countries? To this hour, every one on the surface of the globe.

Had the science of architecture no fixed nomenclature belonging to it – were there no settled names for distinguishing the different sorts of buildings, nor the different parts of the same building from each other – what would it be? It would be what the science of legislation, considered with respect to its *form*, remains at present.

Were there no architects who could distinguish a dwelling-house from a barn, or a side-wall from a ceiling, what would architects be? They would be what all legislators are at present.

From this very slight and imperfect sketch, may be collated not an answer to the questions in the text but an intimation, and that but an imperfect one, of the course to be taken for giving such an answer; and, at any rate, some idea of the difficulty, as well as of the necessity, of the task.

If it were thought necessary to recur to experience for proofs of this difficulty, and this necessity, they need not be long wanting.

Take, for instance, so many well-meant endeavours on the part of popular bodies, and so many well-meant recommendations in ingenious books, to restrain supreme representative assemblies from making laws in such and such cases, or to such and such an effect. Such laws, to answer the intended purpose, require a perfect mastery in the science of law considered in respect of its form – in the sort of anatomy spoken of in the preface to this work: but a perfect, or even a moderate insight into that science, would prevent their being couched in those loose and inadequate terms, in which they may be observed so frequently to be conceived; as a perfect acquaintance with the dictates of utility on that head would, in many, if not in most, of those instances discounsel the attempt. Keep to the letter, and in attempting to prevent the making of bad laws, you will find them prohibiting the making of the most necessary laws, perhaps even of all laws: quit the letter, and they express no more than if each man were to say, *Your laws shall become ipso facto void, as often as they contain any thing which is not to my mind.*

Of such unhappy attempts, examples may be met with in the legislation of many nations: but in none more frequently than in that newly-created nation, one of the most enlightened, if not the most enlightened, at this day on the globe.

Take for instance the *Declaration of Rights*, enacted by the State of North Carolina, in convention, in or about the month of September, 1788, and said to be copied, with a small exception, from one in like manner enacted by the State of Virginia.[a]

The following, to go no farther, is the first and fundamental article:

'That there are certain natural rights, of which men, when they form a social compact, cannot deprive or divest their posterity, among which are the enjoyment of life and liberty, with the means of acquiring, possessing, and protecting property, and pursuing and obtaining happiness and safety.'

Not to dwell on the oversight of confining to posterity the benefit of the rights thus declared, what follows? That – as against those whom the protection, thus meant to be afforded, includes – every law, or other order, *divesting* a man of *the enjoyment of life or liberty*, is void.

Therefore this is the case, amongst others, with every coercive law.

Therefore, as against the persons thus protected, every order, for example, to pay money on the score of taxation, or of debt from individual to individual, or otherwise, is void: for the effect of it, if complied with, is 'to *deprive* and *divest him*,' *pro tanto*, of the enjoyment of liberty, viz. the liberty of paying or not paying as he thinks proper: not to mention the species opposed to imprison-ment, in the event of such a mode of coercion's being resorted to: likewise of property, which is itself a *means of acquiring, possessing, and protecting property*, and *of pursuing and obtaining happiness and safety*.

Therefore also, as against such persons, every order to attack an armed enemy in time of war, it also void: for, the necessary effect of such an order is 'to *deprive* some of them of *the enjoyment of life*.'

The above-mentioned consequences may suffice for examples, amongst an endless train of similar ones.[b]

Leaning on his elbow, in an attitude of profound and solemn meditation, '*What a multitude of things there are*' (exclaimed the dancing-master Marcel) '*in a minuet!*' – May we now add? – and *in a law*.

---

[a] *Recherches sur les Etats Unis*, 8vo, 1788, vol. i, p. 158.

[b] The Virginian Declaration of Rights, said, in the French work above quoted, to have been enacted the 1st of June, 1776, is not inserted in the publication entitled '*The Constitutions of the several independent states of America, &c.*' Published *by order of Congress: Philadelphia printed. Reprinted for Stockdale and Walker, London,* 1782: though that publication contains the form of government enacted in the same convention, between the 6th of May and the 5th of July in the same year.

But in that same publication is contained a *Declaration of Rights*, of the province of *Massachusetts*, dated in the years 1779 and 1780, which in its first article is a little similar: also one of the province of *Pennsylvania*, dated between July 15th and September 28th, in which the similarity is rather more considerable.

Moreover, the famous *Declaration of Independence*, published by Congress July 5th, 1776, after a preambular opening, goes on in these words: '*We hold these truths to be self-evident: that all men are created equal: that they are endued by the creator with certain unalienable rights: that amongst those are life, liberty, and the pursuit of happiness.*'

The Virginian Declaration of Rights is that, it seems, which claims the honour of having served as a model to those of the other Provinces; and in respect of the above leading article, at least, to the above-mentioned general Declaration of Independence. See Recherches &c. i. 197.

Who can help lamenting, that so rational a cause should be rested upon reasons, so much fitter to beget objections, than to remove them?

But with men, who are unanimous and hearty about *measures*, nothing so weak but may pass in the character of a *reason*: nor is this the first instance in the world, where the conclusion has supported the premises, instead of the premises the conclusion.

PRINCIPLES OF THE CIVIL CODE
(from The Theory of Legislation)

PART I – OBJECTS OF THE CIVIL LAW

CHAPTER I

Rights and Obligations

All the objects which the legislator is called upon to distribute among the members of the community may he reduced to two classes:

> 1st   *Rights*.
> 2nd   *Obligations*.

Rights are in themselves advantages, benefits, for him who enjoys them. Obligations, on the contrary, are duties, charges, onerous to him who ought to fulfil them.

Rights and obligations, though distinct and opposite in their nature, are simultaneous in their origin, and inseparable in their existence. In the nature of things, the law cannot grant a benefit to one without imposing, at the same time, some burden upon another; or, in other words, it is not possible to create a right in favour of one, except by creating a corresponding obligation imposed upon another. How confer upon me the right of property in a piece of land? By imposing upon all others an obligation not to touch its produce. How confer upon me a right of command? By imposing upon a district, or a number of persons, the obligation to obey me.

The legislator ought to confer rights with pleasure, since they are in themselves a good; he ought to impose obligations with reluctance, since they are in themselves an evil. According to the principle of utility, he ought never to impose a burden except for the purpose of conferring a benefit of a clearly greater value.

By creating obligations, the law to the same extent trenches upon liberty. It converts into offences acts which would otherwise be permitted and unpunishable. The law creates an offence either by a positive command or by a prohibition.

These retrenchments of liberty are inevitable. It is impossible to create rights, to impose obligations, to protect the person, life, reputation, property, subsistence, liberty itself, except at the expense of liberty.

But every restriction imposed upon liberty is subject to be followed by a natural sentiment of pain, greater or less; and that independently of an infinite variety of inconveniences and sufferings, which may result from the particular manner of this restriction. It follows, then, that no restriction ought to be imposed, no power conferred, no coercive law sanctioned, without a sufficient and specific reason. There is always a reason against every coercive law – a reason which, in default of any opposing reason, will always be sufficient in itself; and that reason is, that such a law is an attack upon liberty. He who proposes a coercive law ought to be ready to prove, not only that there is a specific reason in favour of it, but that this reason is of more weight than the general reason against every such law.

The proposition that every law is contrary to liberty,[1] though as clear as evidence can make it, is not generally acknowledged. On the contrary, those among the friends of liberty who are more ardent than enlightened, make it a duty of conscience to combat this truth. And how? They pervert language; they refuse to employ the word *liberty* in its common acceptation; they speak a tongue peculiar to themselves. This is the definition they give of liberty: *Liberty consists in the right of doing everything which is not injurious to another.* But is this the ordinary sense of the word? Is not the liberty to do evil liberty? If not, what is it? What word can we use in speaking of it? Do we not say that it is necessary to take away liberty from idiots and bad men, because they abuse it?

According to this definition, I can never know whether I have the liberty to do an action until I have examined all its consequences. If it seems to me injurious to a single individual, even though the law permit it, or perhaps command it, I should not be at liberty to do it. An officer of justice would not be at liberty to punish a robber, unless, indeed, he were sure that this

---

1 Those laws must be excepted by which restrictive laws are revoked, laws which *permit* what other laws had forbidden.

punishment could not hurt the robber! Such are the absurdities which this definition implies.

What does simple reason tell us? Let us attempt to establish a series of true propositions on this subject.

The only object of government ought to be the greatest possible happiness of the community.

The happiness of an individual is increased in proportion as his sufferings are lighter and fewer, and his enjoyments greater and more numerous.

The care of his enjoyments ought to be left almost entirely to the individual. The principal function of government is to guard against pains.

It fulfils this object by creating rights, which it confers upon individuals: rights of personal security, rights of protection for honour, rights of property, rights of receiving aid in case of need. To these rights correspond offences of different kinds. The law cannot create rights except by creating corresponding obligations. It cannot create rights and obligations without creating offences. It cannot command nor forbid without restraining the liberty of individuals.

It appears, then, that the citizen cannot acquire rights except by sacrificing a part of his liberty. But even under a bad government there is no proportion between the acquisition and the sacrifice. Government approaches to perfection in proportion as the sacrifice is less and the acquisition more.

CHAPTER II

Ends of Civil Law

In the distribution of rights and obligations, the legislator, as we have said, should have for his end the happiness of society. Investigating more distinctly in what that happiness consists, we shall find four subordinate ends:

> Subsistence.
> Abundance.
> Equality.
> Security.

The more perfect enjoyment is in all these respects, the greater is the sum of social happiness: and especially of that happiness which depends upon the laws.

We may hence conclude that all the functions of law may be referred to these four heads: to provide subsistence; to produce abundance; to favour equality; to maintain security.

This division has not all the exactness which might be desired. The limits which separate these objects are not always easy to be determined. They approach each other at different points, and mingle together. But it is enough to justify this division, that it is the most complete we can make; and that, in fact, we are generally called to consider each of the objects which it contains, separately and distinct from all the others.

Subsistence, for example, is included in abundance; still it is very necessary to consider it separately; because the laws ought to do many things for subsistence which they ought not to attempt for the sake of abundance.

Security admits as many distinctions as there are kinds of actions which may be hostile to it. It relates to the person, to honour, to property, to condition. Acts injurious to security, branded by prohibition of law, receive the quality of offences.

Of these objects of the law, security is the only one which necessarily embraces the future. Subsistence, abundance, equality, may be considered in relation to a single moment of present time; but security implies a given extension of future time in respect to all that good which it embraces. Security, then, is the pre-eminent object.

I have mentioned equality as one of the objects of law. In an arrangement designed to give to all men the greatest possible sum of good, there is no reason why the law should seek to give more to one individual than to another. There are abundance of reasons why it should not; for the advantages acquired on one side, never can be an equivalent for the disadvantages felt upon the other. The pleasure is exclusively for the party favoured; the pain for all who do not share the favour.

Equality may be promoted either by protecting it where it exists, or by seeking to produce it. In this latter case, the greatest caution is necessary; for a single error may overturn social order.[1]

Some persons may be astonished to find that *liberty* is not ranked among the principal objects of law. But a clear idea of liberty will lead us to regard it as a branch of security. Personal liberty is security against a certain kind of injuries which affect the person. As to what is called *political liberty*, it is another branch of security, – security against injustice from the ministers of government. What concerns this object belongs not to civil, but to constitutional law.

---

[1] Equality may be considered in relation to all the advantages which depend upon laws. Political equality is an equality of political rights; civil equality is an equality of civil rights. When used by itself, the word is commonly understood to refer to the distribution of property. It is so used in this treatise.

CHAPTER III

Relations Between These Ends

These four objects of law are very distinct in idea, but they are much less so in practice. The same law may advance several of them; because they are often united. That law, for example, which favours security, favours, at the same time, subsistence and abundance.

But there are circumstances in which it is impossible to unite these objects. It will sometimes happen that a measure suggested by one of these principles will be condemned by another. Equality, for example, might require a distribution of property which would be incompatible with security.

When this contradiction exists between two of these ends, it is necessary to find some means of deciding the pre-eminence; otherwise these principles, instead of guiding us in our researches, will only serve to augment the confusion.

At the first glance we see subsistence and security arising together to the same level; abundance and equality are manifestly of inferior importance. In fact, without security, equality could not last a day; without subsistence, abundance could not exist at all. The two first objects are life itself; the two latter, the ornaments of life.

In legislation, the most important object is security. Though no laws were made directly for subsistence, it might easily be imagined that no one would neglect it. But unless laws are made directly for security, it would be quite useless to make them for subsistence. You may order production; you may command cultivation; and you will have done nothing. But assure to the cultivator the fruits of his industry, and perhaps in that alone you will have done enough.

Security, as we have said, has many branches; and some branches of it must yield to others. For example, liberty, which is a branch of security, ought to yield to a consideration of the general security, since laws cannot be made except at the expense of liberty.

We cannot arrive at the greatest good, except by the sacrifice of some subordinate good. All the difficulty consists in distinguishing that object which, according to the occasion, merits pre-eminence. For each, in its turn, demands it; and a very complicated calculation is sometimes necessary to avoid being deceived as to the preference due to one or the other.

Equality ought not to be favoured except in the cases in which it does not interfere with security; in which it does not thwart the expectations which the law itself has produced; in which it does not derange the order already established.

If all property were equally divided, at fixed periods, the sure and certain consequence would be, that presently there would be no property to divide. All would shortly be destroyed. Those whom it was intended to favour, would not suffer less from the division than those at whose expense it was made. If the lot of the industrious was not better than the lot of the idle, there would be no longer any motives for industry.

To lay down as a principle that all men ought to enjoy a perfect *equality of rights*, would be, by a necessary connection of consequences, to render all legislation impossible. The laws are constantly establishing inequalities, since they cannot give right to one without imposing obligations upon another. To say that all men – that is, all human beings – have equal rights, is to say that there is no such thing as subordination. The son then has the same rights with his father; he has the same right to govern and punish his father that his father has to govern and punish him. He has as many rights in the house of his father as the father himself. The maniac has the same right to shut up others that others have to shut up him. The idiot has the same right to govern his family that his family have to govern him. All this is fully implied in the absolute equality of rights. It means this, or else it means nothing. I know very well that those who maintain this doctrine of the equality of rights, not being themselves either fools or idiots, have no intention of establishing this absolute equality. They have, in their own minds, restrictions, modifications, explanations. But if they themselves cannot speak in an intelligible manner, will the ignorant and excited multitude understand them better than they understand themselves?

CHAPTER IV

Laws Relatively to Subsistence

What can the law do for subsistence? Nothing directly. All it can do is to create *motives*, that is, punishments or rewards, by the force of which men may be led to provide subsistence for themselves. But nature herself has created these motives, and has given them a sufficient energy. Before the idea of laws existed, *needs* and *enjoyments* had done in that respect all that the best concerted laws could do. Need, armed with pains of all kinds, even death itself, commanded labour, excited courage, inspired foresight, developed all the faculties of man. Enjoyment, the inseparable companion of every need satisfied, formed an inexhaustible fund of rewards for those who surmounted obstacles and fulfilled the end of nature. The force of the physical sanction being sufficient, the employment of the political sanction would be superfluous.

Besides, the motives which depend on laws are more or less precarious in their operation. It is a consequence of the imperfection of the laws themselves; or of the difficulty of proving the facts in order to apply punishment or reward. The hope of impunity conceals itself at the bottom of the heart during all the intermediate steps which it is necessary to take before arriving at the enforcement of the law. But the natural effects, which may be regarded as nature's punishments and rewards, scarcely admit of any uncertainty. There is no evasion, no delay, no favour. Experience announces the event, and experience confirms it. Each day strengthens the lesson of the day before; and the uniformity of this process leaves no room for doubt. What could be added by direct laws to the constant and irresistible power of these natural motives?

But the laws provide for subsistence indirectly, by protecting men while they labour, and by making them sure of the fruits of their labour. *Security* for the labourer, *security* for the fruits of labour; such is the benefit of laws ; and it is an inestimable benefit.

CHAPTER V

Laws Relatively to Abundance

Shall laws be made directing individuals not to confine themselves to mere subsistence, but to seek abundance? No! That would be a very superfluous employment of artificial means, where natural means suffice. The attraction of pleasure; the succession of wants; the active desire of increasing happiness, will procure unceasingly, under the reign of security, new efforts towards new acquisitions. Wants, enjoyments, those universal agents of society, having begun with gathering the first sheaf of corn, proceed little by little, to build magazines of abundance, always increasing but never filled. Desires extend with means. The horizon elevates itself as we advance; and each new want, attended on the one hand by pain, on the other by pleasure, becomes a new principle of action. Opulence, which is only a comparative term, does not arrest this movement once begun. On the contrary, the greater our means, the greater the scale on which we labour; the greater is the recompense, and, consequently, the greater also the force of motive which animates to labour. Now what is the wealth of society, if not the sum of all individual wealth? And what more is necessary than the force of these natural motives, to carry wealth, by successive movements, to the highest possible point?

It appears that abundance is formed little by little, by the continued operation of the same causes which produce subsistence. Those who blame abundance under the name of luxury, have never looked at it from this point of view.

Bad seasons, wars, accidents of all kinds, attack so often the fund of subsistence, that a society which had nothing superfluous, and even if it had a good deal that was superfluous, would often be exposed to want what is necessary. We see this among savage tribes; it was often seen among all nations, during the times of ancient poverty. It is what happens even now, in countries little favoured by nature, such as Sweden; and in those where government restrains the operations of commerce, instead of confining itself to protection. But countries in which luxury abounds, and where governments are enlightened, are above the risk of famine. Such is the happy situation of England. With a free commerce, toys useless in themselves have their utility, as the means of obtaining bread. Manufactures of luxury furnish an assurance against famine. A brewery or a starch-factory might be changed into a means of subsistence.

How often have we heard declamations against dogs and horses, as devouring the food of men! Such declaimers rise but one degree above those apostles of disinterestedness, who set fire to the magazines in order to cause an abundance of corn.

CHAPTER VI

Pathological Propositions upon Which the Good of Equality is Founded

Pathology is a term used in medicine. It has not been introduced into morals, where it is equally needed, though in a somewhat different sense. By *pathology*, I mean the study and the knowledge of the sensations, affections, passions, and of their effects upon happiness. Legislation, which hitherto has been founded in a great measure only upon the quicksands of prejudice and instinct, ought at last to be built upon the immoveable basis of sensations and experience. It is necessary to have a moral thermometer to make perceptible all the degrees of happiness and misery. This is a term of perfection which it is not possible to reach; but it is well to have it before our eyes. I know that a scrupulous examination of more or less, in the matter of pain or pleasure, will at first appear a minute undertaking. It will be said that in human affairs it is necessary to act in gross; to be contented with a vague approximation. This is the language of indifference or of incapacity. The sensations of men are sufficiently regular to become the objects of a science and an art. Yet hitherto we have seen but essays, blind attempts, and irregular efforts not well followed up. Medicine has for its foundation the axioms of physical pathology. Morality is the medicine of the soul; and legislation, which is the practical part of it, ought to have for its foundation the axioms of mental pathology.

To judge of the effect of a portion of wealth upon happiness, it is necessary to consider it in three different states:

1st   When it has always been in the hands of the holder.

2nd   When it is leaving his hands.

3rd   When it is coming into them.

It is to be observed in general, that in speaking of the effect of a portion of wealth upon happiness, abstraction is always to be made of the particular sensibility of individuals, and of the exterior circumstances in which they may be placed. Differences of character are inscrutable; and such is the diversity of circumstances, that they are never the same for two individuals. Unless we begin by dropping these two considerations, it will be impossible to announce any general proposition. But though each of these propositions may prove false or inexact in a given individual case, that will furnish no argument against their speculative truth and practical utility. It is enough for the justification of these propositions − 1st, If they approach nearer the truth than any others which can be substituted for them; 2nd, If with less inconvenience than any others they can be made the basis of legislation.

1. Let us pass to the first case. The object being to examine the effect of a portion of wealth, when it has always been in the hands of the holder, we may lay down the following propositions:

1st   *Each portion of wealth has a corresponding portion of happiness.*

2nd   *Of two individuals with unequal fortunes, he who has the most wealth has the most happiness.*

3rd   *The excess of happiness of the richer will not be so great as the excess of his wealth.*

4th   For the same reasons, *the greater the disproportion is between the two masses of wealth, the less is it probable that there exists a disproportion equally great between the corresponding masses of happiness.*

5th   *The nearer the actual proportion approaches to equality, the greater will be the total mass of happiness.*

It is not necessary to limit what is here said of wealth to the condition of those who are called wealthy. This word has a more extensive signification. It embraces everything which serves either for subsistence or abundance. It is for the sake of brevity that the phrase *portion of wealth* is used instead of *portion of the matter of wealth.*

I have said that for *each portion of wealth there is a corresponding portion of happiness.* To speak more exactly, it ought rather to be said, *a certain chance of happiness.* For the efficacy of a cause of happiness is always precarious; or, in other words, a cause of happiness has not its ordinary effect, nor the same effect, upon all persons. Here is the place for making an application of what has been said concerning the sensibility and the character of individuals, and the variety of circumstances in which they are found.

The second proposition is a direct consequence of the first. *Of two individuals, he who is the richer is the happier or has the greater chance of being so.* This is a fact proved by the experience of all the world. The first who doubts it shall be the very witness I will call to prove it. Let him give all his superfluous wealth to the first comer who asks him for it; for this superfluity, according to his system, is but dust in his hands; it is a burden and nothing more. The manna of the desert putrefied, if anyone collected a greater quantity than he could eat. If wealth resembled that manna, and after passing a certain point was no longer productive in happiness, no one would wish for it; and the desire of accumulation would be a thing unknown.

The third proposition is less likely to be disputed. Put on one side a thousand farmers, having enough to live upon, and a little more. Put on the other side a king, or, not to be encumbered with the cares of government, a prince, well portioned, himself as rich as all the farmers taken together. It is probable, I say, that his happiness is greater than the average happiness of the thousand farmers; but it is by no means probable that it is equal to the sum total of their happiness, or, what amounts to the same thing, a thousand times greater than the average happiness of one of them. It would be remarkable if his happiness were ten times, or even five times greater. The man who is born in the bosom of opulence, is not so sensible of its pleasures as he who is the artisan of his own fortune. It is the pleasure of acquisition, not the satisfaction of possessing, which gives the greatest delights. The one is a lively sentiment, pricked on by the desires, and by anterior privations, which rushes toward an unknown good; the other is a feeble sentiment, weakened by use, which is not animated by contrasts, and which borrows nothing from the imagination.

2. Passing to the second case, let us examine the effect of a portion of wealth, when it enters for the first time into the hands of a new possessor. It is to be observed that we must lay expectation out of

view, It is necessary to suppose that this augmentation of fortune comes unexpectedly, as a gift of chance.

1st *A portion of wealth may be so far divided as to produce no happiness at all for any of the participants.* This is what would happen, rigorously speaking, if the portion of each was less in value than the smallest known coin. But it is not necessary to carry the thing to that extreme, in order to make the proposition true.

2nd *Among participants of equal fortunes, the more perfectly equality is preserved in the distribution of a new portion of wealth, the greater will be the total mass of happiness.*

3rd *Among participants of unequal fortunes, the more the distribution of new wealth tends to do away that inequality, the greater will be the total mass of happiness.*

3. The third case requires us to examine the effect produced by a portion of wealth which is leaving the hands of its former possessor. Here, too, we must lay expectation out of view, and suppose the loss to be unforeseen – and a loss almost always is so, because every man naturally expects to keep what he has. This expectation is founded upon the ordinary course of things. For in a general view of human affairs, wealth already acquired is not only preserved, but increased. This is proved by the extreme difference between the primitive poverty of every community and its actual wealth.

1st *The loss of a portion of wealth will produce, in the total happiness of the loser, a defalcation greater or less, according to the proportion of the part lost to the part which remains.*

Take away from a man the fourth part of his fortune, and you take away the fourth part of his happiness, and so on.[1]

But there are cases in which the proportion would not be the same. If, in taking away from me three-fourths of my fortune, you

---

1 It is to this head that the evils of deep play ought to be referred. Though the chances, so far as relates to money, are equal, in regards to pleasure, they are always unfavourable. I have a thousand pounds. The stake is five hundred. If I lose, my fortune is diminished one half; if I gain, it is increased only by a third. Suppose the stake to be a thousand pounds. If I gain, my happiness is not doubled with my fortune; if I lose, my happiness is destroyed; I am reduced to indigence.

take away what is necessary for my physical support, and if, in taking away half of it, you would have left that necessary portion untouched, the defalcation of happiness, instead of being twice as great in the first case as in the second, will be four times, ten times, indefinitely greater.

2nd   *This granted, fortunes being equal, the greater the number of persons among whom a loss is shared, the less considerable will be the defalcation from the sum total of happiness.*

3rd   *After passing a certain point, division renders the several quotas impalpable, and the defalcation in the sum total of happiness amounts to nothing.*

4th   *Fortunes being unequal, the loss of happiness produced by a given loss of wealth will become less in proportion as the distribution of the loss shall tend toward the production of an exact equality.* But in this case we must lay out of view the inconveniences attendant on the violation of security.

Governments, profiting by the progress of knowledge, have favoured, in many respects, the principle of equality in the distribution of losses. It is thus that they have taken under the protection of the laws *policies of insurance*, those useful contracts by which individuals assess themselves beforehand to provide against possible losses. The principle of insurance, founded upon a calculation of probabilities, is but the art of distributing losses among so great a number of associates as to make them very light, and almost nothing.

The same spirit has influenced sovereigns when they have indemnified, at the expense of the state, those of their subjects who have suffered either by public calamities or by the devastations of war. We have seen nothing of this kind wiser or better managed than the administration of the great Frederic. It is one of the finest points of view under which the social art can be considered.

Some attempts have been made to indemnify individuals for losses caused by the offences of malefactors. But examples of this kind are yet very rare. It is an object which merits the attention of legislators; for it is the means of reducing almost to nothing the evil of offences which attack property. To prevent it from becoming injurious, such a system must be arranged with care. It will not do to encourage indolence and imprudence in the neglect of precautions against offences, by making them sure of an indemnification; and it is necessary to guard even more cautiously against fraud and secret connivances which might counterfeit offences, and even produce them, for the sake of the indemnity. The utility of this remedial process would depend entirely on the way in which it was administered; yet the rejection of a means so salutary can only originate in a culpable indifference, anxious to save itself the trouble of discovering expedients.

The principles we have laid down may equally serve to regulate the distribution of a loss among many persons charged with a common responsibility. If their respective contributions correspond to the respective quantity of their fortunes, their relative state will be the same as before; but if it is desired to improve this occasion for the purposes of an approach towards equality, it is necessary to adopt a different proportion. To levy an equal impost, without regard to differences of fortune, would be a third plan, which would be agreeable neither to equality nor security.

To place this subject in a clearer light, I shall present a mixed case, in which it is necessary to decide between two individuals, of whom one demands a profit at the expense of the other. The question is to determine the effect of a portion of wealth which, passing into the hands of one individual under the form of gain, must come out of the hands of another in the form of loss.

1st   *Among competitors of equal fortunes, when that which is gained by one must be lost by another, the arrangement productive of the greatest sum of good will be that which favours the old possessor to the exclusion of the new demandant.*

For, in the first place, the sum to be lost, bearing a greater proportion to the reduced fortune than the same sum to the augmented fortune, the diminution of happiness for the one will be greater than the augmentation of happiness for the other; in one word, equality will be violated by the contrary arrangement.[1]

In the second place, the loser will experience a pain of disappointment; the other merely does not gain. Now the negative evil of not acquiring is not equal to the positive evil of losing. If it were, as every man would experience this evil for all that he does not acquire, the causes of suffering would be infinite,

1 See the note upon gaming. This case is exactly the same.

and men would be infinitely miserable.

In the third place, men in general appear to be more sensitive to pain than to pleasure, even when the cause is equal. To such a degree, indeed, does this extend, that a loss which diminishes a man's fortune by one-fourth, will take away more happiness than he could gain by doubling his property.

2nd   *Fortunes being unequal, if the loser is the poorer, the evil of the loss will be aggravated by that inequality.*

3rd   *If the loser is the richer, the evil done by an attack upon security will be compensated in part by a good which will be great in proportion to the progress towards equality.*

By the aid of these maxims, which, to a certain point, have the character and the certainty of mathematical propositions, there might be at last produced a regular and constant art of indemnities and satisfactions. Legislators have frequently shown a disposition to promote equality under the name of *equity*, a word to which a greater latitude has been given than to *justice*. But this idea of equity, vague and half developed, has rather appeared an affair of instinct than of calculation. It was only by much patience and method that it was found possible to reduce to rigorous propositions an incoherent multitude of confused sentiments.

CHAPTER VII

Of Security

We come now to the principal object of law – the care of security. That inestimable good, the distinctive index of civilization, is entirely the work of law. Without law there is no security; and, consequently, no abundance, and not even a certainty of subsistence; and the only equality which can exist in such a state of things is an equality of misery.

To form a just idea of the benefits of law, it is only necessary to consider the condition of savages. They strive incessantly against famine; which sometimes cuts off entire tribes. Rivalry for subsistence produces among them the most cruel wars; and, like beasts of prey, men pursue men, as a means of sustenance. The fear of this terrible calamity silences the softer sentiments of nature; pity unites with insensibility in putting to death the old men who can hunt no longer.

Let us now examine what passes at those terrible epochs when civilized society returns almost to the savage state; that is, during war, when the laws on which security depends are in part suspended. Every instant of its duration is fertile in calamities; at every step which it prints upon the earth, at every movement which it makes, the existing mass of riches, the fund of abundance and of subsistence, decreases and disappears. The cottage is ravaged as well as the palace; and how often the rage, the caprice even of a moment, delivers up to destruction the slow produce of the labours of an age!

Law alone has done that which all the natural sentiments united have not the power to do. Law alone is able to create a fixed and durable possession which merits the name of property. Law alone can accustom men to bow their heads under the yoke of foresight, hard at first to bear, but afterwards light and agreeable. Nothing but law can encourage men to labours superfluous for the present, and which can be enjoyed only in the future. Economy has as many enemies as there are dissipators – men who wish to enjoy without giving themselves the trouble of producing. Labour is too painful for idleness; it is too slow for impatience. Fraud and injustice secretly conspire to appropriate its fruits. Insolence and audacity think to ravish them by open force. Thus security is assailed on every side – ever threatened, never tranquil, it exists in the midst of alarms. The legislator needs a vigilance always sustained, a power always in action, to defend it against this crowd of indefatigable enemies.

Law does not say to man, *Labour, and I will reward you*; but it says: *Labour, and I will assure to you the enjoyment of the fruits of your labour* – *that natural and sufficient recompense which without me you cannot preserve; I will insure it by arresting the hand which may seek to ravish it from you.* If industry creates, it is law which preserves; if at the first moment we owe all to labour, at the second moment, and at every other, we are indebted for everything to law.

To form a precise idea of the extent which ought to be given to the principle of security, we must consider that man is not like the animals, limited to the present, whether as respects suffering or enjoyment; but that he is susceptible of pains and pleasures by anticipation; and that it is not enough to secure him from actual loss, but it is necessary also to guarantee him, as far as possible, against future loss. It is necessary to prolong the idea of his security through all the perspective which his imagination is capable of measuring.

This presentiment, which has so marked an influence upon the fate of man, is called *expectation*. It is hence that we have the power of forming a general plan of conduct; it is hence that the successive instants which compose the duration of life are not like isolated and independent points, but become continuous parts of a whole. *Expectation* is a chain which unites our present existence to our future existence, and which passes beyond us to the generation which is to follow. The sensibility of man extends through all the links of this chain.

The principle of security extends to the maintenance of all these expectations; it requires that events, so far as they depend upon laws, should conform to the expectations which law itself has created.

Every attack upon this sentiment produces a distinct and special evil, which may be called a *pain of disappointment*.

It is a proof of great confusion in the ideas of lawyers, that they have never given any particular attention to a sentiment which exercises so powerful an influence upon human life. The word *expectation* is scarcely found in their vocabulary. Scarce a single argument founded upon that principle appears in their writings. They have followed it, without doubt, in many respects; but they have followed it by instinct rather than by reason. If they had known its extreme importance they would not have failed to *name* it and to mark it, instead of leaving it unnoticed in the crowd.

CHAPTER VIII

Of Property

The better to understand the advantages of law, let us endeavour to form a clear idea of *property*. We shall see that there is no such thing as natural property, and that it is entirely the work of law.

Property is nothing but a basis of expectation; the expectation of deriving certain advantages from a thing which we are said to possess, in consequence of the relation in which we stand towards it.

There is no image, no painting, no visible trait, which can express the relation that constitutes property. It is not material, it is metaphysical; it is a mere conception of the mind.

To have a thing in our hands, to keep it, to make it, to sell it, to work it up into something else; to use it – none of these physical circumstances, nor all united, convey the idea of property. A piece of stuff which is actually in the Indies may belong to me, while the dress I wear may not. The aliment which is incorporated into my very body may belong to another, to whom I am bound to account for it.

The idea of property consists in an established expectation; in the persuasion of being able to draw such or such an advantage from the thing possessed, according to the nature of the case. Now this expectation, this persuasion, can only be the work of law. I cannot count upon the enjoyment of that which I regard as mine, except through the promise of the law which guarantees it to me. It is law alone which permits me to forget my natural weakness. It is only through the protection of law that I am able to inclose a field, and to give myself up to its cultivation with the sure though distant hope of harvest.

But it may be asked, What is it that serves as a basis to law, upon which to begin operations, when it adopts objects which, under the name of property, it promises to protect? Have not men, in the primitive state, a *natural* expectation of enjoying certain things, — an expectation drawn from sources anterior to law?

Yes. There have been from the beginning, and there always will be, circumstances in which a man may secure himself, by his own means, in the enjoyment of certain things. But the catalogue of these cases is very limited. The savage who has killed a deer may hope to keep it for himself, so long as his cave is undiscovered; so long as he watches to defend it, and is stronger than his rivals; but that is all. How miserable and precarious is such a possession! If we suppose the least agreement among savages to respect the acquisitions of each other, we see the introduction of a principle to which no name can be given but that of law. A feeble and momentary expectation may result from time to time from circumstances purely physical; but a strong and permanent expectation can result only from law. That which, in the natural state, was an almost invisible thread, in the social state becomes a cable.

Property and law are born together, and die together. Before laws were made there was no property; take away laws, and property ceases.

As regards property, security consists in receiving no check, no shock, no derangement to the expectation founded on the laws, of enjoying such and such a portion of good. The legislator owes the greatest respect to this expectation which he has himself produced. When he does not contradict it, he does what is essential to the happiness of society; when he disturbs it, he always produces a proportionate sum of evil.

CHAPTER IX

Answer to an Objection

But perhaps the laws of property are good for those who have property, and oppressive to those who have none. The poor man, perhaps, is more miserable than he would be without laws.

The laws, in creating property, have created riches only in relation to poverty. Poverty is not the work of the laws; it is the primitive condition of the human race. The man who subsists only from day to day is precisely the man of nature – the savage. The poor man, in civilized society, obtains nothing, I admit, except by painful labour; but, in the natural state, can he obtain anything except by the sweat of his brow? Has not the chase its fatigues, fishing its dangers, and war its uncertainties? And if man seems to love this adventurous life; if he has an instinct warm for this kind of perils; if the savage enjoys with delight an idleness so dearly bought; – must we thence conclude that he is happier than our cultivators? No. Their labour is more uniform, but their reward is more sure; the woman's lot is far more agreeable; childhood and old age have more resources; the species multiplies in a proportion a thousand times greater, – and that alone suffices to show on which side is the superiority of happiness. Thus the laws, in creating riches, are the benefactors of those who remain in the poverty of nature. All participate more or less in the pleasures, the advantages, and the resources of civilized society. The industry and the labour of the poor place them among the candidates of fortune. And have they not the pleasures of acquisition? Does not hope mix with their labours? Is the security which the law gives of no importance to them? Those who look down from above upon the inferior ranks see all objects smaller; but towards the base of the pyramid it is the summit which in turn is lost. Comparisons are never dreamed of; the wish of what seems impossible does not torment. So that, in fact, all things considered, the protection of the laws may contribute as much to the happiness of the cottage as to the security of the palace.

It is astonishing that a writer so judicious as Beccaria has interposed, in a work dictated by the soundest philosophy, a doubt subversive of social order. *The right of property*, he says, *is a terrible right, which perhaps is not necessary.* Tyrannical and sanguinary laws have been founded upon that right; it has been frightfully abused; but the right itself presents only ideas of pleasure, abundance, and security. It is that right which has vanquished the natural aversion to labour; which has given to man the empire of the earth; which has brought to an end the migratory life of nations; which has produced the love of country and a regard for posterity. Men universally desire to enjoy speedily – to enjoy without labour. It is that desire which is terrible; since it arms all who have not against all who have. The law which restrains that desire is the noblest triumph of humanity over itself.

CHAPTER X

Analysis of the Evils which Result from Attacks upon Property

We have already seen that subsistence depends upon the laws which assure to the labourer the produce of his labour. But it is desirable more exactly to analyse the evils which result from violations of property. They may be reduced to four heads.

1st. *Evil of Non-Possession.* – If the acquisition of a portion of wealth is a good, it follows that the non-possession of it is an evil, though only a negative evil. Thus, although men in the condition of primitive poverty may not have specially felt the want of a good which they knew not, yet it is clear that they have lost all the happiness which might have resulted from its possession, and of which we have the enjoyment. The loss of a portion of good, though we knew nothing of it, is still a loss. Are you doing me no harm when, by false representations, you deter my friend from conferring upon me a favour which I did not expect? In what consists the harm? In the negative evil which results from not possessing that which, but for your falsehoods, I should have had.

2nd. *Pain of Losing.* – Everything which I possess, or to which I have a title, I consider in my own mind as destined always to belong to me. I make it the basis of my expectations, and of the hopes of those dependent upon me; and I form my plan of life accordingly. Every part of my property may have, in my estimation, besides its intrinsic value, a value of affection – as an inheritance from my ancestors, as the reward of my own labour, or as the future dependence of my children. Everything about it represents to my eye that part of myself which I have put into it – those cares, that industry, that economy which denied itself present pleasures to make provision for the future. Thus our property becomes a part of our being, and cannot be torn from us without rending us to the quick.

3rd. *Fear of Losing.* – To regret for what we have lost is joined inquietude as to what we possess, and even as to what we may acquire. For the greater part of the objects which compose subsistence and abundance being perishable matters, future acquisitions are a necessary supplement to present possessions. When insecurity reaches a certain point, the fear of losing prevents us from enjoying what we possess already. The care of preserving condemns us to a thousand sad and painful precautions, which yet are always liable to fail of their end. Treasures are hidden or conveyed away. Enjoyment becomes sombre, furtive, and solitary. It fears to show itself, lest cupidity should be informed of a chance to plunder.

4th. *Deadening of Industry.* – When I despair of making myself sure of the produce of my labour, I only seek to exist from day to day. I am unwilling to give myself cares which will only be profitable to my enemies. Besides, the will to labour is not enough; means are wanting. While waiting to reap, in the meantime I must live. A single loss may deprive me of the capacity of action, without having quenched the spirit of industry, or without having paralyzed my will. Thus the three first evils affect the passive faculties of the individual, while the fourth extends to his active faculties, and more or less benumbs them.

It appears from this analysis that the two first evils do not go beyond the individual injured; while the two latter spread through society, and occupy an indefinite space. An attack upon the property of an individual excites alarm among other proprietors. This sentiment spreads from neighbour to neighbour, till at last the contagion possesses the entire body of the state.

Power and *will* must unite for the development of industry. Will depends upon encouragement; power upon means. These means are what is called, in the language of political economy, *productive capital*. When the question relates only to an individual, his productive capital may be annihilated by a single loss, while his spirit of industry is not extinguished, nor even weakened. When the question is of a nation, the annihilation of its productive capital is impossible; but a long time before that fatal term is approached, the evil may infect the will; and the spirit of industry may fall into a fatal lethargy, in the midst of natural resources offered by a rich and fertile soil. The will, however, is excited by so many stimulants, that it resists an abundance of discouragements and losses. A transitory calamity, though great, never destroys the spirit of industry. It is seen to spring up, after devouring wars which have impoverished nations, as a robust oak, mutilated by tempests, repairs its losses in a few years and covers itself with new branches. Nothing is sufficient to deaden industry, except the operation of a domestic and permanent cause, such as a tyrannical government, bad legislation, an intolerant religion which drives men from the country, or a minute superstition which stupifies them.

A first act of violence produces immediately a certain degree of apprehension; some timid spirits are already discouraged. A second violence, which soon succeeds, spreads a more considerable alarm. The more prudent begin to retrench their enterprises, and little by little to abandon an uncertain career. In proportion as these attacks are repeated, and the system of oppression takes a more habitual character, the dispersion increases. Those who fly are not replaced; those who remain fall into a state of languor. Thus the field of industry, beaten by perpetual storms, at last becomes a desert.

Asia Minor, Greece, Egypt, the coasts of Africa, so rich in agriculture, in commerce, and in population, at the flourishing epoch of the Roman empire, what have they become under the absurd despotism of the Turkish government? Palaces have been changed into cabins, and cities into hamlets. That government, odious to every thinking man, has never known that a state cannot grow rich except by an inviolable respect for property. It has never had but two secrets of statesmanship, — to sponge the people, and to stupify them. Thus the finest countries of the earth, wasted, barren, and almost abandoned, can hardly be recognised under the hands of barbarous conquerors.

These evils ought not to be attributed to foreign causes. Civil wars, invasions, natural scourges, may dissipate wealth, put the arts to flight, and swallow up cities. But choked harbours are opened again; communications are re-established; manufactures revive; cities rise from their ruins. All ravages are repaired by time, while men continue to be men; but there are no men to be found in those unhappy countries, where the slow but fatal despair of long insecurity has destroyed all the active faculties of the soul.

If we trace the history of this contagion, we shall see its first attacks directed against that part of society which is easy and well off. Opulence is the object of the first depredations. Apparent superfluity vanishes little by little. Absolute need makes itself be obeyed in spite of obstacles. We must live; but when man limits himself to living, the state languishes, and the lamp of industry throws out only a dying flame. Besides, abundance is never so distinct from subsistence, that one can be destroyed without a dangerous blow at the other. While some lose only what is superfluous, others lose a part of what is necessary; for by the infinitely complicated system of economical connections, the opulence of a part of the citizens is the only fund upon which a part more numerous depends for subsistence.

But another picture may be traced, more smiling and not less instructive. It is the picture of the progress of *security*, and of prosperity, its inseparable companion. North America presents to us a most striking contrast. Savage nature may be seen there, side by side with civilized nature. The interior of that immense region offers only a frightful solitude, impenetrable forests or sterile plains, stagnant waters and impure vapours; such is the earth when left to itself. The fierce tribes which rove through those deserts without fixed habitations, always occupied with the pursuit of game, and animated against each other by implacable rivalries, meet only for combat, and often succeed in destroying each other. The beasts of the forest are not so dangerous to man as he is to himself. But on the borders of these frightful solitudes, what different sights are seen! We appear to comprehend in the same view the two empires of good and evil. Forests give place to cultivated fields; morasses are dried up, and the surface, grown firm, is covered with meadows, pastures, domestic animals, habitations healthy and smiling. Rising cities are built upon regular plans; roads are constructed to communicate between them; everything announces that men, seeking the means of intercourse, have ceased to fear and to murder each other. Harbours filled with vessels receive all the productions of the earth, and assist in the exchange of all kinds of riches. A numerous people, living upon their labour in peace and abundance, has succeeded to a few tribes of hunters, always placed between war and famine. What has wrought these prodigies? Who has renewed the surface of the earth? Who has given to man this domain over nature – over nature embellished, fertilized, and perfected? That beneficent genius is *Security*. It is security which has wrought this great metamorphosis. And how rapid are its operations? It is not yet two centuries since William Penn landed upon those savage coasts, with a colony of true conquerors, men of peace, who did not soil their establishments with blood, and who made themselves respected by acts of beneficence and justice.

CHAPTER XI

Opposition Between Security and Equality

In consulting the grand principle of security, what ought the legislator to decree respecting the mass of property already existing?

He ought to maintain the distribution as it is actually established. It is this which, under the name of *justice*, is regarded as his first duty. This is a general and simple rule, which applies itself to all states; and which adapts itself to all places, even those of the most opposite character. There is nothing more different than the state of property in America, in England, in Hungary, and in Russia. Generally, in the first of these countries, the cultivator is a proprietor; in the second, a tenant; in the third, attached to the glebe; in the fourth, a slave. However, the supreme principle of security commands the preservation of all these distributions, though their nature is so different, and though they do not produce the same sum of happiness. How make another distribution without taking away from each that which he has? And how despoil any without attacking the security of all? When your new repartition is disarranged — that is to say, the day after its establishment — how avoid making a second? Why not correct it in the same way? And in the meantime, what becomes of security? Where is happiness? Where is industry?

When security and equality are in conflict, it will not do to hesitate a moment. Equality must yield. The first is the foundation of life; subsistence, abundance, happiness, everything depends upon it. Equality produces only a certain portion of good. Besides, whatever we may do, it will never be perfect; it may exist a day; but the revolutions of the morrow will overturn it. The establishment of perfect equality is a chimera; all we can do is to diminish inequality.

If violent causes, such as a revolution of government, a division, or a conquest, should bring about an overturn of property, it would be a great calamity; but it would be transitory; it would diminish; it would repair itself in time. Industry is a vigorous plant which resists many amputations, and through which a nutritious sap begins to circulate with the first rays of returning summer. But if property should be overturned with the direct intention of establishing an equality of possessions, the evil would be irreparable. No more security, no more industry, no more abundance! Society would return to the savage state whence it emerged.

If equality ought to prevail to-day it ought to prevail always. Yet it cannot be preserved except by renewing the violence by which it was established. It will need an army of inquisitors and executioners as deaf to favour as to pity; insensible to the seductions of pleasure; inaccessible to personal interest; endowed with all the virtues, though in a service which destroys them all. The levelling apparatus ought to go incessantly backward and forward, cutting off all that rises above the line prescribed. A ceaseless vigilance would be necessary to give to those who had dissipated their portion, and to take from those who by labour had augmented theirs. In such an order of things there would be only one wise course for the governed, – that of prodigality; there would be but one foolish course, – that of industry. This pretended remedy, seemingly so pleasant, would be a mortal poison, a burning cautery, which would consume till it destroyed the last fibre of life. The hostile sword in its greatest furies is a thousand times less dreadful. It inflicts but partial evils, which time effaces and industry repairs.

Some small societies, in the first effervescence of religious enthusiasm, have established the community of goods as a fundamental principle. Does anyone imagine that happiness was gained by that arrangement? The alluring power of reward is supplanted by the sad motive of pain. Labour, so easy and so light, when animated by hope, it is necessary under these systems to represent as a penitential means of escaping eternal punishment. So long as the religious impulse preserves its power, all labour, but all groan. So soon as it begins to grow weak, the society divides into two classes: one composed of degraded fanatics, contracting all the vices of an unhappy superstition; the others, lazy rogues, who are supported in a holy indolence by the dupes who surround them. The word equality becomes a mere pretext – a cover to the robbery which idleness perpetrates upon industry.

Those ideas of benevolence and of concord which have seduced some ardent souls into an admiration of this system are only chimeras of the imagination. In the distribution of labours, what motive could determine any to embrace the more painful? Who would undertake gross and disagreeable functions? Who would be content with his lot? Who would not find the burden of his neighbour lighter than his own? How many frauds would be contrived in order to lay upon others the labour from which all would endeavour to exempt themselves? And, in the division, how impossible to satisfy all; to preserve the appearances of equality; to prevent jealousies, quarrels, rivalries, preferences. Who would settle the numberless disputes for ever breaking out? What an apparatus of penal laws would be necessary as a substitute for the sweet liberty of choice, and the natural recompense of labour! One half the society would not suffice to regulate the other half. Thus this absurd and unjust system would only be able to maintain itself by means of a political and religious slavery, such as that of the Helots at Lacedaemon and the Indians of Paraguay, in the establishments of the Jesuits. Sublime invention of legislators, which, to accomplish a plan of equality, makes two corresponding lots of good and of evil, and puts all the pain on one side and all the enjoyment on the other!

CHAPTER XII

Means of Uniting Security and Equality

Is it necessary that between these two rivals, *Security* and *Equality*, there should be an opposition, an eternal war? To a certain point they are incompatible; but with a little patience and address they may, in a great measure, be reconciled.

The only mediator between these contrary interests is time. Do you wish to follow the counsels of equality without contravening those of security? – await the natural epoch which puts an end to hopes and fears, the epoch of death.

When property by the death of the proprietor ceases to have an owner, the law can interfere in its distribution, either by limiting in certain respects the testamentary power, in order to prevent too great an accumulation of wealth in the hands of an individual; or by regulating the succession in favour of equality in cases where the deceased has left no consort, nor relation in the direct line, and has made no will. The question then relates to new acquirers who have formed no expectations; and equality may do what is best for all without disappointing any. At present I only indicate the principle: the development of it may be seen in the second book.

When the question is to correct a kind of civil inequality, such as slavery, it is necessary to pay the same attention to the right of property; to submit it to a slow operation, and to advance towards the subordinate object without sacrificing the principal object. Men who are rendered free by these gradations, will be much more capable of being so than if you had taught them to tread justice under foot, for the sake of introducing a new social order.

It is worthy of remark that, in a nation prosperous in its agriculture, its manufactures, and its commerce, there is a continual progress towards equality. If the laws do nothing to combat it, if they do not maintain certain monopolies, if they put no shackles upon industry and trade, if they do not permit entails, we see great properties divided little by little, without effort, without revolution, without shock, and a much greater number of men coming to participate in the moderate favours of fortune. This is the natural result of the opposite habits which are formed in opulence and in poverty. The first, prodigal and vain, wishes only to enjoy without labour; the second, accustomed to obscurity and privations, finds pleasures even in labour and economy. Thence the change which has been made in Europe by the progress of arts and commerce, in spite of legal obstacles. We are at no great distance from those ages of feudality, when the world was divided into two classes: a few great proprietors, who were everything, and a multitude of serfs, who were nothing. These pyramidal heights have disappeared or have fallen; and from their ruins industrious men have formed those new establishments, the great number of which attests the comparative happiness of modern civilization. Thus we may conclude that *Security*, while preserving its place as the supreme principle, leads indirectly to *Equality*; while equality, if taken as the basis of the social arrangement, will destroy both itself and security at the same time.

CHAPTER XIII

Sacrifice of Security to Security

This title appears at first enigmatical, but the sense of the enigma may easily be found.

There is an important distinction between the ideal perfection of security, and its practicable perfection. The first would demand that nothing should ever be taken from anybody. The second is satisfied, if nothing is taken beyond what is necessary for the preservation of the rest.

This sacrifice is not an attack upon security; it is simply a defalcation. An attack is an unexpected shock, an evil which cannot be calculated, an irregularity which has no fixed principle. It seems to put all the rest in peril; it produces a general alarm. But a defalcation is a fixed, regular, and necessary deduction, which is expected; which produces only an evil of the first order; but no danger, no alarm, no discouragement to industry. The same sum of money, according to the way in which it is levied, will have one or the other of these characters; and will consequently produce either the deadening effects of insecurity, or the vivifying results of confidence.

The necessity of these defalcations is evident. To labour, and to guard the labourers, are two different operations, which cannot be performed at the same time, by the same persons. It is necessary that those who produce wealth by labour should lay aside some portion of it, to support the guardians of the state. Wealth can only be defended at its own expense.

Society, attacked by enemies, whether foreign or domestic, can only maintain itself at the expense of security, – not the security of those enemies alone, but the security even of the very persons to whom protection is extended.

If there are men who do not perceive this necessary connection, it is because in this matter, as in many others, the want of to-day eclipses that of yesterday. The whole of government is but a tissue of sacrifices. The best is that in which these sacrifices are reduced to their lowest term. The practical perfection of security is a quantity which tends without ceasing to approach an ideal perfection.

'It is not necessary to increase the real wants of the people to satisfy imaginary wants of state.'

'Imaginary wants are those created by the passions and the weaknesses of men who govern, by the charm of an extraordinary project, the disordered love of empty glory, and a certain powerlessness of mind to resist the suggestions of fancy. It has often happened that unquiet spirits, placed by the prince at the head of affairs, have imagined that the wants of their own little souls were wants of the state.'[1]

The author of the *Persian Letters* has written too many chapters in the *Spirit of Laws*. What do we learn from this satirical description? If Montesquieu had condescended to give us a simple enumeration of the true wants of the state, we should have known much better what he meant by imaginary wants.

I proceed to give a catalogue of the cases in which the sacrifice of some portion of security, so far as property is concerned, is necessary, to preserve the greater mass of it.

1st. General wants of the state for its defence against exterior enemies.

2nd. General wants of the state for its defence against violators of the laws, or internal enemies.

3rd. General wants of the state to furnish means of affording aid in cases of physical calamity.

4th. Amends levied upon delinquents, either as punishment, or as an indemnity in favour of the parties injured.

5th. A tax upon the property of individuals to furnish the ability of applying remedies to the evils above mentioned, by means of courts of justice, institutions of police, and an armed force.

---

1 Spirit *of Laws*, book xiii. c. i

6th. Limitation of the rights of property, or of the use which each proprietor may make of his own goods, so as to prevent him from employing them to his own injury or to that of others.[1]

In all these cases the necessity is too palpable to need any proofs. But it must be noticed that the same reserves will equally apply to the other branches of security. It is not possible, for example, to maintain the rights of person and of honour, except by penal laws; and penal laws can hardly be executed, except at the expense of person or of honour.

---

1 We possess a general right of property over a thing when we can apply it to every use, except certain uses which are forbidden for special reasons. These reasons may be referred to three heads:

    1st. Private detriment, when a given use of a thing would injure some other individual, either in his fortune or otherwise.

    2nd. Public detriment, that which may result to the community in general.

    3rd. Detriment to the individual himself.

This sword is mine in full property; but however complete that right of property may be, as respects a thousand uses, I ought not to employ it to wound my neighbour, nor to cut his dress, nor to hold it up as a signal of insurrection. If I am a minor or a maniac, it may be taken from me, lest I should injure myself.

An absolute and unlimited right of property over any object, would be the right to commit almost every crime. If I had such a right over a stick which I had cut, I might employ it as a club to beat the passers-by, or convert it into a sceptre as a sign of royalty, or into an idol offensive to the national religion.

CHAPTER XIV

Of Some Cases Liable to be Contested

Ought we to reckon among those wants of the state which ought to be provided for by forced contributions, the care of the indigent, public worship, and the cultivation of the arts and sciences?

1. *Indigence*

In the highest state of social prosperity, the great mass of citizens will have no resource except their daily industry; and consequently will be always near indigence, always ready to be thrown into a state of destitution, by accidents, such as revolutions of commerce, natural calamities, and especially sickness. Infancy has no means of subsisting by its own strength; the feebleness of old age is equally destitute. These two extremes of life are alike in weakness. If natural instinct, humanity, shame, and the aid of the law, assure to children and old men the care and protection of their relatives, still these resources are precarious, and those who give may soon themselves be reduced to want. A numerous family, supported in abundance by the labour of the father and mother, may lose at any instant half its resources by the death of one parent, and the whole by the death of the other.

Old age is yet worse provided for. Love which descends has more force than love which ascends. Gratitude is less powerful than instinct. Hope attaches to feeble beings who are beginning life; it promises nothing for those who are ending it. But suppose – what is not uncommon – suppose all possible care for the old; the idea of changing the part of a giver for that of a receiver will always shed more or less of bitterness into the benefits received, especially at that epoch of decline when the morbid sensibility of the soul renders painful changes indifferent in themselves.

This aspect of society is the saddest of all. It presents that long catalogue of evils which end in indigence, and consequently in death, under its most terrible forms. This is the centre towards which inertia alone, that force which acts without relaxation, makes the lot of every mortal gravitate. Not to be drawn into the abyss, it is necessary to mount up by a continual effort; and we see by our side the most diligent and the most virtuous sometimes slipping by one false step, and sometimes thrown headlong by inevitable reverses.

There are only two means, independently of the laws, of making head against these evils, viz., *savings* and *voluntary contributions*.

If these two resources would always suffice, we ought, by all means, to avoid any legal interference for the succour of the poor. A law which offers to indigence an aid independent of industry is, to a certain extent, a law against industry – or at least against frugality. The motives to labour and economy are – present need and the fear of future need. The law which takes away that need and that fear is an encouragement to idleness and dissipation. Such is the reproach which is cast, and not without reason, upon most of the establishments created in favour of the poor.

But a slight examination will be enough to convince us that the two means of succour, independent of the laws, are not sufficient.

With respect to *savings* – if the greatest efforts of industry will not suffice for the daily support of a numerous class, how can that class lay by for the future? A second class may pay their daily expenses by their daily labour; but they will have nothing superfluous to lay aside against the necessities of a distant day. There will remain then only a third class, which, by economizing during the age of labour, may, perhaps, be able to provide for the time when they can labour no longer. It is only these last to whom poverty can be ascribed as a sort of crime. 'Economy,' it will be said, 'is a duty. If they have neglected it, so much the worse for them. If misery and death await them, they have nobody to accuse but themselves. Their catastrophe, however, will not be an unmixed evil. It will serve as a lesson to prodigals. It is the execution of a law established by nature – a law which is not, like that of men, subject to uncertainty or injustice. Punishment does not fall save on the guilty, and it is exactly proportioned to the fault.'

This severe language might be justifiable if the object of the law were vengeance. But vengeance is condemned by the principle of utility, as an impure motive founded upon antipathy. What will be the fruit of these evils, this abandonment and this indigence, which you regard in your anger as a just punishment of prodigality? Are you sure that these sacrificed victims will prevent, by their example, the faults which have led them into misfortune? To think so would manifest a great ignorance of the human heart. The distress, the death of some prodigals, if we ought so to call those unfortunates who have not known how to deny themselves some of the little pleasures of their condition, who have not known the painful art of striving by reflection against the temptations of every moment – their distress, I say, even their death, will have but little influence, in the way of instruction, upon the laborious classes of society. That sad spectacle, the details of which for the most part would be concealed by shame, would not, like the punishment of malefactors, have a publicity which would attract a general attention, and not suffer its cause to be unknown. Would those to whom the lesson was most necessary know how to give a fit interpretation to the event? Would they always seize upon the supposed connection between imprudence as the cause, and misfortune as the effect? Might they not attribute the catastrophe to accidents unforeseen, and impossible to be foreseen? In place of saying, 'Here is a man who has been the author of his own destruction; his indigence ought to impel me to labour and frugality,' – would they not often say, and with apparent reason, 'Here is an unfortunate man, who has given himself a deal of trouble to no purpose, and whose case is a striking proof of the vanity of human prudence!' This would be bad reasoning, no doubt; but must an error of logic be punished so rigorously – a mere want of reflection, and that too in a class of men more often called upon to exercise their muscles than their minds?

Besides, what shall we think of a punishment delayed in its execution till the very end of life, and which must begin to vanquish, at the other extremity of it – that is, in youth – the influence of the most imperious motives? How feeble grows this pretended lesson in the distance! How little resemblance there is between the old man and the young man! What is the example of the one to the other? In youth the idea of immediate good or evil, occupying all the sphere of reflection, excludes the idea of distant good and evil. If you wish to act upon the young, place the motive near. Show them, for example, a marriage, or some other pleasure, in perspective. But a pain placed at a distance, beyond their intellectual horizon, is quite thrown away. You want to determine men who think very little; and to draw instruction from the misfortunes of others, it is necessary to think much. To what purpose employ a political means, designed to operate upon a class having the least foresight, and yet of a nature to be efficacious only with philosophers?

To recapitulate. The resource of savings is insufficient. 1st, It evidently is so for those who do not gain enough to subsist upon; 2nd, It is equally so for those who gain a mere subsistence. As to the third class, which embraces all not included in the first two, savings are not naturally insufficient, but they become so through the deficiency of human prudence.

Let us now pass to the other resource – *voluntary contributions*. That, too, has many imperfections.

1st. Its uncertainty. It will experience daily vicissitudes, like the fortune and the liberality of the individuals on whom it depends. Is it insufficient? Such junctures are marked by misery and death. Is it superabundant? It will offer a reward to idleness and profusion.

2nd. The inequality of the burden. This supply for the wants of the poor is levied entirely at the expense of the more humane and the more virtuous, often without any proportion to their means; while the avaricious calumniate the poor, to cover their refusal with a varnish of system and of reason. Such an arrangement is a favour granted to selfishness, and a punishment to humanity, that first of virtues.

I say a punishment; for though these contributions are called voluntary, what is the motive whence they emanate? If it is not a religious or a political fear, it is sympathy, tender but sad, which presides over these generous actions. It is not the hope of a pleasure which is bought at this price ; it is the torment of pity, which is sought to be avoided. Thus it has been noticed in Scotland, a country where indigence is limited to this sad resource, that paupers derive their principal support from the class nearest to pauperism.

3rd. The inconveniences of the distribution. If these contributions are abandoned to chance, as in the case of alms asked on the highway; if they are left to be paid, as occasion occurs, without any person intermediate between him who gives and him who asks, the uncertainty as to the sufficiency of these gifts is aggravated by another uncertainty. How appreciate in a multitude of cases the degree of want and of need? May not the poor widow's farthing go to increase the ephemeral treasure of the impure woman? How many generous souls like Sidney will be found, who will repel the vivifying draught from their parched lips, to say, *I can yet wait; first minister to that unfortunate, for his distress is greater than mine.* Everyone knows that in the distribution of these gratuitous gifts, it is not modest virtue, it is not true poverty, often mute and bashful, which obtains the larger part. There needs as much of management and intrigue to succeed upon this obscure theatre, as upon the brilliant scene of the world. He who knows how to importune, to flatter, to lie, to mix boldness with baseness, and to vary his impostures according to the occasion, will have success such as the virtuous poor, devoid of artifice, and preserving their honour in their poverty, will not attain.

> *Les vrais talents se taisent et s'enfuient,*
> *Découragés des affronts qu'ils essuient.*
> *Les faux talents sont hardis, effrontés,*
> *Souples, adroits, et jamais rebutés.*

> Discouraged by affronts, true talents fly,
> And hide themselves in silence.
> Hardy and bold, adroit and supple too,
> False talents brave repulses.

What Voltaire says of talents may be applied to mendicity. In the division of voluntary contributions, the lot of the honest and virtuous poor is seldom equal to that of the impudent and obstreperous beggar.

Suppose that these contributions are put into a common fund to be distributed by persons appointed for that purpose. This method is far preferable, since it admits a regular examination of wants and claims, and tends to proportion the aid accordingly; but it has also a tendency to diminish liberalities. That gift which is going to pass through the hands of a stranger, of which I shall not follow the application, of which I shall not have the pleasure nor the immediate merit, has something abstract about it which chills sentiment. That which I give myself, I give at the moment when I am moved, when the cry of the poor is re-echoed in my heart, when there is only I to succour him. What I put into a general contribution may not have a destination agreeable to my desires; that poor coin which is much for me and my family will be but a drop to that mass of contributions on the one hand, and that multitude of wants on the other; let the rich sustain the poor! This is the way that many people reason, and it is on this account that contributions succeed better when taken for a particular class of individuals, than for an indefinite multitude like the entire mass of the poor; yet it is for that mass that a permanent aid must be provided.

It seems to me, after these observations, that we may lay it down as a general principle that the legislator ought to establish a regular contribution for the wants of indigence, it being understood that those only are to be regarded as indigent who are in want of what is absolutely necessary. From this definition of the indigent, it follows that their title as indigent is stronger than the title of the proprietor of superfluities as proprietor. For the pain of death, which would presently fall upon the starving poor, would be always a more serious evil than the pain of disappointment which falls upon the rich when a portion of his superfluity is taken from him.[1]

In the amount of the legal contribution we ought not to go beyond what is simply necessary. To go beyond that would be taxing industry for the support of idleness. Those establishments which furnish more than is absolutely necessary are not good, except so far as they are supported at the expense of individuals, for individuals can make a discrimination in the distribution of these aids, and apply them to specific classes.

The details of the manner of assessing this contribution, and

---

[1] When this tax is put upon a regular footing, and each proprietor knows beforehand what he must contribute, the pain of disappointment vanishes, and gives place to another, different in its nature, and less in degree.

distributing its produce, belong to political economy, as also the inquiry into the means of encouraging a spirit of economy and foresight in the lower classes of society. We have some instructive memoirs upon this interesting subject, but no treatise which embraces the whole question. Such a work should begin with the theory of poverty – that is, by a classification of the indigent and of the causes which bring on indigence, and thence proceed to suggest precautions and remedies.

2. The Expenses of Public Worship

If the ministers of religion are considered as charged with maintaining one of the sanctions of morality (the religious sanction), the expense of their support ought to be referred to the same branch of administration with justice and the police, viz. the support of internal security. The clergy are a body of inspectors and moral instructors, who form, so to speak, the advanced guard of the law. They have no power against offences, but they combat the vices from which offences originate, and thus render the exercise of authority more rare by maintaining morals and subordination. If they were charged with all the functions which might properly be assigned to them in the education of the inferior classes, in the promulgation of the laws, in the performance of divers public acts, the utility of their ministry would be more manifest. The more real services they rendered to the state the less would they be subject to those maladies of dogmatism and of controversy which spring from the desire of making themselves distinguished and from the want of power to be useful. It is necessary to direct their activity and their ambition towards salutary objects to prevent them from becoming mischievous.

In this point of view, even those who do not acknowledge the truth of religion cannot complain at being called upon to contribute towards its support, since they participate in its advantages.

But if there exists a great diversity of worship and religion, and the legislator is not fettered by an anterior establishment or particular considerations, it will be more conformable to liberty and equality to apply the contributions of each religious community to the support of their own church. It is true that in this arrangement we have cause to fear a spirit of proselytism on the part of the clergy; but it is equally probable that a useful emulation will result from their reciprocal efforts, and that the balance of their influence will establish a kind of equilibrium in that fluid of opinions subject to such dangerous tempests.

We can imagine a very unfortunate case, that of a people to whom the legislator forbids the public exercise of their religion, and at the same time imposes upon them the obligation of supporting a religion which they regard as hostile to their own. This would be a double violation of security. There would gradually be formed among this people an habitual sentiment of hatred against the government, a desire of change, a ferocious courage, a profound secrecy. The people, deprived of all the advantages of a public religion, of known guides and of avowed priests, would be delivered up to ignorant and fanatical leaders. and as the maintenance of their worship would be a school of conspiracy, the faith of oaths, instead of being the safeguard of the state, would become its terror; instead of binding the citizens to the government, it would unite them against it, so much so that such a people would become as formidable through their virtues as their vices. This is not an imaginary case, as the history of Ireland will show.

3. The Cultivation of the Arts and Sciences

I shall not speak here of what ought to be done for what are called the *useful arts and sciences*; nobody doubts that objects of public utility ought to be sustained and encouraged by public contributions.

But when the question relates to the cultivation of the fine arts, the embellishment of a country, edifices of luxury, objects of ornament and pleasure – in one word, to works of superfluity – ought we to raise forced contributions for their support? Can taxes be justified for this brilliant, but superfluous end?

I do not desire to undertake here the support of the agreeable against the useful;[1] nor to argue that the people should be

---

1 Not that there is any real opposition between them; everything that gives pleasure is useful; but in common language, that is exclusively called useful which produces a permanent utility; while the word *agreeable* is limited to an immediate utility, or a present pleasure. Many things, in fact, which we refuse

distressed in order to give *fêtes* to a court, or pensions to buffoons.
But one or two reflections may be offered by way of apology.

1st. The expense which is, or can be, incurred for these objects
is commonly a trifling affair compared to the mass of necessary
contributions. Let anyone undertake to restore to each his quota
of this superfluous expense, and would it not be almost impalpable?

2nd. This superfluous part of the contributions being confounded with the mass of those which are necessary, the levy is
imperceptible; it excites no separate sensation which can give
room to a distinct complaint; and the evil of the first order, limited
to a sum so moderate, is not sufficient to produce an evil of the
second order,

3rd. This luxury of taste may have a palpable utility by bringing
together a concourse of strangers who spend their money in the
country. Little by little all nations become tributary to her who
holds the sceptre of the fashions. A country fertile in amusements
may be looked upon as a great theatre, which is in part supported
at the expense of a crowd of curious spectators drawn to it from all
parts.

It may happen, too, that this pre-eminence in objects of
amusement, literature, and taste, tends to gain for a people the
good will of other nations. Athens, which was called the eye of
Greece, was saved more than once by the sentiment of respect
which superiority of civilization inspired. The halo of glory
which encircled that home of the arts served a long time to hide
its weakness; and everything which was not barbarian was
interested in the preservation of a city, the centre of politeness and
of intellectual pleasures.

But, after all, it must be admitted that this seducing object may
be abandoned without risk to the sole resource of voluntary
contributions, At least, everything essential ought to be provided
for before giving one's self up to expenses of pure ornament. It
will be time to provide for actors, painters, and architects after the
public faith is satisfied; when individuals have been indemnified

---

to call *useful*, have a much more certain utility than some others, to which that
epithet is usually applied.

for the losses occasioned by war, crimes, and physical calamities when the support of the indigent is provided for; till then, all such expense would be an unjust preference granted to brilliant accessaries over objects of necessity.

Such expenses, under such circumstances, are very contrary to the interest of a sovereign, because the reproaches they occasion will always be much exaggerated; for it needs no sagacity to invent them, but only passion and humour to set them distinctly forth. It is well known what efficacy they have had when wrought into pieces of popular eloquence, and employed to stir up the people against regal government. Though it be true that everything conspires to throw kings into this illusion, – so far as regards the luxury of amusements, have they ever fallen into excesses so great as those of many republics? Athens, at an epoch of most pressing dangers, despised alike the eloquence of Demosthenes and the threats of Philip, engrossed with a need more urgent than defence, an object more essential than the maintenance of liberty. The gravest of crimes was the diversion, even for wants of the state, of the funds destined to the support of the theatres. And at Rome, was not the passion for spectacles carried to an equal extreme? It was necessary to lavish the treasures of the world, and the spoils of nations, to captivate the suffrages of the sovereign people. Terror spread through a whole country, whenever a pro-consul was about to give a spectacle at Rome; an hour of the magnificences of the circus cast into despair a hundred thousand inhabitants of the provinces.

CHAPTER XV

Examples of Attacks upon Security

It will be useful to give some examples of what I mean by *attacks upon security*. It will be a means of putting principles in a clearer light, and of showing that what is unjust in morals cannot be innocent in politics. Nothing is more common than to authorize under one name what would be odious under another.

And here I cannot help observing the bad effects of one brand of classical education. We are accustomed from our earliest youth to see in the history of the Roman people public acts of injustice, atrocious in themselves, always coloured with specious names, always accompanied by a proud eulogy on Roman virtues. The abolition of debts plays a great part from the earliest times of the republic. A withdrawal of the people to Mount Aventine, when the enemy was at the gates of Rome, forced the Senate to pass a sponge over the rights of creditors. The historian excites all our interest in favour of the fraudulent debtors who paid their debts by a bankruptcy, and does not fail to render odious those who were despoiled by an act of violence. And what was gained by that injustice? Usury, which had served as a pretext for the robbery, could not but be augmented the very next day after the catastrophe; for the exorbitant rate of interest was only the price of the risk caused by the uncertainty of engagements. The foundation of the Roman colonies has been celebrated as a work of profound policy. It always consisted in despoiling a part of the lawful proprietors of a conquered country to create establishments in the way of favour or reward.

This proceeding, so cruel in its immediate effects, was yet more fatal in its consequences. The Romans, accustomed to violate all the rights of property, knew not where to check themselves in this career. Thence the perpetual demand for a new division of lands, which was ever the fire-brand of the seditious, and which contributed under the triumvirate to a frightful system of general confiscations.

The history of the republics of Greece is full of facts of the same kind, always presented in a manner plausible enough to lead astray superficial inquirers. What abuse of reasoning has there been upon that division of lands brought about by Lycurgus, to serve as a basis for his community of warriors; in which, by an inequality the most shocking, all the rights are on one side, and all the servitude on the other!

These *attacks upon security*, which have found so many officious defenders when the question has been of the Greeks and the Romans, have not experienced the same indulgence when the monarchs of the East have been the actors. The despotism of an individual has nothing seducing in it; because it confines itself too evidently to his person alone; there are a million chances of suffering from it, to one of enjoying. But the despotism exercised by a multitude deceives weak minds by a false image of the public good. We place ourselves in imagination among the great number that commands, instead of supposing ourselves among the small number that yields and suffers. Let us, then, leave in peace the sultans and the viziers. We may be sure their injustice will not be glossed over by the flatteries of historians. Their reputation serves as an antidote to their example.

We may dispense, for the same reason, with insisting upon such attacks upon security as national bankruptcies; but we may remark, in passing, a curious effect of fidelity to engagements upon the authority of the government itself. In England, since the Revolution, the engagements of the state have always been sacred; so that individuals who lend to the government never demand any other pledge than the national credit; and the collection of the imposts assigned to pay the interest of the debt has always remained in the hands of the king. In France, under the monarchy, violations of the public faith were so frequent, that those who made advances to the government were in the habit, from an early period, of requiring the collection of the imposts to be intrusted to them, and of paying themselves with their own hands. But this arrangement cost the people dear; for the public creditor had no interest to consult their convenience; and it cost the prince yet dearer, since it deprived him of the affections of the people. When, in 1787, the

announcement of a deficient revenue alarmed all the creditors of
the state, that class so interested in England, in the maintenance of
government, showed itself in France, ardent for a revolution. All
thought they saw their own security in taking away from the
sovereign the administration of the finances, and placing them in
the hands of a national council. It is well known how far the event
answered to their hopes. But it is not the less interesting to observe
that the fall of that monarchy, which appeared so immoveable, was
owing, in no small measure, to the distrust which so many
violations of the public faith had caused.

But among the many *attacks upon security* committed through
ignorance, inadvertence, or false reasons, it will suffice to note
some individual cases.

1st. We may regard as such, *taxes unequally levied*, – those dis-
proportioned imposts which spare the rich at the expense of the
poor. The weight of this evil is aggravated by the sentiment of
injustice at the idea of paying more than one's fair proportion.

Corvées are the height of inequality; since they fall entirely upon
those who have only their hands for their patrimony.

So are imposts levied upon an uncertain fund; upon persons
who may have nothing to pay with. In that case, the evil takes
another turn. Indigence may protect us from paying the tax, but
it subjects us at the same time to the gravest evils. The sufferings
of want take the place of the inconveniences of the impost. This
is the reason why a poll-tax is so unjust. It is possible to have a
head, and to have nothing else.

Imposts which fetter industry, such as monopolies, and exclusive companies. The true method of estimating these imposts is,
not to consider what income they pay, but what they prevent
from being paid.

Imposts upon necessaries. What physical privations, what maladies, what deaths they produce, no man can tell! These sufferings,
caused by the fault of the government, are confounded with
natural evils which it cannot prevent.

Imposts upon private sales. Generally speaking, it is necessity
which causes these sales; and the tax-gatherer, coming in at an
epoch of distress, levies an extraordinary tribute upon an
unfortunate individual.

Imposts upon public sales, or sales at auction. Here the distress is fully proved; often it is extreme, and the fiscal injustice is most manifest.

Taxes upon law proceedings. They include all kinds of attacks upon security, since they are equivalent to refusing the protection of the law to all those who cannot pay for it. They consequently offer a hope of impunity to crime. It is only necessary to choose as objects of injustice individuals who cannot afford the advances necessary to a judicial prosecution, or who are not rich enough to run the risk.

2nd. *A forced Elevation of the Value of Money.* – This is a bankruptcy, since the government does not pay all that it owes; a fraudulent bankruptcy, since there is a semblance of paying; and a foolish fraud, which deceives nobody. As far as it goes, it is equivalent to an abolition of debts. The theft which the government commits upon its own creditors, it authorizes every debtor to commit upon his, though without any profit from it to the public treasury. And when this course of injustice is completed; after this operation has enfeebled confidence, mined honest men, enriched rogues, deranged commerce, disordered taxation, and caused a thousand individual evils, it does not leave the least advantage to the government which it has dishonoured. Expense and income presently return to the same proportions as before.

3rd. *Forced Reduction of the Rate of Interest.* – Regarded as a question of political economy, reducing the rate of interest by law is injurious to wealth, because it is prohibiting the payment of any premium for the introduction of foreign capital; it is prohibiting, in many cases, new branches of commerce, and even old ones, if the legal interest is not sufficient to balance the risks of the capital employed. But with a more immediate view to security, it is taking away from lenders to give to borrowers. Let the rate of interest be reduced by law a fifth part below its natural level, and the event is the same to the lenders as if they were plundered every year by robbers of the fifth part of their fortunes.

If the legislator finds it good to take away from a particular class of citizens a fifth part of their revenue, why stop there? Why not take away another fifth part, and still another? If the first reduction answered its end, a further reduction will answer it in the same proportion; and if the measure is good in one case, why should it be bad in the other? Wherever we stop, it is necessary to have a reason for stopping; but whatever reason prevents the second step will be just as good to prevent the first. This operation is exactly the same as diminishing rents under the pretext that the proprietors are useless consumers, and the farmers productive labourers. If you shake the principle of security as respects one class of citizens, you shake it for all. The bundle of rods is its emblem.

4th. *General Confiscations.* – I refer to this head vexations exercised upon a sect, upon a party, upon a class of men, under the vague pretext of some political crime – a pretext so vague that, while it is pretended that the confiscation is a punishment, there is often room to believe that the crime has been created for the sake of the confiscation. History presents many examples of such robbery. The Jews have often been its object; they were too rich not to be always guilty. Financiers and farmers of the public revenue, for the same reason, have been often subjected to what were called *chambers of fire* (*chambres ardentes*). While the order of succession remained unfixed, everybody at the sovereign's death might become guilty; and the spoils of the vanquished formed, in the hands of the successor, a treasure of rewards. In a republic torn by factions, each half of the nation denounces the other as traitors; and let the system of confiscations be once introduced, and parties, as at Rome, become in turn the devourers of each other.

The crimes of the powerful, and especially the crimes of the popular party in democracies, have always found apologists. 'The greater part of these great fortunes,' it is said, 'have been founded upon injustice; and what has been plundered from the public may as well be restored to the public.' To reason in this way is to open an unlimited career to tyranny. It is a permission to presume crime instead of proving it. According to this logic, it is impossible for a rich man to be innocent. Ought a punishment so severe as confiscation to be inflicted in gross, without examination, without detail, without proof? Does a procedure which would be declared atrocious if employed against an individual, become lawful when directed against a whole class of citizens? Can we make ourselves deaf to the evil we are doing because of the number of the sufferers whose cries are mingled together in this common shipwreck? To plunder great proprietors, under the pretext that some of their ancestors have acquired their opulence by unjust means, is like bombarding a city because some robbers are thought to be concealed in it.

5th. *Dissolution of Convents and of Monastic Orders.* – The decree for their abolition was signed by reason itself; but its execution should not have been abandoned to prejudice and to avarice. It would have been enough to have forbidden these societies to admit new members. In that case they would have died away gradually. Individuals would have suffered no privation. The revenues as they fell in might have been appropriated to some useful object; and philosophy would have applauded an operation excellent in principle and mild in its execution. But this slow progress is not that which cupidity loves. It would seem as if sovereigns, in dissolving these societies, had wished to punish the members for some wrong they had done, In place of regarding them as orphans and invalids, deserving all the compassion of the legislator, they were looked upon as enemies, who were treated with clemency even when they were stripped of all their wealth and reduced to absolute want.

6th. *Suppression of Pensions and Places without Indemnity to the Possessors.* – This attack upon security merits the rather a particular mention, because, instead of being blamed as an injustice, it is often approved as an act of economy and reform. Envy is never so much at its ease as when it can conceal itself under the mask of patriotism and the public good. But the public good requires only the abolition of sinecures; it does not demand the ruin of the persons who hold them.

The principle of security requires that reform should be attended with complete indemnity. The only benefit that can be lawfully drawn from it is the conversion of a perpetual into a life annuity.

Is it said that the immediate suppression of these places will be a gain to the public? This argument is sophistical. The sum in question would doubtless be a gain, considered in itself, if it came from abroad, or if it were acquired by commerce; but it is not a gain when taken from the hands of certain individuals, who are themselves a part of the public. Would a family be the richer because the father had taken everything from one of his children, the better to endow the others? Even in such a case, the spoils of one child would increase the inheritance of his brothers, and the evil would not be a total loss; it would produce a portion of good.

But when the question is of the public, the profit of a place suppressed is divided among the whole community, while the loss falls entirely upon one. The gain, spread among the multitude, is divided into impalpable parts; the loss is wholly felt by him who alone supports it. The result of the operation is this – it does not enrich the party that gains, and it reduces him who loses to poverty. Instead of one place suppressed, suppose a thousand, ten thousand, a hundred thousand. The total disadvantage will remain the same. The plunder taken from thousands of individuals must be divided among millions. Your streets will everywhere present unfortunate citizens whom you will have plunged into indigence; and you will hardly see an individual who will be sensibly the richer by virtue of these cruel operations Groans of pain and cries of despair will resound on every side. The cries of joy, if there are any, will not be expressions of happiness, but of that antipathy which rejoices in the misery of its victims. Ministers of kings and of the people, it is not by the wretchedness of individuals that you will produce the happiness of nations! The altar of the public good demands barbarous sacrifices as little as the altar of the Divinity.

I cannot yet quit the subject; for the establishment of the principle of security demands that error should be pursued into all its retreats.

What means do men take to deceive themselves or to deceive the people on the subject of such great injustice? They have recourse to certain pompous maxims which are a mixture of truth and falsehood, and which give to a question, simple in itself, an air of depth and political mystery. The interest of individuals, it is said, ought to yield to the public interest. But what does that mean? Is not one individual as much a part of the public as another? This public interest, which you introduce as a person, is only an abstract term; it represents nothing but the mass of individual interests. It is necessary to take them all into account, instead of considering some as all, and the others as nothing. If it is a good thing to sacrifice the fortune of one individual to augment that of others, it will be yet better to sacrifice a second, a third, a hundred, a thousand, an unlimited number; for whatever may be the number of those you have sacrificed, you will always have the same reason to add one more. In one word, the interest of everybody is sacred, or the interest of nobody.

Individual interests are the only real interests. Take care of the individuals; never molest them, never suffer anyone to molest them, and you will have done enough for the public. Would it be believed that there are men so absurd as to love posterity better than the present generation; to prefer the man who is not to the man who is; to torment the living under pretext of doing good to those who are not born, and who perhaps never will be?

Upon a multitude of occasions, men who have suffered by the operation of a law have not dared to complain, or have not been listened to, by reason of this false and obscure notion, that private interest ought to yield to public interest. But if it comes to a question of generosity, who is loudest called upon to exercise it, – the whole towards one, or one towards the whole? An evil felt, and a benefit not felt; such is the result of these admirable operations by which individuals are sacrificed to the public!

I shall conclude by a general observation of great importance. The more the principle of property is respected, the stronger hold it takes on the popular mind. Slight attacks upon this principle prepare the way for heavier ones. A long time has been necessary to carry property to the point where we now see it in civilized societies; but a fatal experience has shown with what facility it can be shaken, and how easily the savage instinct of plunder gets the better of the laws, Governments and the people are, in this respect, like tamed lions; let them but taste a drop of blood, and their native ferocity revives.

Si torrida parvus
Venit in ora cruor, rediunt rabiesque furorque;
Admonitaeque tument gustato sanguine fauces,
Fervet, et a trepido vix abstinet ora magistro.

LUCAN, IV

If but a little blood
Touch his hot mouth, fury and rage return;
His counselled jaws swell with the tasted gore;
He raves; and from his trembling keeper scarce
Restrains his teeth.

CHAPTER XVI

Forced Exchanges

'Astyages, in Xenophon's *Cyropaedia*, asks Cyrus to give an account of his last lesson. Cyrus answers thus: "One of the boys in our school who had a coat too small for him gave it to one of his companions a little smaller than himself, and took away his coat, which was too large. The preceptor made me the judge of this dispute, and I decided that the matter should be left as it was, since both parties seemed to be better accommodated than before. Upon which the preceptor pointed out to me that I had done wrong, for I had been satisfied with considering the convenience of the thing, whereas I ought first to have looked at the justice of it; and justice never would allow violence to be done to anyone's property." ' – Montaigne's *Essays*, book I, ch. xxiv.

What ought we to think of this decision? At the first view it would appear that a forced exchange is not contrary to security, provided an equal value is given. How can I be said to lose in consequence of a law, if, after it has had its full effect, the amount of my property remains the same as before? If one has gained, and the other has not lost, the operation seems to be a good one.

No; it is not. He whom you suppose to have lost nothing by a forced exchange, in reality has lost; since everything moveable or immoveable has different values for different persons, according to circumstances, and everyone expects to enjoy the favourable circumstances which may augment the value of such or such a part of his property. If the house that Peter occupies would be more valuable to Paul, that is no reason why Paul should be gratified by forcing Peter to yield the house to him for the sum which it is worth to himself. That would be to deprive Peter of the benefit which he has a right to derive from the very circumstance that the house is worth more to Paul.

And suppose Paul should say that for the sake of peace he had offered a price above the ordinary value, and that Peter refuses it out of pure obstinacy, still it might be replied to him, 'This surplus of price which you pretend to have offered is only a supposition of yours. The opposite supposition is just as probable. For if you had really offered more than the house is worth, he would have hastened to seize so favourable a circumstance, which might not occur again, and the bargain would have been soon concluded. If he did not accept your offer it is a proof that you were deceived in your estimate, and that if the house were taken from him on the conditions you propose, it would be an injury to his fortune, if not to what he possesses, at least to what he has a right to acquire.'

No, Paul will reply; he knows that my estimate is higher than anything he can expect in the ordinary course of things; but he also knows my necessity, and he refuses a reasonable offer in hopes to derive an unfair advantage from my situation.

I perceive a principle which may serve to settle this difference between Paul and Peter. Things must be distinguished into two classes, those which ordinarily have only their intrinsic value, and those which are susceptible of a value of affection. Houses of the common sort, fields cultivated in the usual way, a crop of hay or corn, and ordinary kinds of manufactures, seem to belong to the first class. To the second may be referred pleasure-grounds and gardens, libraries, pictures, statues, collections of natural history. A forced exchange of such objects should never be permitted. The value they derive from a sentiment of affection cannot be appreciated. But objects of the first class may be submitted to forced exchanges whenever it is the only means to prevent great losses. I possess a piece of land from which I derive a considerable revenue, but which I can approach only by a road running along the edge of a river. The river overflows and washes away the road. My neighbour obstinately refuses me a passage along a strip of land which is not worth the hundredth part of my field. Ought I to lose my all through the caprice or hostility of an unreasonable neighbour?

But to prevent the abuse of a principle so delicate, rigorous rules ought to be laid down. I say, then, that forced exchanges ought to be permitted to prevent a great loss, as in the case of a field rendered inaccessible except by a passage through another.

By observing all the scruples of the English legislators in this behalf, we may perceive the respect which is paid in that country to the rights of property. If a new road is to be opened, an Act of Parliament must be first obtained. All interested are heard, and the legislature, not content with assigning an equitable satisfaction to the proprietors, protects houses, gardens, and such other objects as may have a value of affection, by special exceptions in the Act.

Forced exchanges may also be justified whenever the obstinacy of an individual or of a small number are clearly hostile to the advantage of a great number. So in the matter of the English Enclosure Acts, the opposition of a few has not been suffered to prevail, and the sale of houses is often compelled by the law where the convenience or the health of cities requires it.

The question is of forced *exchanges*, not of forced transfers, for a transfer is not an exchange; and a forced transfer without equivalent, even for the benefit of the state, would be a mere injustice, an act of power devoid of that tenderness which the principle of utility ever demands.

CHAPTER XVII

Power of the Laws over Expectation

The legislator is not master of the dispositions of the human heart, he is only their interpreter and their minister. The goodness of the laws depends upon their conformity to general *expectation*. The legislator ought to be well acquainted with the progress of this expectation, in order to act in concert with it. This should be the end; let us inquire into the conditions necessary to attain it.

1st. The first of these conditions, but at the same time the most difficult to fulful, is this, *that the laws should be anterior to expectation*. If we could suppose a new people, a generation of children, the legislator finding no expectations already formed in contradiction to his views, might fashion them at his pleasure, as the statuary does a block of marble. But as there exists already among all people a multitude of expectations founded upon ancient laws or ancient usages, the legislator is forced to follow a system of conciliation and of humouring which constantly fetters him.

The very first laws found some expectations already formed. For we have seen that prior to laws there existed a feeble kind of property – that is, a sort of expectation of preserving what had been acquired. The laws received their first determination from these anterior expectations, they have produced new ones, and have gradually formed the channel of our desires and hopes. No changes can be made in the laws of property without deranging, more or less, this established current, and without opposing more or less resistance to it.

Do you find it necessary to establish a law contrary to the actual expectations of men? If it is possible, you should so arrange matters that this law will not begin to take effect except at a remote period. The present generation will not feel the change, and the rising generation will be prepared for it. You will find among the young auxiliaries against old opinions, you will not wound actual interests, because time will be allowed to prepare for a new order of things. Everything will become easy to you, because you will have prevented the birth of those expectations which otherwise you would have been compelled to contradict.

2nd. The second condition is, *that the laws should be known.* A law which is unknown can have no effect upon expectation, it will not even serve to prevent a contrary expectation.

This condition, it will be said, does not depend upon the nature of the law, but on the measures which are taken to make it public. These measures may be sufficient for their object, whether the law be so or not.

This reasoning is more specious than true. There are some laws so made as to be more easily known than others. These are laws conformable to expectations already formed, laws which rest upon *natural expectations.* This natural expectation, that is, this expectation produced by previous habits, may be founded upon a superstition, upon a hurtful prejudice, or upon a perception of utility, it makes no difference which, the law which is conformed to it is easily borne in mind; in fact, it was in the mind before it received the sanction of the legislator. But a law contrary to this natural expectation is difficult to be understood, and still more difficult to be remembered. Another arrangement always suggests itself, while the law, strange to all, and without any root in the mind, tends constantly to slip from a place to which it has only an artificial adhesion.

Codes of ritual law have this inconvenience among others, that the fantastic and arbitrary rules of which they are composed, never well known, fatigue the understanding and the memory, so that man, always fearful, always in fault, always defiled by some imaginary sin, can never count upon innocence, and lives in perpetual need of absolution.

Expectation naturally directs itself towards the laws which are most important to society. The stranger who commits a theft, a forgery, an assassination, should not be suffered to plead ignorance of the laws of the country, since he could not be ignorant that acts so manifestly hurtful were crimes everywhere.

3rd. The third condition is, *that the laws should be consistent.* This principle is closely connected with the preceding, but it serves to place a great truth in a new light. When the laws have established a certain arrangement upon a principle generally admitted, every additional arrangement which is consistent with that principle will prove to be conformable to the general expectation. Every analogous law is presumed, as it were, beforehand. Each new application of the principle contributes to strengthen it. But a law which has not this character remains isolated in the mind; and the influence of the principle to which it is opposed is a force which tends, without ceasing, to drive it from the memory.

That upon a man's death his property should go to the next of kin, is a rule generally admitted, and according to which expectations are naturally formed. A law directing the order of succession, which should conform to this principle, would obtain a general approbation, and would be universally understood. But the more this principle is obscured, by admitting exceptions, the more difficult it is to understand the law and to remember it. The English *Common Law* affords us a striking example. It is so complicated in its provisions regulating the descent of property, it admits distinctions so singular, the decisions which serve to regulate it are so subtle, that not only is it impossible for simple good sense to presume its regulations beforehand, but it is very difficult to discover them at all. It is a profound study, like that of the most abstract sciences, confined to a small number of privileged men. It has been even necessary to sub-divide it, for no lawyer pretends to understand the whole of it. Such has been the fruit of too superstitious a respect for antiquity!

When new laws are made in opposition to a principle established by the old ones, the stronger that principle is, the more odious will the inconsistency appear. A contradiction of sentiment results from it, and disappointed expectations accuse the legislator of tyranny.

In Turkey, when an officer of the government dies, the Sultan takes possession of his entire fortune, and his children fall at once from the height of opulence to the depths of poverty. This law, which overturns all natural expectations, was perhaps borrowed from some other oriental government, in which it was less inconsistent and less odious, because the sovereign entrusted employment only to eunuchs.

4th. The fourth condition is, *that the laws should be consistent with the principle of utility*; for utility is a point towards which all expectations have a natural tendency.

It is true that a law conformable to utility may happen to be contrary to public opinion; but this is only an accidental and transitory circumstance. All minds will be reconciled to the law so soon as its utility is made obvious. As soon as the veil which conceals it is raised, expectation will be satisfied, and the public opinion be gained over. Now, it is plain that the more the laws are conformed to utility, the more manifest it is possible for their utility to become. If we ascribe to a thing a quality which it does not possess, the triumph of error can exist but for a time – a single ray of light will suffice to dissipate it. But a quality which actually exists, although not known, may chance to be discovered at any instant. At the first moment, an innovation is surrounded by an impure atmosphere; a mass of clouds formed by caprices and prejudices float about it; and the appearance of things is changed by the refractions it undergoes in the passage through so deceitful a medium. It needs time for the sight to grow strong, and to acquire the power of separating from the object all that is foreign to it. But, little by little, truth gains the ascendant. If the first attempt does not succeed, the second will be more fortunate, because it will be better known where lies the difficulty which it is necessary to conquer. The plan which favours the most interests cannot fail in the end to gain the most suffrages; and the useful novelty, which at first was repulsed with affright, becomes presently so familiar that no one recollects its commencement.

5th. The fifth condition is *method in the laws*. The bad arrangement of a code of laws may produce, by its effect upon expectation, the same inconveniences with incoherence and inconsistency. There may result from it the same difficulty of understanding the law, and of remembering it. Every man has his limited measure of understanding. The more complex the law is, the more it is above the faculties of a great number. In the same proportion it is less known; it has less hold upon men; it does not present itself to their minds upon the necessary occasions; or, what is yet worse, it deceives them, and produces false expectations. Both the style and the method should be simple; the law ought to be a manual of instruction for each individual; and everyone should be enabled to consult it in doubtful cases, without the aid of an interpreter.

The more the laws conform to the principle of utility the simpler they will become; for a system founded upon a single principle may be as simple in form as in substance. It is only such a system which is susceptible of a natural method, and a familiar nomenclature.

6th. To become the controller of expectation, the law ought to present itself to the mind as *certain to be executed*; at least, no reason for presuming the contrary ought to appear.

Is there ground for supposing that the law will not be executed? An expectation is formed contrary to the law itself. The law, then, is useless. It never exercises its power except to punish; and these inefficacious punishments are an additional reproach to the law. Contemptible in its weakness, odious in its force, it is always bad, whether it reaches the guilty or suffers him to escape.

This principle has often been absurdly disregarded. For example, during Law's paper-money system, when the citizens of France were forbidden to keep in their houses more than a certain sum in coin, – could not everybody presume on the success of disobedience?

How many mercantile prohibitions are vicious in this particular! A multitude of rules easily eluded, form, so to speak, a lottery of immorality, in which individuals stake their money against the legislator and the custom-house.

It is in accordance with this principle that the domestic authority has been established in the hands of the husband. If it had been given to the woman, the physical power being on one side, and the legal power on the other, the discord would have been eternal. If an equality had been established between them, this nominal equality could never have been maintained, because of two opposite wills one or the other must have the sway. The existing arrangement is most favourable to the peace of families, because, in making the physical and legal power operate in concert, everything is combined which is necessary for effectual action.

This principle affords a great assistance towards the resolution of certain problems which have very much embarrassed the lawyers; such, for instance, as this – in what cases ought a *thing found* to belong to the finder? The easier it would be to appropriate the thing in spite of the law, the more expedient is it not to make a

law which will disappoint expectation; or in other terms, the
easier it is to elude the law, the more cruel it would be to make a
law which, presenting itself to the mind as almost impossible to be
executed, would do nothing but evil, when by chance it should
happen to be executed. This may be made clearer by an
example: – Should I find a diamond in the ground, my first idea
would be to regard it as my own; and an expectation of keeping
it would be formed at the same instant, not only through the bent
of desire, but also by analogy with habitual ideas of property. 1st.
I have the physical possession of it, and this possession alone is a
title where there is no opposing title. 2nd. There is something of
mine in the discovery; it is I who have drawn this diamond from
the dirt, where, unknown to all the world, it had no value. 3rd. I
may flatter myself with the idea of keeping it, without the aid of
the law, and even in spite of the law; since it will be enough to
conceal it till I have a pretext for producing it under some other
title. Now, should the law undertake to bestow the diamond
upon some other person than me, it could not prevent this first
movement of expectation, this hope of keeping it; and in taking it
away from me, it would make me experience that pain of
disappointment commonly called *injustice* or *tyranny*. This reason
would be sufficient for causing the thing to be given to the finder,
unless some stronger reason can be offered to the contrary.

This rule may vary according to the natural chance of keeping
the thing found without the aid of the law. A shipwrecked vessel
which I may have been the first to see upon the coast; a mine; an
island which I may have discovered; are objects as to which an
anterior law may prevent any idea of property, because it is
impossible for me secretly to appropriate them to my own use.
The law which refused them to me, being easily executed, would
have its full and entire effect upon my mind; to such a degree, that
if the question turned on this principle alone, the legislator would
be at liberty to give or refuse the thing to the discoverer, as he saw
fit. But there is a particular reason for showing some favour to the
discoverer, which is, that a reward given to industry tends to
augment the general wealth. When all the profit of discovery
passes to the public treasury, that all is generally very little.

7th. The seventh and last condition necessary to produce a
conformity between expectation and the laws, requires that the

laws should be literally followed. This condition depends partly on the laws, and partly on the judges. If the laws do not harmonize with the ideas of the people, if the code of a barbarous age still prevails in an era of civilization; the tribunals, little by little, will drop old principles, and insensibly substitute new maxims. Thence will result a kind of contest between laws that are growing obsolete, and usage that is taking their place; and a feebleness in the effect of the laws upon expectation, will be a consequence of this uncertainty.

The word *interpretation* has a very different meaning in the mouth of a lawyer, from what it has when employed by other people. To interpret a passage in an author, is to bring out of it the sense which the writer had in his mind; to interpret a law, in the sense at least of the Roman lawyers, is often to get rid of the intention clearly and plainly expressed, and to substitute some other for it, in the presumption that this new sense was the actual intention of the legislator!

With such a method of proceeding, there is no security. Where the law is fixed, though it be difficult, obscure, incoherent, – the citizen always has a chance to know it. It gives a confused intimation, less efficacious than it might be, yet always useful; we see at least the limits of the evil it can do. But let a judge dare to arrogate to himself the power of interpreting the laws, that is to say, of substituting his will for that of the legislator, and everything becomes arbitrary; no one can foresee the course which caprice will take. The question is no longer of the actual evil; however great that may be, it is small in comparison with the magnitude of possible consequences. The serpent, it is said, can pass his whole body wherever he can introduce his head. As respects legal tyranny, it is this subtle head of which we must take care, lest presently we see it followed by all the tortuous folds of abuse. It is not the evil only which we ought to distrust, – it is the good even which springs from such means. Every usurpation of a power above the law, though useful in its immediate effects, as regards the future ought to be an object of terror. There are bounds, and even narrow bounds, to the good which can result from such arbitrary proceedings; there are no bounds to the possible evil; there are no bounds to the alarm. An indistinct danger hovers over every head.

Without speaking of ignorance and caprice, how many facilities does this arbitrary system afford to partiality! The judge, now conforming to the law, and now explaining it away, can always decide a case to suit his own designs. He is always sure of saving himself, either by the literal sense or the interpretation, He is a charlatan who astonishes the spectators by making sweet and bitter run from the same cup.

One of the most eminent characteristics of the English tribunal is their scrupulous fidelity in following the declared will of the legislator; and in directing themselves as much as possible, by former judgments, in that imperfect part of English legislation which depends upon custom. This rigid observation of the laws may have considerable inconveniences in an incomplete system, but it is the true spirit of liberty which inspires the English with so much horror for what they call *ex post facto laws*.

All the conditions which constitute the goodness of the laws have so intimate a connection that the fulfilment of one supposes the fulfilment of the others. Intrinsic utility; apparent utility; consistency; simplicity; facility of being known; probability of execution; all these qualities may be reciprocally considered as the cause or the effect of each other.

If that obscure system called *custom* were no longer permitted, and everything were reduced to written law; if the laws which concern every member of the community were arranged in one volume, and those which concern particular classes in little separate collections; if the general code were universally disseminated; had it become, as among the Hebrews, a part of worship and a manual of education; if a knowledge of it were required as preliminary to the enjoyment of political rights – the law would then be truly known; every deviation from it would be manifest; every citizen would become its guardian; its violation would not be a mystery, its explanation would not be a monopoly; and fraud and chicane would no longer be able to elude it.

It is further necessary that the style of the laws should be as simple as their provisions; that it should make use of common language; that its forms should have no artificial complexity. If the style of the code differed from that of other books, it should be by a greater clearness, by a greater precision, by a greater familiarity; because it is designed for all understandings, and particularly for the least enlightened class.

After having imagined such a system of laws, if we proceed to compare it with what actually exists, the sentiment that results is far from favourable to our institutions. But however bad existing laws may be, let us distrust the declamations of chagrin and the exaggerations of complaint. He who is so limited in his views, or so passionate in his ideas of reform as to desire a revolt, or to bring the established system into general contempt, is unworthy to be heard at the tribunal of an enlightened public. Who can enumerate the benefits of law, I do not say under the best government, but under the worst? Are we not indebted to it for all we have of security, property, industry, and abundance? Are we not indebted to it for peace between citizens, for the sanctity of marriage, and the sweet perpetuity of families? The good which the law produces is universal; it is enjoyed every day and every moment. Its evils are transient accidents. But the good is not perceived; we enjoy it without referring it to its true cause, as if it appertained to the ordinary course of nature; while evils are vividly felt, and, in the description of them, the suffering which is spread over a great space and a long series of years, is accumulated by the imagination upon a single moment. How many reasons we have to love the laws in spite of their imperfections!

ANARCHICAL FALLACIES

*An Examination of the Declaration of the Rights of the Man
and the Citizen Decreed by the Constituent Assembly in France*

Preamble

'The Representatives of the French people, constituted in National Assembly, considering that ignorance, forgetfulness, or contempt of the Rights of Man, are the only causes of public calamities, and of the corruption of governments, have resolved to set forth in a solemn declaration, the natural, unalienable, and sacred rights of man, in order that this declaration, constantly presented to all the members of the body social, may recall to mind, without ceasing, their rights and their duties; to the end, that the acts of the legislative power, and those of the executive power, being capable at every instant of comparison with the end of every political institution, they may be more respected, and also that the demands of the citizens hereafter, founded upon simple and incontestable principles, may always tend to the maintenance of the constitution and to the happiness of all.

'In consequence, the National Assembly acknowledges and declares, in the presence and under the auspices of the Supreme Being, the following Rights of the Man and the Citizen.' –

From this preamble we may collect the following positions:

1   That the declaration in question ought to include a declaration of all the powers which it is designed should thereafter subsist in the State; the limits of each power precisely laid down, and every one completely distinguished from the other.

2   That the articles by which this is to be done, ought not to be loose and scattered, but closely connected into a whole, and the connexion all along made visible.

3   That the declaration of the rights of man, in a state preceding that of political society, ought to form a part of the composition in question, and constitute the first part of it.

4   That in point of fact, a clear idea of all these stands already imprinted in the minds of every man.

5   That, therefore, the object of such a draught is not, in any part of such a draught, to teach the people anything new.

6   But that the object of such a declaration is to declare the accession of the Assembly, as such, to the principles as understood and embraced, as well by themselves in their individual capacity, as by all other individuals in the State.

7   That the use of this solemn adoption and recognition is, that the principles recognised may serve as a standard by which the propriety of the several particular laws that are afterwards to be enacted in consequence, may be tried.

8   That by the conformity of these laws to this standard, the fidelity of the legislators to their trust is also to be tried.

9   That accordingly, if any law should hereafter be enacted, between which, and any of those fundamental articles, any want of conformity in any point can be pointed out, such want of conformity will be a conclusive proof of two things: 1. Of the impropriety of such law; 2. Of error or criminality on the part of the authors amid adopters of that law.

It concerns me to see so respectable an Assembly hold out expectations, which, according to my conception, cannot in the nature of things be fulfilled.

An enterprise of this sort, instead of preceding the formation of a complete body of laws, supposes such a work to be already existing in every particular except that of its obligatory force.

No laws are ever to receive the sanction of the Assembly that shall be contrary in any point to these principles. What does this suppose? It supposes the several articles of detail that require to be enacted, to have been drawn up, to have been passed in review, to have been confronted with these fundamental articles, and to have been found in no respect repugnant to them. In a word, to be sufficiently assured that the several laws of detail will bear this trying comparison, one thing is necessary: the comparison must have been made.

To know the several laws which the exigencies of mankind call for, a view of all these several exigencies must be obtained. But to obtain this view, there is but one possible means, which is, to take a view of the laws that have already been framed, and of the exigencies which have given birth to them.

To frame a composition which shall in any tolerable degree answer this requisition, two endowments, it is evident, are absolutely necessary – an acquaintance with the law as it is, and the perspicuity and genius of the metaphysician: and these endowments must unite in the same person.

I can conceive but four purposes which a discourse, of the kind proposed under the name of a Declaration of Rights, can be intended to answer: the setting bounds to the authority of the crown; – the setting bounds to the authority of the supreme legislative power, that of the National Assembly; – the serving as a general guide or set of instructions to the National Assembly itself, in the task of executing their function in detail, by the establishment of particular laws; – and the affording a satisfaction to the people.

These four purposes seem, if I apprehend right, to be all of them avowed by the same or different advocates for this measure.

Of the fourth and last of these purposes I shall say nothing: it is a question merely local, dependent upon the humour of the spot and of the day, of which no one at a distance can be a judge. Of the fitness of the end, there can be but one opinion: the only question is about the fitness of the means.

In the three other points of view, the expediency of the measure is more than I can perceive.

The description of the persons, of whose rights it is to contain the declaration, is remarkable. Who are they? The French nation? No; not they only, but all citizens, and all men. By citizens, it seems we are to understand men engaged in political society: by men, persons not yet engaged in political society – persons as yet in a state of nature.

The word men, as opposed to citizens, I had rather not have seen. In this sense, a declaration of the rights of men is a declaration of the rights which human creatures, it is supposed, would possess, were they in a state in which the French nation certainly are not, nor perhaps any other; certainly no other into whose hands this declaration could ever come.

This instrument is the more worthy of attention, especially of the attention of a foreigner, inasmuch as the rights which it is to declare are the rights which it is supposed belong to the members of every nation in the globe. As a member of a nation which with relation to the French comes under the name of a foreign one, I feel the stronger call to examine this declaration, inasmuch as in this instrument I am invited to read a list of rights which belong as much to me as to the people for whose more particular use it has been framed.

The word men, I observe to be all along coupled in the language of the Assembly itself, with the word citizen. I lay it, therefore, out of the question, and consider the declaration in the same light in which it is viewed by M. Turgot, as that of a declaration of the rights of all men in a state of citizenship or political society.

I proceed, then, to consider it in the three points of view above announced:

1.   Can it be of use for the purpose of setting bounds to the power of the crown? No; for that is to be the particular object of the Constitutional Code itself, from which this preliminary part is detached in advance.

2.   Can it be of use for the purpose of setting bounds to the power of the several legislative bodies established or to be established? I answer, No. 1. Not of any subordinate ones: for of their authority, the natural and necessary limit is that of the supreme legislature, the National Assembly. 2. Not of the National Assembly itself: – Why? Such limitation is unnecessary. It is proposed, and very wisely and honestly, to call in the body of the people, and give it as much power and influence as in its nature it is capable of: by enabling it to declare its sentiments whenever it thinks proper, whether immediately, or through the channel of the subordinate assemblies. Is a law enacted or proposed in the National Assembly, which happens not to be agreeable to the body of the people? It will be equally censured by them, whether it be conceived, or not, to bear marks of a repugnancy to this declaration of rights. Is a law disagreeable to them? They will hardly think themselves precluded from expressing their disapprobation, by the circumstance of its not being to be convicted of repugnancy to that instrument; and though it should be repugnant to that instrument, they will see little need to resort to that instrument for the ground of their

repugnancy; they will find a much nearer ground in some particular real or imaginary inconvenience.

In short, when you have made such provision, that the supreme legislature can never carry any point against the general and persevering opinion of the people, what would you have more ? What use in their attempting to bind themselves by a set of phrases of their own contrivance? The people's pleasure: that is the only check to which no other can add anything, and which no other can supersede.

In regard to the rights thus declared, mention will either be made of the exceptions and modifications that may be made to them by the laws themselves, or there will not. In the former case, the observance of the declaration will be impracticable; nor can the law in its details stir a step without flying in the face of it. In the other case, it fails thereby altogether of its only object, the setting limits to the exercise of the legislative power. Suppose a declaration to this effect – no man's liberty shall be abridged in any point. This, it is evident, would be an useless extravagance, which must be contradicted by every law that came to be made. Suppose it to say – no man's liberty shall be abridged, but in such points as it shall be abridged in, by the law. This, we see, is saying nothing: it leaves the law just as free and unfettered as it found it.

Between these two rocks lies the only choice which an instrument destined to this purpose can have. Is an instrument of this sort produced? We shall see it striking against one or other of them in every line. The first is what the framers will most guard against, in proportion to their reach of thought, and to their knowledge in this line: when they hit against the other, it will be by accident and unawares.

Lastly, it cannot with any good effect answer the only remaining intention, *viz*. that of a check to restrain as well as to guide the legislature itself, in the penning of the laws of detail that are to follow.

The mistake has its source in the current logic, and in the want of attention to the distinction between what is first in the order of demonstration, and what is first in the order of invention. Principles, it is said, ought to precede consequences; and the first being established, the others will follow of course. What are the principles here meant? General propositions, and those of the widest extent. What by consequences? Particular propositions, included under those general ones.

That this order is favourable to demonstration, if by demonstration be meant personal debate and argumentation, is true enough. Why? Because, if you can once get a man to admit the general proposition, he cannot, without incurring the reproach of inconsistency, reject a particular proposition that is included in it.

But, that this order is not the order of conception, of investigation, of invention, is equally undeniable. In this order, particular propositions always precede general ones. The assent to the latter is preceded by and grounded on the assent to the former.

If we prove the consequences from the principle, it is only from the consequences that we learn the principle.

Apply this to laws. The first business, according to the plan I am combating, is to find and declare the principles: the laws of a fundamental nature: that done, it is by their means that we shall be enabled to find the proper laws of detail. I say, no: it is only in proportion as we have formed and compared with one another the laws of detail, that our fundamental laws will be exact and fit for service. Is a general proposition true? It is because all the particular propositions that are included under it are true. How, then, are we to satisfy ourselves of the truth of the general one? By having under our eye all the included particular ones. What, then, is the order of investigation by which true general propositions are formed? We take a number of less extensive – of particular propositions; find some points in which they agree, and from the observation of these points form a more extensive one, a general one, in which they are all included. In this way, we proceed upon sure grounds, and understand ourselves as we go: in the opposite way, we proceed at random, and danger attends every step.

No law is good which does not add more to the general mass of felicity than it takes from it. No law ought to be made that does not add more to the general mass of felicity than it takes from it. No law can be made that does not take something from liberty; those excepted which take away, in the whole or in part, those laws which take from liberty. Propositions to the first effect I see are true without any exception: propositions to the latter effect I see are not true till after the particular propositions intimated by the exceptions are taken out of it. These propositions I have attained a full satisfaction of the truth of. How? By the habit I have been in for a course of years, of taking any law at pleasure, and observing that the particular proposition relative to that law was always conformable to the fact announced by the general one.

So in the other example. I discerned in the first instance, in a faint way, that two classes would serve to comprehend all laws: laws which take from liberty in their immediate operation, and laws which in the same way destroy, in part or in the whole, the operation of the former. The perception was at first obscure, owing to the difficulty of ascertaining what constituted in every case a law, and of tracing out its operation. By repeated trials, I came at last to be able to show of any law which offered itself, that it came under one or other of those classes.

What follows? That the proper order is – first to digest the laws of detail, and when they are settled and found to be fit for use, then, and not till then, to select and frame *in terminis*, by abstraction, such propositions as may be capable of being given without self-contradiction as fundamental laws.

What is the source of this premature anxiety to establish fundamental laws? It is the old conceit of being wiser than all posterity – wiser than those who will have had more experience, – the old desire of ruling over posterity – the old recipe for enabling the dead to chain down the living. In the case of a specific law, the absurdity of such a notion is pretty well recognised, yet there the absurdity is much less than here. Of a particular law, the nature may be fully comprehended – the consequences foreseen: of a general law, this is the less likely to be the case, the greater the degree in which it possesses the quality of a general one. By a law of which you are fully master, and see clearly to the extent of, you will not attempt to bind succeeding legislators: the law you pitch upon in preference for this purpose, is one which you are unable to see to the end of.

Ought no such general propositions, then, to be ever framed till after the establishment of a complete code? I do not mean to assert this; on the contrary, in morals as in physics, nothing is to be done without them. The more they are framed and tried, the better: only, when framed, they ought to be well tried before they are ushered abroad into the world in the character of laws. In that character they ought not to be exhibited till after they have been confronted with all the particular laws to which the force of them is to apply. But if the intention be to chain down the legislator, these will be all the laws without exception which are looked upon as proper to be inserted in the code. For the interdiction meant to be put upon him is unlimited: he is never to establish any law which shall disagree with the pattern cut out for him – which shall ever trench upon such and such rights.

Such indigested and premature establishments betoken two things – the weakness of the understanding, and the violence of the passions: the weakness of the understanding, in not seeing the insuperable incongruities which have been above stated – the violence of the passions, which betake themselves to such weapons for subduing opposition at any rate, and giving to the will of every man who embraces the proposition imported by the article in question, a weight beyond what is its just and intrinsic due. In vain would man seek to cover his weakness by positive and assuming language: the expression of one opinion, the expression of one will, is the utmost that any proposition can amount to. Ought and ought not, can and can not, shall and shall not, all put together, can never amount to anything more. 'No law ought to be made, which will lessen upon the whole the mass of general felicity.' When I, a legislator or private citizen, say this, what is the simple matter of fact that is expressed? This, and this only, that a sentiment of dissatisfaction is excited in my breast by any such law. So again – 'No law shall be made, which wlll lessen upon the whole the mass of general felicity.' What does this signify? That the sentiment of dissatisfaction in me is so strong as to have given birth to a determined will that no such law should ever pass, and that determination so strong as to have produced a resolution on my part to oppose myself, as far as depends on me, to the passing of it, should it ever be attempted – a determination which is the more likely to meet with success, in proportion to the influence, which in the character of legislator or any other, my mind happens to possess over the minds of others.

'No law *can* be made which will do as above.' What does this signify? The same will as before, only wrapped up in an absurd and insidious disguise. My will is here so strong, that, as a means of seeing it crowned with success, I use my influence with the persons concerned to persuade them to consider a law which, at the same time, I suppose to be made, in the same point of view as if it were not made; and consequently, to pay no more obedience to it than if it were the command of an unauthorized individual. To compass this design, I make the absurd choice of a term expressive in its original and proper import of a physical impossibility, in order to represent as impossible the very event of the occurrence of which I am apprehensive: occupied with the contrary persuasion, I raise my voice to the people – tell them the thing is impossible; and they are to have the goodness to believe me, and act in consequence.

A law to the effect in question is a violation of the natural and indefeasible rights of man. What does this signify? That my resolution of using my utmost influence in opposition to such a law is wound up to such a pitch, that should any law be ever enacted, which in my eyes appears to come up to that description, my determination is, to behave to the persons concerned in its enactment, as any man would behave towards those who had been guilty of a notorious and violent infraction of his rights. If necessary, I would corporally oppose them – if necessary, in short, I would endeavour to kill them; just as, to save my own life, I would endeavour to kill anyone who was endeavouring to kill me.

These several contrivances for giving to an increase in vehemence, the effect of an increase in strength of argument, may be styled *bawling* upon paper: it proceeds from the same temper and the same sort of distress as produces bawling with the voice.

That they should be such efficacious recipes is much to be regretted; that they will always be but too much so, is much to be apprehended; but that they will be less and less so, as intelligence spreads and reason matures, is devoutly to be wished, and not unreasonably to be hoped for.

As passions are contagious, and the bulk of men are more guided by the opinions and pretended opinions of others than by their own, a large share of confidence, with a little share of argument, will be apt to go farther than all the argument in the world without confidence: and hence it is, that modes of expression like these, which owe the influence they unhappily possess to the confidence they display, have met with such general reception. That they should fall into discredit, is, if the reasons above given have any force, devoutly to be wished: and for the accomplishing this good end, there cannot be any method so effectual – or rather, there cannot be any other method, than that of unmasking them in the manner here attempted.

The phrases *can* and *can not*, are employed in this way with greater and more pernicious effect, inasmuch as, over and above physical and moral impossibility, they are made use of with much less impropriety and violence to denote legal impossibility. In the language of the law, speaking in the character of the law, they are used in this way without ambiguity or inconvenience. 'Such a magistrate cannot do so and so', that is, he has no power to do so and so. If he issue a command to such an effect, it is no more to be obeyed than if it issued from any private person. But when the same expression is applied to the very power which is acknowl-edged to be supreme, and not limited by any specific institution, clouds of ambiguity and confusion roll on in a torrent almost impossible to be withstood. Shuffled backwards and forwards amidst these three species of impossibility – physical, legal, and moral – the mind can find no resting-place: it loses its footing altogether, and becomes an easy prey to the violence which wields these arms.

The expedient is the more powerful, inasmuch as, where it does not succeed so far as to gain a man and carry him over to that side, it will perplex him and prevent his finding his way to the other: it will leave him neutral, though it should fail of making him a friend.

It is the better calculated to produce this effect, inasmuch as nothing can tend more powerfully to draw a man altogether out of the track of reason and out of sight of utility, the only just standard for trying all sorts of moral questions. Of a positive assertion thus irrational, the natural effect, where it fails of producing irrational acquiescence, is to produce equally irrational denial, by which no light is thrown upon the subject, nor any opening pointed out through which light may come. I say, the law cannot do so and so: you say, it can. When we have said thus much on each side, it is to no purpose to say more; there we are completely at a stand: argument such as this can go no further on either side, – or neither yields, – or passion triumphs alone – the stronger sweeping the weaker away.

Change the language, and instead of *cannot*, put *ought not*, – the case is widely different. The moderate expression of opinion and will intimated by this phrase, leads naturally to the inquiry after a reason – and this reason, if there be any at bottom that deserves the name, is always a proposition of fact relative to the question of utility. Such a law *ought not* to be established, because it is not consistent with the general welfare – its tendency is not to add to the general stock of happiness. I say, it ought not to be established; that is, I do not approve of its being established: the emotion excited in my mind by the idea of its establishment, is not that of satisfaction, but the contrary. How happens this? Because the production of inconvenience, more than equivalent to any advantage that will ensue, presents itself to my conception in the character of a probable event. Now the question is put, as every political and moral question ought to be, upon the issue of fact; and mankind are directed into the only true track of investigation which can afford instruction or hope of rational argument, the track of experiment and observation. Agreement, to be sure, is not even then made certain: for certainty belongs not to human affairs. But the track, which of all others bids fairest for leading to agreement, is pointed out: a clue for bringing back the travellers, in case of doubt or difficulty, is presented; and, at any rate, they are not struck motionless at the first step.

Nothing would be more unjust or more foreign to my design, than taking occasion, from anything that has been said, to throw particular blame upon particular persons: reproach which strikes everybody, hurts nobody; and common error, where it does not, according to the maxim of English law, produce common right, is productive at least of common exculpation.

A Critical Examination of the Declaration of Rights

§ Preliminary observations

The Declaration of Rights - I mean the paper published under that name by the French National Assembly in 1791 – assumes for its subject-matter a field of disquisition as unbounded in point of extent as it is important in its nature. But the more ample the extent given to any proposition or string of propositions, the more difficult it is to keep the import of it confined without deviation, within the bounds of truth and reason. If in the smallest corners of the field it ranges over, it fail of coinciding with the line of rigid rectitude, no sooner is the aberration pointed out, than (inasmuch as there is no medium between truth and falsehood) its pretensions to the appellation of a truism are gone, and whoever looks upon it must recognise it to be false and erroneous, – and if, as here, political conduct be the theme, so far as the error extends and fails of being detected, pernicious.

In a work of such extreme importance with a view to practice, and which throughout keeps practice so closely and immediately and professedly in view, a single error may be attended with the most fatal consequences. The more extensive the propositions, the more consummate will be the knowledge, the more exquisite the skill, indispensably requisite to confine them in all points within the pale of truth. The most consummate ability in the whole nation could not have been too much for the task – one may venture to say, it would not have been equal to it. But that, in the sanctioning of each proposition, the most consummate ability should happen to be vested in the heads of the sorry majority in whose hands the plenitude of power happened on that same occasion to be vested, is an event against which the chances are almost as infinity to one.

Here, then, is a radical and all-pervading error – the attempting to give to a work on such a subject the sanction of government; especially of such a government – a government composed of members so numerous, so unequal in talent, as well as discordant in inclinations and affections. Had it been the work of a single hand, and that a private one, and in that character given to the world, every good effect would have been produced by it that could be produced by it when published as the work of government, without any of the bad effects which in case of the smallest error must result from it when given as the work of government.

The revolution, which threw the government into the hands of the penners and adopters of this declaration, having been the effect of insurrection, the grand object evidently is to justify the cause. But by justifying it, they invite it: in justifying past insurrection, they plant and cultivate a propensity to perpetual insurrection in time future; they sow the seeds of anarchy broadcast: in justifying the demolition of existing authorities, they undermine all future ones, their own consequently in the number. Shallow and reckless vanity! – They imitate in their conduct the author of that fabled law, according to which the assassination of the prince upon the throne gave to the assassin a title to succeed him. '*People, behold your rights! If a single article of them be violated, insurrection is not your right only, but the most sacred of your duties.*' Such is the constant language, for such is the professed object of this source and model of all laws – this self-consecrated oracle of all nations.

The more *abstract* – that is, the more *extensive* the proposition is, the more liable is it to involve a fallacy. Of fallacies, one of the most natural modifications is that which is called *begging the question* – the abuse of making the abstract proposition resorted to for proof, a lever for introducing, in the company of *other* propositions that are nothing to the purpose, the very proposition which is admitted to stand in need of proof.

Is the provision in question fit in point of expediency to be passed into a law for the government of the French nation? That, *mutatis mutandis*, would have been the question put in England: that was the proper question to have been put in relation to each provision it was proposed should enter into the composition of the body of French laws.

Instead of that, as often as the utility of a provision appeared (by reason of the wideness of its extent, for instance) of a doubtful nature, the way taken to clear the doubt was to assert it to be a provision fit to be made law for all men – for all Frenchmen – and for all Englishmen, for example, into the bargain. This medium of proof was the more alluring, inasmuch as to the advantage of removing opposition, was added the pleasure, the sort of titillation so exquisite to the nerve of vanity in a French heart – the satisfaction, to use a homely, but not the less apposite proverb, of teaching grandmothers to suck eggs. Hark! ye citizens of the other side of the water! Can you tell us what rights you have belonging to you? No, that you can't. It's *we* that understand rights: not our own only, but yours into the bargain; while you, poor simple souls! know nothing about the matter.

Hasty generalization, the great stumbling-block of intellectual vanity! – hasty generalization, the rock that even genius itself is so apt to split upon! – hasty generalization, the bane of prudence and of science!

In the British Houses of Parliament, more especially in the most efficient house for business, there prevails a well-known jealousy of, and repugnance to, the voting of abstract propositions. This jealousy is not less general than reasonable. A jealousy of abstract propositions is an aversion to whatever is beside the purpose – an aversion to impertinence.

The great enemies of public peace are the selfish and dissocial passions – necessary as they are, the one to the very existence of each individual, the other to his security. On the part of these affections, a deficiency in point of strength is never to be apprehended: all that is to be apprehended in respect of them, is to be apprehended on the side of their excess. Society is held together only by the sacrifices that men can be induced to make of the gratifications they demand: to obtain these sacrifices is the great difficulty, the great task of government. What has been the object, the perpetual and palpable object, of this declaration of pretended rights? To add as much force as possible to these passions, already but too strong, – to burst the cords that hold them in, – to say to the selfish passions, there – everywhere – is your prey! – to the angry passions, there – everywhere – is your enemy.

Such is the morality of this celebrated manifesto, rendered

famous by the same qualities that gave celebrity to the incendiary of the Ephesian temple.

The logic of it is of a piece with its morality: a perpetual vein of nonsense, flowing from a perpetual abuse of words, – words having a variety of meanings, where words with single meanings were equally at hand – the same words used in a variety of meanings in the same page, – words used in meanings not their own, where proper words were equally at hand, – words and propositions of the most unbounded signification, turned loose without any of those exceptions or modifications which are so necessary on every occasion to reduce their import within the compass, not only of right reason, but even of the design in hand, of whatever nature it may be; – the same inaccuracy, the same inattention in the penning of this cluster of truths on which the fate of nations was to hang, as if it had been an oriental tale, or an allegory for a magazine: stale epigrams, instead of necessary distractions, – figurative expressions preferred to simple ones, – sentimental conceits, as trite as they are unmeaning, preferred to apt and precise expressions, – frippery ornament preferred to the majestic simplicity of good sound sense, – and the acts of the senate loaded and disfigured by the tinsel of the playhouse.

In a play or a novel, an improper word is but a word: and the impropriety, whether noticed or not, is attended with no consequences. In a body of laws – especially of laws given as constitutional and fundamental ones – an improper word may be a national calamity: and civil war may be the consequence of it. Out of one foolish word may start a thousand daggers.

Imputations like these may appear general and declamatory – and rightly so, if they stood alone: but they will be justified even to satiety by the details that follow. Scarcely an article, which in rummaging it, will not be found a true Pandora's box.

In running over the several articles, I shall on the occasion of each article point out, in the first place, the errors it contains in theory; and then, in the second place, the mischiefs it is pregnant with in practice.

The criticism is verbal: true, but what else can it be? Words – words without a meaning, or with a meaning too flatly false to be maintained by anybody, are the stuff it is made of. Look to the letter, you find nonsense – look beyond the letter, you find nothing.

§ *Article 1*

Men [all men] are born and remain free, and equal in respect of rights.
Social distinctions cannot be founded, but upon common utility.

In this article are contained, grammatically speaking, two
distinct sentences. The first is full of error, the other of ambiguity.

In the first are contained four distinguishable propositions, all of
them false – all of them notoriously and undeniably false:

1   That all men are born free.
2   That all men remain free.
3   That all men are born equal in rights.
4   That all men remain (*i.e.* remain for ever, for the pro-
    position is indefinite and unlimited) equal in rights.

All men are born free? All men remain free? No, not a single man:
not a single man that ever was, or is, or will be. All men, on the
contrary, are born in subjection, and the most absolute subjection – the subjection of a helpless child to the parents on whom he
depends every moment for his existence. In this subjection every
man is born – in this subjection he continues for years – for a great
number of years – and the existence of the individual and of the
species depends upon his so doing.

What is the state of things to which the supposed existence of
these supposed rights is meant to bear reference? – a state of things
prior to the existence of government, or a state of things
subsequent to the existence of government? If to a state prior to
the existence of government, what would the existence of such
rights as these be to the purpose, even if it were true, in any
country where there is such a thing as government? If to a state of
things subsequent to the formation of government – if in a
country where there is a government, in what single instance – in
the instance of what single government, is it true? Setting aside
the case of parent and child, let any man name that single
government under which any such equality is recognised.

All men born free? Absurd and miserable nonsense! When the
great complaint – a complaint made perhaps by the very same
people at the same time, is – that so many men are born slaves.
Oh! but when we acknowledge them to be born slaves, we refer
to the laws in being; which laws being void, as being contrary to

those laws of nature which are the efficient causes of those rights of man that we are declaring, the men in question are free in one sense, though slaves in another; – slaves, and free, at the same time: free in respect of the laws of nature – slaves in respect of the pretended human laws, which, though called laws, are no laws at all, as being contrary to the laws of nature. For such is the difference – the great and perpetual difference, betwixt the good subject, the rational censor of the laws, and the anarchist – between the moderate man and the man of violence. The rational censor, acknowledging the existence of the law he disapproves, proposes the repeal of it: the anarchist, setting up his will and fancy for a law before which all mankind are called upon to bow down at the first word – the anarchist, trampling on truth and decency, denies the validity of the law in question, – denies the existence of it in the character of a law, and calls upon all mankind to rise up in a mass, and resist the execution of it.

Whatever is, is – was the maxim of Descartes, who looked upon it as so sure, as well as so instructive a truth, that everything else which goes by the name of truth might be deduced from it. The philosophical vortex-maker – who, however mistaken in his philosophy and his logic, was harmless enough at least – the manufacturer of identical propositions and celestial vortices – little thought how soon a part of his own countrymen, fraught with pretensions as empty as his own, and as mischievous as his were innocent, would contest with him even this his favourite and fundamental maxim, by which everything else was to be brought to light. *Whatever is, is not* – is the maxim of the anarchist, as often as anything comes across him in the shape of a law which he happens not to like.

'Cruel is the judge,' says Lord Bacon, 'who, in order to enable himself to torture men, applies torture to the law.' Still more cruel is the anarchist, who, for the purpose of effecting the subversion of the laws themselves, as well as the massacre of the legislators, tortures not only the words of the law, but the very vitals of the language.

All men are born equal in rights. The rights of the heir of the most indigent family equal to the rights of the heir of the most wealthy? In what case is this true? I say nothing of hereditary *dignities* and *powers*. Inequalities such as these being proscribed under and by the French government in France, are consequently proscribed by that government under every other government, and consequently have no existence anywhere. For the total subjection of every other government to French government, is a fundamental principle in the law of universal independence – the French law. Yet neither was this true at the time of issuing this Declaration of Rights, nor was it meant to be so afterwards. The 13th article, which we shall come to in its place, proceeds on the contrary supposition: for, considering its other attributes, inconsistency could not be wanting to the list. It can scarcely be more hostile to all other laws than it is at variance with itself.

. *All men* (*i.e.* all human creatures of both sexes) *remain equal in rights.* All men, meaning doubtless all human creatures. The apprentice, then, is equal in rights to his master; he has as much liberty with relation to the master, as the master has with relation to him; he has as much right to command and to punish him; he is as much owner and master of the master's house, as the master himself. The case is the same as between ward and guardian. So again as between wife and husband. The madman has as good a right to confine anybody else, as anybody else has to confine him. The idiot has as much right to govern everybody, as anybody can have to govern him. The physician and the nurse, when called in by the next friend of a sick man seized with a delirium, have no more right to prevent his throwing himself out of the window, than he has to throw them out of it. All this is plainly and incontestably included in this article of the Declaration of Rights: in the very words of it, and in the meaning – if it have any meaning. Was this the meaning of the authors of it? – or did they mean to admit this explanation as to some of the instances, and to explain the article away as to the rest? Not being idiots, nor lunatics, nor under a delirium, they would explain it away with regard to the madman, and the man under a delirium. Considering that a child may become an orphan as soon as it has seen the light, and that in that case, if not subject to government, it must perish, they would explain it away, I think, and contradict themselves, in the case of guardian and ward. In the case of master and apprentice, I would not take upon me to decide: it may have been their meaning to proscribe that relation altogether; – at least, this may have been the case, as soon as the repugnancy between that institution and this oracle was pointed out; for the professed object and destination of it is to be the standard of truth and falsehood, of right and wrong, in everything that relates to government. But to this standard, and to this article of it, the subjection of the apprentice to the master is flatly and diametrically repugnant. If it do not proscribe and exclude this inequality, it proscribes none: if it do not do this mischief, it does nothing.

So, again, in the case of husband and wife. Amongst the other abuses which the oracle was meant to put an end to, may, for aught I can pretend to say, have been the institution of marriage. For what is the subjection of a small and limited number of years, in comparison of the subjection of a whole life? Yet without subjection and inequality, no such institution can by any possibility take place; for of two contradictory wills, both cannot take effect at the same time.

The same doubts apply to the case of master and hired servant. Better a man should starve than hire himself; – better half the species starve, than hire itself out to service. For, where is the compatibility between liberty and servitude? How can liberty and servitude subsist in the same person? What good citizen is there, that would hesitate to die for liberty? And, as to those who are not good citizens, what matters it whether they live or starve? Besides that every man who lives under this constitution being equal in rights, equal in all sorts of rights, is equal in respect to rights of property. No man, therefore, can be in any danger of starving – no man can have so much as that motive, weak and inadequate as it is, for hiring himself out to service.

Sentence 2. *Social distinctions cannot be founded but upon common utility.* – This proposition has two or three meanings. According to one of them, the proposition is notoriously false: according to another, it is in contradiction to the four propositions that preceded it in the same sentence.

What is meant by *social distinctions*? What is meant by *can*? What is meant by *founded*?

What is meant by *social distinctions*? – Distinctions not respecting equality? – then these are nothing to the purpose. Distinctions in respect of equality? – then, consistently with the preceding propositions in this same article, they can have no existence: not existing, they cannot be founded upon anything. The distinctions above exemplified, are they in the number of the social distinctions here intended? Not one of them (as we have been seeing,) but has subjection – not one of them, but has inequality for its very essence.

What is meant by *can* – can not be founded but upon common utility? Is it meant to speak of what *is* established, or of what *ought to be* established? Does it mean that no social distinctions, but those which it approves as having the foundation in question, are established anywhere? Or simply that none such *ought to be* established anywhere? Or that, if the establishment or maintenance of such dispositions by the laws be attempted anywhere, such laws ought to be treated as void, and the attempt to execute them to be resisted? For such is the venom that lurks under such words as *can* and *cannot*, when set up as a check upon the laws,– they contain all these three so perfectly distinct and widely different meanings. In the first, the proposition they are inserted into refers to practice, and makes appeal to observation – to the observation of other men, in regard to a matter of fact: in the second, it is an appeal to the approving faculty of others, in regard to the same matter of fact: in the third, it is no appeal to anything, or to anybody, but a violent attempt upon the liberty of speech and action on the part of others, by the terrors of anarchical despotism, rising up in opposition to the laws: it is an attempt to lift the dagger of the assassin against all individuals who presume to hold an opinion different from that of the orator or the writer, and against all governments which presume to support any such individuals in any such presumption. In the first of these imports, the proposition is perfectly harmless: but it is commonly so untrue, so glaringly untrue, so palpably untrue, even to drivelling, that it must be plain to everybody it can never have been the meaning that was intended.

In the second of these imports, the proposition may be true or not, as it may happen, and at any rate is equally innocent: but it is such as will not answer the purpose; for an opinion that leaves others at liberty to be of a contrary one, will never answer the purpose of the passions: and if this had been the meaning intended, not this ambiguous phraseology, but a clear and simple one, presenting this meaning and no other, would have been employed. The third, which may not improperly be termed the *ruffian-like* or threatening import, is the meaning intended to be presented to the weak and timid, while the two innocent ones, of which one may even be reasonable, are held up before it as a veil to blind the eyes of the discerning reader, and screen from him the mischief that lurks beneath.

Can and *can not*, when thus applied – *can* and *can not*, when used instead of *ought* and *ought not* – *can* and *can not*, when applied to the binding force and effect of laws, not of the acts of individuals, nor yet of the acts of subordinate authority, but of the acts of the supreme government itself, are the disguised cant of the assassin: after them there is nothing but *do him*, betwixt the preparation for murder and the attempt. They resemble that instrument which in outward appearance is but an ordinary staff, but which within that simple and innocent semblance conceals a dagger. These are the words that speak daggers – if daggers can be spoken: they speak daggers, and there remains nothing but to use them.

Look where I will, I see but too many laws, the alteration or abolition of which, would in my poor judgment be a public blessing. I can conceive some, – to put extreme and scarcely exampled cases, – to which I might be inclined to oppose resistance, with a prospect of support such as promised to be effectual. But to talk of what the law, the supreme legislature of the country, acknowledged as such, *can* not do ! – to talk of a *void* law as you would of a *void* order or a *void* judgment! – The very act of bringing such words into conjunction is either the vilest of nonsense, or the worst of treasons: treason, not against one branch of the sovereignty, but against the whole: treason, not against this or that government, but against *all* governments.

§ *Article 2*

The end in view of every political association is the preservation of the natural and imprescriptible rights of man. These rights are liberty, property, security, and resistance to oppression.

Sentence 1. The end in view of every political association, is the preservation of the natural and imprescriptible rights of man.

More confusion – more nonsense, – and the nonsense, as usual, dangerous nonsense. The words can scarcely be said to have a

meaning: but if they have, or rather if they had a meaning, these
would be the propositions either asserted or implied:

1   That there are such things as rights anterior to the
establishment of governments: for natural, as applied to rights,
if it mean anything, is meant to stand in opposition to *legal* – to
such rights as are acknowledged to owe their existence to
government, and are consequently posterior in their date to
the establishment of government.

2   That these rights *can not* be abrogated by government: for
can not is implied in the form of the word imprescriptible, and
the sense it wears when so applied, is the cut-throat sense
above explained.

3   That the governments that exist derive their origin from
formal associations, or what are now called *conventions*: associations entered into by a partnership contract, with all the
members for partners, – entered into at a day prefixed, for a
predetermined purpose, the formation of a new government
where there was none before (for as to formal meetings holden
under the control of an existing government, they are evidently out of question here) in which it seems again to be
implied in the way of inference, though a necessary and an
unavoidable inference, that all governments (that is, self-called
governments, knots of persons exercising the powers of
government) that have had any other origin than an association of the above description, are illegal, that is, no
governments at all; resistance to them, and subversion of
them, lawful and commendable; and so on.

Such are the notions implied in this first part of the article. How
stands the truth of things? That there are no such things as natural
rights – no such things as rights anterior to the establishment of
government – no such things as natural rights opposed to, in
contradistinction to, legal: that the expression is merely figurative;
that when used, in the moment you attempt to give it a literal
meaning it leads to error, and to that sort of error that leads to
mischief – to the extremity of mischief.

We know what it is for men to live without government – and
living without government, to live without rights: we know
what, it is for men to live without government, for we see
instances of such a way of life – we see it in many savage nations,

or rather races of mankind; for instance, among the savages of New South Wales, whose way of living is so well known to us: no habit of obedience, and thence no government – no government, and thence no laws – no laws, and thence no such things as rights – no security – no property: liberty, as against regular control, the control of laws and government – perfect; but as against all irregular control, the mandates of stronger individuals, none. In this state, at a time earlier than the commencement of history – in this same state, judging from analogy, we, the inhabitants of the part of the globe we call Europe, were; – no government, consequently no rights; no rights, consequently no property – no legal security – no legal liberty: security not more than belongs to beasts – forecast and sense of insecurity keener – consequently in point of happiness below the level of the brutal race.

In proportion to the want of happiness resulting from the want of rights, a reason exists for wishing that there were such things as rights. But reasons for wishing there were such things as rights, are not rights; – a reason for wishing that a certain right were established, is not that right – want is not supply – hunger is not bread.

That which has no existence cannot be destroyed – that which cannot be destroyed cannot require anything to preserve it from destruction. *Natural rights* is simple nonsense: natural and imprescriptible rights, rhetorical nonsense, – nonsense upon stilts. But this rhetorical nonsense ends in the old strain of mischievous nonsense: for immediately a list of these pretended natural rights is given, and those are so expressed as to present to view legal rights. And of these rights, whatever they are, there is not, it seems, any one of which any government *can*, upon any occasion whatever, abrogate the smallest particle.

So much for terrorist language. What is the language of reason and plain sense upon this same subject? That in proportion as it is *right* or *proper*, *i.e.* advantageous to the society in question, that this or that right – a right to this or that effect – should be established and maintained, in that same proportion it is *wrong* that it should be abrogated: but that as there is no *right*, which ought not to be maintained so long as it is upon the whole advantageous to the society that it should be maintained, so there is no right which, when the abolition of it is advantageous to society, should not be abolished. To know whether it would be more for the advantage of society that this or that right should be maintained or abolished, the time at which the question about maintaining or abolishing is proposed, must be given, and the circumstances under which it is proposed to maintain or abolish it; the right itself must be specifically described, not jumbled with an undistinguishable heap of others, under any such vague general terms as property, liberty, and the like.

One timing, in the midst of all this confusion, is but too plain. They know not of what they are talking under the name of natural rights, and yet they would have them imprescriptible – proof against all the power of the laws – pregnant with occasions summoning the members of the community to rise up in resistance against the laws. What, then, was their object in declaring the existence of imprescriptible rights, and without specifying a single one by any such mark as it could be known by? This and no other – to excite and keep up a spirit of resistance to all laws – a spirit of insurrection against all governments – against the governments of all other nations instantly, – against the government of their own nation – against the government they themselves were pretending to establish – even that, as soon as their own reign should be at an end. In us is the perfection of virtue and wisdom: in all mankind besides, the extremity of wickedness and folly. Our will shall consequently reign without control, and for ever: reign now we are living – reign after we are dead.

All nations – all future ages – shall be, for they are predestined to be, our slaves.

Future governments will not have honesty enough to be trusted with the determination of what rights shall be maintained, what abrogated – what laws kept in force, what repealed. Future subjects (I should say future citizens, for French government does not admit of subjects) will not have wit enough to be trusted with the choice whether to submit to the determination of the government of their time, or to resist it. Governments, citizens – all to the end of time – all must be kept in chains.

Such are their maxims – such their premises – for it is by such premises only that the doctrine of imprescriptible rights and unrepealable laws can be supported.

What is the real source of these imprescriptible rights – these unrepealable laws? Power turned blind by looking from its own height: self-conceit and tyranny exalted into insanity. No man was to have any other man for a servant, yet all men were forever to be their slaves. Making laws with imposture in their mouths, under pretence of declaring them – giving for laws anything that came uppermost, and these unrepealable ones, on pretence of finding them ready made. Made by what? Not by a God – they allow of none; but by their goddess, Nature.

The origination of governments from a contract is a pure fiction, or in other words, a falsehood. It never has been known to be true in any instance; the allegation of it does mischief, by involving the subject in error and confusion, and is neither necessary nor useful to any good purpose.

All governments that we have any account of have been gradually established by habit, after having been formed by force; unless in the instance of governments formed by individuals who have been emancipated, or have emancipated themselves, from governments already formed, the governments under which they were born – a rare case, and from which nothing follows with regard to the rest. What signifies it how governments are formed? Is it the less proper – the less conducive to the happiness of society – that the happiness of society should be the one object kept in view by the members of the government in all their measures? Is it the less the interest of men to be happy – less to be wished that they may be so – less the moral duty of their governors to make them so, as far as they can, at Mogadore than at Philadelphia?

Whence is it, but from government, that contracts derive their binding force? Contracts came from government, not government from contracts. It is from the habit of enforcing contracts, and seeing them enforced, that governments are chiefly indebted for whatever disposition they have to observe them.

Sentence 2. These rights [these imprescriptible as well as natural rights] are liberty, property, security, and resistance to oppression.

Observe the extent of these pretended rights, each of them belonging to every man, and all of them without bounds. Unbounded liberty; that is, amongst other things, the liberty of doing or not doing on every occasion whatever each man pleases –

Unbounded property; that is, the right of doing with everything around him (with every *thing* at least, if not with every person,) whatsoever he pleases; communicating that right to anybody, and withholding it from anybody – Unbounded security; that is, security for such his liberty, for such his property, and for his person, against every defalcation that can be called for on any account in respect of any of them – Unbounded resistance to oppression; that is, unbounded exercise of the faculty of guarding himself against whatever unpleasant circumstance may present itself to his imagination or his passions under that name. Nature, say some of the interpreters of the pretended law of nature – nature gave to each man a right to everything; which is, in effect, but another way of saying – nature has given no such right to anybody; for in regard to most rights, it is as true that what is every man's right is no man's right, as that what is every man's business is no man's business. Nature gave – gave to every man a right to everything – be it so – true; and hence the necessity of human government and human laws, to give to every man his own right, without which no right whatsoever would amount to anything. Nature gave every man a right to everything before the existence of laws, and in default of laws. This nominal universality and real nonentity of right, set up provisionally by nature in default of laws, the French oracle lays hold of, and perpetuates it under the law and in spite of laws. These anarchical rights which nature had set out with, democratic art attempts to rivet down, and declares indefeasible.

Unbounded liberty – I must still say unbounded liberty; – for though the next article but one returns to the charge, and gives such a definition of liberty as seems intended to set bounds to it, yet in effect the limitation amounts to nothing; and when, as here, no warning is given of any exception in the texture of the general rule, every exception which turns up is, not a confirmation but a contradiction of the rule: liberty, without any pre-announced or intelligible bounds; and as to the other rights, they remain unbounded to the end: rights of man composed of a system of contradictions and impossibilities.

In vain would it be said, that though no bounds are here assigned to any of these rights, yet it is to be understood as taken for granted, and tacitly admitted and assumed, that they are to have bounds; viz. such bounds as it is understood will be set them by the laws. Vain, I say, would be this apology; for the supposition would be contradictory to the express declaration of the article itself, and would defeat the very object which the whole declaration has in view. It would be self-contradictory, because these rights are, in the same breath in which their existence is declared, declared to be imprescriptible; and imprescriptible, or, as we in England should say, indefeasible, means nothing unless it exclude the interference of the laws.

It would be not only inconsistent with itself, but inconsistent with the declared and sole object of the declaration, if it did not exclude the interference of the laws. It is against the laws themselves, and the laws only, that this declaration is levelled. It is for the hands of the legislator and all legislators, and none but legislators, that the shackles it provides are intended, – it is against the apprehended encroachments of legislators that the rights in question, the liberty and property, and so forth, are intended to be made secure, – it is to such encroachments, and damages, and dangers, that whatever security it professes to give has respect. Precious security for unbounded rights against legislators if the extent of those rights in every direction were purposely left to depend upon the will and pleasure of those very legislators!

Nonsensical or nugatory, and in both cases mischievous: such is the alternative.

So much for all these pretended indefeasible rights in the lump: their inconsistency with each other, as well as the inconsistency of them in the character of indefeasible rights with the existence of government and all peaceable society, will appear still more plainly when we examine them one by one.

1. *Liberty*, then, is imprescriptible – incapable of being taken away – out of the power of any government ever to take away: liberty, – that is, every branch of liberty – every individual exercise of liberty; for no line is drawn – no distinction – no exception made. What these instructors as well as governors of mankind appear not to know, is, that all rights are made at the expense of liberty – all laws by which rights are created or confirmed. No right without a correspondent obligation. Liberty, as against the coercion of the law, may, it is true, be given by the simple removal of the obligation by which that coercion was

applied – by the simple repeal of the coercing law. But as against the coercion applicable by individual to individual, no liberty can be given to one man but in proportion as it is taken from another. All coercive laws, therefore (that is, all laws but constitutional laws, and laws repealing or modifying coercive laws,) and in particular all laws creative of liberty, are, as far as they go, abrogative of liberty. Not here and there a law only – not this or that possible law, but almost all laws, are therefore repugnant to these natural and imprescriptible rights: consequently null and void, calling for resistance and insurrection, and so on, as before.

Laws creative of rights of property are also struck at by the same anathema. How is property given? By restraining liberty; that is, by taking it away so far as is necessary for the purpose. How is your house made yours? By debarring every one else from the liberty of entering it without your leave. But

2. *Property*. Property stands second on the list, – proprietary rights are in the number of the natural and imprescriptible rights of man – of the rights which a man is not indebted for to the laws, and which cannot be taken from him by the laws. Men – that is, every man (for a general expression given without exception is an universal one) has a right to property, to proprietary rights, *a right which* cannot be taken away from him by the laws. To proprietary rights. Good: but in relation to what subject? For as to proprietary rights – without a subject to which they are referable – without a subject in or in relation to which they can be exercised – they will hardly be of much value, they will hardly be worth taking care of, with so much solemnity. In vain would all the laws in the world have ascertained that I have a right to something. If this be all they have done for me – if there be no specific subject in relation to which my proprietary rights are established, I must either take what I want without right, or starve. As there is no such subject specified with relation to each man, or to any man (indeed how could there be?) the necessary inference (taking the passage literally) is, that every man has all manner of proprietary rights with relation to every subject of property without exception: in a word, that every man has a right to every thing. Unfortunately, in most matters of property, what is every man's right is no man's right; so that the effect of this part of the oracle, if observed, would

be, not to establish property, but to extinguish it – to render it impossible ever to be revived: and this is one of the rights declared to be imprescriptible.

It will probably be acknowledged, that according to this construction, the clause in question is equally ruinous and absurd: and hence the inference may be, that this was not the construction – this was not the meaning in view. But by the same rule, every possible construction which the words employed can admit of, might be proved not to have been the meaning in view: nor is this clause a whit more absurd or ruinous than all that goes before it, and a great deal of what comes after it. And, in short, if this be not the meaning of it, what is? Give it a sense – give it any sense whatever, – it is mischievous: to save it from that imputation, there is but one course to take, which is to acknowledge it to be nonsense.

Thus much would be clear, if anything were clear in it, that according to this clause, whatever proprietary rights, whatever property a man once has, no matter how, being imprescriptible, can never be taken away from him by any law: or of what use or meaning is the clause? So that the moment it is acknowledged in relation to any article, that such article is my property, no matter how or when it became so, that moment it is acknowledged that it can never be taken away from me: therefore, for example, all laws and all judgments, whereby anything is taken away from me without my free consent – all taxes, for example, and all fines – are void, and, as such, call for resistance and insurrection, and so forth, as before.

3. *Security*. Security stands the third on the list of these natural and imprescriptible rights which laws did not give, and which laws are not in any degree to be suffered to take away. Under the head of security, liberty might have been included, so likewise property: since security for liberty, or the enjoyment of liberty, may be spoken of as us branch of security: security for property, or the enjoyment of proprietary rights, as another. Security for person is the branch that seems here to have been understood: security for each man's person, as against all those hurtful or disagreeable impressions (exclusive of those which consist in the mere disturbance of the enjoyment of liberty,) by which a man is affected in

his person; loss of life – loss of limbs – loss of the use of limbs – wounds, bruises, and the like. All laws are null and void, then, which on any account or in any manner seek to expose the person of any man to any risk – which appoint capital or other corporal punishment – which expose a man to personal hazard in the service of the military power against foreign enemies, or in that of the power against delinquents: all laws which, to preserve the country from pestilence, authorize the immediate execution of a suspected person, in the event of his transgressing certain bounds.

4. *Resistance to oppression.* Fourth and last in the list of natural and imprescriptible rights, resistance to oppression – meaning, I suppose, the right to resist oppression. What is oppression? Power misapplied to the prejudice of some individual. What is it that a man has in view when he speaks of oppression? Some exertion of power which he looks upon as misapplied to the prejudice of some individual – to the producing on the part of such individual some suffering, to which (whether as forbidden by the laws or otherwise) we conceive he ought not to have been subjected. But against everything that can come under the name of oppression, provision has been already made, in the manner we have seen, by the recognition of the three preceding rights; since no oppression can fall upon a man which is not an infringement of his rights in relation to liberty, rights in relation to property, or rights in relation to security, as above described. Where, then, is the difference? – to what purpose this fourth clause after the three first? To this purpose: the mischief they seek to prevent, the rights they seek to establish, are the same; the difference lies in the nature of the remedy endeavoured to be applied. To prevent the mischief in question, the endeavour of the three former clauses is, to tie the hand of the legislator and his subordinates, by the fear of nullity, and the remote apprehension of general resistance and insurrection. The aim of this fourth clause is to raise the hand of the individual concerned to prevent the apprehended infraction of his rights at the moment when he looks upon it as about to take place.

Whenever you are about to be oppressed, you have a right to resist oppression: whenever you conceive yourself to be oppressed, conceive yourself to have a right to make resistance, and act accordingly. In proportion as a law of any kind – any act of power, supreme or subordinate, legislative, administrative, or judicial, is unpleasant to a man, especially if, in consideration of such its unpleasantness, his opinion is, that such act of power ought not to have been exercised, he of course looks upon it as oppression: as often as anything of this sort happens to a man – as often as anything happens to a man to inflame his passions, – this article, for fear his passions should not be sufficiently inflamed of themselves, sets itself to work to blow the flame, and urges him to resistance. Submit not to any decree or other act of power, of the justice of which you are not yourself perfectly convinced. If a constable call upon you to serve in the militia, shoot the constable and not the enemy; – if the commander of a press-gang trouble you, push him into the sea – if a bailiff, throw him out of the window. If a judge sentence you to be imprisoned or put to death, have a dagger ready, and take a stroke first at the judge.

§ *Article 3*

The principle of every sovereignty [government] resides essentially in the nation. No body of men – no single individual – can exercise any authority which does not expressly issue from thence.

Of the two sentences of which this article is composed, the first is perfectly true, perfectly harmless, and perfectly uninstructive. Government and obedience go hand-in-hand. Where there is no obedience, there is no government; in proportion as obedience is paid, the powers of government are exercised. This is true under the broadest democracy: this is equally true under the most absolute monarchy. This can do no harm – can do no good, anywhere. I speak of its natural and obvious import taken by itself, and supposing the import of the word principle to be clear and unambiguous, as it is to be wished that it were, that is, taking it to mean *efficient cause*. Of power on the one part, obedience on the other is most certainly everywhere the efficient cause.

But being harmless, it would not answer the purpose, as delivered by the immediately succeeding sentence: being harmless, this meaning is not that which was in view. It is meant as an antecedent proposition, on which the next proposition is grounded in the character of a consequent. No body of men, no individual, can exercise any authority which does not issue from the nation in an express manner. *Can* – still the ambiguous and envenomed *can*. What cannot they in point of fact? Cannot they exercise authority over other people, if and so long as other people submit to it? This cannot be their meaning: this cannot be the meaning, not because it is an untrue and foolish one, but because it contributes nothing to the declared purpose. The meaning must be here, as elsewhere, that of every authority not issuing from the nation in an express manner, every act is void: consequently ought to be treated as such – resisted, risen up against, and overthrown. Issuing from the nation in an express manner, is having been conferred by the nation, by a formal act, in the exercise of which the nation, *i.e.* the whole nation, joined.

An authority issues from the nation in one sense, in the ordinary implied manner, which the nation submits to the exercise of, having been in the habit of submitting to it, every man as long as he can remember, or to some superior authority from which it is derived. But this meaning it was the evident design of the article to put a negative upon; for it would not have answered the disorganizing purpose, all along apparent, and more than once avowed. It is accordingly for the purpose of putting a negative upon it, that the word *expressément – in an express way or manner –* is subjoined. Every authority is usurped and void, to which a man has been appointed in any other mode than that of popular election; and popular election made by the nation – that is, the whole nation (for no distinction or division is intimated,) in each case.

And this is expressly declared to be the case, not only in France, under the government of France, but *everywhere*, and under every government whatsoever. Consequently, all the acts in every government in Europe, for example, are void, excepted, perhaps, or rather not excepted, two or three of the Swiss Cantons; – the persons exercising the powers of government in these countries, usurpers – resistance to them, and insurrection against them, lawful and commendable.

The French government itself not excepted: whatever is, has been, or is to be, the government of France. Issue from the nation: that is, from the whole nation, for no part of it is excluded. Women consequently included, and children – children of every age. For if women and children are not part of the nation, what are they? Cattle? Indeed, how can a single soul be excluded, when all men – all human creatures – are, and are to be, equal in regard to rights – in regard to all sorts of rights, without exception or reserve?

§ *Article 4*

Liberty consists in being able to do that which is not hurtful to another, and therefore the exercise of the natural rights of each man has no other bounds than those which insure to the other members of the society the enjoyment of the same rights. These bounds cannot be determined but by the law.

In this article, three propositions are included.

Proposition 1. Liberty consists in being able to do that which is not hurtful to another. What! In that, and nothing else? Is not the liberty of doing mischief liberty? If not, what is it? And what word is there for it in the language, or in any language by which it can be spoken of? How childish, how repugnant to the ends of language, is this perversion of language – to attempt to confine a word in common and perpetual use, to an import to which nobody ever confined it before, or will continue to confine it! And so I am never to know whether I am at liberty or not to do or to omit doing one act, till I see whether or no there is anybody that may be hurt by it – till I see the whole extent of all its consequences? Liberty! What liberty? – as against what power? As against coercion from what source? As against coercion issuing from the law? – then to know whether the law have left me at liberty in any respect in relation to any act, I am to consult not the words of the law, but my own conception of what would be the consequences of the act. If among these consequences there be a single one by which anybody would be hurt, then, whatever the law says to me about it, I am not at liberty to do it. I am an officer of justice, appointed to superintend the execution of punishments ordered by justice: if I am ordered to cause a thief to be whipped, – to know whether I am at liberty to cause the sentence to be executed, I must know whether whipping would hurt the thief: if it would, then I am not at liberty to whip the thief to inflict the punishment which it is my duty to inflict.

Proposition 2. And therefore the exercise of the natural rights of each man has no other bounds than those which insure to the other members of the society the enjoyment of those same rights. Has no other bounds? Where is it that it has no other bounds? In what nation – under what government? If under any government, their the state of legislation under that government is in a state of absolute perfection. If there be no such government, then, by a confession necessarily implied, there is no nation upon earth in which this definition is conformable to the truth.

Proposition 3. These bounds cannot be determined but by the law. More contradiction, more confusion. What then? – this liberty, this right, which is one of four rights that existed before laws, and will exist in spite of all that laws can do, owes all the boundaries it has, all the extent it has, to the laws. Till you know what the laws say to it, you do not know what there is of it, nor what account to give of it: and yet it existed, and that in full force and vigour, before there were any such things as laws; and so will continue to exist, and that for ever, in spite of anything which laws can do to it. Still the same inaptitude of expressions – still the same confusion of that which it is supposed *is*, with that which it is conceived ought to be.

What says plain truth upon this subject? What is the sense most approaching to this nonsense?

The liberty which the law *ought* to allow of, and leave in existence – leave uncoerced, unremoved – is the liberty which concerns those acts only, by which, if exercised, no damage would be done to the community upon the whole; that is, either no damage at all, or none but what promises to be compensated by at least equal benefit.

Accordingly, the exercise of the rights allowed to and conferred upon each individual, ought to have no other bounds set to it by the law, than those which are necessary to enable it to maintain every other individual in the possession and exercise of such rights as it is consistent with the greatest good of the community that he should be allowed. The marking out of these bounds ought not to be left to anybody but the legislator acting as such – that is, to him or them who are acknowledged to be in possession of the sovereign power; that is, it ought not to be left to the occasional and arbitrary declaration of any individual, whatever share he may possess of subordinate authority.

The word *autrui* – another – is so loose, making no distinction between the community and individuals, – as, according to the most natural construction, to deprive succeeding legislators of all power of repressing, by punishment or otherwise, any acts by which no individual sufferers are to be found; and to deprive them beyond a doubt of all power of affording protection to any man, woman, or child, against his or her own weakness, ignorance, or imprudence.

§ *Article 5*

The law has no right to forbid any other actions than such as are hurtful to society. Whatever is not forbidden by the law, cannot be hindered; nor can any individual be compelled to do that which the law does not command.

Sentence 1. The law has no right (*n'a le droit*) to forbid any other actions than such as are hurtful to society. The law has no right (*n'a le droit*, not *ne peut pas*). This, for once, is free from ambiguity. Here the mask of ambiguity is thrown off. The avowed object of this clause is to preach constant insurrection, to raise up every man in arms against every law which he happens not to approve of. For, take any such action you will, if the law have no right to forbid it, a law forbidding it is null and void, and the attempt to execute it an oppression, and resistance to such attempt, and insurrection in support of such resistance, legal, justifiable, and commendable.

To have said that no law ought to forbid any act that is not of a nature prejudical to society, would have answered every good purpose, but would not have answered the purpose which is intended to be answered here.

A government which should fulfil the expectations here held out, would be a government of absolute perfection. The instance of a government fulfilling these expectations, never has taken place, nor till men are angels ever can take place. Against every government which fails in any degree of fulfilling these expectations, then, it is the professed object of this manifesto to excite insurrection: here, as elsewhere, it is therefore its direct object to excite insurrection at all times against every government whatsoever.

Sentence 2. Whatever is not forbidden by the law, cannot be hindered, nor can any individual be compelled to do what the law does not command.

The effect of this law, for want of the requisite exceptions or explanations, is to annihilate, for the time being and for ever, all powers of command: all power, the exercise of which consists in the issuing and inforcing obedience to particular and occasional commands; domestic power, power of the police, judicial power, military power, power of superior officers, in the line of civil administration, over their subordinates. If I say to my son, Do not mount that horse, which you are not strong enough to manage; if I say to my daughter, Do not go to that pond, where there are young men bathing; they may set me at defiance, bidding me show them where there are anything about mounting unruly horses, or going where there are young men bathing, in the laws. By the same clause, they may each of them justify themselves in turning their backs upon the lesson I have given them; while my apprentice refuses to do the work I have given him; and my wife, instead of providing the meals I had desired her to provide for ourselves and family, tells me she thinks fit to go and dine elsewhere. In the existing order of things, under any other government than that which was here to be organized, whatever is commanded or forbidden in virtue of a power which the law allows of and recognises, is virtually and in effect commanded and forbidden by the law itself, since, by the support it gives to the persons in question in the exercise of their respective authorities, it shows itself to have adopted those commands, and considered them as its own before they are issued, and that, whatever may be the purport of them, so long as they are confined within the limits it has marked out. But all these existing governments being fundamentally repugnant to the rights of man, are null and void, and incapable of filling up this or any other gap in the texture of the new code. Besides, this right of not being hindered from doing anything which the law itself has not forbidden, nor compelled to do anything which it has not commanded, is an article of natural, unalienable, sacred, and imprescriptible right, over which political laws have no sort of power; so that the attempt to fill up the gap, and to establish any such power of commanding or forbidding what is not already commanded and forbidden by the law, would be an act of usurpation, and all such powers so attempted to be established, null and void. How also can any such powers subsist in a society of which all the members are free and equal in point of rights?

Admit, however, that room is given for the creation of the powers in question by the spirit, though not by the letter of this clause – what follows? That in proportion as it is harmless, it is insignificant, and incapable of answering its intended purpose. This purpose is to protect individuals against oppressions, to which they might be subjected by other individuals possessed of powers created by the law, in the exercise or pretended exercise of those powers. But it these powers are left to the determination of succeeding and (according to the doctrine of this code) inferior legislatures, and may be of any nature and to any extent which these legislatures may think fit to give them, – what does the protection here given amount to, especially as against such future legislatures, for whose bands all the restraints which it is the object of the declaration to provide are intended? Mischievous or nugatory is still the alternative.

The employment of the improper word *can*, instead of the proper word *shall*, is not unworthy of observation. Shall is the language of the legislator who knows what he is about, and aims at nothing more: can, when properly employed in a book of law, is the language of the private commentator or expositor, drawing inferences from the text of the law – from the acts of the legislator, or what takes the place of the acts of the legislator – the practice of the courts of justice.

§ *Article 6*

The law is the expression of the general will. Every citizen has the right of concurring in person, or by his representatives, in the formation of it: it ought to be the same for all, whether it protect, or whether it punish. All the citizens being equal in its eyes, are equally admissible to all dignities, public places, and employments, according to their capacity, and without any other distinction than that of their virtues and their talents.

This article is a *hodge-podge*, containing a variety of provisions, as wide from one another as any can be within the whole circuit of the law: some relating to the constitutional branch, some to the civil, some to the penal; and, in the constitutional department, some relating to the organization of the supreme power, others to that of the subordinate branches.

Proposition 1. The law is the expression of the general will. The law? What law is the expression of the general will? Where is it so? In what country? – at what period of time? In no country – at no period of time – in no other country than France – nor even in France. As to *general*, it means universal; for there are no exceptions made, – women, children, madmen, criminals – for these being human creatures, have already been declared equal in respect of rights: nature made them so; and even were it to be wished that the case were otherwise, nature's work being unalterable, and the rights unalienable, it would be to no purpose to attempt it.

What is certain is, that in any other nation at any rate, no such thing as a law ever existed to which this definition could be applied. But that is nothing to the purpose, since a favourite object of this effusion of universal benevolence, is to declare the governments of all other countries dissolved, and to persuade the people that the dissolution has taken place.

But anywhere – even in France – how can the law be the expression of the universal or even the general will of all the people, when by far the greater part have never entertained any will, or thought at all about the matter; and of those who have, a great part (as is the case with almost all laws made by a large assembly) would rather it had not taken place.

Sentence 2. Every citizen has the right of concurring in person, or by his representatives, in the formation of it.

Here the language changes from the enunciation of the supposed practice, to the enunciation of the supposed matter of right. Why does it change? After having said so silly a thing as that there is no law anywhere, but what was the expression of the will of every member of the community, what should have hindered its going on in the same silly strain, and saying that everybody did concur – did join in the formation of it? However, as the idea of right is, in this second sentence at any rate, presented by its appropriate term, the ambiguity diffused by the preceding sentence is dissipated; and now it appears beyond a doubt, that every law in the formation of which any one citizen was debarred from concurring, either in person or by his representatives, is, and ever will be, here and there and everywhere, a void law.

To characterize proxies, the French language, like the English, has two words – representatives and deputies: the one liable to misconstruction, the other not, – to misconstruction, and such misconstruction as to be made expressive of a sense directly opposite to that which appears here to have been intended; the one tainted with fiction as well as ambiguity, the other expressing nothing but the plain truth. Being so superior to imitation – so free to choose – not tied down by usage as people in Britain are – how come they to have taken the English word representatives, which has given occasion to so many quibbles, instead of their own good word deputies, which cannot give occasion to anything like a quibble? The king of Great Britain is acknowledged to be the representative of the British nation, in treating with foreign powers; but does the whole nation ever meet together and join in signing an authority to him so to do? The king of Great Britain is acknowledged, in this instance, to represent the British nation; but, in this instance, is it ever pretended that he has been deputed by it? The parliamentary electors have been said to represent the non-electors; and the members of parliament to represent both; but did anybody ever speak of either members or electors as having been deputed by the non-electors? Using the improper word representatives, instead of the proper word deputies, the French might be saddled with the British constitution, for anything there is in this clause to protect them from so horrible a grievance. Representatives sounded better, perhaps, than deputies. Men who are governed by sounds, sacrifice everything to sound: they neither know the value of precision, nor are able to attain it.

Sentence 3. It [the law] ought to be the same for all, whether it protect or whether it punish [*i.e.* as well in respect of the protection it affords, as in respect of the punishment it inflicts.]

This clause appears reasonable in the main, but in respect to certain points it may be susceptible of explanations and exceptions, from the discussion of which it might have been as well if all posterity had not been debarred.

As to protection, English law affords a punishment, which consists in being put out of the protection of the law; in virtue of which a man is debarred from applying for redress from any kind of injury. For my own part, I do not approve of any such punishment: but perhaps they do, who having it in their power to abrogate it, yet retain it. In France, I suppose it is approved of, where, in a much severer form than the English, it has been so much practised. This species of punishment is inhibited for ever, by the letter at least of this clause. As to the spirit of it, one of the ruling features of this composition from end to end is, that the spirit of it is incomprehensible.

Under the English law, heavier damages are given in many instances to the ministers of justice, acting as such, in case of ill-founded prosecutions against them, for supposed injuries to individuals, than would be given to private individuals aggrieved by prosecutions for the same injuries. The notion evidently is, that the servants of the public, not having so strong an interest in defending the rights of the public as individuals have in defending their own, the public man would be apt to be deterred from doing his duty if the encouragement he have to do it were no greater than the encouragement which the individual has to defend his right. These examples, not to plunge further into details, appear sufficient to suggest a reasonable doubt, whether, even in this instance, the smack-smooth equality, which rolls so glibly out of the lips of the rhetorician, be altogether compatible with that undeviating conformity to every bend and turn in the line of utility which ought to be the object of the legislator.

As to punishment, a rule as strictly subordinate to the dictates of utility, as the doctrine of undeviating equality is congenial to the capricious play of the imagination, is, not in any instance to employ more punishment than is necessary to the purpose. Where, as between two individuals, the measure of sensibility is different, a punishment which in name – that is, according to every description which could be given of it in and by the law – would be equal in the two instances, would in effect be widely different. Fifty lashes may, in the estimation of the law, be equal to fifty lashes; but it is what no man can suppose, that the suffering which a hard-working young man, or even a young woman of the hard-working class, would undergo from the application of fifty lashes, could be really equal in intensity to that which must have been endured from the same nominal punishment (were even the instrument and force applied the same) by the Countess Lapuchin, till then the favourite, and one of the finest ornaments of the court of a Russian empress. Banishment would, upon the face of the law, be equal to banishment: but it will not readily be admitted, that to a servant of the public, who happens to have nothing to live upon but a salary, the receipt of which depends upon attendance at his office, it would be no greater punishment than to a sturdy labourer, who in one country as well as in another, may derive an equal livelihood from the labour of his hands.

Those, if any such there are, to whom distinctions such as these would appear consonant to reason and utility, might perhaps regard them as not irreconcilable with the language of this clause, But others might think them either not reasonable, or, though reasonable, not thus reconcilable. And were any such distinctions to be ingrafted into the law by any succeeding legislators, those who did not approve of the alteration would, if at all actuated by any regard to the tenor and spirit of this declaration, raise a cry of aristocracy, and pronounce the alteration void: and then comes resistance and insurrection, and all the evils in their train.

Sentence 4. All the citizens being equal in its eyes, are all of them admissible to all dignities, public places, and employments, according to their capacity, and without any other distinction than that of their virtues and their talents.

This is one of the few clauses, not to say the only one, which does not seem liable to very serious objection: there is nothing to object to in its general spirit and meaning, though perhaps there is something as to the expression. In general, it were to be wished that no class of men should stand incapacitated with regard to any object of competition by any general law: nor can anything be said in favour of those hereditary incapacitations which suggested and provoked this clause. Yet as governments are constituted, and as the current of opinion runs, there may be cases where some sorts of incapacitation in regard to office seem called for by the purpose which operated as the final cause in the institution of the office. It seems hardly decent or consistent, for example, to allow to a Jew the faculty of presenting to a Christian benefice with cure of souls: though, by a judgment of no very ancient date, the law of England was made to lend its sanction to an appointment of this sort. As inconsistent does it appear to admit a Catholic patron to appoint to a Protestant, or a Protestant to a Catholic benefice; at least so long as diversities in matters of religious profession continue to have ill-will for their accompaniment. Ecclesiastical patronage in the hands of individuals, is indeed one of the abuses, or supposed abuses, which it was the object of this code to eradicate: and since then, the maintenance of an ecclesiastical establishment of any kind at the expense of the state, has, in France, been added to the catalogue of abuses. But at the time of the promulgation of this code, the spirit of subversion had not proceeded this length: ecclesiastical offices were still kept up; though, in relation to all these, together with all other offices, the right of nomination was given to assemblies of the people. The incongruity of admitting the professor of a rival religion to the right of suffrage, would therefore be the same in this instance as in the case where the nomination rested in a single breast, though the danger would seldom be of equal magnitude.

Madmen, and criminals of the worst description, are equally protected against exclusion from any office, or the exercise of any political right. As to offices which under this system a man cannot come into possession of but by election, the inconvenience, it may be said, cannot be great; for though not incapable of being elected, there is no danger of their being so. But this is not the case with regard to any of those political privileges which this system gives a man in his own right, and as a present derived from the hands of nature – such as the right of suffrage with regard to offices. Were an assassin, covered with the blood of the murdered person, and ordered for execution on the second of the month – or, which is doubtless esteemed worse, a royalist convicted of adherence to the government under which his country had existed for so many hundred years – to put in his claim for admittance to give his suffrage in the election of a deputy to the convention, or of a mayor of the Paris municipality, I see not how his claim could be rejected without an infringement of this clause. Indeed, if this right, like all the others, be, as we are told over and over again, a present of the goddess Nature, and proof against all attacks of law, what is to be done, and what remedy can be administered by the law? Something, it is true, is said of talents and of virtues; and the madman, it may be said, is deficient in talents, and the criminal in point of virtues. But neither talents nor virtues are mentioned otherwise than as marks of pre-eminence and distinction, recommending the possessors to a proportionable degree of favour and approbation with a view to preference: nothing is said of any deficiency in point of talent or virtue as capable of shutting the door against a candidate: distinction is the word, not exception, – distinction among persons all within the list, not exception excluding persons out of the list.

So far from admitting the exclusion of classes of men, however incompetent, the provision does not so much as admit of the exclusion of individuals from any office. An individual, or a knot of individuals, bent upon affording a constant obstruction to all business, and selected perhaps for that very purpose, might be returned to the supreme assembly, or any other; nor could they be got rid of without a breach of the natural and inviolable rights of man, as declared and established by this clause.

What makes the matter still the clearer is, that the particular provision is given in the character of a consequence of, that is, as being already included in the preceding article, declaring the perfect and unchangeable equality of mankind in respect of all manner of rights: 'The citizens being all of them equal in its sight, are all of them equally admissible', and so forth. As the general proposition, therefore, admits of no exception to it, no more can this particular application of it have one. Virtues and talents sound prettily, and flatter the imagination, but in point of clearness, had that been the object, the clause, such as it is, would have been all the better had it ended with the words public places and employments; and had all that is said about capacity, and distinction, and virtues, and talents, been left out.

§ *Article 7*

No one can be accused, arrested or detained, but in the cases determined by the law, and according to the forms prescribed by the law. Those who solicit, issue, execute, or cause to be executed, arbitrary orders, ought to be

punished; but every citizen, summoned or arrested in virtue of the law,
ought to obey that instant: he renders himself culpable by resistance.

Sentence 1. No one can be accused, arrested, or detained, but in
the cases determined by the law, and according to the forms
prescribed by the law.

Here again we have the improper word *can*, instead of *ought*.
Here, however, the power of the law is recognized, and passes
unquestioned: the clause, therefore, is in so far not mischievous
and absurd, but only nugatory, and beside the purpose. The
professed object of the whole composition is to tie the hands of
the law, by declaring pretended rights over which the law is never
to have any power, – liberty, the right of enjoying liberty: here
this very liberty is left at the mercy and good pleasure of the law.
As it neither answers the purpose it professes to have in view, so
neither does it fulfil the purpose which it ought to have had in
view, and might have fulfilled, – the giving the subject, or, to
speak in the French style, the citizen, that degree of security
which, without attempting to bind the hands of succeeding
legislators, might have been given him against arbitrary mandates.

There is nothing in this article which might not be received, and
without making any alteration, into the constitutional codes of
Prussia, Denmark, Russia, or Morocco. It is or is not law – (no
matter which, for I put it so only for supposition sake) – it is law,
let us say, in those countries, that upon order signed or issued by
any one of a certain number of persons – suppose ministers of state
– any individual may be arrested at any time, and detained in any
manner and for any length of time, without any obligation on the
part of the person issuing the order to render account of the issuing
or of the execution of it to anybody but the monarch. If such were
the law in these countries respectively, before the establishment of
such a law as this clause imports, such may it remain, and that
without effecting any abridgment of the powers of the ministers in
question, or applying any check to the abuses of those powers, or
affording the subject any security or remedy against the abuses of
those powers, after the introduction of such article.

The case in which it is determined by the law, that a man may
be so arrested and detained, is the case of an order having been
issued for that purpose by any one in such a list of ministers; and

the form in which the order for that purpose must be conceived, is the wording in the form in which orders to the purpose in question have been in use to be worded, or, in short, any other form which the ministers in question may be pleased to give it. If to this interpretation any objection can be made, it must be grounded on the ambiguity of the word *the law* – an ambiguity resulting from the definition above given of it in this declaratory code. If the laws are all of them *ipso facto* void, as this manifesto has, by the preceding article, declared them to be in all countries where the laws are made by other authority than that of the whole body of the people, then indeed the security intended to be afforded is afforded; because in that case no arrest or detention can be legal, till the ground and form of it have been preordained by a law so established. On the contrary, if that article be to be explained away, and countries foreign to France are to be left in possession of their laws, then the remedy and security amounts to nothing, for the reason we have seen. Nugatory or mischievous: such is the option everywhere else – such is the option here.

Sentence 2. Those who solicit, issue, execute or cause to be executed, arbitrary orders, ought to be punished.

Yes, says a Moullah of Morocco, after the introduction of this article into the Morocco code, – yes, if an order to the prejudice of the liberty of the subject be illegal, it is an arbitrary order, and the issuing of it is an offence against the liberty of the subject, and as such ought to be, and shall be punished. If one dog of an infidel presume to arrest or detain another dog of an infidel, the act of arrest and detention is an arbitrary one, and nothing can be more reasonable than what the law requires, viz. that the presuming dog be well bastinadoed. But if one of the faithful, to every one of whom the sublime emperor, crowned with the sun and moon, has given the command over all dogs, think fit to shut up this or that dog in a strange kennel, what is there of arbitrariness in that? It is no more than what our customs, which are our laws, allow of everywhere, when the true believers have dogs under them.

The security of the individual in this behalf depends, we see, upon the turn given to that part of the law which occupies itself in establishing the powers necessary to be established for the furtherance of justice. Had the penners of this declaration been contented with doing what they might have done consistently with reason and utility, in this view they might have done thus: they might have warned and instructed them to be particular in the indication of the cases in which they would propose to grant such powers, and in the indication of the forms according to which the powers so granted should be exercised; – for instance, that no man should be arrested but for some one in the list of cases enumerated by the law as capable of warranting an arrest; nor without the specification of that case in an instrument, executed for the purpose of warranting such arrest; nor unless such instrument were signed by an officer of such a description; and so on: not to attempt to exhibit a code of such importance, extent, and nicety, in the compass of a parenthesis. In doing so, they would have done what would at least have been innocent, and might have had its use – but in doing so, they would not have prosecuted their declared purpose; which was not only to tutor and lecture their more experienced and consequently more enlightened successors, but to tie their hands, and keep their fellow-citizens in a state of constant readiness to cut their throats.

Sentence 3. But every citizen summoned or arrested in virtue of the law, ought to obey that instant: he renders himself culpable by resistance.

This clause is mighty well in itself: the misfortune is that it is nothing to the purpose. The title of this code is the Declaration of Rights; and the business of it is accordingly, in every other part of it, to declare such rights, real or supposed, as are thought fit to be declared. But what is here declared is for once a *duty*; the mention of which has somehow or other slipt in, as it were through inadvertence. The things that people stand most in need of being reminded of, are, one would think, their duties: for their rights, whatever they may be, they are apt enough to attend to of themselves. Yet it is only by accident, under a wrong title, and as it were by mistake, and in this single instance, that anything is said that would lend the body of the people to suspect that there were any such things appertaining to them as *duties*.

He renders himself culpable by resistance: Oh yes – certainly, unless the law for the infringement of which he is arrested, or attempted to be arrested, be an oppressive one: or unless there be anything oppressive in the behaviour of those by whom the arrest or detention is performed. If, for instance, there be anything of the insolence of office in their language or their looks, – if they lay hold of him on a sudden, without leaving him time to run away, – if they offer to pinion his arms while he is drawing his sword, without waiting till he have drawn it, – if they lock the door upon him, or put him into a room that has bars before the window, – or if they came upon him the same night, while the evidences of his guilt are about him and all fresh, instead of waiting on the outside of the door all night till he have destroyed them.[1] In any of these cases, as well as a thousand others that might be mentioned, can there be any doubts about the oppression? But by Article 2 of this same code – an article which has already been established and placed out of the reach of cavil, the right of resistance to oppression is among the number of those rights which nature hath given, and which it is not in the power of man to take away.

1 By a subsequent decree of the Convention, this silly provision was actually made law, under the notion of favouring liberty. The liberty of doing mischief, it certainly does favour, as certainly as it disfavours the liberty of preventing it. Ask for a reason: *a man's house* you are told, *is his castle*. Blessed liberty! – where the trash of sentiments – where epigrams, pass for reasons, and poetry gives rule to law! But if a man's house be his castle by night, how comes it not to be so by day? And if a house be a castle to the owner, why not to everybody else in whose favour the owner chooses to make it so? By day or by night, is it less hardship to a suspected person to have his house searched, than to an unsuspected one? Here we have the mischief and the absurdity of the ancient ecclesiastical asylums, without the reason.

The course of justice in England is still obstructed to a certain degree by this silly epigram, worthy of the age which gave it birth. Delinquents, like foxes, are to have law given them: that is, are to have chances of escape given them on purpose, as if it were to make the better sport for the hunters – for the lawyers, by and for whom the hunt is made.

§ *Article 8*

The law ought not to establish any other punishments than such as are strictly and evidently necessary; and no one can be punished but in virtue of a law established and promulgated before the commission of the offence, and applied in a legal manner.

Sentence 1. The law ought not to establish any other punishments than such as are strictly and evidently necessary.

The instruction administered by this clause is not great: so far, however, is well, that the purpose declared in this instrument is departed from, and nothing but instruction is here attempted to be given; and which succeeding legislators may be governed by or not as they think fit. it is well, indeed, that penal laws not conforming to this condition are not included in the sentence of nullity so liberally dealt out on other occasions, since, if they were, it would be difficult enough to find a penal law anywhere that would stand the test, from whatever source – pure or impure, democratical, aristocratical, or monarchical – it were derived.

No rules of any tolerable degree of particularity and precision have ever yet been laid down for adjusting either the quantum or the quality of punishments – none such at least could have been in the contemplation of the framers of this code: and supposing such rules laid down, and framed with the utmost degree of particularity and precision of which the nature of the subject is susceptible, it would still be seen in most instances, if not in every instance, that the offence admitted optionally of a considerable variety of punishments, of which no one could be made to appear to be strictly and evidently necessary, to the exclusion of the rest.

As a mere *memento*, then, of what is fit to be attended to, a clause to this effect may be very well; but as an instruction, calculated to point out in what manner what is so fit to be attended to may be accomplished, nothing can be more trifling or uninstructive: anarchical fallacies it is even erroneous and fallacious, since it assumes, and that by necessary implication, that it is possible, in the case of every offence, to find a punishment of which the strict necessity is capable of being made evident, – which is not true. Unfortunately, the existence of a system of punishments of which the absolute necessity is capable of being made evident, with reference to the offences to which they are respectively annexed, is not altogether so clear as the existence of the article by which succeeding legislators are sent in quest of such a system by these their masters and preceptors. One thing is but too evident, that the attention bestowed by the penner of this article, on the subject on which he gives the law to posterity so much at his ease, was anything but strict. It was the Utopia created by the small talk of Paris that was dancing before his eyes, and not the elementary parts of the subject-matter he was treating of – the list of possible punishments, confronted with the list of possible offences. He who writes these observations has bestowed a closer and more minute inquiry into the subject than anybody who has been before him – he has laid down a set of rules, by which, as be conceives, the disproportion but too generally prevalent between punishments and offences, may be reduced within bounds greatly more narrow than it occupies anywhere at present in any existing code of laws – and what he would undertake for is, not to make evident any such list of strictly necessary punishments, but the impossibility of its existence.

Sentence 2. No one can be punished but in virtue of a law established and promulgated before the commission of the offence, and applied in a legal manner.

This clause – if instead of the insurrection-inviting word *can*, the word *ought* had been employed, as in the preceding clause of this same article – would, as far as it goes, have been well enough. As it is, while on the one hand it not only tends to bring in the everlasting danger of insurrection, – on the other hand, it leaves a considerable part of the danger against which it is levelled, uncovered and unprovided against.

Numerous are the occasions on which sufferings as great as any that, being inflicted with a view to punishment, go under the denomination of punishment, may be inflicted without any such view. These cases a legislator who understood his business would have collected and given notice of, for the purpose of marking out the boundaries and confines of the instruction in question, and saving it from misapplication. Laying an embargo, for instance, is a species of confinement, and, were a man subjected to it with a view to punishment, might in many cases be a very severe punishment: yet if the providence of the legislator happen not to have provided a general law empowering the executive authority to lay an embargo in certain cases, the passing of a special law for that purpose, after the incident which calls for it has taken place, may be a very justifiable, and even necessary measure; for instance, to prevent intelligence from being communicated to a power watching the moment to commence hostilities, or to prevent articles of subsistence or instruments of defence, of which there is a deficiency in the country, from being carried out of it.

Banishment must, in a certain sense, be admitted to be equally penal, whether inflicted for the purpose of punishment, or only by way of precaution, – for the purpose of prevention, and without any view to punishment. Will it be said, that there is no case in which the supreme government of a country ought to be trusted with the power of removing out of it, not even for a time, any persons, not even foreigners, from whom it may see reason to apprehend enterprises injurious to its peace? So in the case of imprisonment, which, though in some instances it may be a severer, may in others be a less severe infliction than banishment. Even death, a suffering which, if inflicted with a view to punishment, is the very extremity of punishment, and which, according to my own conception of the matter, neither need nor ought to be inflicted in any instance for the purpose of punishment, may, in some certain instances perhaps, be highly necessary to be inflicted without any view to punishment – for example, to prevent the diffusion of the plague.

Thus it is, that while the clause passing censure on *ex post facto* penal laws (a censure in itself, and, while it confines itself to the cases strictly within its declared subject, so highly reasonable) is thus exhibited with the insurrection-inciting *can* in it, and without the explanations necessary, as we have seen, to guard it against misapplication, the country is exposed to two opposite dangers: one, that an infliction necessary for the purpose of prevention should be resisted and risen up against by individuals, under the notion of its being included in the prohibition given by this clause; the other, that the measure, how necessary soever, should be abstained from by the legislature through apprehension of such resistance.

As to the concluding epithet, *and legally applied*, it might have been spared without any great injury to the sense. If the law referred to in justification of an act of power have not been legally applied in the exercise of that act of power, the act has not been exercised in virtue of that law.

§ *Article 9*

Every individual being presumed innocent until he have been declared guilty, – if it be judged necessary to arrest him, every act of rigour which is not necessary to the making sure of his person, ought to be severely inhibited by the law.

This article being free from the insurrection-exciting particle, and confining itself to the office of simple instruction, is so far innocent: the object of it is laudable, though the purport of it might have been expressed with more precision.

The maxim it opens with, though of the most consummate triviality, is not the more conformable to reason and utility, and is particularly repugnant to the regulation in support and justification of which it is adduced. That every man *ought* to be presumed innocent (for 'is presumed innocent' is nonsense,) until he have been *declared* (that is, adjudged) guilty, is very well so long as no accusation has been preferred against him, – or rather, so long as neither that nor any other circumstance appears to afford reason for suspecting the contrary – but very irrational, after that ground for supposing he may have been guilty has been brought to light.

The maxim is particularly misapplied and absurd when applied to the case where it has been judged proper (on sufficient grounds we are to suppose) to put him under arrest, to deprive him of his power of locomotion. Suppose him innocent, and the defalcation made from his liberty is injurious and unwarrantable. The plain truth of the matter is, that the only rational ground for empowering a man to be arrested in such a case, is its not being yet known whether he be innocent or guilty; suppose him guilty, he ought to be punished – suppose him innocent, he ought not to be touched. But plain unsophisticated truth and common sense do not answer the purpose of poetry or rhetoric; and it is from poetry and rhetoric that these tutors of mankind and governors of futurity take their law. A clap from the galleries is their object, not the welfare of the state.

As for the expression, *ought to be severely repressed* (by punishment I suppose,) it is as well calculated to inflame (the general purpose of this effusion of matchless wisdom) as it is ill calculated to instruct. A rather more simple and instructive way of stating it would have been to say, in relation to every such exercise of rigour which goes beyond what appears necessary to the purpose in question – that of making sure of the person, that not coming within the ground of justification taken from that source, it remains upon the footing of an offence of that description of delinquency, whatever it be, of an injury of the species in question, whatever it may be. The satisfaction and punishment annexed to it will come of course to be of the same nature and extent as for an injury of the same nature and extent having no such circumstance to give occasion to it. Should the punishment in such case be greater or less than the punishment for the same injury would be if altogether divested of the justification which covers the remainder of the unpleasant treatment? Should the punishment of the minister of justice exceeding his authority, be greater or less than that of the uncommissioned individual doing the same mischief without any authority? On some accounts (as would be found upon proper inquiry,) it should be greater: on other accounts, not so great. But these are points of minute detail, which might surely as well have been left to the determination of those who would have had time to give them due examination, as determined upon at random by those who had no such time. The words of this article seem to intimate, that the punishment for the abuse of power by the minister of justice ought to be the greater of the two. But why so? You know better where to meet with the minister of justice than with an offending individual taken at large; the officer has more to lose than the individual: and the greater the assurance you have that a delinquent, in case of accusation, will be forthcoming, in readiness to afford satisfaction in the event of his being sentenced to afford it, the less the alarm which his delinquency inspires.

§ *Article 10*

No one ought to be molested [meaning, probably, by government] *for his opinions, even in matters of religion, provided that the manifestation of them does not disturb* [better expressed perhaps by saying, except in as far as the manifestation of them disturb, or rather tends to the disturbance of] *the public order established by the law.*

Liberty of publication with regard to opinions, under certain exceptions, is a liberty which it would be highly proper and fit to establish, but which would receive but a very precarious establishment from an article thus worded. Disturb the public order? – what does that mean? Louis XIV need not have hesitated about receiving an article thus worded into his code. The public order of things in this behalf was an order in virtue of which the exercise of every religion but the Catholic, according to his edition of it, was proscribed. A law is enacted, forbidding men to express a particular opinion, or set of opinions, relative to a particular point in religion: forbidding men to express any of those opinions, in the expression of which the Lutheran doctrine, for example, or the Calvinistic doctrine, or the Church of England doctrine consists: in a prohibition to this effect, consists the public order established by the law. Spite of this, a man manifests an opinion of the number of those which thus stand prohibited as belonging to the religion thus proscribed. The act by which this opinion is manifested, is it not an act of disturbance with relation to the public order thus established? Extraordinary indeed must be the assurance of him who could take upon him to answer in the negative.

Thus nugatory, thus flimsy, is this buckler of rights and liberties, in one of the few instances in which any attempt is made to apply it to a good purpose.

What should it have done, then? To this question an answer is scarcely within the province of this paper: the proposition with which I set out is, not that the Declaration of Rights should have been worded differently, but that nothing under any such name, or with any such design, should have been attempted.

A word or two, however, may be given as a work of supererogation: that opinions of all sorts might be manifested without fear of punishment; that no publication should be deemed to subject a man to punishment on account of any opinions it may be found to contain, considered as mere opinions, but at the same time, that the plea of manifesting religious opinions, or the practising certain acts supposed to be enjoined or recommended in virtue of certain religious opinions as proper or necessary to be practised, should not operate as a justification for either exercising, or prompting men to exercise, any act which the legislature, without any view or reference to religion, has already thought fit, or may hereafter think fit, to insert into the catalogue of prohibited acts or offences.

To instance two species of delinquency, – one of the most serious, the other of the slightest nature – acts tending to the violent subversion of the government by force – acts tending to the obstruction of the passage in the streets: An opinion that has been supposed by some to belong to the Christian religion, is, that every form of government but the monarchical is unlawful: an opinion that has been supposed by some to belong to the Christian religion – by some at least of those that adhere to that branch of the Christian religion which is termed the Roman Catholic – is, that it is a duty, or at least a merit, to join in processions of a certain description, to be performed on certain occasions.

What, then, is the true sense of the clause in question, in relation to these two cases? What ought to be the conduct of a government that is neither monarchical nor Catholic, with reference to the respective manifestation of these two opinions?

First, as to the opinion relative to the unlawfulness of a government not monarchical. The falsity or erroneousness which the members of such a government could not but attribute in their own minds to such an opinion, is a consideration which, according to the spirit and intent of the provision in question, would not be sufficient to authorize their using penal or other coercive measures for the purpose of preventing the manifestation of them. At the same time, should such manifestation either have already had the effect of engaging individuals in any attempt to effect a violent subversion of the government by force, or appear to have produced a near probability of any such attempt – in such case, the engagement to permit the free manifestation of opinions in general, and of religious opinions in particular, is not to be understood to preclude the government from restraining the manifestation of the opinion in question, in every such way as it may deem likely to promote or facilitate any such attempt.

Again, as to the opinion relative to the meritoriousness of certain processions. By the principal part of the provision, government stands precluded from prohibiting publications manifesting an opinion in favour of the obligatoriness or meritoriousness of such processions. By the spirit of the same engagement, they stand precluded from prohibiting the perform- ance of such processions, unless a persuasion of a political inconvenience as resulting from such practice – a persuasion not grounded on any notions of their unlawfulness in a religious view – should come to be entertained: as if, for example, the multitude of the persons joining in the procession, or the crowd of persons flocking to observe them, should fill up the streets to such a degree, or for such a length of time, and at intervals recurring with such frequency, as to be productive of such a degree of obstruc- tion to the free use of the streets for the purposes of business, as in the eye of government should constitute a body of inconvenience worth encountering by a prohibitive law.

It would be a violation of the spirit of this part of the engagement, if the government – not by reason of any view it entertained of the political inconveniences of these processions (for example, as above,) but for the purpose of giving an ascend- ency to religious opinions of an opposite nature (determined, for example, by a Protestant antipathy to Catholic processions) – were to make use of the real or pretended obstruction to the free use of the streets, as a pretence for prohibiting such processions.

These examples, while they serve to illustrate the ground and degree and limits of the liberty which it may seem proper, on the score of public tranquillity and peace, to leave to the manifesta- tion of opinions of a religious nature, may serve, at the same time, to render apparent the absurdity and perilousness of every attempt on the part of the government for the time being, to tie up the hands of succeeding governments in relation to this or any other spot in the field of legislation. Observe how nice, and incapable of being described beforehand by any particular marks, are the lines which mark the limits of right and wrong in this behalf – which separate the useful from the pernicious – the prudent course from the imprudent! – how dependent upon the temper of the times – upon the events and circumstances of the day! – with how fatal a certainty persecution and tyranny on the one hand, or revolt and civil war on the other, may follow from the slightest deviation from propriety in the drawing of such lines! – and what a curse to any country a legislator may be, who, with the purest intentions, should set about settling the business to all eternity by inflexible and adamantine rules, drawn from the sacred and inviolable and imprescriptible rights of man, and the primeval and everlasting laws of nature!

I give the preference, for the purpose of exemplification, to one of those points of all others, in relation to which it would give me pleasure to see liberty established for ever, as it could be established consistently with security and peace. My persuasion is, that there is not a single point with relation to which it can answer any good purpose to attempt to tie the hands of future legislators; and so, that as there is not a single point, not even of my own choosing, in relation to which I would endeavour to give any such perpetuity to a regulation even of my own framing, it is still less to say – strong as it may appear to say – that were it to depend upon me, I would sooner, were the power of sanctioning in my hands, give my sanction to a body of laws framed by any one else, how bad soever it might appear to me, free from any such perpetuating clause, than a body of laws of my own framing, how well soever I might be satisfied with it, if it must be incumbered with such a clause.

§ *Article 11*

The free examination of thoughts and opinions is one of the most precious rights of man: every citizen may therefore speak, write, and print freely, provided always that he shall be answerable for the abuse of that liberty in the cases determined by the law.

The logic of this composition is altogether of a piece with its policy. When you meet with a *therefore* – when you meet with a consequence announced as drawn from the proposition immediately preceding it, assure yourself that, whether the propositions themselves, as propositions, are true or false – as ordinances, reasonable or unreasonable, expedient or inexpedient – that the consequent is either in contradiction with the antecedent, or has nothing at all to do with it.

The liberty of communicating opinions is one branch of liberty; and liberty is one of the four natural rights of man, over which human ordinances have no power. There are two ways in which liberty may be violated: by physical or bodily coercion, and by moral coercion or demonstration of punishment; – the one applied before the time for exercising the liberty – the other to be applied after it, in the shape of punishment, in the event of its not producing its intended effect in the shape of prohibition.

What is the boon in favour of the branch of liberty here in question, granted by this article? It saves it from succeeding legislators in one shape – it leaves it at their mercy in the other. Will it be said, that what it leaves exposed to punishment is only the abuse of liberty? Be it so. What then? Is there less of liberty in the abuse of liberty than in the use of it? Does a man exercise less liberty when he makes use of the property of another, than when he confines himself to his own? Then are liberty and confinement the same thing – synonymous and interchangeable terms.

What is the abuse of liberty? It is that exercise of liberty, be it what it may, which a man who bestows that name on it does not approve of. Every abuse of this branch of liberty is left exposed to punishment; and it is left to future legislators to determine what shall be regarded as an abuse of it. What is the security worth, which is thus given to the individual as against the encroachments of government? What does the barrier pretended to be set up against government amount to? It is a barrier which government is expressly called upon to set up where it pleases. Let me not be mistaken: what I blame these constitution-makers for, is not the having omitted to tie the hands of their successors tight enough, but the suffering themselves to entertain a conceit so mischievous and so foolish as that of tying them up at all; and in particular for supposing, that were they weak enough to suffer themselves to be so shackled, a phrase or two of so loose a texture could be capable of doing the business to any purpose.

The general notion in regard to offences – a notion so general as to have become proverbial, and even trivial – is, that *prevention is better than punishment*. Here prevention is abjured, and punishment embraced in preference. Once more, let me not be mistaken. In the particular case of the liberty of communicating opinions, there most certainly are reasons, for giving up the object of prevention, and in the choice of the means of repression, confining the repressive operations of the legislator to the application of punishment, which do not apply to other offences. A word or two to this purpose, and to justify the seeming inconsistency, would have been rather more instructive than most of those other instructions of which the authors of this code have been so liberal.

Not only is the consequent of these two propositions, clogged with the proviso at the tail of it, repugnant to the antecedent, but in itself it is much more extensive – it extends a vast way beyond what is intended as a covering for it. The free communication, of thoughts, and of opinions, I presume are here put as synonymous terms: the free communication of opinions, says the antecedent, is one of the most valuable of the rights of man – of those unalienable rights of man. What says the consequent of it? Not only that a man may communicate opinions without the possibility of being prevented, but that he is to be at liberty to communicate what he will, without the possibility of being prevented, and in any manner, – false allegations in matters of fact, and known to be such – for true, false allegations to the prejudice of the reputation of individuals – in a word, slander of all sorts – and that in all manner of ways, – by speech, by writing, and even in the way of printing, without the possibility of stopping his mouth, destroying his manuscript, or stopping the press.

What then? Does it follow, that because a man ought to be left at liberty to publish opinions of all sorts, subject not to previous prevention, but only to subsequent punishment, that therefore he ought to be left at equal liberty to publish allegations of all sorts, false as well as true – allegations known by him to be false, as well as allegations believed by him to be true – attacks which he knows to be false, upon the reputation of individuals, as well as those which he believes to be true? Far is it from my meaning to contend in this place, especially in a parenthesis, much more to take for granted, that the endurance of even these mischiefs, crying as they are, may not be a less evil than the subjecting the press to a previous censure, under any such restrictions on the exercise of that power as could be devised – at any rate, under any as have ever hitherto been proposed. All I mean to say is, that whether a man ought or ought not to be left at liberty to publish private slander without the application of anything but subsequent punishment to stop the progress of it, it does not follow that it ought to be left in his power to publish such allegations, because it ought to be left in like manner in his power to publish whatever can come under the denomination of opinions. As for the word thoughts, which is put in a line with the word opinions, as if thoughts were something different from opinions, I shall lay it out of the question altogether, till I can find somebody who will undertake to satisfy me, in the first place, that it was meant to denote something in addition to opinions, and in the next place, that that something was meant to include allegations, true and false, in relation to matters of fact.

Is it, or is it not, a matter to be wished, in France for example, that measures were taken by competent authority – whatever authority be deemed competent, to draw the line between the protection due to the useful liberty, and the restraint proper for the pernicious licence of the press? What a precious task would the legislator find set for him by this declaration of sacred, inviolable, and imprescriptible rights! The protectors of reputation on one side of him: the idolators of liberty on the other: each with the rights of man in his mouth, and the dagger of assassination in his hand, ready to punish the smallest departure from the course marked out in his heated imagination for this unbending line.

§ Article 12

The guarantee of the rights of the man and of the citizen necessitates a public force: this force is therefore instituted for the advantage of all, and not for the particular utility [advantage] *of those to whom it is intrusted.*

The general purpose of the whole performance taken together, being mischievous and pestilential, this article has thus much to recommend it, that it is nothing to the purpose – no declaration of inviolable rights – no invitation to insurrection. As it stands, it is a mere effusion of imbecility – a specimen of confused conception and false reasoning. With a little alteration, it might be improved into a commonplace memento, as stale, and consequently as useless, as it is unexceptionable: to wit, that the employment given to the public force, maintained as it is at the expense of the public, ought to have for its object the general advantage of the whole body of the public taken together, not the exclusive private advantage of particular individuals.

This article is composed of two distinct propositions. In the first, after throwing out of it as so much surplusage, the obscure part about the guarantee or maintenance of the right of the man and the citizen, there will remain a clear and intelligible part, a declaration of opinion asserting the necessity of the public force: to this, hooked on in the shape of an inference, of a logical conclusion, a vague assertion of an historical matter of fact, which may have been true in one place, and false in another – the truth of which is incapable of being ascertained in any instance – an operation, the labour of which may be spared with the less loss, from its being nothing to the purpose.

This matter of fact is neither more nor less than the main end in view which happened to be present in the minds of the several persons to whose co-operation the public force was respectively indebted for its institution and establishment in the several political communities in the world, and which officiated in the character of a final cause in every such instance. This final cause, the penner of the article – such is his candour and good opinion of mankind – pronounces without hesitation or exception to have been the pure view of the greatest good of the whole community – public spirit in its purest form, and in its most extensive application. Neither Clovis, Pepin, nor Hugh Capet, had the smallest preferable regard to the particular advantage of themselves or their favourites, when they laid the foundations of the public force in France, nor any other consideration in view than what might be most conducive to the joint and equal advantage of the Franks, Gauls, and Gallo-Romans upon the whole. As little partiality existed in the breast of William the Conqueror, in favour of himself, or any of his Normans, on the occasion of his sharing out England among those Normans, and dividing it into knight's fees: freemen and villains, barons and yeomen, Normans, Danes, and English, collectively and individually, occupying one equal place in his affections, and engaging one equal portion of his solicitude.

According to this construction, the inference, it must be

confessed, may be just enough. All you have to suppose is, that the greatest good of the whole community taken together was in every instance the ruling object of consideration in the breast of the institutors of the public force: the pursuit of that greatest good, in a certain shape not perfectly explained, being the ruling object with these worthy men. As they did institute this public force, it seems to follow pretty accurately that the attainment of that general advantage was the end in view, in each instance, of its being instituted.

Should the two propositions, the antecedent and the consequent, in this their genuine signification, appear too silly to be endurable, the way to defend it may be to acknowledge that the man who penned it knew no difference between a declaration of what he supposed was or is the state of things with regard to this or that subject, and a declaration of what he conceived ought to have been, or ought to be that state of things; and this being the case, it may be supposed that in saying such was the end in view upon the several occasions in question, what he meant was, that such it ought to have been. If this were really his meaning, the propositions are such, both of them, as we may venture to accede to without much danger. A public force is necessary, we may say; and the public is the party for whose advantage that force ought to be employed. The propositions themselves are both of them such, that against neither of them, surely, can any objection be produced: as to the inference by which they are strung together, if the application made of it be not exactly of the clearest nature, you have only to throw it out, and everything is as it should be, and the whole article is rendered unexceptionable.

§ *Article 13*

For the maintenance of the public force, and for the expenses of administration, a common contribution is indispensable: it ought to be equally divided among all the citizens in proportion to their faculties.

In the first part of this article two propositions are contained. One is, that a common contribution is indispensable for the maintenance of the public force. If by this be meant, that raising money upon all, for the maintenance of those whose individual forces are employed in the composition of the public force, is proper, I see no reason to dispute it: if the meaning be, that this is the only possible way of maintaining a public force, it is not true. Under the feudal system, those whose individual forces composed the public force, were maintained, not at the expense of the community at large, but at their own expense.

The other proposition is, that a common contribution is indispensable for the expenses (meaning the other expenses) of administration. Indispensable? Yes, certainly: so far as these other branches of administration cannot be carried on without expense – if they are carried on, the defraying of that expense is indispensable. But are these nameless branches of administration necessary? For if they are not, neither is a common contribution for the defraying of the expense. Are they then necessary? – these unnamed and unindicated branches of administration, which in this mysterious manner are put down on the list of necessary ones, is their title to be there a just one? This is a question to which it is impossible to find an answer: yet, till an answer be found for it, it is impossible to find a sufficient warrant for admitting this proposition to be true. From this proposition, as the matter stands upon the face of it, it should seem that one of these sacred and inviolable and imprescriptible rights of a man consists in the obligation of contributing to an unknown mass of expense employed upon objects not ascertained.

Proposition 3. It (the common contribution in question) ought to be equally divided amongst all the citizens, in proportion to their faculties.

Partly contradiction – a sequel to, or rather repetition of preceding contradiction: partly tyranny under the mask of justice.

By the first article, human creatures are, and are to be, all of them, on a footing of equality in respect to all sorts of rights. By the second article, property is of the number of these rights. By the two taken together, all men are and are to be upon an equal footing in respect of property: in other words, all the property in the nation is and is to be divided into equal portions. At the same time, as to the matter of fact, what is certain is, that at the time of passing this article, no such equality existed, nor were any measures so much as taken for bringing it into existence. This being the case, which of the two states of things is it that this article supposes? – the old and really existing inequality, or the new and imaginary equality? In the first case, the concluding or explanatory clause is in contradiction to the principal one: in the other case, it is tautological and superfluous. In the first case, the explanatory clause is in contradiction to the principal one; for, from unequal fortunes if you take equal contributions, the contributions are not proportional. If from a fortune of one hundred pounds you take a contribution of ten pounds, and from a fortune of two hundred pounds, ten pounds and no more, the proportion is not a tenth in both cases, but a tenth in the one, and only a twentieth in the other.

In the second case – that is, if equality in point of property be the state of things supposed – then, indeed, equality of contribution will be consistent with the plan of equalization, as well as consonant to justice and utility; but then the explanatory clause, *in proportion to their faculties*, will be tautologous and superfluous, and not only tautologous and superfluous, but ambiguous and perplexing: for proportionality in point of contribution is not consistent with equality in point of contribution, on more than one out of an infinity of suppositions, viz. that of equality in point of fortune: nor, in point of fact, was the one consistent with the other in the only state of things which was in existence at the time.

Men's *faculties* too! What does that word mean? This, if the state of things represented as actually existing, as well as always having existed, and for ever about to exist, had been anything more than a sick man's dream, would have required to be determined, had it been at all a matter of concern to prevent men from cutting one another's throats, and must have been determined before this theory could have been reduced to practice. In the valuation of men's faculties, is it meant that their possessions only, or that their respective wants and exigencies, as well as their ways and means, should be taken into account? In the latter case, what endless labour! In the former case, what injustice!

In either case, what tyranny! An inquisition into every man's exigencies and means, – an inquisition which, to be commensurate to its object, must be perpetual, – an inquisition into every man's circumstances, one of the foundation stones in this plan of liberty!

To a reader who should put an English construction upon this plan of taxation – (masked by the delusive term contribution, as if voluntary contributions could be a practicable substitute for compulsory,) – to a reader who should collect from the state of things in England the construction to be put upon this plan of taxation, the system here in view would not show itself in half its blackness. To an English reader it might naturally enough appear that all that was meant was, that the weight of taxation should bear in a loose sense as equally, or rather as equitably – that is, as proportionably, as it could conveniently be made to do; – that taxes, a word which would lead him directly and almost exclusively to taxes upon consumption, should be imposed – for example, upon superfluities in preference to the necessaries of life. Wide indeed would be his mistake. What he little would suspect is, that taxes on consumption, the only taxes from which arise the contributions that in plain truth, and not in a sophistical sense, are voluntary on the part of the contributor, are carefully weeded out of the book of French finance. Deluded by the term *indirect*, imposed as a sort of term of proscription upon them by a set of muddy-headed metaphysicians – little does he think that the favourite species of taxation in that country of perfect liberty, is a species of imposition and inquisition, which converts every man who has any property into a criminal in the first instance, which sends the tax-gatherer into every nook and corner of a man's house, which examines every man upon interrogatories, and of which a double or treble tithe would be an improved and mollified modification.

§ *Article 14*

All the citizens have the right to ascertain by themselves, or by their representatives, the necessity of the public contribution – to give their free consent to it – to follow up the application of it, and to determine the quantity of it, the objects on which it shall be levied, the mode of levying it and getting it in, and the duration of it.

Supposing the author of this article an enemy to the state, and his object to disturb the course of public business, and set the individual members of the state together by the ears, nothing could have been more artfully or more happily adapted to the purpose. Supposing him a friend, and his object to administer either useful instruction or salutary controul, nothing more silly or childish can be imagined.

In the first place, who is spoken of – who are meant, by all the citizens? Does it mean all, collectively acting in a body, or every citizen, every individual, that is, any one that pleases? This right of mine, – is it a right which I may exercise by myself at any time whenever it happens to suit me, and without the concurrence of anybody else, or which I can only exercise if and when I can get everybody else, or at least the major part of everybody else, to join me in the exercise of it? The difference in a practical view is enormous; but the penners of this declaration, by whom terms expressive of aggregation, and terms expressive of separation, are used to all appearance promiscuously, show no symptoms of their being aware of the smallest difference. If in conjunction with everybody else, I have it already by the sixth article. Laws imposing contributions are laws: I have already, then, a right of concurring in the formation of all laws whatever: what do I get by acquiring the right of concurring in the formation of the particular class of laws which are employed in imposing contributions? As a specification, as an application of the general provision to the particular subject, it might be very well. But it is not given as a specification, but as a distinct article. What marks the distinction the more forcibly, is the jumbling in this instance, and in this instance only, acts of another nature with acts of legislation – the right of examining into the necessity of the operation, and of following up such examination with the right of performing the operation – the right of observing and commenting on the manner in which the powers of government are exercised, with the right of exercising them.

Make what you will of it, what a pretty contrivance for settling matters, and putting an end to doubts and disagreements! This, whatever it is, is one of the things which I am told I have a right to do, that is, either by myself, or by certain persons alluded to under the denomination of my representatives, – either in one way or the other; but in which? This is exactly what I want to know, and this is exactly what I am not told. – Can I do it by myself, or only by my representatives; that is to say, in the latter case by a deputy in whose election I have perhaps had a vote, perhaps not – perhaps given the vote, perhaps not – perhaps voted for, perhaps voted against; and who, whether I voted for or against him, will not do either this, or any one other act whatsoever, at my desire? Have I, an individual – have I in my individual capacity – a right when I please, to ascertain, that is, to examine into the necessity of every contribution established or proposed to be established? Then have I a right to go whenever I please, to any of the officers in the department of the revenue, – to take all the people I find under my command, – to put all the business of the office to a stand, – to make them answer all my questions, – to make them furnish me with as many papers or other documents as I desire to have? – You, my next neighbour, who are as much a citizen as I am, have as much of this right as I have. It is your pleasure to take this office under your command, to the same purpose at the same time. It is my pleasure the people should do what I bid them, and not what you bid them; it is your pleasure they should do what you bid them, and not what I bid them: which of us is to have his pleasure? The answer is, – he who has the strongest lungs, or if that will not do, he who has the strongest hand. To give everything to the strongest hand is the natural result of all the tutoring, and all the checking and controuling of which this lecture on the principles of government is so liberal; but this is the exact result of that state of things which would have place, supposing there were no government at all, nor any such attempt as this to destroy it, under the notion of directing it.

The right of giving consent to a tax, – the right of giving consent to a measure, – is a curious mode of expression for signifying assent or dissent as a maim thinks proper! It is surprising that a man professing and pretending to fix words – to fix ideas – to fix laws – to fix everything – and to fix them to all eternity, should fix upon such an expression, and should say the right of giving consent, instead of the right of giving a vote – the right of giving consent, and consent only, instead of the right of giving consent or dissent, or neither, as a man thinks proper.

§ *Article 15*

Society has a right to demand from every agent of the public, an account of his administration.

Society? What is the meaning – what is the object here? Different, where it ought to be identical – identical, where it ought to be different – ever inexplicit – ever indeterminate, using as interconvertible, expressions which, for the purpose of precision and right understanding, require the most carefully to be set and kept in opposition: such is the language from the beginning of this composition to the end!

Is it, that superiors in office have a right to demand such an account of their subordinates? Not to possess such a right, would be not to be a superior: not to be subject to the exercise of it, would be not to be a subordinate. In this sense, the proposition is perfectly harmless, but equally nugatory. Is it, that all men not in office have this right with respect to all men, or every man in office? Then comes the question as before – each in his individual capacity, or only altogether in their collective? If in their collective, whatever this article, or any other article drawn up in the same view, does or can do for them, amounts to nothing: whatever it would have them do, it gives them no facilities for doing it, which they did not possess without it. Whatever it would have them do, if one and all rise for the purpose of doing it, bating what hindrance they may receive from one another, there will be nobody to hinder them. But is there any great likelihood of any such rising ever taking place? And if it were to take place, would there be any great use in it?

If the right be of the number of those which belongs to each and every man in his individual capacity, then comes the old story over again of mutual obstruction, and the obstruction of all business, as before.

The right of demanding an account? What means that, too? The right of simply putting the question, or the right of compelling an answer to it – and such an answer as shall afford to him that puts it, the satisfaction he desires? In the former case, the value of the right will not be great; in the latter case, he who has it, and who, by the supposition, is not in office, will in fact be in office; and, as everybody has it, and is to have it, the result is, that everybody is in office; and those who command all men are under the command of every man.

Instead of meaning stark nonsense, was the article meant after all simply to convey a memento to those who are superiors in office, to keep a good look-out after their subordinates? If this be the case, nothing can be more innocent and unexceptionable. Neither the child that is learning wisdom in his horn-book, nor the old woman who is teaching him, need blush to own it. But what has it to do in a composition, the work of the collected wisdom of the nation, and of which the object is, throughout and exclusively, to *declare rights*?

Silly or pestilential – such, as usual, is here the alternative. In the shape of advice, a proposition may be instructive or trifling, wholesome or insipid. But be it the one or the other, the instant it is converted, or attempted to be converted, into a law, of which those called legislators are to be the objects, and those not called legislators to be the executors, it becomes all sheer poison, and of the rankest kind.

§ *Article 16*

Every society in which the warranty of rights is not assured, ['la garantie des droits n'est pas assurée',] nor the separation of powers determined, has no constitution.

Here we have an exhibition: self-conceit inflamed to insanity – legislators turned into turkey-cocks – the less important operation of constitution-making, interrupted for the more important operation of bragging. Had the whole human species, according to the wish of the tyrant, but one neck, it would find in this article a sword designed to sever it.

This constitution, – the blessed constitution, of which this matchless declaration forms the base – the constitution of France – is not only the most admirable constitution in the world, but the only one. That no other country but France has the happiness of possessing the sort of thing, whatever it be, called a constitution, is a meaning sufficiently conveyed. This meaning the article must have, if it have any: for other meaning, assuredly it has none.

Every society in which the warranty of rights is not assured (*toute société dans laquelle la garantie des droits n'est pas assurée*,) is, it must be confessed, most rueful nonsense; but if the translation were not exact, it would be unfaithful: and if not nonsensical, it would not be exact.

Do you ask, has the nation I belong to such a thing as a constitution belonging to it? If you want to know, look whether a declaration of rights, word for word the same as this, forms part of its code of laws; for by this article, what is meant to be insinuated, not expressed (since by nonsense nothing is expressed,) is the necessity of having a declaration of rights like this set by authority in the character of an introduction at the head of the collection of its laws.

As to the not absolutely nonsensical, but only very obscure clause, about a society's having 'the separation of powers determined', it seems to be the result of a confused idea of an intended application of the old maxim, *Divide et impera*: the governed are to have the governors under their governance, by having them divided among themselves. A still older maxim, and supposing both maxims applied to this one subject, I am inclined to think a truer one, is, that a house divided against itself cannot stand.

Yet on the existence of two perfectly independent and fighting sovereignties, or of three such fighting sovereignties (the supposed state of things in Britain seems here to be the example in view,) the perfection of good government, or at least of whatever approach to good government can subsist without the actual adoption *in terminis* of a declaration of rights such as this, is supposed to depend. Hence, though Britain have no such thing as a constitution belonging to it at present, yet, if during a period of any length, five or ten years for example, it should ever happen that neither House of Commons nor House of Lords had any confidence in the King's Ministers, nor any disposition to endure their taking the lead in legislation (the House of Commons being all the while, as we must suppose, peopled by universal suffrage,) possibly in such case, for it were a great deal too much to affirm, Britain might be so far humoured as to be allowed to suppose herself in possession of a sort of thing, which, though of inferior stuff, might pass under the name of a constitution, even without having this declaration of rights to stand at its head.

That Britain possesses at present anything that can bear that name, has by Citizen Paine, *following*, or *leading* (I really remember not, nor is it worth remembering,) at any rate *agreeing* with this declaration of rights, been formally denied.

According to general import, supported by etymology, by the word *constitution*, something *established*, something *already* established, something possessed of *stability*, something that has given *proofs* of stability, seems to be implied. What shall we say, if of this most magnificent of all boasts, not merely the simple negative, but the direct converse should be true? and if instead of France being the only country which has a constitution, France should be the only country that has none! Yet, if government depend upon obedience – the stability of government upon the permanence of the disposition to obedience, and the permanence of that disposition upon the duration of the habit of obedience – this most assuredly must be the case.

§ *Article 17*

Property being an inviolable and sacred right, no one can be deprived of it, unless it be when public necessity, legally established, evidently requires it [*i.e.* the sacrifice of it,] *and under the condition of a just and previous indemnity*.

Here we have the concluding article in this pile of contradictions; it does not mismatch the rest. By the first article, all men are equal in respect of all sorts of rights, and so are to continue for evermore, spite of everything which can be done by laws. By the second article, property is of the number of those rights. By this seventeenth and last article, no man can be deprived of his property – no, not of a single atom of it, without an equal equivalent paid – not when the occasion calls for it, for that would not be soon enough, but beforehand; all men are equal in respect of property, while John has £50,000 a-year, and Peter nothing: all men are to be equal in property, and that for everlasting; at the same time that he who has a thousand times as much as a thousand others put together, is not to be deprived of a single farthing of it, without having first received an exact equivalent.

Nonsense and contradiction apart, the topic touched upon here is one of those questions of detail that requires to be settled, and is capable of being settled, by considerations of utility deducible from quiet and sober investigation, to the satisfaction of sober-minded men; but such considerations are far beneath the attention of these creators of the rights of man.

There are distinctions between species of property which are susceptible, and species of property which are not susceptible, of the *value of affection*; between losses in relation to which the adequacy of indemnification may be reduced to a certainty, and losses in respect of which it must remain exposed to doubt: there may be cases in which a more than equivalent gain to one individual will warrant the subjecting another individual, with or without compensation, to a loss. All these questions are capable of receiving a solution to the satisfaction of a man who thinks it worth his while to be at the pains of comparing the feelings on one side with the feelings on the other, and to judge of regulations by their effect on the feelings of those whom they concern, instead of pronouncing on them by the random application of declamatory epithets and phrases.

Necessity? What means necessity? Does necessity order the making of new streets, new roads, new bridges, new canals? A nation which has existed for so many ages with the stock of water-roads which it received from Nature, – is any addition to that stock *necessary* to the continuation of its existence? If not, there is an end to all improvement in all these lines. In all changes there are disadvantages on one side, there are advantages on the other: but what are all the advantages in the world, when set against the sacred and inviolable rights of man derived from the unenacted and unrepealable laws of Nature?

§ *Conclusion*

On the subject of the fundamental principles of government, we have seen what execrable trash the choicest talents of the French nation have produced.

On the subject of chemistry, Europe has beheld with admiration, and adopted with unanimity and gratitude, the systematic views of the same nation, supported as they were by a series of decisive experiments and conclusive reasonings.

Chemistry has commonly been reckoned, and not altogether without reason, among the most abstruse branches of science. In chemistry, we see how high they have soared above the sublimest knowledge of past times; in legislation, how deep they have sunk below the profoundest ignorance – how much inferior has the maturest design that could be furnished by the united powers of the whole nation proved, in comparison of the wisdom and felicity of the chance-medley of the British Constitution.

Comparatively speaking, a select few applied themselves to the cultivation of chemistry – almost an infinity, in comparison, have applied themselves to the science of legislation.

In the instance of chemistry, the study is acknowledged to come within the province of science: the science is acknowledged to be an abstruse and difficult one, and to require a long course of study on the part of those who have had the previous advantage of a liberal education; whilst the cultivation of it, in such manner as to make improvements in it, requires that a man should make it the great business of his life; and those who have made these improvements have thus applied themselves.

In chemistry there is no room for passion to step in and to confound the understanding – to lead men into error, and to shut their eyes against knowledge: in legislation, the circumstances are opposite, and vastly different.

What, then, shall we say of that system of government, of which the professed object is to call upon the untaught and unlettered multitude (whose existence depends upon their devoting their whole time to the acquisition of the means of supporting it,) to occupy themselves without ceasing upon all questions of government (legislation and administration included) without exception – important and trivial, – the most general and the most particular, but more especially upon the most important and most general – that is, in other words, the most scientific – those that require the greatest measures of science to qualify a man for deciding upon, and in respect of which any want of science and skill are liable to be attended with the most fatal consequences?

What should we have said, if, with a view of collecting the surest grounds for the decision of any of the great questions of chemistry, the French Academy of Sciences (if its members had remained unmurdered) had referred such questions to the Primary Assemblies?

If a collection of general propositions, put together with the design that seems to have given birth to this performance – propositions of the most general and extensive import, embracing the whole field of legislation – were capable of being so worded and put together as to be of use, it could only be on the condition of their being deduced in the way of abridgment from an already formed and existing assemblage of less general propositions, constituting the tenor of the body of the laws. But for these more general propositions to have been abstracted from that body of particular ones, that body must have been already in existence: the general and introductory part, though placed first, must have been constructed last; – though first in the order of communication, it should have been last in the order of composition. For the framing of the propositions which were to be included, time, knowledge, genius, temper, patience, everything was wanting. Yet the system of propositions which were to include them, it was determined to have at any rate. Of time, a small quantity indeed might be made to serve, upon the single and very simple condition of not bestowing a single thought upon the propositions which they were to include: and as to knowledge, genius, temper, and patience, the place of all these trivial requisites was abundantly supplied by effrontery and self-conceit. The business, instead of being performed in the way of abridgment, was performed in the way of anticipation – by a loose conjecture of what the particular propositions in question, were they to be found, might amount to.

What I mean to attack is, not the subject or citizen of this or that country – not this or that citizen – not citizen Sieyes or citizen anybody else, but all anti-legal rights of man, all declarations of such rights. What I mean to attack is, not the execution of such a design in this or that instance, but the design itself.

It is not that they have failed in their execution of the design by using the same word promiscuously in two or three senses – contradictory and incompatible senses – but in undertaking to execute a design which could not be executed at all without this abuse of words. Let a man distinguish the senses – let him allot, and allot in variably a separate word for each, and he will find it impossible to make up any such declaration at all, without running into such nonsense as must stop the hand even of the maddest of the mad.

Ex uno, disce omnes – from this declaration of rights, learn what all other declarations of rights – of rights asserted as against government in general, must ever be, – the rights of anarchy – the order of chaos.

It is right I should continue to possess the coat I have upon my back, and so on with regard to everything else I look upon as my property, at least till I choose to part with it.

It is right I should be at liberty to do as I please – it would be better if I might be permitted to add, whether other people were pleased with what it pleased me to do or not. But as that is hopeless, I must be content with such a portion of liberty, though it is the least I can be content with, as consists in the liberty of doing as I please, subject to the exception of not doing harm to other people.

It is right I should be secure against all sorts of harm.

It is right I should be upon a par with everybody else – upon a par at least; and if I can contrive to get a peep over other people's heads, where will be the harm in it?

But if all this is right now, in what time was it ever otherwise? It is now naturally right, and at what future time will it be otherwise? It is then unalterably right for everlasting.

As it is right I should possess all these blessings, I have a right to all of them.

But if I have a right to the coat on my back, I have a right to knock any man down who attempts to take it from me.

For the same reason, if I have a right to be secure against all sorts of harm, I have a right to knock any man down who attempts to harm me.

For the same reason, if I have a right to do whatever I please, subject only to the exception of not doing harm to other people, it follows that, subject only to that exception, I have a right to knock any man down who attempts to prevent my doing anything that I please to do.

For the same reason, if I have a right to be upon a par with everybody else in every respect, it follows, that should any man take upon him to raise his house higher than mine, – rather than it should continue so, I have a right to pull it down about his ears, and to knock him down if he attempt to hinder me.

Thus easy, thus natural, under the guidance of the selfish and anti-social passions, thus insensible is the transition from the language of utility and peace to the language of mischief. Transition, did I say? – what transition? – from right to right? The propositions are identical – there is no transition in the case. Certainly, as far as words go, scarcely any: no more than if you were to trust your horse with a man for a week or so, and he were to return it blind and lame: it was your horse you trusted to him – it is your horse you have received again – what you had trusted to him, you have received.

It is in England, rather than in France, that the discovery of the *rights of man* ought naturally to have taken its rise: it is we – we English, that have the better *right* to it. It is in the English language that the transition is more natural, than perhaps in most others: at any rate, more so than in the French. It is in English, and not in French, that we may change the sense without changing the word, and, like Don Quixote on the enchanted horse, travel as far as the moon, and farther, without ever getting off the saddle. One and the same word, right – right, that most enchanting of words – is sufficient for operating the fascination. The word is ours, – that magic word, which, by its single unassisted powers, completes the fascination. In its adjective shape, it is as innocent as a dove: it breathes nothing but morality and peace. It is in this shape that, passing in at the heart, it gets possession of the understanding: it then assumes its substantive shape, and joining itself to a band of suitable associates, sets up the banner of insurrection, anarchy, and lawless violence.

It is right that men should be as near upon a par with one another in every respect as they can be made, consistently with general security: here we have it in its adjective form, synonymous with desirable, proper, becoming, consonant to general utility, and the like. I have a right to put myself upon a par with everybody in every respect: here we have it in its *substantive* sense, forming with the other words a phrase equivalent to this, – wherever I find a man who will not let me put myself on a par with him in every respect, it is right, and proper, and becoming, that I should knock him down, if I have a mind to do so, and if that will not do, knock him on the head, and so forth.

The French language is fortunate enough not to possess this mischievous abundance. But a Frenchman will not be kept back from his purpose by a want of words: the want of an adjective composed of the same letters as the substantive *right*, is no loss to him. Is, has been, ought to be, shall be, can, – all are put for one another – all are pressed into the service – all made to answer the same purposes. By this inebriating compound, we have seen all the elements of the understanding confounded, every fibre of the heart inflamed, the lips prepared for every folly, and the hand for every crime.

Our right to this precious discovery, such as it is, of the rights of man, must, I repeat it, have been prior to that of the French. It has been seen how peculiarly rich we are in materials for making it. *Right*, the substantive *right*, is the child of law: from *real* laws come *real* rights; but from *imaginary* laws, from laws of nature, fancied and invented by poets, rhetoricians, and dealers in moral and intellectual poisons, come *imaginary* rights, a bastard brood of monsters, 'gorgons and chimeras dire'. And thus it is, that from *legal rights*, the offspring of law, and friends of peace, come *anti-legal rights*, the mortal enemies of law, the subverters of government, and the assassins of security.

Will this antidote to French poisons have its effect? – will this preservative for the understanding and the heart against the fascination of sounds, find lips to take it? This, in point of speedy or immediate efficacy at least, is almost too much to hope for. Alas, how dependent are opinions upon sound! Who shall break the chains which bind them together? By what force shall the associations between words and ideas be dissolved – associations coeval with the cradle – associations to which every book and every conversation give increased strength? By what authority shall this original vice in the structure of language be corrected? How shall a word which has taken root in the vitals of a language be expelled? By what means shall a word in continual use be deprived of half its signification? The language of plain strong sense is difficult to learn; the language of smooth nonsense is easy and familiar. The one requires a force of attention capable of stemming the tide of usage and example; the other requires nothing but to swim with it.

It is for education to do what can be done; and in education is, though unhappily the slowest, the surest as well as earliest resource. The recognition of the nothingness of the laws of nature and the rights of man that have been grounded on them, is a branch of knowledge of as much importance to an Englishman, though a negative one, as the most perfect acquaintance that can be formed with the existing laws of England.

It must be so: Shakspeare, whose plays were filling English hearts with rapture, while the drama of France was not superior to that of Caffraria, – Shakspeare, who had a key to all the passions and all the stores of language, could never have let slip an instrument of delusion of such superior texture. No: it is not possible that the rights of man – the natural, pre-adamitical, ante-legal, and anti-legal rights of man – should have been unknown to, have been unemployed by Shakspeare. How could the Macbeths, the Jaffiers, the Iagos, do without them? They present a cloak for every conspiracy – they hold out a mask for every crime; – they are every villain's armoury – every spendthrift's treasure.

But if the English were the first to bring the rights of man into the closet from the stage, it is to the stage and the closet that they have confined them. It was reserved for France – for France in her days of degradation and degeneration – in those days, in comparison of which the worst of her days of fancied tyranny were halcyon ones – to turn debates into tragedies, and the senate into a stage.

The mask is now taken off, and the anarchist may be known by the language which he uses.

He will be found *asserting rights*, and acknowledging them at the same time not to be recognised by government. Using, instead of *ought* and *ought not*, the words *is* or *is not* – *can* or *can not*.

In former times, in the times of Grotius and Puffendorf, these expressions were little more than improprieties in language, prejudicial to the growth of knowledge: at present, since the French Declaration of Rights has adopted them, and the French Revolution displayed their import by a practical comment, – the use of them is already a *moral crime*, and not undeserving of being constituted a legal crime, as hostile to the public peace.

LEADING PRINCIPLES OF A
CONSTITUTIONAL CODE

I *Ends aimed at*

1. This Constitution has for its general end in view, the greatest happiness of the greatest number;[1] namely, of the members of this political state: in other words, the promoting or advancement of their interests. By *the universal interest*, understand the aggregate of those same interests. This is the all-comprehensive end, to the accomplishment of which, the several arrangements contained in the ensuing code are all of them directed.

2. Government cannot be exercised without coercion; nor coercion, without producing unhappiness. Of the happiness produced by government, the net amount will be – what remains of the happiness, deduction made of the unhappiness.

3. Of the unhappiness thus produced, is composed, in the account of happiness, the *expense* of government. Of the happiness produced by government, the gross amount being given, the net amount will be inversely as this expense.

---

1 If the nature of the case admitted the possibility of any such result, the endeavour of this constitution would be – on each occasion, to maximize the felicity of *every one* of the individuals, of whose interests the universal interest is composed; on which supposition, the greatest happiness of *all*, not of the greatest number only, would be the end aimed at.

But such universality is not possible. For neither in the augmentation given to the gross amount of *felicity*, can all the individuals in question ever be included; nor can the *infelicity*, in which the *expense* consists, be so disposed of, as to be borne in equal amount by all: in particular, such part of that same expense, as consists in the suffering produced by *punishment*.

Thus it is, that to provide for the greatest felicity of the greatest number, is the utmost that can be done towards the maximization of universal national felicity, in so far as depends on government.

4. Of the members of this, as of other states in general, the great majority will naturally, at each given point of time, be composed of the several persons who, having been born in some part or other of the territory belonging to the state, have all along remained inhabitants of it. But, to these, for the purpose of benefit, of burden, or of both, will be to be added sundry other classes of persons, of whom designation is made in an appropriate part of the ensuing code.

5. Immediately specific, and jointly all-comprehensive, ends of this constitution are − subsistence, abundance, security, and equality; each maximized, in so far as is compatible with the maximization of the rest.

6. (I) As to *Subsistence*.[1] This speaks for itself.

7. (II) As to *Abundance*. This is an instrument of felicity on two accounts: on its own account, and as an instrument of security for subsistence. In this latter character, its usefulness may be still greater to those who possess it not, than to those who possess it.

8. (III) As to *Security*.[2] This *is for* good, or *against* evil. Security for good is − either for the matter of subsistence, or for the matter of abundance.

---

1 By *subsistence* − or say *matter of subsistence* − may be understood everything, the non-possession of which would be productive of positive physical suffering: that, and nothing more. In so far as distinct from, and not comprehended in, the corresponding branch of security, namely, security for subsistence − subsistence itself must be understood as being, in the field of time, limited to a single instant − any instant taken at pleasure.

Accordingly, of the several elements or dimensions of value, to *extent* alone, as measured by the *number* of the individuals in question, can *maximization*, on this occasion, be applicable.

2 In the words *good* and *evil*, apt additaments being employed, may be seen two appellatives, which, − opposite as are the sensations and other objects which they are employed to designate, − are, as to no small part of their extent, inter-convertible: by ablation of *good*, evil is produced; by ablation of *evil*, good. But, on some occasions, the one is the more convenient appellative; on others, the other; on others again, both. Infinite, and in no small degree perhaps irremoveable, are the ambiguity and obscurity produced at every turn by the imperfections of *language*: language, that almost exclusively applicable, though so deplorably inadequate, instrument of human converse.

Of *security* – considered in so far as it belongs to government to afford it, – the several *subject-matters*, corporeal, incorporeal, or say fictitious, taken together, have been found comprehendible under the five following heads:

1. *Person*: the security afforded in this case, is security *against* evil, in whatever shape a man's *person*, body and mind included, stands exposed to it.

2. *Property*: under which denomination, the matter of *subsistence* and the matter of *abundance*, as above, are comprehended.

3. *Power*: considered in its two distinguishable branches – the *domestic* and the *political*.

4. *Reputation*: a fictitious entity, the value of which, considered in the character of a subject-matter of possession and security, consists in its being a source of respect, or love, or both: and as being, in either case, an eventual source of *good offices*, or say of *services*, receivable from other persons, by the person by whom it is possessed. Take away all services, eventual as well as actual, you strip it of all intelligible value.

5. *Condition in life*: a factitious and fictitious entity, compounded of *property*, *power*, and *reputation*, in indeterminate and indefinitely diversifiable proportions. In the idea *of power*, that of *right* – meaning legal *right*, as being a particular modification of it – a sort of *eventual power* is included.

Examples of condition in life are: – 1. Those constituted by the several genealogical relations, expressed by the words, *husband, wife, son, daughter, father, mother*, and so on, throughout the whole genealogical tree; 2. The several distinguishable *occupations*, profit-seeking ones included; and the several *political situations*, corresponding to the several offices, with the powers and functions respectively attached to them.

Taken together, – the injuries, *against* which, security *for* these five several subject-matters is requisite to happiness, constitute the most obvious, and as it were tangible, portion of the matter of the *Penal code*: as does the detailed description of the several *cases*, in which a man has a *right to security* against these several injuries, those to property in particular, that of the *civil code*: right to *security*, that is to say, to the eventual appropriate *services*, of the several classes of public functionaries – that is to say, judges and their subordinates, by the exercise of whose functions it is afforded.

A distinction – which must here be kept in view, or a conception, as afflictive as it would be erroneous, will be entertained, is – *that* between a defalcation made from a subject-matter of security (say, for example, from *property*,) and a defalcation from security itself: in which latter case, in the phrase commonly employed, a *shock* is spoken of as being given to security. Howsoever the subject-matter of security be lessened, security itself will not be lessened , if by means of the defalcation made from the subject-matter, the probability of retaining what remains of it, be not lessened. By any such defalcation made from the subject-matter of security taken in the aggregate, so far is security itself from being necessarily lessened, that without such defalcation it could not have existence. Witness *taxation*: without which, nowhere could the business of government be carried on: nowhere could security against adversaries of any class have place: nowhere could security against calamity in any shape be afforded by government.

9. Security against evil, is either against evil from calamity,[1] or against evil from hostility.

10. By *calamity*, understand human suffering, in the case in which, by its magnitude and indeterminateness in respect to extent, it stands distinguished from, and above, the quantity ordinarily produced by one and the same cause.

11. By evil from calamity, understand evil from purely physical agency: by evil from hostility, evil from human agency. But, by purely physical agency, no evil is producible, which may not, from human agency, receive its commencement or its increase.

12. Of calamity, the principal sources are — inundation, conflagration, collapsion, explosion, pestilence, and famine.

13. The evil-doers, against whose hostility, that is to say, against whose evil agency, security is requisite, are either external or internal. By the external, understand those adversaries who are commonly called *enemies*.

14. Internal adversaries, against whose evil agency security is requisite, are the *unofficial* and the *official*.

15. By the *unofficial* adversaries, understand those evil-doers who are ordinarily termed *offenders*, *criminals*, *malefactors*. These are resistible, everywhere resisted, and mostly with success.

16. The *official* are those evil-doers whose means of evil-doing are derived from the share they respectively possess in the aggregate of the powers of government. Among these, those of the highest grade, and in so far as supported by those of the highest, those of every inferior grade, are everywhere irresistible.

17. To provide, in favour of the rest of the community, security against evil in all its shapes, at the hands of the above-mentioned

---

1 The giving execution and effect to precautionary arrangements, taken with a view to calamity, belongs to one branch of that part of the business of the executive department, which in the ensuing code is styled the *preventive service*: the giving the like support to such precautionary arrangements as are taken with a view to hostility at the hands of the unofficial and resistible class of adversaries, belongs to the other branch of that same service.

internal, and, so long as they continue in such their situation, irresistible adversaries, – is the appropriate business of the constitutional branch of law, and accordingly of this code.

18. As in difficulty so in importance, this part of the business of law far surpasses every other. Of the danger to which an assemblage of individuals stand exposed, the *magnitude* will be in the joint ratio of the *intensity* of the evil in question on the part of each, the *duration* of it, the *propinquity* of it, the *probability* of it; and, on the part of all, the *extent* of it; the extent, as measured by the *number* of those who stand exposed to it. Measuring it in every one of these *dimensions*, – taking into account every one of these *elements of value* in both cases, – minute will be seen to be the danger to which the other members of the community stand exposed at the hands of those their resistible, in comparison with that to which they stand exposed at the hands of these their irresistible, adversaries. In the first case, it has place on no other than an individual scale; in the other, on a national scale.

19. Inferior even is the danger to which they stand exposed at the hands of foreign and declared enemies, in comparison with that to which they stand exposed at the hands of their everywhere professed protectors. Foreign enemies, in the event of their obtaining the object of their hostility, withdraw most commonly from whatever territory they invade, leaving the inhabitants thenceforward unmolested. At the worst, they keep possession of it: and in that case, from the external and resistible, become the internal and irresistible adversaries, such as those above mentioned.

20. On the texture of the *constitutional* branch of law, will depend that of every other. For on this branch of law depends, in all its branches, the *relative and appropriate aptitude* of those functionaries, on whose will depends, at all times, the texture of every other branch of law. If, in the framing of this branch of law, the greatest happiness of the greatest number is taken for the end in view, and that object pursued with corresponding success, so will it be in the framing of those other branches: if not, not.

21. (IV) Lastly, as to *Equality*. In the instances of *subsistence*, *abundance*, and *security*, the title of the object to the appellation of

an instrument of felicity, is stamped, as it were, upon the face of it – designated by the very name. Not so in the case of equality.

22. In the idea of *equality*, that of *distribution* is implied. Distribution is either of *benefits* or of *burdens*: under one or other of these names, may every possible subject-matter of the operation be comprised. Benefits are distributed by *collation* made of the instruments of felicity – burdens by the *ablation* of them, or by the *imposition* of positive hardship.

23. (I) In proportion as equality is departed from, inequality has place: and in proportion as inequality has place, evil has place. First, as to inequality, – in the case where it is in the *collation* made of those same instruments that it has place. In this case, it is pregnant with two distinguishable evils: the one may be styled the *domestic* or *civil*; the other, the *national* or *constitutional*.

24. The *domestic* evil is that which has place in so far as the subject-matter of the distribution is the matter of wealth – matter of subsistence and abundance. It has place in this way: The more remote from equality are the shares possessed by the individuals in question, in the mass of the instruments of felicity, – the less is the sum of the felicity produced by the sum of those same shares.

25. The national or constitutional evil is that which has place, in so far as the subject-matter of the distribution is *power*. It has place in this way: The greater the quantity of power possessed, the greater the facility and the incitement to the abuse of it. In a direct way, this position applies only to *power*. But, between *power* and *wealth* such is the connexion that each is an instrument for the acquisition of the other: in this way, therefore, the position applies to *wealth* likewise.

26. Of inequality as applied to both subjects, – and of the evil with which, in both the above shapes, it is pregnant, – the case of *monarchy* may serve for exemplification: for exemplification, and thereby for proof.

27. Of the maximum of inequality, every monarchy affords an example. Of the matter of wealth, to the monarch is allotted a mass as great as suffices for the subsistence of from 10,000 to 100,000 of the individuals from whom, amongst others, after

being produced by their labour, it is extorted. Yet does it still remain matter of doubt, whether the quantity of felicity thus produced in the breast of that one, be greater than that which has place in the breast of one of those same labourers taken on an average, – has place, or at least would have had, but for the extortion thus committed.

28. What is certain is – that the quantity of felicity habitually experienced by a gloomy, or ill-tempered, or gouty, or otherwise habitually diseased monarch, is not so great as that habitually experienced by an habitually cheerful, and good-tempered, and healthy, labourer.

29. True it is, that if, *per contra*, by a monarch maintained at an expense such as the above, good is, by means of that same expense, produced in greater quantity than by a commonwealth chief whose maintenance will not be a hundredth part of the monarch's; – true it is, that on this supposition, the excess of expense, vast as it is, may be not ill-bestowed. But, by whomsoever the existence of any such excess of good is asserted, upon him does it rest to prove or probabilize it.

30. If, in the case of those whose share in the *instruments* of felicity is *greatest*, the excess of *felicity itself* is, on an average, so small, – and, in some individuals out of the small number belonging to this class, the non-existence of any such excess certain – still less and less will be the probable amount of the excess of felicity, in the case of those whose share in the instruments of felicity is *less* and *less*. And thus it is, that as, in a pure *monarchy*, the distribution made of the external instruments of felicity is in the highest degree – so, in a pure *aristocracy*, is it in the next highest degree – unfavourable to the maximization of felicity itself.

31. Hence, throughout the whole population of a state, the less the inequality is between individual and individual, in respect of the share possessed by them in the aggregate mass or stock, of the instruments of felicity, – the greater is the aggregate mass of felicity itself: provided always, that by nothing that is done towards the removal of the inequality, any shock be given to security, – security, namely, in respect of the several subjects of possession above mentioned.

More shortly thus –

32. The less unequal the distribution of the external instruments of felicity is – the greater, so as security be unshaken, will be the sum of felicity itself.

33. On the occasion of the distribution made of a mass of burdens, *delinquency* either is, or is not, in question: is not – as where it is for defraying the expense of government that the burdens are imposed.

34. A burden imposed on the occasion of delinquency, is imposed either for the purpose of its operating in the way of *punishment*, or for the purpose of conferring a correspondent *benefit* on some other person or persons, in *compensation* for damage sustained – sustained, namely, in consequence of the delinquency.

35. Correspondent to the evil produced by inequality in the case of *collation*, is the evil produced by it in the case of *ablation*, – ablation made of a mass of the external instruments of felicity in any shape, and in particular in the shape of *wealth*. Other circumstances the same, – the smaller the mass a man possesses of the instruments of felicity in this shape, the greater is the loss of felicity produced in his instance by the ablation of any given mass of them. By the ablation of fifty pounds, more felicity will be abstracted from the breast of a man who has but one hundred pounds for his whole property, than from the breast of one who has two hundred pounds; much more would it, if, instead of the hundred pounds, he had but that same fifty pounds.

36. (II) So much for felicity, considered as the product of government. Now as to infelicity, considered as the *expense* by means of which that same felicity is produced. Maximization was the object in regard to the desired product: *minimization* is the object in regard to the expense. Now as to the *elements* of that same expense.

37. The expense is evil – evil produced either for the exclusion of greater evil, or for the production of more than equivalent good: it may be distinguished into *punishment* and *hardship*.

38. *Punishment* is evil, produced under the notion of its being a

direct instrument, or efficient cause, of some good *thereby* desired
and intended to be produced.

39. *Hardship* is evil, produced as a collateral result of some
operation employed for the exclusion of evil, or for the production of good: a collateral result, not an efficient cause.

40. In respect of its shape, expense employed by government, as
above, is either *non-pecuniary* or *pecuniary*.

41. The non-pecuniary expense of government is *hardship at
large*: the principal modification of it is that produced by forced
personal service: and, of forced personal service, that produced by
forced *military* service.

42. As to the matter of expense, in no shape can it ever be
procurable by government, in anything like sufficient quantity,
without hardship, or punishment, or the fear of it, or both.

43. Whatever is done by government is done – partly by means of
the matter of *punishment*, or the *fear* of it, partly by means of the
matter of *reward*, or the *hope* of it.

44. The matter of reward is a portion of the matter of good,
considered as employed in the production of felicity in the breast
of some individual, in consideration of some act done or supposed
to be done by him, or about to be done by him.

45. The matter of reward is not, in any sufficient quantity,
procurable by government without expense – expense, as above,
in the shape of hardship and punishment.

46. Accordingly, on no occasion, and for no purpose, is *good*
producible by government, but through *evil*, as above.

47. Hence, in so far as may be without detriment to the net
amount of good produced, the maximization of national felicity
requires that *factitious reward* (reward applied by the hand of
government, at the expense of the community) be in every shape
minimized, as well as the matter of punishment.

II *Principal means employed for the attainment of the above ends*

1. These means are comprisable, all of them, in one expression: maximization of *appropriate official aptitude* on the part of rulers.

2. Of this aptitude, three branches are distinguishable: 1. appropriate *moral* aptitude; 2. appropriate *intellectual* aptitude; 3. appropriate *active* aptitude.

3. Of appropriate intellectual aptitude there are two distinguishable branches: 1. appropriate *knowledge*; 2. appropriate *judgment*.

4. By appropriate moral aptitude, understand – disposition to contribute, on all occasions and in all ways, to the greatest happiness of the greatest number; in other words, to the promoting or advancement of the universal interest.

5. If appropriate *moral* aptitude be to a certain degree deficient, – the consequence is, that by abundance of appropriate aptitude in those other shapes, the aggregate of appropriate aptitude will naturally, instead of being increased, be diminished. If hostile to the interests of the greatest number, – the more able the functionary, the more mischievous.

6. To the different branches of appropriate official aptitude, apply correspondently different means. Expressed in the shortest manner, indication may be given of them by the following rules.

7. (I) Means applying to appropriate *moral* aptitude:
Rule 1. In the hands of those of whose happiness the universal happiness is composed, keep at all times the choice of those agents, by whose operations that happiness is to be promoted.[1]

---

1 To this arrangement, no objection, wearing the face of a rational one, could

8. Rule 2. In the hands of each such agent, minimize the power of doing *evil*.

9. Rule 3. Leave, at the same time, as little diminished as may be, the power of doing good.

10. Rule 4. Minimize the quantity of public money at his disposal.

11. Rule 5. Minimize the time during which it remains at his disposal.

12. Rule 6. Minimize the number of hands through which it passes in its way to the hand by which it is received in payment.

13. Rule 7. Extra-reward give none, without proportionable extra-service — extra-service *proved*, and *that* by evidence not less conclusive than that which is required to be given of *delinquency*, with a view to *punishment*.

14. Rule 8. Maximize each man's *responsibility* with respect to the power and the money with which he is entrusted.

15. Rule 9. Means by which such responsibility is maximized, are — 1. constant dislocability; 2. eventual punibility.[1]

---

ever be made, other than that *of impracticability* — an objection formed by the assertion, that, consistently with internal peace and security, no such arrangement can have place. But, in the case of the Anglo-American United States, the groundlessness of this objection has been completely demonstrated by experience — demonstrated by the very first experiment ever made; while, to the purpose of all such persons as had a new constitution to make, this same arrangement, even on the supposition that the experiments made of it had, in a considerable number, all of them failed, might still have remained the only eligible one: for, as will be seen below, the above-mentioned constitution is one, which, bating irresistible force from without, affords a reasonable promise of everlasting endurance; whereas every other form of government contains, in the very essence of it, the seeds of its own dissolution — a dissolution which, sooner or later, cannot but have place.

1 Namely, immediately or unimmediately, at the hands of those by whom the responsible agents in question were chosen; as is the case in the Anglo-American United States. Say — dislocability, immediately: punibility, unimmediately; namely, by the hands of other agents.

16. Rule 10. By the several means above mentioned, – so order matters that, in the instance of each such agent, the course prescribed by his particular *interest* shall on each occasion coincide, as completely as may be, with that prescribed by his *duty*: which is as much as to say, with that prescribed by his share in the universal interest.

(II) Means applying to appropriate intellectual and active aptitude:

17. Rule 1. For appropriate intellectual and active aptitude, – establish, throughout the whole field of official duty, appropriate preliminary *tests* and *securities*. For these, see the code itself.

18. Rule 2. Maximize, throughout, the efficiency of these same tests and securities.

19. Rule 3. Minimize, in the instance of each office, the pecuniary inducements for the acceptance of it.

20. Follow the observations on which Rule 3 is grounded.
   (I) The less the money required by a man for subjecting himself to the *obligations* attached to the office, the stronger the proof afforded by him of his relish for the *occupations*.

21. Still stronger, and in a proportionable degree, will be the proof, – if, instead of receiving, he is content to *give*.

22. Every penny – added to whatsoever remuneration is, as above, sufficient, – adds strength to predatory appetites, and to the means of gratifying them.

23. A throne, – seat of the most extravagantly fed, – is so, everywhere, of the most invariably insatiable, appetites.

24. As to the means, applying, as above, to appropriate moral aptitude, – there is not one of them, of which an exemplification may not be seen, in the constitution of the Anglo-American United States.

25. Under that constitution, in so far as depends on government, – has uncontrovertibly been, and continues to be, – enjoyed, a greater quantity of happiness, in proportion to population, than in any other political community in these or any other times.

26. By that one example is excluded, and for ever, all ground for any such apprehension, real or pretended, as that of inaptitude, on the part of the people at large, as to the making choice of their own agents, for conducting the business of government.

27. Nowhere else has such universal satisfaction been manifested: satisfaction with the form of the government – satisfaction with the *mode* in which, satisfaction with the *hands* by which, the business of it has been carried on. No other political community is there, or has there ever been, – in which, by so large a proportion of the population, so large a part has been constantly taken in the conduct and examination of the affairs of government; – no other, in which the part so taken has been so perfectly unproductive of disorder and suffering in every shape.

28. No other constitution is there, or has there been, under which, in anything like so small a degree (slave-purchasing and pertinaciously slave-holding States always excepted,) the interest and happiness of the many have been sacrificed to those of the ruling and influential few; – no other, under which what yet remains of that sinister sacrifice, will, with so little difficulty, and sooner or later with such perfect certainty, be abolished.

29. Thus much as to the *all-comprehensive* end of government, in so far as the government is *good*. As to the several above-mentioned *specific* ends, – the means for compassing them would not here have been in their place. The description of them will be found to be in great measure different, according to the differences between the respective ends: they will form the subject-matter – in the first place, of the constitutional – in the next place, of the penal and non-penal, codes.

WORDSWORTH CLASSICS
OF WORLD LITERATURE

REQUESTS FOR INSPECTION COPIES   Lecturers wishing to obtain copies of Wordsworth Classics, Wordsworth Poetry Library or Wordsworth Classics of World Literature titles on inspection are invited to contact: Dennis Hart, Wordsworth Editions Ltd, Crib Street, Ware, Herts SG12 9ET; E-mail: dennis.hart@wordsworth-editions.com. Please quote the author, title and ISBN of the titles in which you are interested; together with your name, academic address, E-mail address, the course on which the books will be used and the expected enrolment.

Teachers wishing to inspect specific core titles for GCSE or A level courses are also invited to contact Wordsworth Editions at the above address.

Inspection copies are sent solely at the discretion of Wordsworth Editions Ltd.

APULEIUS
The Golden Ass

ARISTOTLE
The Nicomachean Ethics

MARCUS AURELIUS
Meditations

FRANCIS BACON
Essays

JAMES BOSWELL
The Life of Samuel Johnson
(UNABRIDGED)

JOHN BUNYAN
The Pilgrim's Progress

BALDESAR CASTIGLIONE
The Book of the Courtier

CATULLUS
Poems

CERVANTES
Don Quixote

CARL VON CLAUSEWITZ
On War
(ABRIDGED)

CONFUCIUS
The Analects

CAPTAIN JAMES COOK
The Voyages of Captain Cook

DANTE
The Inferno

CHARLES DARWIN
The Origin of Species
The Voyage of the Beagle

RENÉ DESCARTES
Key Philosophical Writings

FYODOR DOSTOEVSKY
The Devils

ERASMUS
Praise of Folly

SIGMUND FREUD
The Interpretation of Dreams

EDWARD GIBBON
*The Decline and Fall of the
Roman Empire*
(ABRIDGED)

GUSTAVE FLAUBERT
A Sentimental Journey

KAHLIL GIBRAN
The Prophet

JOHANN WOLFGANG
VON GOETHE
Faust

HERODOTUS
Histories

HOMER
The Iliad and The Odyssey

HORACE
The Odes

BEN JONSON
Volpone and Other Plays

KENKO
Essays in Idleness

WILLIAM LANGLAND
Piers Plowman

LAO TZU
Tao Te Ching

T. E. LAWRENCE
Seven Pillars of Wisdom